The Birth of Modernism

The Birth
of Modernism

Ezra Pound, T.S. Eliot, W.B. Yeats, and the Occult

LEON SURETTE

McGill-Queen's University Press
Montreal & Kingston • London • Buffalo

Legal deposit second quarter 1993
Bibliothèque nationale du Québec

Printed in Canada on acid-free paper

This book has been published with the help of a grant from the Canadian Federation for the Humanities, using funds provided by the Social Sciences and Humanities Research Council of Canada. Publication has also been supported in part by the Smallman fund administered by the Faculty of Arts, The University of Western Ontario.

Canadian Cataloguing in Publication Data

Surette, Leon, 1938–
    The birth of modernism: Ezra Pound, T.S. Eliot, W.B. Yeats, and the occult
    Includes bibliographical references and an index.
    ISBN 0-7735-0976-3
    1. Modernism (Literature) – Europe. 2. European literature – 20th century – History and criticism. 3. European literature – 19th century – History and criticism. 4. Pound, Ezra 1885–1972 – Criticism and interpretation. 5. Eliot, T.S. (Thomas Stearns), 1888–1965 – Criticism and interpretation. 6. Yeats, W.B. (William Butler), 1865–1939 – Criticism and interpretation. 7. Theosophy in literature. I. Title.

PN56.M54S77 1993   809'.91   C92-090710-5

Typeset in Palatino 10/12 by Caractéra production graphique inc., Quebec City

Grateful acknowledgment is given to New Directions Publishing Corporation and Faber & Faber Ltd for permission to quote from the following copyrighted works of Ezra Pound: *The Cantos* (copyright © 1934, 1937, 1940, 1948, 1956, 1959, 1962, 1963, 1966, and 1968 by Ezra Pound); *Guide to Kulchur* (copyright © 1970 by Ezra Pound); *Pavannes and Divigations* (copyright © 1958 by Ezra Pound); *Selected Prose 1909–1965* (copyright © 1960, 1962 by Ezra Pound, copyright © 1973 by the Estate of Ezra Pound); *The Spirit of Romance* (copyright © (1953 by the Trustees of the Ezra Pound Literary Property Trust; used by permission of New Directions Publishing Corporation agents).

Grateful acknowledgment is given to Faber and Faber Ltd and Harcourt Brace Jovanovich for permission to quote from the following material by T.S. Eliot: *Collected Poems 1909–1962, Knowledge and Experience in the Philosophy of F.H. Bradley, Notes Toward the Definition of Culture, Selected Essays* and *The Waste Land: A Facsimile and Transcript of the Original Drafts*, ed. Valerie Eliot.

To my father, Rudy Surette,
and the memory of my mother, Agnes Surette

Contents

Preface

I wrote *The Birth of Modernism* during a sabbatical leave I enjoyed in the academic year of 1989–90. It represents a radical revision of the standard view of literary modernism. When I wrote *A Light from Eleusis: A Study of the Cantos of Ezra Pound* in the mid-1970s, I held the conventional view that literary modernism belonged to twentieth-century scientific materialism. On this view, the mythological and Eleusinian elements of such representative modernist works as *The Waste Land* and *The Cantos* were considered to be factitious formal and thematic devices. This aestheticization of the apparently mystical or noumenal content of literary modernism was achieved through the tactic of Joyce's so-called mythological method. The argument of *The Birth of Modernism* is that the ubiquity of myth in modernist literature must be attributed at least in part to the occult belief that myths represent a record of contact between mortals and the *au delà*.

I would probably have persisted in a secular and aesthetic reading of modernist discourse to this day were it not for a series of phone calls and letters I received in 1980 from William French of Vienna, Virginia. French had been a member of Pound's entourage during his St Elizabeth's years. He was then, and is today, an unashamed occultist. He phoned me to discover if I, too, was an initiate into arcane wisdom. He apparently thought that I must have been to have penetrated the arcanum of *The Cantos* to the degree I had done in *A Light from Eleusis*. When I assured him that I was just a literary scholar without any knowledge of arcana, he enjoined me to read H.P. Blavatsky and Annie Besant where all would be made plain.

I have not followed Bill French's advice for a research program, but his intervention did cause me to re-examine those mythical and visionary elements of Pound's work that – like everyone else – I had thought to be factitious and rhetorical. I could hardly do otherwise, since French pointed out that G.R.S. Mead, whose influence on

Pound I had demonstrated in *A Light from Eleusis*, was himself a theosophist and was secretary to Mme Blavatsky. The fact that I had ignored the colophon of the Theosophical Publishing Society on Mead's books indicates the extent to which in the 1970s I too wore the blinkers that continue to protect the scholarly community from any exposure to the occult components of literary modernism.

My title is a self-conscious echo of Nietzsche's epochal work, *The Birth of Tragedy out of the Spirit of Music*. The echo is appropriate, I think, for Nietzsche has been an important hinge between occult and mainstream culture from the 1880s to the present. He was read by occultists such as Yeats, A.R. Orage, and Edouard Schuré as a witness on the noumenal, and by others much as he is read today – as an iconoclastic sceptic rejecting equally metaphysics, religion, and science. Given the current vogue of Nietzsche among avatars of the postmodern, the ambivalent reception of Nietzschean discourse is of particular interest. By the time I finished this study, I realized that we could use a cultural history of the period entitled *The Birth of Modernism out of the Spirit of Hegel*, for Hegel is a ghostly presence behind most of the generation of Pound and Eliot. Hegel remains a ghostly presence in *The Birth of Modernism*, only dimly perceived by its author until very late stages.

I am grateful to McGill-Queen's University Press for the courage to publish such a controversial study and to the Canadian Federation for the Humanities for a subvention to help defray the costs of publication. My own institution, the University of Western Ontario, also has contributed to the costs of publication, as well as permitting me a sabbatical leave during which I wrote the book. In addition, I held a Social Sciences and Humanities Research Council research time stipend during 1988–89, which enabled me to conduct much of the research. I have revised the study since its acceptance, incorporating some of the research I have conducted since 1990 with the assistance of a Social Sciences research grant that I currently hold.

Writing a book is always lonely work, and it is especially lonely when one is out of step with the scholarly community. For these reasons I am more than usually grateful to Demetres Tryphonopoulos, who has worked with me on these topics as student, research assistant, and colleague since 1986. His place has been taken as student and research assistant during the past two years by Andrzej Sosnowski. I also want to thank my colleague Stephen Adams, who has gradually come round to some acceptance of my eccentric view of modernism, for his interest and support.

I also want to thank Patricia Willis, curator of the American Literature Section of the Beinecke Rare Book Room and Research

Library at Yale, Dennis Cosgrove of the Humanities Research Center at Austin, and the staff of the Manuscript Room of the British Museum and of the Lilly Library at Bloomington for their gracious and effective assistance. Everyone who studies the poetry of Ezra Pound owes a debt to Mary de Rachelwitz. I am particularly grateful to her for showing me some books in her father's library at Brunnenberg of which I had no previous knowledge.

Portions of chapter 4 first appeared in *Twentieth Century Literature*. I thank the editors for permission to republish. I also thank the trustees of the Ezra Pound Literary Property Trust for permission to quote from Pound's published and unpublished works. All previously unpublished materials from the pen of Ezra Pound are the copyright of the trustees of the Ezra Pound Literary Property Trust.

The Birth of Modernism

Introduction

Now that the twentieth century is drawing to a close, we can truly begin to write the history of modernism. Until the present, modernism has been allowed to write its own history – a role that cannot be denied a cultural movement. But now that postmodernism has bared the particularity and partiality of modernist claims to universality and impartiality, as well as all other such claims, we can for the first time put under scrutiny the paradigms, mind-sets, or *Weltanschauungen* that made up literary modernism.

In a sense, the history of modernism is still dark and hidden, even now as we abjure it. Modernism presented itself as the end, the conclusion – even the fulfilment – of history and therefore as the end of historical writing. It would be difficult to find any modernist flatly expressing such a claim, but the claim is implicit in the *echt* modernist principle of the autonomy of the work of art, which has been deployed within literary scholarship to liberate the work of art from the tyranny of authorial intention and hence from the cult of personality.

The principle of aesthetic autonomy is even more firmly attached to the central tenet of philosophical modernism, namely, the context-independence of knowledge. Context-free knowledge is relieved of the burden of historical contingency but without at the same time being placed in some metaphysical or ideal realm beyond history. It is, in a word, positive knowledge, as opposed to historical, relative, or subjective knowledge. Such knowledge has no history, no past, and no future but enjoys an absolute status that Richard Rorty has dubbed "incorrigibility" (Rorty 1979, esp. 88–98).

Although the term "modern" has been current in English with its present meaning since at least the seventeenth century, no school of philosophy or artistic movement took the term as a label before this century. To be "modern" is not just to be postclassical, still less just to be up to date. To be "modern" in the modernist sense is to have transcended history, to have climbed out of history into an unmediated, incorrigible realm of knowledge, and in that sense to have fulfilled history. Postmodernism – whatever this volatile force might eventually turn out to be – clearly has as a common element the rejection of the modernist fantasy of decontextualized or positive knowledge and the adoption of a relativism or perspectivism that is most commonly traced to Friedrich Nietzsche (see, for example, Nehemas 1985). The modernists have become "adopted" as the self-assured, oppressive fathers of the postmodernists, just as the Victorians were for the modernists themselves.

This study is not a postmodern critique of modernism. That is, it is not my intention to unveil the errors, self-deceptions, and vices of those geniuses whose impossibly great achievements oppress us all. Most particularly, it is not my purpose to expose the folly of all claims to positive, context-free knowledge. While I share some of postmodernism's sense of the hubris of modernism's fantastic claims to have transcended historical contingency, I do not share its conviction that to expose the excesses of modernist positivism will reveal a highroad to wisdom. And although I also share the postmodernists' conviction that all knowledge is contingent and relative, I cannot share their joy in the consequent liberation from the risk of oppressive attributions of error.

Nietzsche's oft-cited remark, "Nothing is true, everything is permitted" (*On the Genealogy of Morals*, 3.24), is an expression of the liberating effect of cognitive relativism that should give us pause. A student of the first half of this century cannot take much comfort from such a slogan of liberation – particularly when one remembers that Nietzsche cited it as the *secretum* of the assassins, "that order of free spirits *par excellence*" (3.24), and further that it was often invoked by Nazis as justification for whatever brutality they had in mind.

Nor is the following discussion a New Historicist exposure of the unrecognized and self-serving motivations endemic in the culture and society that produced them and their capitalist, absolutist, or logocentric prejudices. Clearly, such forces must have played on modernist artists as they do on all of us, and they may well account for modernist style and theme as well as for the degree of success that modernism achieved in competition with other styles and attitudes. I have no quarrel with such Foucauldian or neo-Marxist analyses of cultural phenomena, but I am not currently engaged in such an enterprise.

The rationale of this study is much closer to the old method of the history of ideas. My hope is to identify both the nature and the provenance of a set of ideas, attitudes, and concerns that are ubiquitous in modernism and are particularly strong in William Butler Yeats, in his protégé, Ezra Pound, and, to a much lesser extent, in Pound's sometime protégé, T.S. Eliot. These ideas, attitudes, and concerns I call "the occult," deliberately choosing a strong term instead of more honorific terms such as the "wisdom tradition," "Platonism," "symbolism," or even "the literary tradition" – or simply, and more obscurely, "the tradition." Although these terms are not all equivalent, they are commonly used as a kind of code for beliefs that might more properly be called the occult and are employed to darken a scene that might not comfortably bear the harsh light of day.

It is my intention to bring the occult provenance of portions of literary modernism into a harsher light than literary scholarship has so far permitted. It is my hope that such an indiscretion might now be tolerated just because we have at last decided that modernism is behind us. On the other hand, my descent into the dark realms of the occult – like all descents – is fraught with dangers. The two greatest, like Scylla and Charybdis, threaten from opposite sides of the gulf. To borrow from Joyce's symbolism, Scylla is the rock of scientific materialism, and Charybdis is the whirlpool of mysticism and occultism.

The modernist scholars, who as a group have long been loath to grant any serious attention to the acknowledged occult provenance of Yeats's poetry and drama, are the rock of Scylla. Most will not be pleased to hear "allegations" that Ezra Pound was as thoroughly imbued with the occult as Yeats himself was. Eliot scholars may well not be "interested" in an argument claiming that *The Waste Land* should be placed within the occult enterprise of assembling the fragments of a lost faith rather than within the Nietzschean enterprise of "calling into question" all religious faith. The whirlpool of Charybdis is, of course, the postmodern perception that modernism was a coherent cultural movement identifiable with bourgeois, capitalist, paternalist, ethnocentrist, phallocentrist, and logocentrist ideologies which modernist artists shared with positivist philosophers and empirical scientists. In many respects, the postmodern story of modernism corresponds to the one that the modernists themselves put out. This fact alone should be enough to make postmodernists suspicious of its trustworthiness. In any event, the following account gives no support to a postmodern critique of literary modernism's positivistic tendencies. On the contrary, it suggests that positivism was never more than protective colouring for literary modernism's more "romantic" and mystical tendencies. Nor will my story give much comfort to those postmodern revisionists (such as Kathryne Lindberg) who wish to co-opt modernism as a precursor – rather than the antagonist – of postmodern cognitive relativism and scepticism. For if the modernism that issues from the following investigations is, indeed, a precursor of the postmodern, then postmodernism must face its own occult roots.

WHAT IS THE OCCULT?

Even without the complications of the current polemic between the defenders of "classical" modernism and its assailants, a discussion of the relations between the occult movement and literary movements calls for unusually careful explanation. One needs to clarify just what is meant by the occult and to explain why a scholarly audience should be interested in learning about such a disreputable subject. It will become clear that these two issues are really one and the same, for an understanding of what I mean by the occult will go a long way towards explaining why it should be of interest to literary scholars.

In ordinary marketplace usage, "occult" is very nearly synonymous with black magic, sorcery, devil worship, voodoo, and the like, and includes various supernatural entities such as poltergeists, ghosts, zombies, vampires, and devils. This "occultism" is the current stock-in-trade of the horror genre of film and pulp fiction. While these sensational activities and Zoroastrian beliefs cannot be excluded from the sense of the term "occult" as used in this study, they are far less characteristic of occultism than such popular manifestations would suggest. Demonology (the study of malign divinities) is a lunatic fringe even of occultism. Theurgy, or the production of magical phenomena, is more mainstream within the occult, but an excessive enthusiasm for such things is thought by occultists to be rather vulgar. My interest is neither in the subgenre of horror literature nor in the shady world of "phenomena," but in the relation between occult speculation and mainstream aesthetic theory and practice.

It has long been recognized, even if largely evaded in commentary, that W.B. Yeats fully participated in occult ideas and even engaged regularly in theurgic activities. Although Yeats's occult interests and activities are now universally acknowledged, the fact that he "dabbled" in the occult remains an uncomfortable problem for Yeats scholarship. If the literary community were better versed in occult literature, it would recognize that Yeats's occultism is not nearly as eccentric as it has been thought to be. This is not to say that a treasure house of wisdom is awaiting discovery in a body of back-stairs literature and speculation. On the contrary, most occult literature is of little or no intrinsic value. However, occultism as a movement draws into itself texts and ideas that have a very long history in Western literary culture. The occultists include in their canon not only the *Corpus Hermeticum* and the works of Paracelsus and Swedenborg, but also the works of Plato, Plotinus, Iamblichus, Dante, Blake, Shelley, and Balzac (see Schuré [1889] 1927 and 1904; Saurat 1930 and 1934).

On the question of the Hellenic sources of the modern occult, Eliade observes, with much greater authority than I can pretend to, that "all the beliefs, theories, and techniques covered by the terms occult and esoteric were already popular in late antiquity" (Eliade 1976, 49). All varieties of occultism claim to represent a single tradition reaching back into the remotest antiquity. Yeats, for example, devoted much of his life to the study of that tradition. He began with Blake and Shelley, and reached Plotinus only in his later years. Yeats clearly regarded his occult studies as a central component of his literary education.

This assessment contradicts the view vigorously held by Richard Ellmann, who argued that Yeats kept his poetry and occultism separate. Ellmann's theory has recently been reiterated by Graham Hough in *The Mystery Religion of W.B. Yeats*, even in the face of his own survey of Yeats's occult "researches." I cannot attack this strategy in detail, but the thrust of my study is to displace the old posture which sought to inoculate Yeats, as the most exposed modernist, against the more virulent forms of infection by admitting his occultism but somehow isolating it from the poetry, despite the fact that everyone knows that the poetry is manifestly occult in topic and imagery. The evidence marshalled in George Mills Harper's collection, *Yeats and the Occult*, militates against the "saving the appearances" arguments of Ellmann and Hough. Yeats even considered Nietzsche, whom he studied in the early years of the century, to be a fellow occultist (Thatcher 1970, 148).

Occultism sees itself as the heir of an ancient wisdom – either passed on from adept to adept or rediscovered in each new generation by mystical illumination. This self-perception generates a bookishness within the occult that brings it into contact with imaginative literature and authors at many points. The most important point of contact is in the field of myth studies, for the occult movement regards myths as records of contacts between the human and the divine.

There have been frequent suggestions in scholarly writing over the years that modernists other than Yeats were "infected" by occult influences. Occult influence on D.H. Lawrence is well documented and widely discussed (see Whelan 1988, 1–8 for a survey of scholarship on Lawrence and the occult). The attention Joyce gave to occult figures – especially George Russell – and the occurrence of occult ideas in *Ulysses* have prompted speculation about his interest in the occult (see Jenkins 1969; B.K. Scott 1978; Tedlock 1960; Tindall 1954). Lyndall Gordon has demonstrated beyond reasonable doubt that Eliot had a strong interest in mystical literature, and it has been suggested that he was also drawn to the occult (Materer 1988; Senior 1959; Surette 1988). Pound, it is now becoming increasingly clear, shared Yeats's interest in occult topics from early in his career to the very end (Surette 1979, 1986; Materer 1984; Materer and French 1982; Longenbach 1988; Tryphonopoulos 1989). Joseph Conrad, too, echoes occult themes and topoi (Henricksen 1978). Less controversially, the influence of the occult on such premoderns as Edgar Allan Poe and the *Symbolistes* is well recognized by French scholarship (see Viatte [1928] 1965; Amadou and Kanters 1955).

The bibliography of literature on relations between modernist literature and painting on the one hand and the occult or secret societies on the other is very large and is growing. Nor, of course, is such scholarship confined to modernism. Blake, Christopher Smart, Robert Burns, Shelley, and even Kipling have been drawn into the net of occult influence (Roberts 1986). No author seems safe from allegations of occultism, or of membership in a secret society, or of infection by theosophical ideas. Even Wallace Stevens, the consummate sceptic, has been found to indulge in Hermetic ideas (Woodman 1983). For the most part, such studies have been left to languish in obscurity if not oblivion. Some of the authors are themselves members of the occult movement. Kathleen Raine is one such individual, as was the French scholar Denis Saurat of the University of London. However, others – such as John Senior, Timothy Materer, and myself – are interested in the topic only because the historical evidence of its pertinence to literary modernism is overwhelming.

The scandal is not that scholars have dared to suggest that canonized authors such as Conrad, Yeats, Lawrence, Pound, Eliot, and Stevens – to mention only those so far invoked – were tainted by occult influences. On the contrary, the scandal is scholarship's longstanding avoidance of the topic. The evident motive for its avoidance is noble enough. Much of the literature "exposing" occultism in canonized authors is of poor quality or on the margins of scholarship, or is written by individuals whose enthusiasm for the topic often outreaches their caution. At the same time, even with an author whose occult interests were as public and overt as Yeats's were, the scholarly community considers it poor form to dwell upon such an aberration. Like Pound's fascism, Yeats's occultism has been a subject not to be raised in polite company. To do so could only serve to discredit an accredited genius of the modern age and give aid and comfort to the enemies of the modernist enlightenment.

Literary scholars have long been joined together in an exercise of damage control on the issue of Yeats's occultism as they have for Pound's fascism. Of course, there were a few renegades and mavericks who would not close ranks. In the case of Yeats's occultism, these voices were successfully pushed to the margins of the scholarly community. This strategy, I think, can no longer be maintained. The spectre of the occult is now being raised on clear-cut evidence for Pound as well as for Yeats. Lofty disregard is no longer appropriate. (For examples of lofty disregard, see H. Bloom 1964 and Davie 1972.)

There have been two general approaches to the topic of relations between the occult and mainstream literature. The "official" manner is to admit the fact of some infection or relationship but to argue that occult ideas are absorbed into an aesthetic or psychological theory and are thereby rendered "harmless." This is the manner adopted by Abrams for Romanticism in *Natural Supernaturalism*, by Ellmann for Yeats in both of his major studies of Yeats, and most recently by Graham Hough. The second approach has been to bring occult sources and ideas to the interpretation of the literary texts, thereby at least implicitly legitimizing the occult elements. This approach is adopted by F.A.C. Wilson in his studies of Yeats and by Kathleen Raine in her studies of Blake and Yeats.

Within these general approaches, one finds two strategies commonly deployed. The one most vulnerable to destructive analysis focuses rather narrowly on some particular point of similarity between a theme, or topos, common to the occult and to poetry or fiction, and alleges an influence or at least a shared belief based on these similarities. The second strategy is to select some particular occult source – for example, the tarot pack, Masonry, Blavatsky, Ouspensky, or Edward Carpenter – and to seek evidence of that source's reflection in particular texts. In many cases, there is good evidence for contact between the author and the occult source but only a rather shaky indication that this contact is reflected in the poetry or fiction. Cases in point here are Robert Burns and Rudyard Kipling, for whom there is good evidence that both were Freemasons, and yet there are no clear manifestations of peculiarly masonic ideas in their poetry. (In the case of Masonry, there is great difficulty in discovering what might count as a specifically masonic idea.) In other cases – such as Joseph Conrad and Wallace Stevens – there are ample indications of occultlike themes and topoi in the fiction or poetry, but there is not such good evidence of contact between the authors and occult sources.

Scholarship has now reached the point where the question of the relevance of occultism to Yeats, Pound, Lawrence, and even Eliot is no longer open. While not all the evidence is in, enough is in to render the strategy of scholarly avoidance obsolete. If we cannot expunge the occult from the history of modernism (and we cannot), then the sensible thing is to learn more about the occult so that we can not only recognize it when we meet it in a literary setting but also have a clearer sense of what it is that mainstream literary scholarship has been avoiding for the past fifty years and more.

On this point, I find – somewhat to my chagrin – that Herbert Schneidau has anticipated me by some twenty years. Schneidau remarked in his 1969 study of Pound and Imagism that "literary and religious thought are as intertwined in the twentieth century as they were in the seventeenth" (173). He goes on to observe, in a note, that he could not believe that "the developments in the theories of myth and religion which were stimulated in those years, by scholars and charlatans, had no effect on modern literature" (174). His note then mentions "Cambridge anthropologists" and Madame Blavatsky, and predicts that "we will find ways to avoid the obscuring" of these sources of modernism. Elsewhere in his study, Schneidau gives some attention to G.R.S. Mead, editor of the *Quest*, a theosophical review in which Pound published "Psychology and Troubadours," and to Allen Upward, an occultist and the man who introduced Pound to Chinese literature (118–30). Schneidau also mentions Joséphin Péladan, a French occultist who influenced Pound (120), and he has a long note on the relevance of Nietzsche to modernism (199). Although I had previously read Schneidau's study, that was nearly twenty years ago, and I remembered it as a J. Hillis Miller–inspired examination of Imagist rhetorical theory and practice. I had no recollection of the above remarks and was reminded of them only during late revisions of my own study. However, Schneidau did not carry out the investigation he foresaw. That work has been left for me to accomplish.

Learning more about the occult will not demonstrate that scholarship's cautious isolation of aesthetic modernism from the occult was ill advised. That is, it will not demonstrate that occult speculation is sober and profound – as the occultists and some of their champions maintain. The occult, alas, is full of ideas to which few educated men and women could subscribe. However, we shall discover that not all occultists are habitually engaged in conversing with ghosts and demons, transmigrating from Dublin to Tibet, running naked in the moonlight, or signing pacts with the devil, as Hollywood and pulp fiction would lead one to believe. But it must be admitted that such perceptions of the occult are supported by the behaviour of some prominent occultists, the most notorious perhaps being Joséphin Péladan, Mme Blavatsky, and Aleister Crowley. Even sober scholarly works are inclined to a little sensationalism when they approach the occult. Mario Praz's study, soberly entitled *The Romantic Agony* in its English translation, was more spectacularly titled in Italian *La Carne, la morte e il diavolo* ("Flesh, death and the devil").

If we were to call our subject Perennial Philosophy, Gnosticism, Neoplatonism, or Hermeticism, some of the contempt and fear prompted by the label "occult" might be allayed, for these terms isolate the occult from ghosts, poltergeists, witches, vampires, werewolves, and the like. Certainly, it is not my contention that such supernatural phenomena or beings are important to the history of modernism. But at the same time, it is the case that the occult community on the whole believes in such things, and therefore it would be misleading to pretend that we are dealing with "excited" philosophy when we speak of the occult.

Gnosticism, Neoplatonism, and Hermeticism are proper names applying to particular – if rather ill-defined – bodies of doctrine and opinion of the late classical period. Perennial Philosophy is Aldous Huxley's label for a set of beliefs that I call "occultism." Both Perennial Philosophy and the occult claim for themselves whatever enlightenment is thought to be contained in Gnosticism, Neoplatonism, Hermeticism, or any other mystical, illuminated, pneumatic, or visionary tradition whatsoever – including those of Hinduism, Judaism, Buddhism, Christianity, and Islam, as well as Swedenborgianism, spiritualism, and theosophy. They are, in short, synoptic belief systems.

Scholarly ignorance of the occult results from a largely justifiable contempt for the set of beliefs it represents. Although occultism is marginal to aesthetic culture, it is not as clearly isolated from it as might at first appear, or as one might wish. If we draw the horizons of the occult as the occultists themselves do, it possesses a long history running parallel to mainstream aesthetic culture, intersecting with it at many points. The intersections of which I speak are not just resemblances between the themes and beliefs of occult writers and poets or artists; they include clear-cut cases of artists who adopt and accept occult beliefs and formulations. Occultism has much the same relation to nineteenth- and twentieth-century literature as

Hermetic and Neoplatonic ideas have to the painting and architecture of the Italian Renaissance – as has been well recognized for Blake, the *Symbolistes*, and Yeats, but not yet for modernism as a whole. (For a discussion of the history of occultism and its affiliation with literature, see Tryphonopoulos 1992, 23–38.)

Claims for the ubiquity of occult influence on aesthetic culture are commonly received as allegations, reflecting scholarly fear of the occult. It seems to be widely believed that any contact with the occult is rather like contact with an infectious and incurable disease. The response to Yeats's indubitable occultism is a case in point. Modernist writers who are connected in one way or another with Yeats have been careful to dissociate themselves from his occultism. Pound, Joyce, and Eliot are all on record with disparaging remarks about Yeats's ghosts. We have no reason to doubt the candour of Joyce and Eliot, but Longenbach's recent study demonstrates beyond doubt that Pound was far more sympathetic to Yeats's occultism and even his "ghosts" than his public remarks would lead one to believe (Longenbach 1988, esp. 30–3).

But before we can even begin to ground such claims, we need to have some idea of what is meant by the term "occult." A tight definition of doctrine or practice is not to be expected, for the occult movement is highly eclectic in doctrine and varied in practices. Although it does throw up institutionalizations of itself – such as Blavatsky's Theosophical Society, Joséphin Péladan's Rose-Croix Catholique, and Yeats's Order of the Golden Dawn – occultists tend to follow their own bent: everyone is his or her own prophet. Clearly, to identify some belief or practice as occult is to discriminate it from more acceptable beliefs and practices related to the transcendental. The occult may share many beliefs and practices with Muslims, Christians, Buddhists, Hindus, or Jews, but it remains distinct from institutionalized religions. One way of formulating the relationship is to consider the occult as a pathological form of religion like devil worship, voodoo, and witchcraft. There is no question but that these pathological beliefs and practices are found within the network that I identify as the occult, but I would argue that they are just as pathological for the occult as for religion, and not definitional for it.

Occultism seems to be an exclusively Western phenomenon (if one counts the whole Mediterranean littoral as Western). The dominant Western religious culture has long been monotheistic and doctrinally intolerant. These features are shared by Judaism, Christianity, and Islam in all their varieties. The occult is often not theistic at all, and even when it is monotheistic it retains all sorts of supernatural agencies in addition to God. These are features it shares with Indian

religious culture and all varieties of shamanism. An equally fundamental feature of Western religions is a dualistic ontology – that is,
the postulation of a spiritual and a material realm. The occult is
almost invariably monist, assuming a single realm modulating from
material or "hylic" thickness through mental or psychic attenuation
to spiritual or noumenal reality. Because of this monism, the modern
occult thought it had found an ally in materialist science's discovery
of radiation and the nonparticulate nature of quantum physics (see
Chiari 1970, 19).

However, the occult can hardly be adequately characterized by
theological and philosophical positions. It is much less coherent and
perhaps more interesting than that. Denis Saurat's characterization
of the occult as the "strange and monstrous alliances" of "all the
conquered religions: Gnostic beliefs, Neo-platonism, Hermeticism,
Manicheanism, Mithraism, Zoroastrianism" is as true and accurate a
definition as we are likely to get (Saurat 1929, 225). He is right to
remind us that the occultist creates strange and monstrous alliances
of these various beliefs and doctrines – many of them known only
in fragments, and all of them subtle or obscure even when known.

Occultism, then, can reasonably be regarded as metaphysical speculation – speculation about the nature of ultimate reality and of our
relation to it. Typically nontheistic and monistic, it is also typically
mystical. All varieties of occultism of which I am aware assume the
possibility of direct contact between living human beings and ultimate reality, the noumenal, the transcendent, or the divine. Contact
with ultimate reality can be achieved either through a spontaneous
mystical revelation or through some ritual initiation such as those of
the mysteries at Eleusis. The possibility of illumination through initiation distinguishes the occult from mysticism and connects it to
secret societies such as Masonry.

However achieved, occultism holds that the revelation is preserved
and handed down in written texts and in the oral traditions of
communities of initiates and adepts. In all cases the wisdom (that is,
the content of the revelation) is thought to be incomprehensible to
all but the enlightened. That is to say, the wisdom is "occult" or
hidden from all but the initiates. Hence, human society is divided
into the enlightened, the "seekers," and the benighted. The incommunicable nature of the enlightenment justifies the label "occult" and
distinguishes occultism from other postclassical Western religions
which, although they have mysteries or incomprehensible dogmas,
do not have *secrets* – teachings revealed only to a select group of
initiates. The touchstone for the occult is neither mysticism (which
it shares with most world religions) nor, of course, a belief in the

divine (which it shares with all religions) but rather a belief that throughout human history certain individuals have had intimate contact with the divine and from this contact have gained special knowledge (wisdom, or gnosis), which they have preserved in a form comprehensible only to the already enlightened and which is passed on in texts whose esoteric interpretation is preserved by secret societies.

It is in the nature of a religion to have mediatory rites designed to maintain contact with or to propitiate the divinity. The faithful are enjoined to participate in these rites on a regular basis. The occult has only one rite, the rite of initiation. Once initiated, the occultist is enlightened, is one with God, and has no further need of the mediation of rites – although there usually are degrees or grades of enlightenment. So far as we can tell, this feature of a one-time initiation into a profound mystery was also the distinguishing property of the ancient mystery religions – Eleusis, Mithraism, Orphism, and Gnosticism. To this extent, the occult's claim to descend from these ancient mystery religions is well founded.

Because of occultism's focus on a mystery or incommunicable wisdom, occult writing has two principal themes: contact with the noumenal, or "reality"; and the secret tradition, namely, the lives and teachings of enlightened individuals and of the communities of "seekers" after illumination. These latter may practise rites of illumination or study the literature of illumination.

The first theme is mystical and has considerable overlap with the mysticism of major religions. Occultists invariably include the founders and mystics of major religions within their canons of the enlightened. Within the occult, mystical illumination permanently transforms the individual. The illuminated soul is henceforth superior to ordinary mortals in cognitive capacity and often possesses supernatural powers. Séraphita, the eponymous (and androgynous) hero of Balzac's Swedenborgian novel (1833) is one such illuminated soul, as is Mejnour, the magus in Bulwer-Lytton's 1845 novel, *Zanoni*. Glyndon, the protagonist of *Zanoni* wonders if Mejnour belongs to a mystical fraternity that "boasted of secrets of which the Philosopher's Stone was but the least; who considered themselves the heirs of all that the Chaldaeans, the Magi, the Gymnosophists, and the Platonists had taught; and who differed from all the darker Sons of Magic in virtue of their loves, the purity of their doctrines, and their insistence, as the foundation of all wisdom, on the subjugation of the senses, and the intensity of Religious Faith" (Bulwer-Lytton [1845] 1853, 98). Apollonius of Tyana, who appears in the *Thrones* section of Pound's *Cantos* (cantos 91 and 94), is another. All three of these figures have superhuman intellect, are capable of metempsychosis, can perform magical feats, and are no longer mortal.

Such figures can perform all sorts of magic feats, as Fabre d'Olivet explains: "The will of man can have an influence on Providence, when, acting in a lofty soul, it is assisted by succour from heaven and operates with it. This was a part of the doctrine taught in the mysteries, whose divulgence to the profane was forbidden. According to this doctrine, of which sufficiently strong traces can be recognized in Plato, the Will exerting itself by faith, was able to subjugate Necessity itself, to command Nature, and to work miracles" ([1813] 1925, 172). This transformation is quite different from that of the ordinary mystic, which is moral and emotional rather than cognitive and psychic. It also distinguishes the occult from orthodox Judaism, Christianity, and Islam, none of which allow for a gradation of human souls between mortals and God.

The motif of transformation, of being "born again," is a constant in the occult tradition although not exclusive to it. Charismatic, pneumatic, or "born again" versions of Christianity share the notion of such a transformation through some individual experience, such as having "met Christ." The occult tradition regards all religions as popular, profane, or corrupted institutionalizations of the ineffable illuminations experienced by their founders, who are usually conceded to be illuminated souls. Only the initiated can understand the truth, the gnosis. This insistence on the ineffability of genuine revelation is another factor distinguishing the occult from standard religions, which we might characterize as a set of doctrines and practices concerned with the divine or supernatural and man's relation to it. The occult is generally very thin on dogma and practice, since the gnosis is directly received by the initiate.

Following Richard Reitzenstein, and in conformity with Demetres Tryphonopoulos, I shall call the motif of transformation *palingenesis*, literally "backward birth" or rebirth; a death to the old life and rebirth to a new, higher one. As Reitzenstein points out, within literature and the arts palingenesis is commonly represented as metamorphosis. Thus, the metamorphoses in Circe's palace (*Odyssey* 9), Ovid's *Metamorphoses*, and *The Golden Ass* of Apuleius can all be read as accounts of palingenesis (Reitzenstein [1911] 1978, 39). It is this reading of metamorphosis that Pound had in mind when he wrote, "A great treasure of verity exists for mankind in Ovid and in the subject matter of Ovid's long poem, and … only in this form could it be registered" (Pound 1938, 299). An equally ubiquitous representation of palingenesis is the *hieros gamos*, or divine marriage. Sexual copulation is literally a "backward birth" for the male partner who synecdochically re-enters the womb of his partner. The sexual motif in Yeats, Pound, and Lawrence is, I believe, best understood under the rubric of palingenesis.

Within the Hellenic world, initiations into mystery cults also commonly adopt a palingenetic structure or paradigm (see Nock [1928] 1964, esp. 109–45). Sometimes the rites involved dressing in animal costume in a mock or theatrical metamorphosis (Reitzenstein [1911] 1978, 38–44) and sometimes ritual copulation, miming the *hieros gamos*. More commonly, however, initiation rites mimed palingenesis itself as a ritual death and rebirth. The mystic nights at Eleusis appear to have taken this form. Certainly, the myth of Persephone was celebrated at Eleusis as a ritual descent to the underworld and a subsequent return to the world of the living (Paul Foucart, Goblet d'Alviella, K. Kerényi). And as Arthur Darby Nock points out, in contrast to Christian ritual practice the initiation rite in a Hellenic mystery religion took place only once for any individual. Most of the community of worshippers of a mystery religion consisted of non-initiates (Nock [1928] 1964, 109–45). Modern occultism for the most part models its dogmas and practices on its own understanding of Hellenic religious thought and regards itself as the preserver of an ancient wisdom largely suppressed by Christianity. Blavatsky's location of higher wisdom in India, for example, can already be found in Philostratus, who has Apollonius of Tyana journey to India to gain this wisdom.

The topos of descent and death has been far more popular in the modern world than that of metamorphosis, which was favoured in the ancient world. The motif of descent and death is prominent in the Grail literature adopted by Tennyson, Wagner, and Eliot. The descent invariably involves a journey – either to the mouth of the underworld, as in Odysseus's voyage from Circe's palace to the River of Ocean, or a journey within the underworld itself, as in Dante's dream vision. Obviously the descent has more resonance for a Christian culture than metamorphosis. Christ's passion, death, and resurrection fits the motif of descent perfectly and is self-consciously mimicked in the Grail literature. D.H. Lawrence's *Women in Love* enacts several descents involving Gerald Crich, a coal mine owner, and the Persephone figure, Gudrun Brangwen. (Interestingly, it is finally Gerald who is the victim, and Gudrun the victimizer.) Authors more remote from Christianity, such as W.B. Yeats and Ezra Pound, find the topos of metamorphosis more congenial. The topoi of metamorphosis and descent – ubiquitous in modernist literature – are equally ubiquitous in occult literature, where they are esoterically understood as accounts of palingenesis.

G.R.S. Mead is a little-known London occultist who had an important influence on Ezra Pound. Born in 1863, Mead was more than twenty years Pound's senior and was a close friend of Olivia Shakespear, Pound's mother-in-law. Educated at Cambridge, he joined the Theosophical Society in 1884, shortly after graduating. His engagement in theosophy led him to pursue philosophical studies as a graduate at Oxford. He also studied spiritualism in France, at Clermont-Ferrand. He met Mme Blavatsky in 1887, shortly after she came to London from Ceylon (1884), and was her London secretary from 1889 until her death in 1891. He was subeditor of the theosophical journal, *Lucifer*, and chief editor of its successor, the *Theosophical Review*. He remained prominent in the Theosophical Society until he broke with it over a homosexual scandal involving C.W. Leadbeater. He then formed his own Quest Society in 1897 and his own journal, the *Quest*. No full bibliography of Mead's publications exists, but he published dozens of books and hundreds of articles. All of them are of a scholarly nature in that they are either commentaries on or editions of what he calls in one title "fragments of a faith forgotten." Titles from which Pound is known to have borrowed are *Simon Magus* (1892) and *Apollonius of Tyana* (1901). Dorothy Shakespear was reading *Fragments of a Faith Forgotten* during September 1912 (Pound 1984, 160). In the 1950s Pound returned to his interest in Mead and recommended *Echoes from the Gnosis* to Virginia Cazort (letter of 11 April 1955, Pound-Cazort corr. HRC, Austin). Mead died on 28 September 1933. (For a fuller consideration of Mead's impact on Pound, see Tryphonopoulos 1992.)

Mead and Yeats were well known to one another, although Yeats did not much admire Mead. Yeats was expelled from the Esoteric Section of the society in 1890. The year before, he had complained in a letter that "Mead, whose intellect is that of a good size whelp, was a little over righteous as usual." However, the animosity was not lasting, for Mead was a regular participant at Yeats's Monday evenings during the 1910s, when Pound was also a regular. Mead and his wife socialized with the Shakespears too, and he was still corresponding with Dorothy, Pound's wife, in the late twenties when they were in Rapallo.

Mead describes the topoi of metamorphosis and descent quite clearly and succinctly in the *Quest* (just two numbers after he had published Pound's "Psychology and Troubadours"). He observes that "mind is spiritual intuitive mind, the human counterpart of that Mind or Divine Monad in which we are to be dowsed or baptised," and explains that among the higher Hellenistic religions "gnosis was operated by means of an essential transformation or transmutation leading to a transfiguration. There was first of all a 'passing out through oneself,' a mystical death, and finally a rebirth into the nature of a spiritual being or of a god." This illumination is a return to God "symbolised indifferently as a path, a voyage, or the ascent of a mountain" (Mead 1913, 683, 685, 687).

In most cases it is not possible to trace an influence between an occultist and an artist as determinately as can be done with Mead and Pound. But when we consider the extent of personal and literary contacts between major figures of modernism and the occult, it is difficult to avoid the conclusion that the ubiquity of mythological allusion within modernism cannot be entirely attributed to anthropology, as literary scholarship has tended to argue. James B. Vickery's influential *Literary Impact of the Golden Bough* (1973) is one of many examples of this tendency.

The examination of contact between literary and occult literature that follows calls into question the adequacy of this long-established account of the provenance of mythopoeia within literary modernism. Instead of a modernist break with a Romantic and symbolist past, I find a continuity between modernism and its precursors, much like that postulated by early observers such as Edmund Wilson in *Axel's Castle*. However, I go behind *Symbolisme* to its own inspiration in Wagnerian, Nietzschean, and occult ideas, attitudes, and concerns. The relation between modernism and the occult is complex and intricate, but one line of filiation is clearly the importance of myth as both stylistic resource – as in the "mythical method" – and as a source of inspiration and thematic enrichment.

The first, and most difficult, step in illuminating the relationship between modernism and the occult is to educate ourselves about the occult. If literary scholarship knew more about the occult, it would perhaps be less cautious about admitting occult influence on literary modernism. Scholarship's phobia of the occult is illustrated by the misfire of John Senior's "discovery" in *The Way Down and Out* (1959) that Jessie Weston's *From Ritual to Romance* was a theosophical rather than an anthropological study, as Eliot scholarship has taken it to be. My own study of *The Cantos* has been treated with caution by Pound scholars because it is perceived to make Pound too "romantic," if not outright occult.

Modernist scholarship has certainly not ignored the topic of mythopoeia – to use Nietzsche's term – but it has tended to approach it in an explicatory rather than investigative spirit. Although early studies – for example, Edmund Wilson's *Axel's Castle* (1933) and Mario Praz's *The Romantic Agony* (1948, trans. 1951) – did stress the continuity between the overtly occult French symbolist movement and modernism, later studies tended to be almost entirely explicatory. Examples of the latter are Lillian Feder's *Ancient Myth in Modern Poetry* (1971), Daniel Hoffman's *Barbarous Knowledge* (1967), M.B. Quinn's *The Metamorphic Tradition in Modern Poetry* (1955), and Philip Wheelwright's *The Burning Fountain* (1954). This shift from accounts of filiation of modernist mythopoeia with earlier varieties was no doubt prompted by the New Critical doctrine of textual autonomy and New Critical hostility towards scholarship itself – often dismissed as "source hunting."

Mythology is not the only subject of occult speculation. The occult is equally concerned with history. Occultists typically seek to establish a line of transmission of the gnosis from high antiquity, through the classical and medieval worlds, to the present. This line of descent is the "secret tradition." The secret tradition most clearly distinguishes occultists from ordinary mystics whose revelations conform to the dogmas of the religion to which they belong, be it Hindu, Buddhist, Christian, Hebrew, or Islamic – revelations that may be mysteries but are not secrets. (Christian mysteries are "open secrets" that test the strength of the believers' faith, whereas occult secrets are revealed to the initiates, who are sworn to secrecy.) The occult theme of the secret tradition coincides and overlaps with broader trends in modern literary and aesthetic culture: historicism, speculative philosophy of history, and metahistory. Since there does not seem to be any firm consensus on just what these terms represent, let me attempt to sketch my use of them.

"Historicism" is ineluctably linked to Popper's assault in *The Poverty of Historicism* on the claim that large-scale historical movements can be brought under general laws such as those governing physical events, a claim that he attributes to the social sciences generally. However, the hermeneutical historical relativism of Schleiermacher and Dilthey is also often called historicism, even though it isolates the human sciences from the natural sciences precisely on Popper's point that no universal laws govern human behaviour. "New Historicists" in literary studies appear to have adopted the term from Schleiermacher and Dilthey, but they draw their inspiration more proximately from Michel Foucault. Foucault's theory is virtually the inverse of the German hermeneutical historicists in that – under Hegelian and Nietzschean inspiration – he assumes that *Weltanschauungen* largely determine historical event (for a survey, see Dray 1964).

The term "metahistory" has recently been given renewed currency by Hayden White (in his *Metahistory: The Historical Imagination in Nineteenth-Century Europe* (1973). For White, "metahistory" means the "deep structure of the historical imagination" (ix) which formulates and guides the narratives which we call "history." My use of the term is divergent from White's and applies to the structure of the past rather than to the structure of accounts of the past. In this I follow the older usage described by George Mosse in his introduction to Houston Stewart Chamberlain's *Foundations of the Nineteenth Century*: (1968). "Metahistory" designates for him "a synthesis of all historical events and trends of the past – and on the basis of such a truly cosmic construct ... [forms] dogmatic conclusions about the future of man and his world" (vi). Mosse's sense makes metahistory much closer to Hegelian philosophy of history than is the case with White. However, it is distinct, for the metahistorian's preoccupation is to demonstrate the pattern displayed in recorded historical event – a concern rather beneath the notice of Hegelian philosophers of history. Other metahistorians are Oswald Spengler, Arnold Toynbee, Artur de Gobineau, and Paul de Lagaarde.

Gobineau and Lagaarde are proto-Nazi racial theorists who attribute the efflorescence and degeneration of civilizations to the admixture of superior "blood" with inferior. For example, the flowering of Greece is said to be the result of the invasion of Aryan Hellenes into the territory of the indigenous Pelasgians. The subsequent decline is explained by the "exhaustion" of the Hellenic blood in a sea of Pelasgian and other inferior Mediterranean "races." Some of the racial theories combine a racist explanation of historical event with conspiracy theory, for example, *The Protocols of Zion*. Gobineau unites racism with a degenerative theory of history, and Chamberlain unites racism with a "man of destiny" theory.

Nothing is more characteristic of post-Renaissance thinking than the notion that cultural and political change through time is comprehensible and will yield its secrets to scholarly or theoretical investigation. This supposition is shared by such diverse theorists as Vico, Rousseau, Herder, Burke, Hegel, Burckhardt, Nietzsche, and Marx. It is what I would like to designate by the general term "historicism," recognizing that an almost inevitable corollary of such a belief is an "epochal" view of historical event, because if the past is to be comprehensible it must be divisible into components such as epochs. The epochal model is especially identified with the hermeneutical historicists. Through Thomas Kuhn, it has invaded the history of science, where the epoch is replaced by the "paradigm" (Kuhn 1970, 208).

Philosophers of history tend to privilege teleological explanatory models, while metahistorians more commonly present aeteleological accounts. The hermeneutical historians fall in between, providing cyclical accounts which presume that epochs or cultures have a natural term or cycle. However, any given thinker can mix and match these models. For example, the unmistakably metahistorical account that Yeats gives in *A Vision* shows a hermeneutical influence in its insistence on mutually incommensurable cycles, or "gyres." On these grounds Nietzsche's historicism can be characterized as both epochal and teleological in *The Birth of Tragedy* and *Thus Spake Zarathustra*.

Fabre d'Olivet (1767–1825), who has a good claim to be the earliest theosophist or modern occultist, would qualify as a metahistorian. He was in Paris in July 1789 and joined the Jacobin club in 1790 (Cellier 1953, 33–45). He coined the term "theosophy" in his translation of the "Golden Verses of Pythagoras" (1813), a work that proleptically contains most of the elements of Blavatskian theosophy. The origin of the modern occult is thus nearly contemporaneous with the birth of Romanticism, with the triumph of Jacobinism, and with the early metahistorical speculation of Rousseau and Vico. One might even consider theosophy to be a pathological instance of philosophy of history, for in both the Fabrean and Blavatskian versions it couches its teaching in a reformulated history of the world.

Fabre d'Olivet's metahistory still has a Christian, providential cast, but it is very clearly a precursor of philosophy of history – especially of the organicist variety of Frobenius and Spengler:

It is of the past that the future is born, of the future that the past is formed, and of the union of both that is engendered the always existent present, from which they draw alike their origin: a most profound idea that the Stoics had adopted. Thus, following this doctrine, liberty rules in the future, necessity in the past, and Providence over the present. Nothing that exists happens by chance but by the union of the fundamental and providential law with the human will which follows or transgresses it by operating upon necessity. The harmony of the Will and Providence constitutes Good; Evil is born of their opposition. (Fabre d'Olivet [1813] 1925, 168)

Madame Blavatsky and William Butler Yeats were both metahistorians. Yeats's *Vision* is an unmistakably metahistorical work and is modelled in important respects on Blavatsky's *Secret Doctrine*, itself a pot-pourri of Paracelsus, Swedenborg, Fabre d'Olivet, and others. Pound's *Cantos* are an obvious candidate for inclusion in this group. *The Cantos* claim to embody an economic explanation of historical event. However, Pound's epic belongs to secret history rather than metahistory. The historical patterns surveyed in *The Cantos* are not at all deterministic or even providential. The poem permits – indeed, insists upon – chance and accident. *The Cantos* explains historical event through its exposure of a malignancy blocking the creative forces that also are identified and celebrated in the poem. Pound calls the malignancy "Usura." The creative forces are called "amor" and "Eleusis."

Both of Joyce's major works – *Ulysses* and *Finnegans Wake* – are historical, and even *A Portrait of the Artist as a Young Man* has a strong element of historical and mythical parallel. *Ulysses* might be considered as itself a contribution to metahistory in that it applies the pattern of Achaea and Troy to England and Ireland. But, of course, the novel is satirical and comic, and the patterns elaborated are deliberately factitious. *Finnegans Wake*, on the other hand, can be read as a parody of modern philosophy of history and metahistory – explicitly invoking Vico, the grandfather of metahistory. Such diverse modernists as T.S. Eliot, D.H. Lawrence, W.C. Williams, and Virginia Woolf all devoted much of their energy to the problem of history – of the relation between the present, the past, and the future. However, of this group, only Lawrence engaged in anything that could be considered philosophy of history – most notably in "The Crown" and "Apocalypse."

The historical theme within the occult gravitates more to secret history than to philosophy of history or metahistory, but the two approaches – one empirical, the other theoretical – are not always easy to keep separate. The most important sources for secret history – the Abbé Barruel, masonic literature, and Gabriele Rossetti – are themselves mixed, typically citing the same texts as the occultists do but as evidence of secret societies, which are either deplored as anarchic and seditious or celebrated as progressive and liberating. Secret history, then, can be either euhemeristic (that is, allegorical and secular) or esoteric (that is, symbolic and sacred). Euhemeristic secret history easily modulates into conspiracy theory, as in the case of the forged *Protocols of Zion*.

Pound read the *Protocols*, but not until April 1940, very late in the development of his historical fantasy. He spoke of them shortly after in a letter to Odon Por, saying that he had long been put off them by the "rumour that they were fake." Although he found them dull and badly written, he judged them to contain the "complete code, and absolute condensation of history of the U.S.A. for the past 50 years" (Redman 1991, 202). He went on to observe that John Drummond had found their source in a pamphlet written against Napoleon III, a datum that ought to have persuaded him to acknowledge that they were indeed a forgery. The letter remains ambivalent but is certainly not dismissive.

Redman observes that Pound's copy of the *Protocols* is unmarked, suggesting a less than robust interest in this particular conspiracy theory, despite an anti-Semitism that was pretty well full blown by 1941. Another book of conspiracy theory in Pound's library at his daughter's home at Dorf Tirol, which is very well marked, is Nesta H. Webster's *Secret Societies and Subversive Movements*. This book has John Drummond's name in the flyleaf and was probably read about the same time at the *Protocols*, since it identifies in an appendix the source of the *Protocols* in Maurice Joly's 1864 pamphlet, *Dialogues aux enfers intre Machiavel et Montesquieu*. Webster insists on the plausibility of the *Protocols*, despite her knowledge of their source in a political satire directed at Napoleon III (409–10).

The Abbé Barruel's *Memoirs* present the French Revolution as the outcome of an ancient conspiracy more or less identified with Masonry. Gabriele Rossetti – who is the ultimate source of Pound's notion of "a conspiracy of intelligence" – postulates a secret tradition nearly congruent with Barruel's, but where Barruel finds sedition and heresy, Rossetti finds a persecuted society of enlightened individuals.

The occult, then, shares with the mainstream an interest in philosophy of history, in secret history, and in the history of religion and mythology. Literary modernism also participates in these interests. It is no small task to attempt to disentangle all of these threads, but it is one that must be undertaken if we are to have a better understanding of the phenomenon of literary modernism. At least, this is so if one subscribes – as I do – to an empirical notion of historiography. Such a notion has, of course, long been denigrated by literary modernism and New Criticism, both of which adopted (under the rubric of textual autonomy) the positivist principle that only decontextualized knowledge counts as knowledge. Empirical historiography assumes that history *is* context and that contexts can be reconstituted within some useful limits of accuracy. The project of this study is to reconstitute the intellectual context in which literary modernism was born by investigating the occult, mystical, and secret history literature that has been ignored by literary scholarship, even though it was known to Yeats, Pound, Hulme, Lawrence, Joyce, and Eliot to a greater or lesser degree.

There is also, it must be admitted, a branch of the occult more interested in magic and communication with spirits or gods than in metaphysics or history. W.B. Yeats's participation in séances, spirit manipulations, evocations, and the like is unusual for the occult artist. However, a much more extreme case is Yeats's London contemporary, Aleister Crowley (1874–1947), a notorious magician of the day. Crowley claimed to be the reincarnation of the French occultist Eliphas Lévi (1810–75) despite the inconvenient tardiness of Lévi's death. His most spectacular stunt was the performance of the rites of Eleusis on seven consecutive evenings in Caxton Hall, London, in 1909. Price of admission was five guineas (McIntosh 1972, 226–7; King 1970, 115–17). An earlier instance of spiritual manifestation is the reported appearance of the ghost of Apollonius of Tyana to Bulwer-Lytton and Eliphas Lévi in 1854 (Mercier 1969, 1:64–5).

Such activities are quite unlike the ritual practices of religions. They are not forms of worship but are more like athletic contests or spectacular shows. Typically, the object is to induce a ghost or divinity to inform the theurgist on some topic – the future, the past, or the nature of the world beyond the grave. Indeed, we are told that the point of the ancient mystery initiations was to learn of the world beyond the grave, a knowledge which bestows *soteria*, or "salvation," usually understood to mean immortality (Reitzenstein [1911] 1978, 64).

The theurgic practices of such occultists as Crowley, Lévi, and Joséphin Péladan were quite distinct in provenance from spiritualist séances, even though the latter were very common throughout Europe and North America during the late nineteenth and early twentieth century. Spiritualism was initiated by the Fox sisters of Hydesville, New York, who in 1848 began to receive visitations from deceased relatives. A doctrine of spiritualism was elaborated by Andrew Jackson Davis, who patched together a spiritualist theory from Mesmer and Swedenborg in a series of books beginning with *The Principles of Nature* (1847). Spiritualism, however, communicates exclusively with deceased humans and with neither gods nor demons. Nor is the séance truly theurgic, for it does not produce magical events – except, of course, for the apparitions and voices. The Fox sisters themselves communicated with the dead only by asking questions and receiving answers in series of knocks or bangs.

Mme Blavatsky learned of spiritualism when she came to New York in 1873. She soon began to attend séances reported upon by Colonel Olcott. Up to that time she had been just a typical fortune teller, bilking the credulous with predictions and tricks. She embellished spiritualism by adding her special discarnate teachers – the Hindu, Master Morya, and the Tibetan, Koot Hoomi – and other "manifestations" and by redubbing the movement "Theosophy." Most importantly, she ransacked occult literature to produce her first – and very little read – "scripture," *Isis Unveiled* (Meade 1980, 173–4). Blavatsky's success depended upon her talents as a self-promoter and especially on her move to Ceylon with Colonel Olcott in 1878 shortly after the "foundation" of Theosophy. This move legitimated her adoption of Indian wisdom, a strategy that was Blavatsky's greatest contribution to European occultism. (This account is based on Meade 1980. The interpretation is my own.)

The most overt distinction between Blavatskian and Fabrean theosophy is the place assigned in each to India and China. Fabre d'Olivet privileges China and Israel over India as a fount of wisdom, whereas Blavatsky ignores both, privileging India and the Tibetan Buddhists. In addition, Fabre d'Olivet's esotericism takes a linguistic turn. Both of his major studies are linguistic in nature, rather than mythological. His first book is a commentary on *The Golden Verses of Pythagoras* (1813), and the second is an amateur etymological treatise, *The Hebraic Tongue Restored* (1815), which is indebted to Sir William Jones and Court de Gebelin. He argues for three Ur-languages: Sanskrit, Hebrew, and Chinese. Pound reflects the Fabrean privileging of China and of metaphorical etymology – a preference he also found in his friend Allen Upward, particularly in *The New Word*. (So far as I can make out, Pound was ignorant of Fabre d'Olivet.) The hostility towards Indian mysticism and friendliness towards Confucianism evident in the Chinese cantos should be read not as evidence of hostility towards occultism as such but as a reflection of Pound's preference for a Fabre/Upward language-based theosophy over a Blavatsky/Olcott theosophy based on direct communication with spirits. Olcott preferred to call their movement "Esoteric Buddhism," and both Blavatsky's "teachers" were Buddhists. (Pound's hostility to Buddhism also reflects the anti-Buddhist bias of his source for the Chinese cantos, Moyriac de Mailla's *Histoire générale de la Chine*.)

Yeats copied Blavatsky's form of revelation from discarnate masters for *A Vision* – as he revealed in "A Packet for Ezra Pound." Swedenborg is the European prototype for such revelations, and is the model for Blake, who is the most important recipient of astral communications in English literary history prior to Yeats. Fabre d'Olivet, in contrast to Swedenborg, Blake, and Yeats, is essentially a theorist of religion and a disencrypter of texts, much like his contemporary, the English Neoplatonist, Thomas Taylor. Mead, Upward, Edouard Schuré, and Joséphin Péladan are like Fabre d'Olivet in this respect and unlike Swedenborg and Blavatsky. Although all of them are mystics in that they experienced visions, the discourses of the "scholars" are text-based, whereas the others transcribe celestial messages or report on other-worldly experiences, journeys, or conversations. Pound belongs to the text-based group and thus sometimes speaks derisively of Yeats's "ghosts." (The prominence Pound assigns to Greek myth derives proximately from Mead and Frazer, indirectly from Nietzsche, and more remotely from Friedrich Creuzer, whose monumental

Symbolik und Mythologie der alten Völker, besonders der Griechen preceded Fabre's d'Olivet's *Golden Verses* by only three years.)

If we take a very lofty and general view, the occult can be considered a religion in that it is a bundle of teachings about the divine or the noumenal. Most European and North American occultists are content to call themselves theosophists on these grounds, for "theosophy" means "god-wisdom." However, Madame Blavatsky chose "Theosophy" for her movement, making it the proper name for her particular brand of occultism. Blavatsky claimed to have coined the term, but she was anticipated by Fabre d'Olivet, who, as already noted, had labelled the tradition lying behind all world religions "theosophy" as early as 1813 (Fabre d'Olivet [1813] 1925, esp. 159). It would avoid confusion if I could restrict my use of "theosophy" to Blavatsky's movement, but occultists themselves use the term in its descriptive sense rather than as a proper name. I compromise by using "occult" and "theosophy" interchangeably whenever it will not cause confusion.

The occult, then, as we are interested in it in this study, is "god-wisdom"; teachings about the supernatural, the other world, the noumenal, the *au delà*; teachings that are said to embrace the doctrines of all world religions and to be based on direct knowledge of – or privileged access to – the noumenal. Blavatsky's instruction by the discarnate souls, Koot Hoomi and Master Morya, and Yeats's attribution of the metahistory of *A Vision* to unnamed masters of similar provenance are examples of privileged access. Pound's visionary cantos are examples of direct knowledge or vision.

Aldous Huxley catches the essence of the occult very well with his term "empirical theology," by which he means a clear and immediate apprehension of the "ultimate reality." The central occult claim, then, is that all of the world's religions are partial, popularized, or even corrupt versions of a revelation, gnosis, or wisdom that is fully possessed only by a few extraordinary mortals – if, indeed, mortals they be. For some, it is accessible only (to quote Huxley again) to "those who have made themselves loving, pure in heart and poor in spirit" (Huxley [1946] 1985, 12–14). For others – such as Bulwer-Lytton's Mejnour – the wisdom is accessible to those who have the courage and ability to seize it.

In any case, those who acquire wisdom are enlightened – if not beatified – and can speak to the unenlightened only in figures, only darkly and obscurely. The occult believes that gnosis or revelation can be *communicated* only to those who already understand, to initiates or adepts. Pound's translation of Cavalcanti's "Dona mi prega" in canto 36 is thus addressed to "present knowers." Once again,

Huxley succinctly expresses the relation between the enlightened and the rest of us: "If one is not oneself a sage or saint, the best thing one can do, in the field of metaphysics, is to study the works of those who were and who, because they had modified their merely human mode of being, were capable of more than merely human kind and amount of knowledge" (14–15).

OCCULT HERMENEUTICS

The problematic nature of the communicability of occult knowledge – of wisdom or gnosis – is one key to an understanding of the relation between the occult and literature, because it makes a hermeneutic or theory of interpretation an invariable component of occultism, just as it must be of literary theory. Occultism needs a hermeneutic that will explain the general ignorance of an occult revelation contained in various well-known texts. Although some occultists receive the revelation directly in visions, most are initiated into it by instruction or rite. The revelation must remain forever ineffable, hidden, and unspeakable, but it must also be shown to be of great antiquity. As a result, a major class of occult writing is made up of interpretations of texts, hinting at the esoteric meaning hidden or occluded beneath an exoteric surface. There is also, of course, the other class of writing, recording direct revelations. Swedenborg, Blake, and Yeats belong to this class. But visionaries are very much the exception rather than the rule. Fabre d'Olivet, Schuré, Mead, A.R. Orage, Upward, MacGregor Mathers, and George Russell all tended to be scholarly and interpretive in their occult speculation. Pound's "scholarly" approach to the generation of his epic is of a piece with these occultists.

Much occult writing, then, tends to be very like literary criticism or philology. Aldous Huxley's *Perennial Philosophy* is a fairly typical example. It is an anthology of allegedly enlightened texts with commentary. The commentary draws out the esoteric meaning, and the anthology establishes the canon of texts containing the revelation or wisdom.

The occult hermeneutic is based upon a relatively simple binary set of an exoteric or manifest meaning apparent to the uninitiated, and on an esoteric or latent meaning encrypted "beneath" the "surface" meaning. It was the standard hermeneutic of Hellenistic Neoplatonism, which read Mediterranean mythology as a vast allegory, which – if properly understood – revealed the nature of the divine. Plutarch's *Isis and Osiris* and Porphyry's commentary on the Cave of the Nymphs in the *Odyssey* are two well-known applications of such a hermeneutic. The Neoplatonic mythographers believed that mythology darkly revealed the relationship between the human and the divine or the hylic and the astral.

Plutarch, a priest of Apollo at Delphi, found divine revelation in those myths the Christian fathers would soon be condemning as the work of the devil. The Neoplatonist Porphyry regarded Jewish and Christian scripture as a rival textual tradition and – in a now lost treatise – exposed the Old and New Testaments as fraudulent. The theosophists – particularly under the tutelage of G.R.S. Mead – revived much of the Neoplatonic literature on mythology and added their own commentary on the esoteric content of medieval legend. Like the Neoplatonists, the theosophists regarded Christianity as their chief rival and were moderately hostile towards it.

Another parallel between occult and mainstream speculation is found in the theosophical rejection of Christianity in favour of paganism (or Hinduism) and the similar opposition that was expressed by Nietzsche in *The Birth of Tragedy* (1872) and was intensified fifteen years later in *On the Genealogy of Morals* (1887). Blavatsky's *Isis Unveiled* was published five years later than *The Birth of Tragedy*, and the more successful *Secret Doctrine* (1888) was published just the year after *Genealogy*. Blavatsky denounced Christian dualism and adopted Hindu monism, as well as Hindu cosmological and racial theories. Nietzsche and Richard Wagner (Nietzsche's mentor at the time of *The Birth of Tragedy*) were both heavily influenced by Arthur Schopenhauer and transmitted his Hindu-tinged philosophy to Europe at large.

The following sample of Schopenhauer's interpretation of Christian scripture would not look out of place in a work by Mead, Upward, or Schuré:

Now if we keep in view the Idea of man, we see that the Fall of Adam represents man's finite, animal, sinful nature in respect of which he is just a being abandoned to limitation, sin suffering, and death. On the other hand, the conduct, teaching and death of Jesus Christ represent the eternal, supernatural side, the freedom, the salvation of man. Now, as such and *potentiâ*, every person is Adam as well as Jesus, according as he comprehends himself, and his will thereupon determines him. ([1958] 1966, 2:628).

Schopenhauer goes on to observe that "these truths were completely new, both in the allegorical and in the real sense, as regards the Greeks and Romans," but were known to the Druids, Christians, Hindus, and Buddhists (2:628).

Nietzsche and Blavatsky – even though it would be difficult to imagine two figures more remote from one another – almost simultaneously promulgated views that challenged Christianity and proposed to supplant it by a return to antique paganism and Indian mysticism. Of course, Nietzsche was a powerful and highly educated thinker, and Blavatsky an undisciplined autodidact, plagiarist, and charlatan. Nonetheless, both the renegade philologist and the mystical mountebank assisted at the birth of literary modernism in ways that are not always easy to disentangle.

The relationships between Nietzscheanism, occultism, and modernism are complex and intricate but not especially tenuous. The most obvious cases are those where prominent modernists are also avowed occultists or Nietzscheans, or both. Yeats is well known to have been both (Thatcher 1970, 1139–74; Oppel 1987). Wassily Kandinsky and Piet Mondrian were self-declared theosophists (Long 1980, esp. ch. 2). We know D.H. Lawrence to have been deeply influenced by Wagnerian and occult thought (Martin 1982; Whelan 1988). A.R. Orage, editor of the *New Age* and an important influence on Pound, was both a theosophist and a Nietzschean (Thatcher 1970, 219–68). Both of Pound's recent biographers take note of his occult interests and associations, but they make no effort to incorporate this datum into their assessment of the man and his work. They do not even register surprise, despite the general silence of Pound scholarship on the point (Carpenter 1988, 67, 167; Tytell 1987, 57, 69–70, 141–3). And apart from such cases of direct filiation, it can be argued that there existed a modernist *Weltanschauung* shared by occultism, Nietzscheans, Wagnerians, anthropology, philosophy of history, and literary modernism. This claim flies in the face of the standard view first formulated by T.E. Hulme, and endorsed by Eliot, that modernism was a turn away from the mysticism and emotionalism of Romanticism and towards the hard, dry, clear edges of classicism.

The ancient world, like the modern, was not of one mind on the nature and meaning of myths and rituals. Just as modern positivist anthropology interprets myths and rituals as transformed accounts of perfectly natural behaviour or phenomena, so the ancient world had its "positivists" who offered physical, psychological, moral, geographical, and historical allegoresis of myth, ritual, and literature. Such sceptical allegoresis appeared as early as the sixth century BC. The geographical allegoresis is usually traced to Euhemerus (311–298 BC) and the historical or political to Strabo (64 BC to AD 21) (Pépin 1976, 477). I shall follow the common practice of employing "euhemerism" as a label for any naturalistic account that strips myth and ritual of all transcendental or religious significance.

Modern euhemerism is much more varied than the ancient. Sir James Frazer's positivism is close to the ancient euhemerism. He considered all myths to have been explanations or justifications of ritual practices grounded in political practicalities. He thought that kings were originally regarded as gods whose sexual prowess guaranteed fertility for farmers and herdsmen. Since the "gods" were in fact mortal men, primitive societies were obliged to kill old kings and replace them with young virile ones. In the spirit of Strabo, Frazer concluded that stories of the death and rebirth of gods – such as the myths of Attis, Osiris, and Adonis – were devised to "cover" these ritual murders. Frazer's theory was first published in 1890 but was prominent during the birth of modernism, for he kept adding to it. A two-volume expansion of *The Golden Bough* was published in 1900, and the great twelve-volume expansion appeared between 1911 and 1915. It was this expanded version that was read by Eliot and his contemporaries. An abridged edition appeared in 1922 – which coincidentally was also the year of publication of *Ulysses* and *The Waste Land*, and of Mussolini's march on Rome which ushered in the *era fascista*.

Other anthropologists sought to derive all myths from a single event, such as the diurnal round, the seasonal cycle, or gestation. E. B. Tylor – more philosophically – argued in *Primitive Culture* (published in 1871, the same year as *The Birth of Tragedy*) that myths and their accompanying rituals were clumsy attempts to develop rational accounts of observed natural events such as birth and death. Max Müller, at about the same time as Frazer first published his euhemeristic account of myth (the Gifford Lectures, "Natural Religion," were delivered in 1888), argued that myths were essentially a disease of language and that they would disappear as a consequence of our improved understanding of the cognitive imperfections and ambiguities of language. Müller's argument anticipates Freud's in that he sees myths as the product of a pathology rather than as wilfully symbolic or allegorical – as both euhemerism and Straboism tend to argue. Freud, of course, understood myth as a pathological product of human nature itself rather than of language. For Freud, myth arose from the suppression of "taboo" impulses – a term he borrowed from anthropological attempts to understand the "primitive" past of human history. Although Freud turned his attention to the personal past of the individual instead of the fossilized "primitive" cultures studied by nineteenth-century anthropology and ethnology, his mind-set clearly shares much with the cultural theorists, especially with Nietzsche and Max Müller. (For the disputed relationship between Freud and Nietzsche, see Assoun 1980. Freud himself invokes Nietzsche as a predecessor in *The Interpretation of Dreams*; see below, p. 53.)

Neither Müller nor Freud can be thought of as euhemeristic, still less as Straboistic. Nonetheless, anthropology and psychoanalysis shared the notion that present conditions could be causally explained by past conditions – whether it be the survival of religion in modern rational culture or the survival of infantile behaviour in adults. And they all share the conviction that myths, rituals, and other religious practices are merely disguised, transformed, confused, or pathological accounts of ordinary, unmystical, human behaviour.

Occult allegoresis is adamantly opposed to all these varieties of positivistic interpretations of myth and ritual. The occult adopts the symbolic theory of Friedrich Creuzer and reads myths as accounts of transcendental experiences that have been esoterically concealed beneath an exoteric surface. Creuzer applied Romantic theories of symbolic expression to the history of religions and mythology. His "symbolic" or "mythopoeic" allegoresis was adopted by Wagner and, through Wagner, by Nietzsche. In a slightly less transcendental form, it is at the heart of the Romantic hermeneutics of Schelling and Coleridge. French *Symbolisme* directly adopts Creuzer's theory that myths, rituals, and even some secular literature express an ineffable wisdom or revelation that cannot be translated, paraphrased, or otherwise made explicit or manifest. They even adopt his term, "symbol," together with his theory of its nature as the esoteric expression of the ineffable. For the occult, for the *Symbolistes*, and for Creuzer, the literal sense of myths and poetry is merely an *exoteric* surface clothing an ineffable *esoteric* message known only to initiates.

Pound unmistakably echoes Creuzer's symbolic theory of myth in "Psychology and Troubadours," an essay he wrote at Mead's instigation and read to the Quest Society before publishing it in the *Quest*: "I believe in a sort of permanent basis in humanity, that is to say, I believe that Greek myth arose when someone having passed through delightful psychic experience tried to communicate it to others and found it necessary to screen himself from persecution. Speaking aesthetically, the myths are explications of mood: you may stop there, or you may probe deeper. Certain it is that these myths are only intelligible in a vivid and glittering sense to those people to whom they occur" ([1929] 1953, 92). Except for the omission of the idea of cultic initiation, this account is *echt* Creuzerian. Creuzer's symbolism can be contrasted with the Wagner-coloured French *Symbolisme* in which Yeats participated by its privileging of the visual over the auditory and hence of clarity over intensity. These Creuzerian biases are reflected by Pound in his theory of the image.

Although literary symbolism comes down to us from Schelling, Creuzer, the Romantic poets, and the *Symbolistes*, a line can be drawn between literary symbolism and occult allegoresis. The latter holds that the esoteric sense of rites, myths, and poems is perfectly comprehensible to initiates and is obscure only to the unenlightened.

Literary symbolism also maintains that there are mysteries, but it holds that they are ineffable to everyone and not just to the uninitiated. Literary symbolism claims only that the mystery can in some indistinct way be figured forth for everyone in the symbolic structures of myth and literature.

Christianity can be distinguished from the occult in much the same way. As Mircea Eliade observes, "It is primarily the attraction of a *personal* initiation that explains the craze for the occult. As is well known, Christianity reflected the mystery-religion type of secret initiation. The Christian 'mystery' was open to all; it was 'proclaimed upon the housetops,' and Gnostics were persecuted because of their secret rituals of initiation" (1976, 64).

Gilbert Durand's definition of the symbol is almost exactly that which Creuzer elaborated more than a century and a half earlier: "Unable to figure the unfigurable transcendence, the symbolic image is the transfiguration of a concrete representation by a meaning that is never abstract. The symbol is a representation that makes manifest a secret meaning; it is the epiphany of a mystery" (1976, 12–13; my translation). In addition to their theoretical proximity, occult esotericism and literary symbolism share the same hermeneutic antagonists – positivist euhemerism on the one hand and Christian allegory on the other.

Despite clearly articulable distinctions between various symbolic hermeneutics, it is extremely difficult to assign a particular interpretive discourse or theoretical posture to its proper realm: (1) positivistic euhemerism, (2) secular literary symbolism, (3) transcendental mysticism, and (4) occult esotericism; or some combination of these four main types. For example, I could not assign Evelyn Underhill's mythological theory to any one of these with any confidence. She appears to combine (1) and (3). One might characterize Pound's aesthetic as a combination of (2) and (4) plus the Image; Yeats's of (3) and (4) plus Blavatskian communications; Joyce's of (1) and (4) plus Catholic liturgical allegory; and Eliot's of (2) and (3) plus Anglican and Dantescan Christian allegory. I make no extravagant claims for the utility of this fourfold division of hermeneutic schemata, but it is important that one has some sense of the complexity of symbolic or mythopoeic techniques, and the subtlety of the distinctions between them.

Occultism is rather less subtle. Correct understanding of occult texts is held to be dependent upon a profound familiarity with the doctrines and "philosophy" that these texts express. Hence, occultist hermeneuts – who generally do not claim to be enlightened in an occult sense – behave much like literary hermeneuts. They study collateral texts and read everything by a particular author or school so that they can understand the cognitive universe implied in each and every component of the object texts. Occult authors – that is, the enlightened souls who register their enlightenment exoterically in texts (whether sermons, stories, or fantasies) – express themselves in conventional or "traditional" forms, often resorting to allusion and even citation.

Although it is to anticipate our argument, it takes no great familiarity with modernist literature in English to recognize that *Ulysses*, *The Waste Land*, and *The Cantos* all lend themselves to such exegesis in ways that "The Prelude" and even *The Idylls of the King* do not. One of the questions I hope this study will help to answer is to what extent this similarity is merely a matter of style – as Ellmann and Hough argue for Yeats and as Longenbach argues for Pound – and to what extent it is integral to the "vision" of these authors.

Occult exegesis does not deploy some key or code, the knowledge of which would permit anyone to reveal the secret meaning of encoded texts. Such allegoresis is attributed to secret societies by Barruel and Rossetti. Freemasons are the secret society of choice, but Eleusinian initiates, the Albigenses, Rosicrucians, Knights Templar, and Jacobins are commonly said to belong to a perennial secret society communicating in a code, or *gergo*. We will find Pound struggling against such a reading of Dante and Cavalcanti when he encounters it in Luigi Valli. On the other hand, occult exegesis is unlike literary symbolism in that there is held to be a single esoteric meaning which can be cleanly and unambiguously derived by those competent to do so, that is, the enlightened or initiated.

Euhemerism is most vigorous among masonic writers or those inspired by them. The only leading modernist strongly drawn to the secret society and secret history hypothesis was Ezra Pound, and he vacillated about it until he succumbed entirely in his Fascist phase. We shall examine some of the most influential euhemeristic allegorists and their mutual influence in the following pages: the Abbé Barruel, Gabriele Rossetti, Reghellini da Schio, Eugène Aroux, Joséphin Péladan, and Luigi Valli. Of course, euhemerism can coincide with a symbolic or metaphysical hermeneutic – as it certainly does in Pound and in the passage from Bulwer-Lytton's *Zanoni* cited above. The secret society Bulwer-Lytton invents is made up of enlightened souls who possess superhuman powers of whom Mejnour is one. Nietzsche, so far as I can determine, is completely free of either euhemeristic or Straboistic tendencies. Instead of secret societies with secret codes, he stresses the solitary nature of the Superman. Thatcher points out that Nietzscheans were prone to fold together the occult or theosophical superior soul with Nietzsche's Superman. Edwin Ellis did this in his *Savoy* articles of 1896, and Orage explicitly links Nietzsche's Superman to Mejnour, the Magus in *Zanoni* (Thatcher 1970, 112–13, 219–20).

Occult literature contains as much religious history, anthropology, and ethnology as it does ghost stories, visions, and prophecies. The occultist is typically an autodidact and often very prolific. (Heavy borrowing from predecessors seems unobjectionable among occult scholars.) Mead is a typical occult author – as, indeed, is Madame Blavatsky. Joséphin Péladan is another occultist of the period whose bibliography is vast. Unlike Mead, Péladan was a novelist and dramatist as well as an amateur scholar. Allen Upward, mentioned above, was well known to both Ezra Pound and Yeats. His output was small for an occultist but was typical in other respects. He wrote poetry, fiction, and religious history and he translated Chinese poetry. (For Péladan, see Surette 1979; for Mead, see Surette 1979 and Tryphonopoulos 1992; for Upward, see Knox 1974, Bush 1976, and Surette 1979.)

Pound came into contact – either personally or through publications – with all of these occultists. After Yeats, Pound's closest association during his London years was with a very atypical occultist, A.R. Orage, editor of the *New Age*, a journal in which Pound published at least one piece virtually every week from 1912 to 1920. As a Nietzschean as well as an occultist, Orage introduced Pound to a much "harder" brand of occultism than that he had found in Yeats. More importantly for Pound's future career, Orage also introduced him to political and economic radicalism. Orage and his journal were the driving force behind Major Douglas and his economic theory, known as Social Credit.

Orage, Upward, Evelyn Underhill, and Weston were frequent participants in the Quest Society meetings organized by Mead in Kensington Town Hall. Other participants included Ezra Pound, Dorothy Shakespear, W.B. Yeats, Harriet Shaw Weaver, Wyndham Lewis, Rebecca West, and T.E. Hulme. Many of these names are mentioned by Pound in the unpublished correspondence with Patricia Hutchins (British Museum, Add. 57725). Although not all of these individuals were occultists, their attendance indicates that they were not ashamed to be associated with the kind of "excited philosophy" they would hear at these meetings. As we have seen, one of the talks they would have heard was Pound's "Psychology and Troubadours." The ideas and prose style of this much-cited Pound essay does not look at all out of place in the *Quest*.

The crossover between occult and imaginative literature occurs in two distinct but perfectly clear-cut ways. Occult writers take literature as part of their subject and write commentaries upon it. Jessie Weston, for example, takes the Grail literature as her subject. Homer, Ovid, and Dante are favourite subjects of occult exegesis. Among English authors, Blake and Shelley are favourites, though Shakespeare and Browning are also sometimes studied as authors who either share the theme of illumination with the occult or who are themselves illuminated. Secondly, poets and novelists themselves read occult authors and treat occult themes. Edward Bulwer-Lytton's *Zanoni* is overtly occult in theme, as are Honoré de Balzac's *Séraphita* and Huysmans's *Là-Bas*. Pound brought *Séraphita* – along with Swedenborg, Ibsen, Maeterlinck, Shaw, William Morris, and "Yogi books" – to Hilda Doolittle during their courting days in Pennsylvania (Doolittle 1979, 46–7).

More rarely it happens that a poet or novelist is himself or herself an occult visionary and registers an illumination directly experienced in his or her literary works. Blake and Yeats are well recognized instances of such cases. Blake regarded himself as illuminated in that he had visions and sought to convey their message in his poetry. But, of course, Blake also read Boehme and Swedenborg and learned much Zoroastrian and gnostic lore from them (Saurat 1929). Yeats was a different sort. He adopted the Blavatskian model and communicated with "masters," illuminated ones from beyond the grave, who taught him the system published in *A Vision*. Yeats also experienced some visions, but they remained incidental to his poetry – as in the image out of "Spiritus Mundi" that appears in "The Second Coming." Blake is a very rare case in that he was an accomplished artist who sought to elaborate his own "revelation" in his art. D.H. Lawrence is another such figure, but the occult nature of Lawrence's vision is not so well recognized (see Whelan 1988, 1–8).

Pound, I will argue, is a figure rather more like Blake than Yeats, and not at all the sceptical relativist that he is sometimes portrayed as being. Because there is relatively little of the mystical visionary in Pound's poetry – and still less in his prose – he has not been read in the tradition to which he truly belongs. I shall argue that Pound's message is *echt* occult and that its representation in *The Cantos* is also characteristic of the occult, being hidden as it is in an obscurity of surface for which Pound is notorious. In effect, *The Cantos* are intended only for initiates or – perhaps more accurately – for those whom the poem itself can initiate into the mysteries it obscurely manifests (see Tryphonopoulos 1992, esp. 1–18). It is not an allegory but an esoteric compendium of "modern thought" – just as Pound said it was in the 1917 "Canto One." The surprise, however, is that by "modern thought" Pound meant essentially what I mean by the term "occult." *The Cantos* were designed as an esoteric poem *lacking* an exoteric surface or packaging. They can be understood only esoterically, only by initiates.

The purpose of *The Cantos* was to herald the new age that was impatiently awaited by the whole nineteenth century, by Spencerians, Marxists, and Fabians, as well as by occultists. The esoteric content of the poem is not just – or even principally – an ineffable or metaphysical revelation; rather, it is the hidden dynamic of world history. Alas, Pound's belief that he understood the *au delà*, the world, and history was a fantasy. He was, after all, just a very talented poet, not a prophet or a seer. Once we familiarize ourselves with the occult speculation in which Pound was steeped, we can see that the esoteric meaning of *The Cantos* is essentially an occult interpretation of history together with some beatific visions. Students of *The Cantos* will not find a revelation of the secret springs of the clockwork of history which Pound promised and which he believed he could deliver. But even though the poem's interpretation of history is not authoritative (or even presentable), *The Cantos* survive as a fascinating and labyrinthine testimony to the passion and folly of the occult revival and of its nearly complete conquest of the arts at the birth of modernism.

Pound's arrogance and intransigence are characteristic of those who are convinced that the secrets of cosmology, psychology, aesthetics, history, and economics have been revealed to them. Pound imbibed the "knowledge" and the arrogance from his occult mentors – most especially from Yeats, Orage, Mead, and Upward. Pound's occultism, as we shall see, was both overt and covert. It could not have been unrecognized by his contemporaries, even though it has gone largely unremarked. However, it did not go entirely unremarked. I hope to show that what I call the "occult" was so ubiquitous in *fin de siècle* Europe and America that Pound's occultism was hardly worth remarking upon. Everyone "dabbled" in the occult. Only theurgy or magic would be remarked upon, and Yeats was the only important figure who had any interest in such things. Everything else that I identify as the occult commonly passed muster as symbolism, philosophy, romanticism, aestheticism, or – a little more obscurely – "visionary."

CHAPTER ONE

Discovering the Past

SECRET HISTORY

Although literary scholarship has not ignored occult and mystical elements in the literary canon, almost all of the attention is directed at the mystical and transcendental aspects of the occult. Such a concentration of attention is perfectly reasonable, but it has left out of account the political and cultural history that makes up a large part of occult literature. No doubt this neglect has been motivated by the bizarre and untrustworthy nature of occult historical specu-lation, which relies on ancient principles of historiography and schol-arly procedures that have long been discredited. But literature is a repository for all sorts of archaic cultural detritus – myths, religious beliefs, and legendary history, for example. Scholarship is not shy of discussing these components of the literary. The occult is a repository for the same detritus, but because in that realm these archaisms are without the prophylactic protection of ironic detachment, scholarship is shy about these elements.

It is not too much to say that the historical sense of key modernists was very strongly touched by occult political and cultural historical speculation. The historiography and much of the content of W.B. Yeats's *Vision* is clearly derived from occult historical literature. And Ezra Pound's *Cantos*, which Pound himself described as "a poem including history," can be seen to express the occult version of the secret history of Europe (enlarged to include America and China) once we are familiar with occult historiography. This affinity between Yeats's *Vision* and Pound's *Cantos* – that is, the narratization of civili-zation and culture within the ambience of occult historiography – explains why Yeats prefaced his own universal history with "A Packet for Ezra Pound." The packet not only implicates Pound in his own project of universal history, but Yeats also attempts to explain the plan and project of *The Cantos* as if it were somehow a companion work to *A Vision*.

D.H. Lawrence, too, was attracted to the idea of an antique wisdom occluded or suppressed by centuries of European civilization. His search for the springs of that wisdom in Etruscan Italy, in St John the Evangelist, and in Mexico fits the paradigm of occult scholarship. In addition to the influence of the occult on literary figures, it has frequently been alleged that nazism grew out of the occult. (Goodrick-Clarke 1985 gives a balanced assessment of the evidence; for a less measured assessment, see Frère 1974.) Although there is no question of Hitler's contact with occult circles and knowledge of occult publications during his youth in Austria, there is little reason to suppose that nazism itself was an outgrowth of occultism as some credulous works claim. Nonetheless, the historical fantasies of a Nordic or Aryan race articulated by Houston Stewart Chamberlain and Alfred Rosenberg bear a family relationship with the historiography of Mme Blavatsky and her theosophical followers. In all cases, history is seen as a story of conflict between superior individuals of small number ("the few," whether defined genetically or by enlightenment) and an oppressive inferior mass (whether defined genetically or by ignorance). The few are identifiable by their cultural attributes. For the avant garde, these attributes are almost the diametrical opposite of what they are for Fascists and Nazis, but in both cases society is bifurcated into the worthy few and the unworthy many, who must be controlled, directed, or even – in the case of nazism – exterminated.

It can be plausibly argued that T.S. Eliot formulated his cultural theories in the shadow of occult scholarship. His notion of a tradition that subsists somehow independently of official institutions and dogmas, carried by extraordinary individuals (*Kulturträger*) who acquire it by dint of energetic effort is an idea that bears strong affinities with occult notions of a secret tradition. Indeed, the strong anti-establishment cast of aesthetic culture in Europe since the Romantics is mirrored in occult history, which is always a history of an oppressed and enlightened alternate culture perpetuating itself only surreptitiously and with great difficulty. And, of course, the romantic nostalgia for the past is echoed in occultism's adherence to the ancient view of historical process as degenerative, in contrast to the Christian providential view and its Jacobin and Darwinian heirs.

Occult history is founded upon the supposition that an underground elite has maintained itself throughout history and is present amongst us at this very moment. Whenever historical circumstances are favourable, the elite manifests itself. These historical moments – so the theory goes – are marked sometimes by cultural efflorescence, sometimes by political and social change, sometimes by philosophical and scientific achievements, and sometimes by religious reformation. Thus, the occultists have an explanation for historical change that privileges individual agency: once in a while, enlightened individuals achieve positions of power and influence, and the results are momentous. Nietzsche's argument in *The Birth of Tragedy out of the Spirit of Music* that Apollonian culture was introduced by Socrates fits this paradigm, and his argument for the Superman in *Thus Spake Zarathustra* is an even more extreme version of it.

Of course, the historical agent need not be an individual; it can be an instance of dissemination of the tradition. The common hypothesis that the Italian Renaissance was set off by the arrival of Greek scholars from the destroyed Byzantine empire also fits the paradigm. Those scholars were not creators but were merely transmitters of the tradition and wisdom that the West had supposedly lost through the triumph of patristic culture in the West and the consequent isolation of Western Europe from archaic Greek wisdom.

Of course, occult scholarship is not all historiography. Much of it is concerned with the content of the mystery whose periodic efflorescence explains the ups and downs of human history. Since the content of the secret tradition is *ex hypothesi* ineffable, the very notion of such scholarship might seem inconsistent. As Evelyn Underhill puts it (speaking of the mystic), true knowledge is "the piercing vision of the desirous heart" rather than "the squirrel-work of the industrious brain" ([1911] 1960, 13). But even Underhill devotes her life to "squirrel work," making arguments for the facticity of mystic visions and collecting reports on these visions in the hope of leading others to similar illumination.

The occult student of the ineffable is in a similar position. She studies texts just like any other scholar. The only difference is that the occult scholar is seeking confirmation in the documentary record of a knowledge that is already privately vouchsafed to the "desirous heart." The goal of occult scholarship is to bring into the light this noumenal wisdom, a wisdom supposed either to have been deliberately suppressed by official scholarship or to have been hidden from the eyes of the profane by deliberate and clever disguise. Although Evelyn Underhill is a Christian and not an occultist, as a scholar of mystical vision, her scholarship overlaps with the occultists.

The difference between a Christian mystic such as Evelyn Underhill and an occultist such as Jessie Weston is largely doctrinal. Both believe in the possibility of direct, unmediated knowledge of absolute reality, but they privilege different texts as records of this illumination, and they seek confirmation of different truths. In both cases, their scholarship seeks either to confirm or to formulate a revelation given directly to the illuminated – or "initiates," as Underhill calls fellow mystics. Underhill and Weston had enough in common to make it possible for both of them to contribute regularly to Mead's theosophical journal, the *Quest*.

Although the two topics – transmission of the secret tradition and the nature of the revelation transmitted – necessarily overlap, I shall consider them separately in this chapter, examining first the scholarship on the secret tradition, which I call the secret history of Europe. This scholarship divides into two main varieties: (1) euhemeristic studies seeking to discover – or to expose – secret societies maintaining themselves against political and religious oppression; and (2) occult history proper, which traces the transmission of the wisdom through texts disguising an esoteric message. Euhemeristic histories gravitate irretrievably towards accounts of conspiracies and secret societies, and hence never cross easily into the mainstream. By contrast, the histories of the tradition are less tendentious, and they easily mix with cultural history. Part of the purpose of this chapter is to detail the crossovers between occult history, philology, anthropology, and religious history. Jessie Weston is our principal example of this variety of scholarship, but detailed discussion of her work will be postponed until we examine her relation to *The Waste Land*.

The euhemerists study the same mystical writing, mystery rites, and myths singled out by occultists for attention. These scholars explain the marvels reported in the literature by supposing that it is in a jargon or secret code. They further suppose that such a code is necessary because the texts are communications between members of secret and seditious societies. The euhemerists themselves divide into several warring camps. Some, like the Abbé Barruel and Eugène Aroux, are conservatives who seek to expose the invidious nature of these secret societies. Others, like Gabriele Rossetti and Luigi Valli, are friends of the revolution, seeking to demonstrate the antiquity of their Jacobin views and thereby justify them. Still others, like Reghellini da Schio and Jean Ragon, are Masons glorifying the antiquity and influence of the institution of Freemasonry. All of these scholars are amateurs and autodidacts whose writing is motivated by a passionate conviction that they have discovered a truth unknown to the scholarly community. They read one another and repeat the same historical evidence – some of it of very dubious authenticity – and each gives it his own particular interpretation. Between them, these euhemeristic scholars generate an untrustworthy body of knowledge that both occultists and artists continue to drawn upon.

Sedition or Revolution

The story of this secret history begins, for our purposes, with the Abbé Barruel, whose *Memoirs Illustrating the History of Jacobinism* purported to expose the French Revolution as the culmination of a long history of heresy stretching back through the Freemasons all the way to the Manicheans of late antiquity. The abbé wrote his exposé in exile in England, where it appeared in both French and English. The English translation appeared in four volumes in 1797 and 1798, just two years after the French edition. So far as I am aware, Barruel's anti-Jacobin exposé had no influence on literature until late in the nineteenth century, when Gabriele Rossetti discovered it and gave Barruel's secret history some currency through an extraordinary series of events.

Barruel's work stands at the head of occult scholarship because he invented the secret history of Europe. He did so in order to trace the history of an alleged long-term conspiracy against church and king culminating in the French Revolution of 1789. His invention has animated virtually all subsequent versions of occult and secret history. Prior to Barruel, the occult tradition was content to trace its origin to Egypt, Persia, pre-Socratic Greece, or India. Even Barruel's contemporary, Fabre d'Olivet, did not include medieval heresies in his version of the tradition, although he added China to the list of nations possessing the wisdom. Barruel was the first to turn his attention to the problem of the transmission of theosophical or occult wisdom through the Middle Ages to the eighteenth century.

Barruel's argument for a continuity between the classical past and the revolutionary present contradicted the standard Enlightenment view of a medieval hiatus – the superstitious Dark Ages – between themselves and the classical world. His motive was to discredit Jacobinism by exposing it as the survival of dark and anarchic paganism. That he should have supposed that this strategy would work shows how little Barruel understood the romantic and revolutionary forces that he opposed. He apparently could not imagine that the continuity of Jacobinism with a dark and remote past would be received by the romantic imagination as a legitimation of that very Jacobinism he sought to discredit. But so it was.

It is perhaps worth noting here that the notion of a cultural "renaissance" conforms to the occult paradigm of change – itself modelled on the ancient cultic practices of palingenetic initiation – and is in strong contrast to the Enlightenment notion of a revolution, or over-turning, of the status quo to form a new order. A revolution is a willed act that requires decisions, effort, and purpose. In contrast, a second birth – like a first birth – is a natural, unwilled event. The initiate dies to his old life and is reborn to a higher plane of existence, incommunicable to the uninitiated. As the adept is led through a series of ritual experiences representing and often mimicking death and rebirth, so Europe itself was imagined to have "died" during the Dark Ages and to have been reborn, no longer the old classical culture, but transformed or "reborn" as a higher Christian reformu-lation of classical culture. The Italian Renaissance certainly had this view of itself, but in the north the notion of rebirth was taken as a mere rhetorical figure. When the forces of the Italian Renaissance reached Paris and London, they were ripe to be converted by the Enlightenment into neoclassicism, with its program of a willed and planned restoration of classical culture, instead of the more mystical Italian paradigm of a rebirth. Of course, it was the Romantics who labelled the sixteenth century recovery of classical art a "renaissance." They viewed their Enlightenment elders as opponents and called them "neoclassical." Eliot and Hulme's decision to call themselves "classical" was a self-conscious reversal of the Romantic polemic.

This discussion brings us into deep waters involving theories of cultural change that we cannot adequately explore in these pages. Nonetheless, they cannot be ignored, for they are close to the heart of the issue addressed by occultists and euhemerists. Moreover, the whole of modernism is dependent upon a theory of cultural change. Modernism defines itself as an instance of cultural change, just as virtually every other cultural movement in Europe since the Renais-sance has done. We rarely question the facticity of cultural change, and disagree only about the mechanisms governing change. Revo-lution and sedition, the two mechanisms relevant to this discussion, both impute voluntary action to individuals and groups.

Revolution supposes a sudden adoption of a new set of values by the general population. Such an event is analogous to conversion or to what Thomas Kuhn calls a "paradigm shift" – when scientists abandon one set of presuppositions in favour of a newly articulated set. The notion of revolution belongs to Romantic cultural theory and is a model of change that requires no leader but postulates automatic and impersonal mechanisms. The Renaissance is commonly thought to have been such a revolution. An earlier and even more radical shift was the conversion of the ancient world to Christianity. The Reformation was an analogous event, except that it was unable to dispose of Catholicism and hence led to division and war. The Romantic movement suffered no such territorial constraint and is therefore arguably a third such paradigm shift. The point of this survey of "pop" history is to place modernism's self-image as a fourth such revolution into the appropriate ideological context. George Steiner beautifully reflects this kind of historicist thinking in *After Babel* when he divides all of Western literature into "a literature essentially housed in language" that subsisted from the beginning until about 1870, and "one for which language has become a prison" for the period since 1870 – or since Rimbaud and Mallarmé (Steiner 1975, 176). (The phrase "the prison house of language" is from Nietzsche.)

Sedition or conspiracy theories suppose that some individual or group seizes the reigns of power and then carries out a program of reform aided by the power of the state – or some other institution. Sedition is in some ways a more rational theory of cultural change than revolution, for it identifies the mechanisms. However, since the mechanisms are clandestine, sedition theories are prone to attract paranoid personalities. For Barruel, the French Revolution was the result of such a seditious plot, and in this he was probably representative of conservative thought of the day.

Ezra Pound, too, favoured sedition theories. He understood the Renaissance to be the result of the importation of Greek learning and Greek scholars consequent upon the fall of Byzantium (Pound [1929] 1953, 214). He also clearly thought of modernism itself as a "conspiracy of intelligence." Mussolini, Hitler, and Lenin also adhered to a sedition theory of cultural change, and they acted on the theory through their own sedition. The greatest exponents of a sedition theory of cultural change were Marx and Engels. They regarded capitalists as a cabal of zealots protecting their own interests, and concluded that only a counter cabal could bring about change. Of course, Marx and Engels saw capitalism as an open conspiracy – in contrast to such conspiracy theorists as Rosenberg and Hitler, who imagined a secret Jewish plot to control the world.

Both revolution and sedition assume that changes are abrupt rather than gradual. Both, in other words, are contradictory of the evolutionary theory of cultural and historical change, which has been mainstream in the West since Darwin. Of course, the evolutionary theory of social and cultural change is older than Darwin, originating in its modern form with Edmund Burke. As one of the most articulate opponents of the French Revolution, Burke is inevitably associated with conservative positions. However, Burke's gradualism was adopted by nineteenth-century liberal thinkers under the influence of Herbert Spencer and Darwin. The current notion of "progress" is derived from Spencer's adoption of that label for a Burkean theory of gradual social and political change. The phrase "survival of the fittest," which is so firmly identified with liberal capitalism, is Spencer's coinage and was reluctantly adopted by Darwin only in later editions of *The Origin of Species*.

Nietzsche's cultural theory also is relevant to our story, since his influence on this century is as ubiquitous and "systemic" as was Darwin's influence on the latter half of the nineteenth. His theory, like Marx's, involves an abrupt or cataclysmic change. Chronology is of some interest and importance here. *The Origin of Species* first appeared in 1859. The *Communist Manifesto* was promulgated in 1848, and *Das Kapital* appeared in 1867. *The Birth of Tragedy* is the last of these texts, appearing in 1872. Despite the chronology, and the claims of some of their followers, neither Marx nor Nietzsche based his arguments on the Darwinian principle of random selection. Dialectical materialism and the Superman (from *Thus Spake Zarathustra*, 1883, 1884, and 1887) are both teleological theories that are incompatible with Darwinian environmentally driven random selection.

Nietzsche's argument is the contrary of Darwinism. He maintains that the spirit of tragedy, which gave birth to Athenian culture, became degenerate very early – with Euripides. He attributes the degeneration to the triumph of Socratism or "optimistic dialectic" (*Birth of Tragedy*, s14). No mechanism for this triumph is mentioned; but, once achieved, it seems to have been maintained up to the time of Nietzsche himself.

Having established that the essence of Greek culture was destroyed by Socratism, he announces the rebirth of "Hellenic antiquity" in the music of Wagner (s20). It seems that for Nietzsche such great cultural moments depend upon the presence of some genius or group of geniuses, and this impression is very much reinforced by *Thus Spake Zarathustra*. Socrates by his teaching alone brought an end to the true Greek civilization, and Wagner – with the assistance of Nietzsche – was to bring about its rebirth. No further explanation is offered. Apparently, Nietzsche felt that none was required or desired. Modernism participates completely in such a notion of cultural change.

Nietzsche's genius or Superman theory of cultural change is very similar to the sedition theory of Barruel and is as close to a pure contrary of the Hegelian and Marxist understanding of historical process as one could desire. No dialectic – whether material or spiritual – is involved. We have just the accident of an extraordinary individual or group of individuals dominating historical process. Nietzsche does not imagine any "conspiracy of intelligence" as Pound does, but his influence certainly strengthened the sedition theory of cultural change to which Pound subscribed. Instead of a conspiracy such as both Barruel and Pound saw as the essential agent of cultural change, Nietzsche speaks of the enlightened man who "breaks the history of mankind in two. One lives before him, or one lives after him" (*Ecce Homo*, "Why I Am a Destiny," s8). Nietzsche tells us that he himself became enlightened, receiving his revelation "as a sudden birth that occurred in February of 1883" (*Ecce Homo*, "Thus Spoke Zarathustra," s1).

While the political provenance of the sedition theory of cultural change is freely variable, the theory seems always to possess a political or ideological component. Occultism, too, is frequently accompanied by some variety of political radicalism or subversion and, like the sedition theory, does not appear to have any particular ideological preferences. As with Nietzscheanism, the occult finds adherents across the whole political spectrum, from conservative authoritarians to revolutionary anarchists. A case in point is the admiration that Allen Ginsberg, a left-wing Jewish poet, maintains for the right-wing and anti-Semitic Ezra Pound. Despite these differences, they share a sedition theory of history and culture, and a belief in the power of poetry to communicate revelations of ultimate reality.

On the question of political affiliation, Gabriele Rossetti is an interesting case in point. Rossetti spent much of his adult life attempting to prove that Dante was party to Barruel's Jacobin conspiracy and that the *Commedia* was a revolutionary document written in a secret code. Barruel's memoirs do not even mention Dante, but Rossetti – regarding himself as a Jacobin – recruited the great Catholic poet for the antipapal forces. Rossetti discovered the hypothesis of a medieval origin for the Jacobin conspiracy in Barruel. The addition of Dante to Barruel's conspiracy was Rossetti's signal contribution to the secret history of Europe. In so doing, he united heresy, political sedition, and poetic vision, completely inverting the partisan force of Barruel's argument. Barruel and Rossetti were clearly motivated by political partisanship. Both men wrote while in exile in England as the result of political revolution – Barruel at some time in the early 1790s and Rossetti about thirty years later, after Ferdinand I retook his Neapolitan throne (1821). Barruel was a counterrevolutionary facing a successful revolution, while Rossetti was a revolutionary fleeing a failed insurgency.

Another such partisan private scholar, who adopted the sedition theory and disseminated Barruel's exposé of Jacobinism, is the French Catholic, Eugène Aroux. Aroux's partisanship was motivated by religious rather than political considerations. Like Barruel, he was politically conservative and Catholic. Aroux published four books during the Second Empire (1854, 1856, 1857, 1857). In each of them he adopted Rossetti's hypothesis that Dante was a Jacobin. However, in contrast to Rossetti's praise of Dante as an apostle of political freedom, Aroux condemned him as a seditious heretic.

The story of how Aroux came to be involved in his exposé of Dante's heresy is an interesting case study in itself. It sheds some light on the obsessive personality that becomes involved in occult scholarship, but more importantly it demonstrates the ideological neutrality of the sedition theory. In 1851 Rossetti sent Aroux part of the manuscript of his study *La Beatrice di Dante* in the hope that Aroux, who had translated Dante into French, would be interested in translating it. Rossetti continued to send chapters until, by April 1852, Aroux had the whole manuscript. Aroux was so astonished and incensed by Rossetti's claims that the *Commedia* was a political and antipapal allegory that he promptly plagiarized Rossetti's work for his Catholic exposé, *Dante hérétique* (1854). Rossetti had already published a portion of his study in 1842 under the title *La Beatrice di Dante*, but the full work that he sent to Aroux was never published in his lifetime (Rossetti 1935, i–xii). As a consequence, Rossetti's theories were better known in France and Britain by way of Aroux's Catholic attack on Dante than in his own Jacobin celebration of him – which remained untranslated from Italian.

Akiko Miyake has recently devoted an entire book to the hypothesis that *The Cantos* are inspired root and branch by Rossetti's last book, *Il Mistero dell' amor platonico del medio evo*. She argues in *Ezra Pound and the Mysteries of Love* (1991, 227 n. 10) that in 1906 Pound read one of the British Museum's two copies of this work, most copies of which were destroyed by Rossetti. She maintains this postulate in the face of Pound's silence about it until after he became acquainted with Rossetti's granddaughter, Olivia Rossetti Agresti, about 1937. In the summer of 1990 when I first learned of her argument, I pointed out to Dr Miyake the evidence in the Agresti correspondence that runs counter to her thesis. Although she dutifully examined this correspondence, she has chosen to construe it as supportive of an unbelievably early familiarity with this massive work written in Italian – a language, incidentally, with which Pound was far from comfortable in 1906. Dr Miyake's case is further weakened by her ignorance of the dissemination of Rossetti's ideas amongst the occult by Aroux and others discussed below. She tends to undermine her own case by stressing the Plotinian provenance of Rossetti's ideas while ignoring the fact that everyone in Rossetti's day

– and Pound's day – had access to Plotinian speculation without recourse to Rossetti.

Despite her zeal, Dr Miyake fails to find any detailed or circumstantial correspondence between Pound's poetry and prose and Rossetti. She prefers to resort to their putative common source in Plotinus, thereby ignoring the historical facticity of both Pound and Rossetti. Nonetheless, it must be admitted that Dr Miyake and I are in agreement about the centrality of the noumenal theme in *The Cantos* and of Pound's interest in the transcendent throughout his life. However, her penchant for a single-factor explanation of this fact vitiates much of her study. But she brings together many features of Pound's so-called arcanum which support the argument put forward here.

We do know that Pound read Nesta Webster's *Secret Societies and Subversive Movements* – some time around 1940. John Drummond's copy of the fourth edition of that work is in Pound's library at his daughter's home at Dorf Tirol. It is heavily marked in Pound's hand. (I had the opportunity to examine this book only in 1991, when the present study was completed and in circulation, so I have been unable to incorporate it smoothly into this discussion.) Webster was a disgruntled theosophist who entirely accepted the secret history we are placing under examination here. The book is overtly anti-Semitic, "exposing" a Jewish conspiracy even at the heart of the occult. Webster's argument against theosophy is that it was infected at an early stage by Kabbalism and is therefore polluted by Jewish ideas. Nonetheless, she does not dismiss the esoteric; she merely puts it aside, explicitly excluding "theories of occultism" and "the secrets of Freemasonry" as objects of attention ([1924] 1946, xii). It is clear from the frequent markings that Pound read this book with great interest, even though he would not have been friendly to the accusation that all of the secret and esoteric cults were "infected" with Kabbalism.

On the other hand, Webster's concluding praise for Mussolini would have been welcome. And the following statement of a hardcore conspiracy view of history is one echoed in *The Cantos*: "How is it possible to ignore the existence of an Occult Power at work in the world? Individuals, sects or races fired with the desire of world-domination, have provided the fighting forces of destruction, but behind them are the veritable powers of darkness in eternal conflict with the powers of light" (Webster [1924] 1946, 405). In *Guide to Kulchur*, which was written before Pound read Webster (if I am correct in dating the reading as *c.* 1940), Pound contrasts benign and malign conspiracies, and declares his interest in the former: "Secret history is at least twofold. One part consists in the secret corruptions, the personal lusts, avarices, etc. that scoundrels keep hidden, another part is the 'plus,' the constructive urges, a *secretum* because it passes unnoticed or because no human effort can force it on public attention" (Pound 1938, 264). The cantos following the Pisan section, however, tend to reflect more and more the anti-Semitic paranoia of Webster. But that is another story.

The following paragraph from *Secret Societies*, marked by Pound, is an excellent summary of Webster's argument and of the secret history tradition under consideration here, and it includes the bifurcation into malign political and benign esoteric components found in *Guide to Kulchur*:

It has been shown in the foregoing chapters that from very early times occult sects had existed for two purposes – esoteric and political. Whilst the Manicheans, the early Ismailis, the Bogomils, and the Luciferians had concerned themselves mainly with religious or esoteric doctrines, the late Ismailis, the Fatimites, the Karmathites, and Templars had combined secrecy and occult rites with the political aim of domination. We shall find this double tradition running through all the secret society movements up to the present day. (Webster [1924] 1946, 74)

Although neither Barruel nor Rossetti are cited by her, Webster belongs very much to the same tradition, relying on Ragon and the post-Rossetti occultists, Eliphas Lévi, A.E. Waite, John Yarker, and Kenneth Mackenzie. Hence, she is a legitimate heir of Rossetti and is a more definite source for his ideas than some supposed reading of Rossetti by Pound during his brief visit to London in 1906.

Rossetti himself was an assembler of the opinions he encountered in his reading in scholarly bywaters – particularly masonic works – in the course of his obsessive endeavour to defend his original hypothesis in his first scholarly endeavour and his only work translated into English, *Disquisition on the Antipapal Spirit which Produced the Reformation; Its Secret Influence on the Literature of Europe in General and of Italy in Particular* (trans. 1834). In these works Rossetti found hypotheses of secret history that were reflected in Pound but were unremarked by Dr Miyake.

The so-called speculative Masons fill in the fantasy history of Freemasonry between its mythical origin in an incident during the construction of Solomon's temple (preserved in masonic ritual) and the nineteenth century with a history of secret societies and heresies. The nineteenth-century Masons repeat Barruel's account of a continuity between late classical paganism and medieval heresies. The most prominent figures here are Reghellini de Schio and Jean Marie Ragon.

Reghellini was a Venetian who had emigrated to Belgium and wrote in French. His *La Maçonnerie considerée comme le résultat des religions égyptiens, juives et chrétiennes* (1829) was an important source for Rossetti. Its wonderful title is an inverse paradigm of the general hypothesis of occult scholarship. The occultist would substitute "theosophy," "perennial philosophy," Gnosticism, "*l'amour courtoise*," or some such for Masonry as the source rather than the result of Egyptian, Jewish, and Christian religions. Reghellini published three books of the same ilk, but he was a piker compared with the French Mason, Jean Marie Ragon (d.1867) who is Reghellini's major source. Ragon has some twenty titles in *La Catalogue générale*. The eldest of these masonic scholars is Jonathan Ashe, whose *Masonic Manual* of 1814 sets out the "official" history of Masonry upon which Ragon and Reghellini ring fanciful changes, and which in turn is indebted to Barruel, the Holy Ghost of the secret history of Europe.

Ragon, Reghellini, and Barruel are important sources for Rossetti, who in turn is the principal channel for the transmission of Barruel's secret history into the nineteenth century. Although Rossetti's arguments were rejected by mainstream scholars, his attachment of Barruel's secret history to Dante brought his secret history into the realm of literary history. As we shall see, once Dante was attached to a tradition of religious resistance, it was not long before a link was drawn between the Albigensian heretics and the troubadours – a link that has now become almost canonical but was not dreamed of by Barruel or even by his contemporary occult historian, Fabre d'Olivet.

The questionable link between the Albigenses and the troubadours was an essential step in the formulation of the tradition that combines political sedition, religious heresy, and the arts. Aroux's piously orthodox exposure of Dante as a heretic had the undesired effect of disseminating Rossetti's eccentric ideas in France, where they were picked up by the occultist Joséphin Péladan. Thanks to Aroux, by the time Pound joined Yeats's circle of "excited reverie," the notion that the troubadour poets were Albigensian heretics and therefore initiates in the secret doctrine was already standard belief in occult circles.

The Secret Church

Occultism's claim to belong to a tradition much older than Christianity cannot be taken seriously. It is, in fact, an attempt to *recover* older, pagan beliefs and practices from *within* Christianity. It is for this reason that occultists characteristically attribute the survival of their cult to secret, underground societies and are typically hostile to the Christian church and often to Christian beliefs as well. Their understanding of historical process tends to derive from the paradigmatic case of an archaic wisdom or practice suppressed – and often oppressed – by authorities committed to a degenerative or corrupt version of the true, pure, archaic faith. The occult scholar is typically engaged in an effort to recover an ancient wisdom that survives only in scattered fragments and in the practice of marginalized or secret societies. Once collected, these fragments are, to paraphrase *The Waste Land*, "shored" against the ruins of modern civilization. Viewed from this angle, Eliot's poem is a sort of elegiac epic, lamenting the failure of the attempt to recover the past – or perhaps lamenting the impossibility of reassembling the Humpty Dumpty of Christian European culture now that it has been broken. In contrast both to the occult and to Eliot, Reghellini is thoroughly modern – that is to say, meliorist – in his understanding of historical process, regarding Freemasonry as a superior development of ancient pagan religions rather than as the custodian of the surviving fragments of a lost wisdom.

As we shall see, these contrary historical attitudes are very difficult to discriminate cleanly from one another because occultists – Orage and Mead are typical examples – frequently assert that the fragments have now, finally, been sufficiently recovered for the ancient wisdom to be reconstituted, making them appear to be modern progressive thinkers. One touchstone that can help to identify the occultist is his tendency to speak of a cultural "rebirth," "return," or *risorgimento*. Of course, some of them – Mead and Yeats are cases in point – display their occult beliefs quite openly, but others do not – Orage, for example.

The notion of history as the story of the loss and recovery of an antique wisdom has been ably discussed by Jeffrey M. Perl in *The Tradition of Return*. Perl argues that modernism itself and modernist scholarship both accept what he calls an A B A historical paradigm. He traces this scheme to Burckhardt and German art history. The model case is the revival of classical aesthetic standards in the Italian Renaissance. Perl's strong account of the ubiquity of the *nostos*, or "return," paradigm is parallel to this account. I do not deny the presence of the *nostos* paradigm, but I think that the occult paradigm of palingenesis, or rebirth, is equally ubiquitous and moreover is often difficult to distinguish from the *nostos*. Within the horizon of an esoteric hermeneutics such as that employed by Mead and Weston, one would naturally understand the *nostos* to be a secularization or exoteric version of palingenesis. Perl's account does overlap with the occult story in that he accepts the standard view that modernism is post-Christian. He makes Christianity the B phase in his A B A scheme. Modernism and paganism are corresponding A phases for Perl, as they are for Nietzsche, for the occult, and for modernism.

The occult scholars proper try to trace the transmission of an occult tradition and practice from remote antiquity in order to establish a kind of apostolic succession. Like Weston, they not infrequently pass muster as anthropologists, classical philologists, or religious historians. Indeed, I so mistook Mead when writing *A Light from Eleusis*, where I argued for his importance to the representation of European history in Pound's *Cantos*. Of course, Mead and Weston both draw on mainstream scholars – church historians, classicists, mythographers, and folklorists. But in contrast to secular scholars, their clear and overt intention is to discover the secret history of a faith, practice, and revelation in which they are adepts.

Unlike philosophy or history and metahistory, secret history is a distortion, or perhaps a disease, of empirical history in that it assumes that the free, or at least undetermined, decisions of individuals – particularly great leaders such as Alexander, Caesar, and Napoleon – are important causal factors in history. In accounts of secret history, events are determined by small groups or coteries of extraordinary individuals that from time to time achieve positions of power and influence. These conspiracies may be either malign, as in Webster's fantasies of a Jewish conspiracy, or benign, as in Pound's fantasies of illuminated heroes such as Odysseus, Malatesta, John Adams, and Apollonius. As a disease of empirical history, secret history is far less respectable than either metahistory of the Toynbee variety or philosophy of history – even in extreme forms such as that represented by the most recent contribution to it, Francis Fukayama's *The End of History and the Last Man*.

The Tradition

When occult secret history is adopted by poets, painters, and musicians, creative artists become the elite group that carries on the sacred and secret tradition. Shelley's bold assertion that "artists are the unacknowledged legislators of the world" was an early manifestation of this *ars victrix* sentiment. Exactly fifty years after Shelley, Nietzsche – under the influence of Wagner and Schopenhauer as well as of Shelley himself – made the even stronger claim that "it is only as an *aesthetic phenomenon* that existence and the world are *eternally justified*" (*Birth of Tragedy*, s5). Nietzsche later abjured this "romantic" evaluation of the aesthetic, but it became a foundational axiom of symbolism, aestheticism, and modernism. This very same anti-Enlightenment valuation has recently been revived in its full early-Nietzschean guise by postmodernists and deconstructors. The post-modernists – in contrast to the modernists – have not, however, adopted Nietzsche's endorsation of the great-man theory of historical change.

A little earlier than Nietzsche, Pater observed that "every one of those impressions [of experience] is the impression of the individual in his isolation, each mind keeping as a solitary prisoner in its own dream of a world" (Pater 1910, 235). These remarks were first widely read in the concluding essay of the collection called *Studies in the Renaissance*, published in 1873, the same year as *The Birth of Tragedy*. Like Nietzsche, Pater thought of the aesthetic realm as a dream world to which the individual has unmediated and unqualified access. And like Nietzsche, he drew moral conclusions from this observation, suggesting that the highest moral value was to live life to the full, to "burn always" with a "hard, gemlike flame." For both men, a life of passion was the highest and best life. Pater's belief that "poetic passion, the desire of beauty, the love of art for its own sake" were most likely to lead to the wisdom of "a quickened, multiplied consciousness" (238–9) is the essence of aestheticism.

It would be too much to suggest that Shelley, the occult, Pater, and Nietzsche all preach the same doctrine derived from the same mixture of Hindu, Hellenistic, and Neoplatonic sources. Wolfgang Iser, for one, argues against such a conclusion and claims that many of the more striking similarities between Pater and Nietzsche are inessential (Iser 1960, 169–70). On the other hand, André Gide wickedly remarked on the most famous of Pater's disciples, Oscar Wilde, that many of Nietzsche's aphorisms might have been expressed by Wilde and many of Wilde's by Nietzsche (Ellmann 1969, x).

Although Nietzsche's famous bifurcation of the Greek *paideia* into rational and irrational impulses is not a component of aestheticism, it is certainly parallel to aestheticism's bifurcation of the cognitive realm into warm, moist, and suggestive "aesthetic" components and hard, dry, precise "scientific" ones. Pater's French biographer, Germain d'Hangest, observes that this bifurcation is found not only in Nietzsche and Pater at about the same time but also earlier, in Karl Ottfried Müller's *Die Dorier* (1824), and in Ruskin – both of whom were known to Pater, whereas Nietzsche was not; d'Hangest concludes that Pater was faced with an embarrassment of choices with respect to the splitting of European culture between a rational, clear,

Apollonian strain and an ecstatic, dark, Dionysian strain that is now ineluctably associated with Nietzsche (Hangest 1961, 363 n.3).

It is worth noting here – although it is getting somewhat ahead of our story – that the attention that Müller gave to the ecstatic and irrational elements of Greek religion and myth, and the prominence that he (and Pater) gave to the Eleusinian myth of Demeter and Persephone, is derived from another German classical philologist, Friedrich Creuzer. Although little known today, Creuzer's *Symbolik und Mythologie* (1810–12) went through three editions (1819–21 and 1837–43), each one larger than its predecessor. Despite its controversial reception, it permanently altered the way in which ancient myth was studied in Europe. K.O. Müller, Jane Harrison, and the whole Cambridge school of anthropology were following Creuzer's lead when they studied pagan myths in art and literature as records of religious revelation rather than as simply literary fancy and imagination.

However, the scholarly community did reject important components of Creuzer's argument – notably his Christian synopticism and his insistence that myths were priestly encryptions of an ancient religious revelation. On the other hand, the occult found Creuzer's synoptic and diffusionist version of European religious history much to their liking. His account presented European and Near Eastern religion as a single revelation preserved by Egyptian, Hebrew, and Greek priestly classes, finally reaching its fulfilment in Christianity. Ernst Renan, the principal French student of Creuzer, summarizes the theory as follows in his long review of Guigniault's translation of Creuzer's massive *Symbolik des Alten Volker*: "M. Creuzer constructed the history of paganism in the same way that the ancient school constructed the history of Christianity – that is to say, as if it were a body of doctrines, always remaining identical, and crossing the centuries without any vicissitudes but those which sprung from from exterior circumstances" (Renan 1853, 35). This is exactly the way the occult constructs its own history. All the occult had to do was to replace Christianity with its own particular set of beliefs.

Despite disassociating himself from Creuzer's synopticism, Renan observed that

it was like a revelation, a grand lesson, to see, for the first time, united in a scientific pantheon, all the gods of humanity – Indian, Egyptian, Persian, Phoenician, Etruscan, Greek, Roman. The sustained elevation, the religious and profound tone, the perception of the higher destinies of humanity, which breathe throughout this book, announced that a great revolution had been accomplished, and that to an irreligious age – because it was exclusively analytic – there was about to succeed a better school, reconciled by synthesis, with human nature in its entirety. The Neo-platonist spirit of Plotinus, of Porphyry and of Proclus seemed to revive in that grand and philosophical manner of explaining the ancient symbols. (9–10)

Creuzer's diffusionist argument is virtually definitional for the occult. It can be found in his French contemporary, the occultist Fabre d'Olivet – in *The Golden Verses of Pythagoras* (1813) and *The Hebraic Tongue Restored* (1815). As Renan implies, it is the standard hypothesis for the Neo-platonic synopticists Plutarch and Porphyry, as well as for Philostratus – all writing in the patristic period. Edouard Schuré, whom we discuss below as one of the formulators of the occult ambience, was a reader and admirer of both Creuzer and Fabre d'Olivet. Another of Creuzer's readers important to the history of literary modernism is Carl Jung. Jung credits Creuzer with leading him to the discovery of "the close relationship between ancient mythology and the psychology of primitives" (Jung 1965, 162). Nietzsche, too, was a reader of Creuzer. *The Birth of Tragedy* is essentially a revisionist reading of Creuzer, denouncing his alien, Apollonian priests for the suppression of an indigenous Greek, Dionysian religion. However, Nietzsche's avoidance of Creuzerian arguments supporting the unity of paganism and Christianity did not prevent him from being roundly – and justly – attacked for rendering intuitive rather than scholarly judgments, much as Creuzer had been attacked by Voss a half century earlier (see Münch 1976, 101–39; Ratschow 1985, 45).

While no single genealogy of the ideas and attitudes found in Yeats, Pound, and modernism is possible, it is time that literary history considered the relevance of those occult ideas and philological speculations that were demonstrably known to the modernists but have so far been almost totally neglected or avoided by modernist literary scholarship. As a preliminary move in this project, it is heuristically useful to draw attention to the similarities between the occult and better-known mainstream authors. These similarities are, I think, strong enough to account for the difficulty of distinguishing between manifestations of Paterian aestheticism, *Symbolisme*, Nietzscheanism, Wagnerism, and occult esotericism in the literary production of the modernist poets, painters, and musicians. And perhaps more to the point, they are strong enough that the poets, painters, and musicians sometimes themselves failed to perceive any differences and often regarded the whole mixture as a single cultural movement.

Scholarship has tended to isolate these elements from one another. For example, Wagner and Nietzsche are both ignored in *The Orphic*

Vision, Gwendolyn Bays's study of literature and the occult. Stoddard Martin scarcely mentions Nietzsche or the occult in *Wagner to "The Waste Land."* Neither of them consider Pound at all.

Art and Anthropology

Just at the time the popular understanding of the nature and role of art was undergoing mystification in England at the hands of Pater (and, later, of Wilde), the academic understanding of the history of art and culture also was undergoing a transformation that moved it towards the obscurity and esotericism of the occult. Particularly important is the notion of the autonomy of the arts as first developed by the German critical historians of art. Karl Schnaase argued that since art (that is, the graphic arts) has its own "language" – its own forms and modes of meaning independent of verbal language, music, and mathematics – it must also have its own logic of development and its own history (Podro 1982, 40–2). The immediate goal of this theory was to unite the "spiritual" meaning of Christian and pagan art, but its long-term effect was to isolate the arts from the historical nexus and to license the now standard view that the arts have no history in the sense of evolution or development along the type of time line that is manifested in the fields of politics, science, and philosophy. (For a provocative attack on the notion of the ahistoricality of aesthetic value and value judgments, see Godlovitch 1987.) Ahistoricism is not equivalent to the degenerative view of historical change adopted by the occult, but both views are hostile to the dominant historical meliorism of the Enlightenment, of Comtean positivism, and of Darwinism, as well as to Hegelian and Marxist dialectical and to Christian providential views of historical *telos*.

As noted above, a degenerative understanding of the historical process is not unique to the occult. It is in fact the standard view of pagan Europe, and it survived well into the modern period. A notable late proponent of such a Golden Age sense of history is Giambattista Vico, whose *New Science* (1725) is not new in this respect. Joyce's *Finnegans Wake* parodies Vico's understanding of history as a *ricorso*, a view not unlike the *nostos* that Jeffrey Perl ascribes to modernism. *Ulysses*, as well as *Finnegans Wake*, is built around the Homeric *nostos*, which can be thought of as a less abstract version of Viconian *ricorso*. Joyce's satirical target here was the modern developmental view of historical change – even though Joyce did not spare the antique degenerative view either.

The question of history, historicity, and "narratizing" is very tangled and polemical today. I still find Sidney Pollard's discussion in

The Idea of Progress (1968) helpful. Pollard traces the idea of progress back to the late sixteenth century – in particular to Jean Bodin, Le Roy, and Francis Bacon – but points out that it was not dominant until the triumph of Cartesianism and Lockeanism in the Enlightenment (8–11). Pollard also detects a strong resistance to the notion of progress in the early part of this century amongst those "doubters" and "pessimists" such as Spengler whom he sees "as very much part of that revolt against reason which affected a distinct sector of European society around the turn of the century, and brought forth the ideas of Freud, of Pareto, of Bergson, and of Sorel" (163). Pollard's empirical bias is no longer in fashion, and his story leaves Hegel out of account. My story tries to fill in those rebels against reason whom Pollard too easily dismisses.

There was nothing occult about the synoptic and synchronic (or ahistorical) theory of Schnaase and Semper, but their great influence on the writing of cultural history made the occult scholars appear far less idiosyncratic than they might otherwise have done, and it fitted into the general Hegelian shift in which history became a history of spirit, rather than merely a chronicle of political and martial event. Occultists appeared to be applying this historiography to literature, myths, and folklore. Spirit could manifest itself there, too, just as in the formal elements of art and architecture. After all, even the thoroughly positivistic and euhemeristic Sir James Frazer discovered hidden meanings in myths and rituals long known to European scholarship but previously dismissed by the pious as devilish practices or by the sceptical as puzzling barbarisms.

If Frazer's investigation of the strange night vigils of the priests of Nemi could lead to a general theory of the origin of a whole class of myths, then surely an inquiry into the Grail stories might well uncover ancient pagan ritual practices that were unwittingly transmitted by the Christian redactors of myths and fantasies. These stories might reveal themselves as in-truth garbled accounts of forgotten or suppressed rituals. In the same way, the Cambridge anthropologists sought to discover genuine religious beliefs and ritual practices hidden in classical myths. The assumption that the past hides a *veiled* wisdom is the contrary of the Enlightenment assumption that the past is barbaric and benighted, and it easily modulates into the Romantic belief that the past is "truer" because closer to origins, and thence into the ubiquitous occult belief that true wisdom belongs to a remote past when man was close to his divine origin.

Jane Harrison, one of the best known of the Cambridge anthropologists, reflects some of this sentiment in the preface to the 1911 edition of *Themis*, where she explicitly isolates herself from Spencer's progressivism. "The material of religion," she writes, "is essentially the uncharted, the ungrasped, as Herbert Spencer would say, though with a somewhat different connotation, the 'unknowable.'" She speaks of the meaning of religious ritual in immanentist terms with which any contemporary occultists would have been perfectly comfortable: "The only intelligible meaning that ritual has for me, is the keeping open of the individual soul – that bit of general life which life itself has fenced in by a separate organism – to other souls, other separate lives, and to the apprehension of other forms of life" ([1911] 1963, xxiii). Although no occultist, Jane Harrison's interest in myth is of a piece with that of theosophists and the occult revival. An earnest of the proximity of such mainstream views and occultist views is the fact that reviewers and readers of Weston's *From Ritual to Romance* almost never remarked upon its clearly occult nature (F.L. Lucas and John Senior being significant exceptions).

Sir James Frazer's *Golden Bough* (1890, rev. 1900, rewritten in 12 vols. 1911–15), although resolutely positive and euhemeristic, can be read as a revelation of the secret history of European religion. Frazer's findings reduced the putatively unique event of Christ's passion, death, and resurrection to just one of hundreds, perhaps thousands, of such deaths and resurrections that have been enacted around the world from the earliest times. Frazer's revelation that the solemn Christian mass is a survival of bloody ritual murder and ritual cannibalism – even though he was careful to avoid explicitly drawing this obvious conclusion – can clearly count as the revelation of a secret history, even though of a type remote from that invented by Barruel. Common to the Critical Historians, to the Frazerians and Nietzscheans, to Barruel, Rossetti, Aroux, and to the occultists proper, then, is the conviction that things are not what they seem, that there is a hidden or occluded truth to be discovered through an appropriately directed study of the past.

Almost as important is the belief common to all of these groups that some universal and *unitary* explanation of history should be discoverable. Except for Frazer, they all share the antique, unchristian, and un-Hegelian notion that history is degenerative. The Cambridge anthropologists – who include Gilbert Murray, W.C K. Guthrie, and F.M. Cornford, as well as Harrison – participated in this degenerative view of human history in the face of their mentor's (Frazer's) unmistakably euhemeristic and empirical understanding of myth and ritual.

However, in contrast to Nietzsche and Spengler, the Frazerians, the aesthetes, Pound, and the occult clung to the belief that some of the lost virtue or wisdom of the past could be recovered through scholarship or meditation, thereby saving civilization. This is the sense of Pound's much-cited slogan from Mencius: "Make it New." Pound does not mean – as some reader's perversely suppose – "Throw it away and replace it!" Obviously he means that we should recover the old for use in the present by patching, polishing, or even reforging it.

As Ernst Cassirer has observed, positivism has always considered myth and religion to be pathological conditions which society would eventually outgrow or be cured of by intellectual therapy (Cassirer 1946, 21). Against the positive historians were ranged, on the one hand, the euhemerists Barruel, Frazer, and Aroux; and on the other hand, the more credulous Nietzscheans, Wagnerians, and the Cambridge anthropologists. Rossetti and the theosophists Mead and Schuré found themselves precariously situated in the no-man's-land between these warring scholarly factions. Friendly poets and artists most typically situated themselves alongside the theosophists on this point, even if they were quite innocent of any direct knowledge of occult speculation.

Jane Harrison's preface to *Themis* admirably illustrates the special kind of historicism that dominated the period. She seeks revelation in the ancient, discarded, suppressed, forgotten, or misunderstood works of the human imagination: "I have come to see in the religious impulse a new value. It is, I believe, an attempt, instinctive and unconscious, to do what Professor Bergson bids modern philosophy do consciously and with the whole apparatus of science behind it, namely to apprehend life as one, as indivisible, yet as perennial movement and change" (Harrison [1911] 1963, xxii). The mystical and transcendental cast of this remark cannot be mistaken. It accurately represents, I think, a powerful wave of academic research and speculation into myth as revelation that was a constant force in Europe from the beginning of the Romantic period to the present. It was particulary vigorous around the turn of the century, and hence was contemporaneous with the occult revival and the birth of modernism.

Just the year before *Themis*, Lucien Lévy-Bruhl published *La Mentalité primitive* (1910), in which he argued that primitives employed different cognitive processes from civilized men and women. It was his belief that myths were the products of this primitive mentality, characterized by a *participation mystique* (Lévy-Bruhl [1910] 1985, esp. 36–8, 176–7, 368–9). Lévy-Bruhl is not just an illustrative case. He had a direct influence on literary modernism through T.S. Eliot, who knew his theories and was strongly attracted to them. Tellingly, Eliot's principal disagreement with Lévy-Bruhl was with his contention that

civilized man had completely lost the capacity for "mystical participation" possessed by the primitive (Skaff 1966, 67; Harmon 1976).
Eliot, like Blake, Wordsworth, Shelley, and Pater before him, believed
that the poet retained those cognitive properties that Lévy-Bruhl
assigned to the primitive – particularly the primitive's special kind
of memory. Lévy-Bruhl describes the primitive memory in terms very
friendly to Eliot's theories of poetic composition: "In prelogical mentality both the aspect and tendencies of memory are quite different
because its contents are of a different character. It is both very accurate and very emotional. It reconstructs the complex collective representations with a wealth of detail, and always in the order in which
they are traditionally connected, according to relations which are
essentially mystic" (110). We shall return to Eliot's connection with
all of this speculation in a later chapter, but it is important to have
before us the fact that the ideas and attitudes under discussion were
not just "in the air." They were explicit components of the mental
baggage of the principal players in the development of literary modernism.

Lévy-Bruhl's theory contradicted the Enlightenment view of man
as the rational animal and tended to support the Rousseauean view
that the onset of civilization involved an irreversible loss of insight
or wisdom. Lévy-Bruhl was one more voice entrenching this view in
the academic community. As an anthropologist rather than an archaeologist, Lévy-Bruhl relativized the "past" through an ahistorical perception characteristic of modernism. For him, the extraordinary
insight or wisdom of the primitive mind is to be found not in the
temporal past but in the cultural "past," among "primitives" in Africa,
the Americas, and Polynesia.

One could construct an argument that some *Weltanschauung* dominated European thought in the late nineteenth and early twentieth
century, and that occultism participated in this spirit of the age. Such
an argument would be an instance of the mind-set I hope to bring
under examination, rather than an analysis or explanation of it. What
I do want to claim is that the notion of an insight or wisdom surviving in some occluded or secret form from a remote historical,
cultural, or genetic past was neither sinister nor particularly idiosyncratic from the 1880s to perhaps as late as the 1930s. On the contrary,
this supposition was rather mainstream.

The "secret" of the German critical historians, of Frazer, of the
Cambridge anthropologists, or of Lévy-Bruhl was not a deliberately
hidden message or story – as both theosophy and the children of
Barruel believed. However, for them, as for the occult, the true history
was hidden by an imperfect understanding of the import of the

record. They all argued that the significance of the record was not self-evident, that it required a general theory to make the latent meaning manifest. Such a rational and positive approach to the study of an occluded past is not easy to distinguish from the occultist's general interpretive practice, in which he or she assumes an esoteric meaning that is plain to initiates but is occluded behind the misleading exoteric sense apparent to the profane. Indeed, as the examples of Jessie Weston and Jane Harrison attest, it was difficult even for the participants themselves to keep scholarly and missionary motives distinct.

THE PHILOSOPHY OF HISTORY

Pound was, I think, genuinely interested in benign conspiracies, as he claimed in *Guide to Kulchur* – in contrast to Barruel, Aroux, and Webster who were interested in malignant conspiracies, or "secret corruptions." Rossetti's inclinations were of the same nature. His discovery of Dante's Ghibelline sympathies hidden in a secret code – which Aroux took as an exposé – was intended as a sort of Jacobin or masonic rehabilitation of Dante. However, all three secret historians were speaking of a purely secular and political secret. For the theosophists, the *secretum* was a religious mystery or revelation, not a political secret or a philosophical illumination, and so it was for Pound (and Rossetti also moved progressively towards an esoteric rather than political version of the secret).

At about the same time as modernism was being formulated by Pound, Eliot, Joyce, and Wyndham Lewis in London, more profound and more sinister personalities also were borrowing from and contributing to these streams of secret history, metahistory, and Hegelian philosophy of history. Having sketched a little the ambience of historical and cultural speculation at the birth of modernism, I would like to turn again to Barruel's *Memoirs* and their extraordinary legacy.

Although not the sole inventor of the secret history that descends from him, Barruel stands at the head of a vogue for secret history that has been fairly continuous to the present day. Secret history had been a preoccupation of the occult since the late eighteenth century, which produced not only Barruel's *Memoirs* but also Bailly's *Lettres sur l'Atlantide* (1777). Bailly constructed a complete history of preclassical antiquity, including sunken continents and an account of the dissemination of civilization by the dispersed Atlanteans to Greece, India, and China. This bizarre theory was attacked by Voltaire and by l'Abbé Beaudeau. Tellingly, unlike Voltaire, the abbé was not offended at the fantastic nature of the theory. He attacked it because it challenged French claims that the Celtic Druids were the origin of all civilization (Saurat 1929, 54–5).

Rather risibly for us, in the nineteenth century the hot issue was between blond Aryans as originators of Western civilization (favoured by the Germans, the English, and those of the French who stressed France's Frankish origins) and the red-headed Celts (favoured by those French who follow Beaudeau and stressed France's Gallic origin). Perhaps it could have been foreseen that the rather comical "racialization" of national and imperial conflict contained the seeds of the Nazi holocaust, but no one did foresee it. These ill-attested racial speculations were echoed in Mme Blavatsky's cultural theories, but they were not confined to such bywaters (see Barzun [1937] 1965).

A constant characteristic of both Enlightenment and occult historical theory is the adherence to the principle of cultural diffusion. Diffusionism is a natural correlate of the Platonic theory of knowledge to which all occultists subscribe. In both cases, one accounts for present knowledge or cultural practice by postulating a provenance reaching back to some authentic origin. It is obviously contrary to the empirical and Lockean supposition that knowledge arises from experience.

A Lockean cultural theory would assign similarities of cultures around the world to constants in the terrestrial environment and in the biological endowment of human beings. Local differences would be explained by variations in these two factors – environment and genetics – plus the accidents of history. There is no need to assume some ancient origin as an explanation of widely disseminated cultural practices and beliefs, or of myths and legends.

However, the "consequences" of Lockean environmentalism were not fully appreciated until Darwin applied them to the biological realm in *The Origin of Species* (1859). Until that time, the more "rational" Lamarckian model of challenge and response dominated empirical cultural speculation. On Lamarckian grounds, superior ideas, species, or races would naturally dominate inferior ones and spread over the globe. Until Darwin, diffusionist accounts of cultural history seemed the most plausible on either empirical or Hegelian idealist grounds. After the triumph of Darwinism in cultural theory, diffusionism was restricted to an eccentric fringe of the intellectual community. But – like Lamarckianism itself – it did not disappear, for both diffusionism and Lamarckianism appeal to a widespread taste for simpler "top-down" accounts in which events are treated as *acts*, as voluntary behaviour of some agent.

Rousseau – an Enlightenment thinker almost despite himself – focused his attention on the human environment into which men and women were invariably born. That environment was thought to be the residue of some primordial event – a social contract – which had to be abrogated or overturned before men and women could be free to participate in the "natural" environment and thereby achieve full development through free Lockean interchange with an environment not specifically designed to mould them into obedient subjects. Thus, the past was still perceived through diffusionist eyes by the Enlightenment, while the future was to be invented, designed, and fabricated like a work of art.

Jacob Burckhardt might be considered an exception, for he attributed the discovery that the state could be invented like a work of art to the Italian Renaissance. However, there is a degree of anachronism to his claim, for the Renaissance required other modes of legitimation for the state than its mere rationality, and these modes were typically dependent on diffusionist principles. Surely the scandal of Machiavelli was his denial of the principle that all legitimacy derived ultimately from God, and therefore proximately from the church (Burckhardt 1935, esp. part 1, "The State as a Work of Art").

Thor Heyerdahl of the Kon-Tiki expedition is an example of a contemporary diffusionist. His expedition was designed to prove that Amerindian culture was transplanted from the Old World, in contradiction of the Darwinian notion that it was spontaneously generated in the New World. Another such modern diffusionist is Joseph Campbell. The argument of his major work, *Masks of God*, is in a direct line with the diffusionist theories of Creuzer. Giambattista Vico also gives a diffusionist account of human prehistory in *The New Science* (1725, rev. 1744). Although Vico explicitly dismisses those sources that are standard for the occult – Zoroaster, the Corpus Hermeticum, the Orphics, the Golden Verses of Pythagoras, and the Egyptian hieroglyphs (para. 128), he nonetheless asserts that "the entire original human race was divided into two species: the one of giants, the other of men of normal stature; the former gentiles, the latter Hebrews" (para. 173). Such speculations seem wild and irresponsible in the last quarter of the twentieth century, but they were typical of the infant social sciences of the Enlightenment.

Mme Blavatsky was sufficiently ill-educated to adopt the outmoded style of Vico, Bailly, and Beaudeau as late as 1888. Artur de Gobineau's notoriously racist and unscientific *Essai sur l'inégalité des races* was published in 1853, only six years before *The Origin of Species*. In this massive work, Gobineau accounts for the rise and fall of civilizations by the admixture of the blood of a superhuman white race of divine origin (as revealed by Genesis) with inferior black and yellow races of merely terrestrial provenance. Believing the white race to have been diluted so that contemporary Europeans are scarcely as much divine as animal, Gobineau painted a pessimistic picture of irreversible genetic and cultural decline. He was much admired by Richard Wagner and is often said to have influenced Houston Stewart Chamberlain, the son-in-law of Wagner and the leading racial theorist for the Nazis. However, Chamberlain in fact had no use for Gobineau's work. The allegation is a result of the enthusiasm of his father-in-law, Richard Wagner, and Cosima Wagner for both "theorists" (Gobineau 1983, ed's note on p. 1250).

Gobineau is also said to have influenced Nietzsche (Barzun [1937] 1965, 62–3). The facts are difficult to establish, but Gobineau's ideas reappear in recognizable form in Pound's *Patria Mia*. Pound found them in A.R. Orage, an early English translator and excerpter of Nietzsche (see below, "Nietzsche and Orage" in chapter 3). Barruel, Ragon, Reghellini, and Rossetti – eccentric as they are – are sober scholars in comparison with Vico, Bailly, Beaudeau, Chamberlain, Gobineau, and Blavatsky.

So far as its fondness for aeteological accounts of culture is concerned, it would not be too much to say that the nineteenth-century occult is a legitimate heir of the Enlightenment. However, the occult retained the least disciplined and most synthetic productions of the Age of Reason's speculation on human history undertaken within the horizon of a pre-Darwinian diffusionist and degenerative understanding of human history. Oswald Spengler's hugely successful *Decline of the West* combined the old degenerative understanding of human history with Romantic organicism to produce a fatalistic metahistorical and pessimistic account of the birth, maturation, and decay of cultures.

Spengler's theories were derived in large part from those of Leo Frobenius, a German anthropologist of the late nineteenth and early twentieth century who adhered to a diffusionist theory long after it had ceased to be fashionable. Joseph Campbell considers himself to be continuing Frobenius's work (Campbell 1976, 15). Ezra Pound was a great admirer and booster of Frobenius from his first knowledge of him early in the 1930s. Speaking of *Guide to Kulchur*, Pound told Eliot that he claims "to get on from where Frobenius left off, in that his Morphology was applied to savages and my interest is in civilizations at their *most*" (Pound 1951, 434).

And we should not forget that the second (1938) version of Yeats's contribution to metahistory, *A Vision*, was largely undertaken at Rapallo during a long visit with Ezra and Dorothy Pound. Yeats lists Giambattisa Vico, Henry Adams, Leo Frobenius, and Oswald Spengler as scholars whose writings confirm the historical patterns revealed to him by his astral teachers, clearly marking the diffusionist provenance of his own more "metaphysical" metahistory (Yeats [1938] 1956, 258–62).

The 1938 version of *A Vision* was prefaced by "A Packet for Ezra Pound." In the "packet" Yeats attempted to explain the aim and structure of Pound's *Cantos*, which then amounted to only 27 cantos (*A Draft of Sixteen Cantos* and *Eleven New Cantos*). Over the years Pound scholars, including myself, have attempted to discover some key to Pound's epic in these remarks. No one – once again, including myself – has bothered to notice the implication that *The Cantos* and *A Vision* are both metahistorical works. That is, both Yeats and Pound are endeavouring to compose the genuine history of Europe and the world, a history to be found only in obscure sources antipathetic to what Yeats calls the "happy counter-myth of progress" (Yeats [1938] 1956, 262). Their history will be dependent upon some metahistorical patterns or forces such as those discovered by Vico, Gobineau, Spengler, or Houston Stewart Chamberlain.

Yeats identifies Vico as the master source for his cyclical view of history and asserts that "half the revolutionary thoughts of Europe are a perversion of Vico's philosophy," and he cites Benedetto Croce as his authority (Yeats [1938] 1956, 261). Presumably, the other half derive from Locke and Rousseau. Although it would be unwise to accept Yeats's own account of the agreement between himself, Vico, Henry Adams, Frobenius, and Spengler, it is certainly true that all these men developed universal theories of cyclical historical development – as did the more respectable Arnold Toynbee, whom Yeats also invokes (268).

Vico expressed the basic concept as succinctly as possible: "Our Science [the "New Science," or social science] therefore comes to describe at the same time an ideal history traversed in time by the history of every nation in its rise, development, maturity, decline, and fall" (Vico [1744] 1961, para. 349). As I noted above, Joyce adopted Vico's historical schemata and linguistic theories for *Finnegans Wake*. In the light of these observations it begins to appear that virtually all of modernism is drawn either to metahistory or to Hegelian philosophy of history. The appearance is not misleading.

Oddly enough, Pound's *Cantos* do not really qualify as metahistorical. They are not Viconian, Hegelian, Blavatskian, or Spenglerian in their treatment of history. Pound's epic does not present a universal explanation of history as the others do. Nor are *The Cantos* a parody of metahistory like *Ulysses* and *Finnegans Wake*. They belong, rather, to secret history. They are intended to reveal the hidden truth about the conspiracies – both malign and benign – that have formulated the past, control the present, and generate the future. In Pound's

poem, the force that formulates history is neither an Hegelian disembodied spirit nor divine providence, nor even the historical dialectic; on the contrary, it is embodied in individuals and societies.
Pound's epic must be placed in the tradition of secret history rather
than either philosophy of history or metahistory.

Although secret history need not adopt any particular historical
pattern or causal principle, it is unlikely to be friendly to either a
progressive or a cyclical view. Instead, the avatar of secret history
will expect events to unfold randomly and capriciously according to
the accidents of birth and opportunities for cooperation of those
superior individuals who determine the course of events. In this
respect, as I have already noted, it has affinities with liberal historiography. There is, however, a real and important distinction in that
the secret or occult historian – like the metahistoricist who reveals
the inescapable pattern of history – is convinced that the standard
chronicle veils a deeper story. And he is also much friendlier to a
degenerative and diffusionist view just because it is evident to him
that wisdom can be preserved against the ravages of time and the
veniality of men only with the greatest of difficulty – hence the need
of a secret "tradition."

Mainstream nineteenth- and twentieth-century historiography has
rejected the various deterministic cyclical views of the Enlightenment
and all varieties of conspiracy history, as well as Hegelian philosophy
of history, in favour of a mildly Darwinian and progressive story.
That story is now under severe attack from a variety of neo-Marxist
perspectivism, which tends to overlook the fact that mainstream
historiography never abandoned the Aristotelian principle that ran-
domness and accident are the very essence of the historical. It was
perhaps the logical tension between two such apparently contrary
assumptions that permitted the survival of the old degenerative and
diffusionist view alongside the new "evolutionary" view – particularly
within theological and aesthetic realms.

The production of secret histories based on the old, discredited
historiography seems to have been tolerated amongst theologians
and poets as harmless eccentricities. After all, traditional poetry had
been made up in great part of historical fantasies. As a matter of
course, poets had long filled their verses with stories of gods and
heroes who had never existed. What did it matter if they found some
new fables in the pages of eccentric scholars or imaginative prose-
lytizers of new religions of the likes of Emanuel Swedenborg and
Mme Blavatsky?

Yeats is a paradigmatic case. When he offered to "spend what
remained of life explaining and piecing together those scattered

sentences" written and spoken by his wife in trance, his astral teachers replied, "No, we have come to give you metaphors for poetry" (Yeats [1938] 1956, 8). Literary scholarship has been content to accept such justifications for otherwise unacceptable beliefs and practices. It did not seem to matter very much until the rise of totalitarianism in the 1920s and 1930s and the adoption of such "histories" by the Fascist parties. Marxist historical determinism almost simultaneously became much more powerful and dangerous with the Bolshevik victory in Russia.

As Paul Fussell noted in *The Great War and Modern Memory*, the war did great damage to the meliorist and progressive sense of history that had dominated the nineteenth century (Fussell 1975, 8). However, Fussell does not take note of the degree to which social Darwinism, Hegelian idealism, Fabian socialism, and Marxism – different as these philosophies are in other respects – shared a meliorist understanding of the historical process. Literary scholarship has long recognized that the "conservatism" of T.E. Hulme, Wyndham Lewis, T.S. Eliot, and Ezra Pound involved a rejection of such meliorist views, and it has castigated them as "reactionary" (see Chace 1973; John Harrison 1966; Longenbach 1987; Viereck 1961). But the ubiquity of historical pessimism in the aesthetic circles of the period has not been adequately acknowledged. Nor has there been adequate discussion of the degree to which this historical pessimism was confirmed by World War I.

The long-running conflict between meliorist views of historical process and either degenerative or cyclical views has been obscured by the "hot" conflict between left and right, between progressives and reactionaries. On the one hand we have Karl Popper, who traced to Hegel the belief that the direction of historical change was knowable and inevitable and who labelled it "historicism" in *The Poverty of Historicism*. Popper directed his attack primarily at Marxism, but he makes it clear in the preface that fascism and nazism are also caught in his historicist net. Popper, of course, has been perceived as conservative and has had the whole weight of progressive and neo-Marxist polemic ranged against him.

It would be quixotic to attempt to resolve the ongoing conflict between left, right, and centre, but I cannot avoid running into the dust and smoke as I attempt to retrace some of the paths followed by literary modernism. Hence, while I endorse Popper's claim that both Marxism and nazism appeal to the inevitability of history in order to justify their programs, it does not appear to me that Marxism and nazism are equally "historicist." It would be more accurate to place the Nazi sense of historical change in the context of the older degenerative view of history which we have found in Vico and the occult and which – together with Schopenhauer – informs Nietzsche's famous pessimism. Marxist historical determinism is quite a different thing, having its provenance in Hegel's idealistic philosophy of history. Since, for Hegel, history is the story of the growth of spirit, his historicism – like Marx's – is optimistic and progressive.

But despite the cultural hegemony of Hegel, Darwin, and Marx, the shock of the Great War permitted the older cyclical and degenerative historical theories to become fashionable once again. The system elaborated by Yeats in *A Vision* is only one of many manifestations of "poetic" or invented history between the wars. His system describes a cyclical pattern which, much like Spengler's, mirrors the biological cycle of birth, maturation, and death. For Yeats, history is the playing out of an endless, and therefore meaningless, drama composed and staged in the *anima mundi*, in contrast to Hegel's and Marx's idea of a story with a predetermined and logical conclusion.

Pound's *Cantos*, begun during the winters of 1914–15, 1915–16, and 1916–17, which he and Yeats spent together at Stone Cottage, are another manifestation of the period's obsession with historical process. However, as we have seen, Pound's epic does not present either a degenerative or a cyclical view of historical process but treats the past as a story of the capricious flourishing of genius. Perhaps the most striking feature of the epic – which he defined as "a poem including history" – is its un-Nietzschean optimism. *The Cantos* are designed to announce the birth of a new age. They are the contrary of Joyce's *Ulysses* and of Eliot's *Waste Land*, which Pound read as the burial and the "lancing" of the old age. In *Guide to Kulchur* (1938), he recalls the experience of receiving drafts of Joyce's novel to pass on to Margaret Anderson and the *Little Review*: "The karthasis of *Ulysses*, the joyous satisfaction as the first chapters rolled into Holland Place, was the feel that here was the JOB DONE and finished, the diagnosis and cure was here. The sticky, molasses-covered filth of current print, all the fuggs, all the foetors, the whole boil of the European mind, had been lanced" (96). Pound's historical optimism has permitted him to pass muster with some as a progressive despite his undeniable entanglement with fascism. Of course, this is not to deny that many denounce him as a reactionary, as was noted above.

On the question of Pound's fascism, the most recent and I think most judicious assessment of his politics is Tim Redman's *Ezra Pound and Italian Fascism* (1991). Redman concludes: "Pound's support for Italian fascism was not the result of psychosis but was consistent with and developed from his thought about social and economic issues. Certainly there were flaws in his character and in his judgment, but they are not sufficient to explain his support of Mussolini's regime. To do this we must look carefully at Pound's own ideology" (7). This study puts under examination the historical provenance of that "ideology" – a provenance that has heretofore gone largely unexamined.

Among the features of Mussolini's fascism that appealed to Pound was its pretension to be the beginning of a new and wonderful era, the *era fascista*. Pound's historical optimism is not based on an Enlightenment faith in the perfectibility of man, nor on Spencerian notions of automatic progress through evolution, and still less on Christian, Hegelian or Marxist providentialism. On the contrary, it is simply the inverse of Yeats's pessimism. Whereas Yeats was held enthralled and half terrified by the coming of the new age, Pound innocently and uncomplicatedly saw himself as its herald. Pound thought Mussolini was his man of destiny (Pound 1938, 44–9). He believed that the past holds the key to a glorious future (129) but that the key has been bent by stupidity and veniality (30–1). He thought that if we could identify and assemble those ideas suited to "go into action," if we could support the geniuses who produce those ideas, and if we could promulgate them to the world, we could probably generate a utopian future, a new age (34, 43). But, of course, the "ifs" could not be cashed out.

The Cantos begin with Pound's translation of the *nekuia* from the *Odyssey*. The *nekuia*, or "calling forth of the dead," serves as a paradigm of ritual enlightenment. The poem as a whole can be thought of as a long *nekuia*, cataloguing in a seemingly random manner the struggle of enlightened individuals to bring their wisdom into the world in the face of the hostility of an indifferent populace and corrupt authorities. Among these heroes are Sigismundo Malatesta, Thomas Jefferson, John Adams, Yong Tching, Apollonius of Tyana, and Abd-el-Melik. The order of appearance of these heroes is out of historical sequence because they appear in the unpredictable and unstructured manner of ghosts in a séance, the modern variation of the Homeric *nekuia*.

The Cantos can be read as a history of the *secretum* presented in the guise of a séance or *nekuia*. Pound inserts himself and his contemporaries into the story as if they were the participants in the séance. This aspect of the poem is most apparent, and most poignant, in *The Pisan Cantos*. Unlike the rest of the poem, the Pisan section has a setting – the American military detention camp near Pisa where Pound was held awaiting transfer to the United States and indictment for treason. In this section, the poet's activities and surroundings are mixed with memories, visions, and citations. In the rest of the poem, the poet's activities and surroundings are seldom specified or invoked, obscuring the sense of the poem as time-travel – as opposed to mere history.

Pound began *The Cantos* in 1915, six years before Eliot asked him to comment on the manuscript of *The Waste Land*, but he entirely recast its beginning after the fantastic success of Eliot's poem. As Pound received it, *The Waste Land* also had some of the marks of a séance, with its random jumps in time and space as well as multiple disembodied voices. Quite apart from its organization, *The Waste Land* must have been immediately recognized by Pound as growing out of occult speculation such as that which he and Yeats had been reading at Stone Cottage.

We shall return in a later chapter to a discussion of *The Waste Land*'s relation to occult speculation on history and revelation, but I should note here that I do not believe that Eliot was ever persuaded by these studies – as Pound certainly was. However, *The Waste Land* certainly expresses the general despair consequent on the failure of historical optimism after the debacle of the Great War. Most probably, Eliot chose Weston's history and Wagnerian *liebestod* as vehicles to express this despair, much as Joyce selected the Odyssean *nostos* as a vehicle of modern alienation in *Ulysses*, and not at all as the figure of an occult palingenesis. Like the occult studies proper – in contrast to both Yeats and Pound at that date – *The Waste Land* concentrates on spiritual or mental states rather than on political, social, or even cultural states. Although it has a place within the ambience of the secret spiritual history of Europe, it is not a contribution to it. Apart from *The Waste Land*, Eliot shows no interest in occult or secret histories.

In sharp contrast to Eliot, but in conformity with "orthodox" occult opinion, Yeats believed that the Christian era was coming to the end of its two-thousand-year cycle, and in his later verse he conflated his own advancing age and decrepitude with that of the era. Yeats's imagination dwelt upon the pain and terror of the passing of the old era more than on the joy and glory of the birth of the new. Pound, twenty years younger than Yeats, seems to have equated his own youth and the critical success of the modernists with the imminent arrival of a new age. He determined to be its Virgil and rashly began to write the epic of an age still waiting to be born.

Pound and Eliot were profoundly influenced by the example of Joyce in their attempts to grapple with the puzzle of history. Both men had been reading *Ulysses* from 1917 when it began to appear in the *Little Review*. Joyce's masterpiece also takes history as its principal vehicle. In addition, the technique that Eliot dubbed the "mythological method" is clearly a variant of the double hermeneutic common to Creuzerian mythography, *Symbolisme*, occult esotericism, and psychoanalysis. In the case of *Ulysses*, everything has a manifest and a latent sense – both of them tied to history, Irish or Homeric. There is no ineffable truth to be revealed. The manifest or exoteric sense is Leopold Bloom's day in Dublin, 16 June 1904. The esoteric or latent sense is Odysseus's wanderings over the entire world known to Homer in his attempt to return to Ithaca from Troy. The correspondences permit Joyce to fold virtually the whole history of Europe into a carefully contrived network of allusions – some historical, some fabulous, and some fictional.

Of course, "nesting" is permitted in the exoteric/esoteric hermeneutic. We can interpret Ulysses' *nostos* as representing the effort of the Irish to regain their own land from the British, and at the same time we can read Leopold's wanderings as a representation of the wanderings of the homeless Jews of Europe. The virtual inexhaustibility of *Ulysses* as an interpretand is well known, and my remarks are not intended to limit its interpretation to a duple schema, even though a duple schema such as the exoteric/esoteric permits endless nesting or "bracketing."

Although *Ulysses* is in no sense a contribution to the secret history of Europe, it nonetheless co-opts two elements characteristic of such histories: the technique of allegoresis, and the conflation of history with fiction, myth, and ritual. But *Ulysses* is essentially a work of art, and a satirical one at that. In contrast to Weston's *From Ritual to Romance* or Chamberlain's *Myth of the Nineteenth Century*, it weaves a magic circle about itself that protects it from leaking into the real historical world as Yeats, Pound, and Eliot all permitted their works to do. *Finnegans Wake*, the last and most ambitious of Joyce's works, is probably the most sustained, the most detailed, and the most eccentric of all the metahistories produced in the period – even including those of the occultist themselves. But like *Ulysses*, it is a parody of such histories and a satire on their speculative content.

Joyce did not take *his* history to be a trustworthy account of the world. He was so absorbed by the game of correspondences that he scarcely noticed the more literal-minded players until the advancing Germans chased him out of Paris and back to Switzerland. Joyce belongs in the story, not because he was touched by the occult but because he, too, participated in the general preoccupation with the collapse of progressive theories of history which coincided with a period of strife and social collapse in Europe unexampled since the Thirty Years War. The one universal feature of modernism was its epochal thinking. All "ideologies" or "philosophies" defined themselves as either the end or the beginning of an era. The age was eager to contemplate its relation to the past and to the future.

Pound is a different case entirely from Joyce. As I have suggested, he saw himself as the herald of the new age. He took his "insights" into the historical process so seriously that he abandoned his nation, and his political culture, to adopt fascism. He believed Mussolini to be the man of destiny who would bring about the new age that *The Cantos* were designed to celebrate.

In *A Light from Eleusis*, I described the historical drama represented in *The Cantos* as breaking into two movements, with the fissure being World War II. Pound's conversion to fascism was well entrenched by 1935 when he wrote *Jefferson and/or Mussolini*. In *Eleven New Cantos* (1934) he had memorialized Jefferson as a hero whose revolution had been betrayed. Thus, Jefferson became a failed hero – an American analogue of Sigismundo Malatesta, the Italian *condottiere* celebrated in cantos 8 to 11. (The Malatesta cantos were first published in 1923, in the fourth [July] number of Eliot's *Criterion*.)

The Fifth Decad of Cantos (1937), the first section to be published after Pound's discovery of Mussolini, draws parallels between American and Italian history. At this point the poem seemed to be heading for a smooth rise through history to Mussolini and the *era fascista*. Such a rise would have fulfilled an historical paradigm – set up in *A Draft of Sixteen Cantos* (1925) – of correspondences between the Trojan War, perceived in a Virgilian manner as a prelude to the founding of Rome, and the Albigensian crusade in twelfth-century Provence.

The historical paradigm that animates the early cantos is quite simple: a military defeat leads to the diffusion of the cultural and spiritual wisdom possessed by the defeated group. It is a paradigm with provenance in theosophical and masonic historiography, as well as in the Virgilian reading of the fall of Troy and in the Christian reading of the history of the Jews. The chosen people are always weak or defeated, confronting or fleeing superior hostile forces. In the Virgilian account, the fall of Troy led to the foundation of Rome. Similarly, the defeat of the Albigenses at Montségur led to the Tuscan renaissance led by Cavalcanti and Dante. On the same pattern, the fall of Byzantium is seen to have transmitted Neoplatonic and Hermetic wisdom to Florence, producing the glories of the Italian *cinquecento* (see Pound 1938, 45, and the Malatesta cantos). The "failure" of America to live up to Jeffersonian ideals caused its geniuses to leave, producing high modernism. Some of these geniuses invoked frequently by Pound are Whistler, James, and Eliot.

This obviously factitious pattern was not uncontroversially fulfilled by the 1914–18 conflict. Pound was too close to the event to be sure which of the two leading groups competing for the role of defeated underdog was the true one. The claimants were communism and fascism. Some of the theosophical avant garde were attracted to Lenin as the man of destiny – for example Wassily Kandinsky returned to Bolshevik Russia for a period. Pound was also attracted to Lenin and bolshevism for a while, but in the end he chose Mussolini, the anticommunist, as his man of destiny.

However, the outbreak of a war with Germany and Italy allied against France and Britain gave Pound some difficulties, for his personal loyalties were in conflict with his ideological commitment. These difficulties explain the peculiar hiatus in *The Cantos* during the war years. Instead of suspending work, Pound turned into the barren detour of the Adams and Chinese cantos, uninspired redactions from single sources. In these twenty cantos he continued his world history without any interleaving of contemporary events, such as had characterized earlier sections of the poem. It seems that he was marking time as he waited to discover where destiny would take the world and Mussolini.

His prose of the period and the broadcasts over Rome radio suggest that he was in no doubt about which camp had destiny on its side. But his confidence that Mussolini and Hitler were men of destiny seems not to have been strong enough for the permanence of poetry, for it does not appear in *The Cantos*. When it became clear in 1945 that the future was not yet to be born, despite so much vigorous beating of drums, the poem turned lyrical and nostalgic in *The Pisan Cantos* (1948). Tellingly, it is only after he has been defeated and "martyred" that Mussolini takes his place as a failed hero. He is entered into the canon with Malatesta, Dionysus, and Manes, the founder of Manicheanism (Pound 1973a, 425).

After the lyrical interlude of *The Pisan Cantos*, Pound turned once again to the remote past, to China, to Apollonius, a Levantine magus of the patristic period, and to the banking controversy of Andrew Jackson's presidency in *Section: Rock-Drill* (1955). Pound now permitted the occult nature of his story to become far more explicit than he had previously done by drawing on sources of undoubted occult provenance (for details, see Terrell 1984). He continued in the same vein in the last full section of the poem, *Thrones* (1959).

Because of the portrait that scholarship has painted of Pound as a prophet of modern Nietzschean scepticism, Poundians have been completely baffled by the appearance of these kinds of sources and themes in the so-called late cantos. On the reading offered here, they are not at all puzzling but are a quite understandable retreat from the intolerable debacle of the occult revival. In the later cantos, the contemporary world is present only to be excoriated in passages so shrill that Pound's publishers have marked them off in italics. Visions are more ubiquitous, more cryptic, and more insistent than ever before, and occult material more prominent. A case in point is the Restoration wizard, John Heydon, whom Pound resurrected in cantos 87 and 91 from "Canto Three."

MODERNISM AND IDEOLOGY

Scholarly ignorance of the imaginative and "speculative" history circulating in the early twentieth century, and New Criticism's ahistorical bias, have conspired to disguise the extent to which the paradigmatic products of literary modernism are historiographic and political in inspiration. They are historical and political to much the same extent as the paradigmatic products of Romanticism are personal and lyrical. Indeed, much of the hostility of modernism towards Romanticism stems from this very contrast between the preoccupations of the two periods. The modernists, I think, failed to understand that English Romanticism bore much the same relationship to the French Revolution and the Terror as English modernism bears towards World War I and its totalitarian aftermath. Just as Robespierre and the Terror drove the Romantics away from a belief in historical redemption into private and lyric meditations, into soul-making, so Hitler and Stalin drove modernism into ahistoricism and the doctrine of aesthetic autonomy.

If I can be permitted some rather Hermetic drawing of historical analogy, we can see that political events have moved rather more slowly in the twentieth century than they did in the eighteenth and nineteenth centuries. The Terror followed the French Revolution almost within months, and Napoleon became emperor within less than a decade. Hitler (Robespierre and Napoleon combined in one demonic package) came to power almost two decades after 1914. As a result, the shock of Hitler and nazism was not absorbed by the "men of 1914" – Joyce, Eliot, Pound, and Wyndham Lewis – until they were well into middle age.

It may be protested that the proper analogue of the French Revolution in the twentieth century is the Communist revolution in Russia and not the Fascist revolution, which can be dismissed as mere reaction. I would argue, however, that while it may be that communism ought to have been the revolutionary force in Western Europe in this century, in fact it turned out not to be. Communist revolutions took place in Asia and in the Caribbean, but not in Western Europe. I should note that I attach no privilege to the term "revolution." My point holds even if we consider fascism and nazism to be "counter-revolutionary." The point is that it turned Europe upside down. The question of which side is truly "right side up" I leave to philosophers and political scientists.

Fascism and communism presented themselves in the 1930s as rival revolutionary movements. It was fascism, not communism, that swept over Europe from modest beginnings with Mussolini's 1922 march on Rome to its traumatic demise in the unconditional surrender of Germany in 1945. Germany and German culture played the same role in this twentieth-century convulsion as France and French culture had played in the nineteenth-century spread of revolution throughout Europe.

If Hitler was the demonic Napoleon of the twentieth century, Churchill was the Wellington. Like Wellington, Churchill represented a conservatism. He was just as opposed to communism as he was to fascism. For Churchill, as for many liberal European politicians of the period, fascism and communism were twin threats to democracy and liberty. The conflict of the thirties was not, in their view, between the progressive left and the reactionary right, but rather between democracy and liberty on the one hand and totalitarian dictatorship on the other. By contrast, the standard view today – at least among literary scholars – is that the real struggle was between socialism and capitalism. Since both Churchill and Hitler were capitalists, and both Stalin and Léon Blum were socialists, this view does not aid us in understanding the political landscape that Eliot, Pound, and Wyndham Lewis would have had before them in the interwar period. Both views, it has to be noted, leave out of account old national rivalries, rivalries that surely played as great a role as ideological disagreements did.

If we say that Locke and Rousseau were the philosophers who presided *in absentia* over the French (and American) revolutions, and that Hegel and Marx were the philosophers who presided (also *in absentia*) over the Russian Revolution, it might be appropriate to say that Nietzsche and Rosenberg presided over the fascist revolution. In the last case, only Nietzsche was *in absentia*. Thus, while it may be true to say that fascism – in contrast to Jacobinism and communism – had no presentable political theory, it is not true that it was without philosophical or intellectual content. If we grant fascism some filiation with Nietzsche, it could be considered even more profoundly revolutionary than either Jacobinism or Marxist communism. Where Locke and Rousseau overturned the sanctity of the past, and Hegel and Marx overturned the sanctity of property, Nietzsche overturned the sanctity of human rationality itself.

Viewed in such a way, all three of these revolutions are still locked in conflict. It appears that the military and political confrontation on the world stage between Locke and Marx under the labels of capitalism and communism is now over, with the triumph of Locke. However, the conflict between Locke and Nietzsche, between empirical positivism and sceptical rationalism, has increased in ferocity as the geopolitical conflict has waned. Its field of confict so far has been the academy, where Hegelian philosophy of history dominates New Historicism and where Nietzschean scepticism under the label of "deconstruction" does battle with Lockean empiricism denounced as "logocentrism." The nature and history of literary modernism is one of the battlegrounds for this conflict.

In this conflict, modernism is accused on varied grounds of being reactionary and retrograde. This charge is, of course, telling, for modernism claimed to be progressive and revolutionary. The accusation has some bite, for modernism does hold to the sanctity of the past, of property, and of rationality, and in so doing preserves a continuity with the political, cultural, and even religious thought of the European past. If such a posture is reactionary and retrograde, then modernism must stand guilty as accused. But the revolutionary values – liberty, equality, fraternity – also belong to the past, and they are invoked by liberals and revolutionaries alike. If we are to come to any understanding of our own history, we must abandon the notion that we can decide complex moral, political, and social issues with a simple binary scheme, approving a break with the past and disapproving continuity with it. That modernism, fascism, and nazism all revere aspects of the past is surely not sufficient grounds on which to equate them with one another.

Even though we ought not to find modernism guilty simply on grounds of association, it must be admitted that the conspiracy view of European history – like much else – was deprived of its innocence in the 1930s by its implication in the rise of fascism and nazism in the interwar period. We cannot dismiss such characters as Nesta Webster as harmless kooks in the face of the horrors of the Nazi death camps.

The phony *Protocols of Zion* is an instance of the same sort of fantasy that Barruel had indulged in a century and a half earlier. The putative Zionist plot against the established order was very much a copy of Barruel's Jacobin plot, and the consequences of the false allegation were unqualifiedly malignant (see Heiden [1944] 1969, 1–18). Of course, despite Hitler and Webster, Zionism was not the only conspiracy that Europeans were enjoined to fear. Communists and anarchists were alleged to be everywhere, organized into cabals of zealots plotting the overthrow of governments. It is a curiosity that in the eighteenth century the counterrevolution invented a conspiracy theory of the revolution, but in the twentieth century it has frequently been those who would overthrow the status quo – whether Communists or Fascists – who subscribe to conspiracy theories. Even Pound and Nesta Webster supposed that the status quo needs to be overthrown because it is controlled by malign interests or groups.

The revolution most feared by democratic and capitalist Europe in this century was the Communist revolution. Fascism represented itself as conservative. However, it managed to appear revolutionary at the same time, for its task was, like Hercules, to cleanse. Fascism's mission was to restore a lost past, not to preserve a corrupt present. In the period between the wars, the Communist revolution in Russia was feared as an analogue of the French Revolution whose sedition would spread (Parker 1969). Indeed, at the time this study was first completed, Western Europe and America were still frozen in a posture of vigilant watch against the spread of Communist revolution either by war or by insurrection. This confrontation is not yet fully extinguished, but it seems to be drawing to a close a century and a half after publication of the *Communist Manifesto*. In the interwar period the Communist revolution was forestalled everywhere in Western Europe – either by the pre-emptive action of the Fascist movement (as in Italy, Germany, and Spain) or by the perilous vitality of democracy in France, Britain, and the former British colonies in America, Asia, and Australia. In the thirties, the Fascist revolution successfully drove communism out of Western Europe. Of course, it also drove out democracy, liberty, and human decency. Mussolini was the first Fascist leader to export his revolution by arms – to Ethiopia. Spain was next on the list of recipients of Fascist revolution, and soon Hitler (with Mussolini along for the ride) had conquered pretty much the same territory as Napoleon had done. England and Russia remained beyond the grasp of both of them.

Barruel had offered the counterrevolution, a fabricated fantasy of a Jacobin conspiracy surviving from pagan antiquity. The Nazis, not content with the very real bogeyman of Communist revolution – a threat that had been adequate to Mussolini's needs for a decade – adopted the analogous fabrication of a Zionist plot to rule the world. Unlike the Zionist plot, the Communist and anarchist "plots" invoked by Mussolini, Hitler, Franco, and Oswald Mosley did have some basis in fact, even though they were hardly conspiracies. Far from being surreptitious infiltrators of positions of power and influence, anarchists and Communists were rag-tag groups of malcontents, agitators, and terrorists.

European racism has a very intricate provenance, as I have tried to indicate. Part of that provenance is Nietzsche's writing, which was very popular in Nazi circles. Nietzsche has many defenders, among them Walter Kaufman, who gives a concise, albeit very partisan, account of Nietzsche's racism – see the long note to "blond beast" in Kaufmann's translation of *Genealogy* (Nietzsche 1969, 40–1). The whole of the first essay in *Genealogy* endeared Nietzsche to the Nazis. Whatever Nietzsche's final position on the question of race, this essay seems to be indebted to Gobineau, who bids fair to be the ultimate source of the Nazi doctrine that the Germans were descended from a super race that was in partial decline because of miscegenation with inferior non-Aryan stock. (See Viereck 1961 for a discussion of the Wagnerian provenance of Nazi racism and nationalism. For the importance of Chamberlain, see George L. Mosse's, introduction in Chamberlain 1968.)

Blavatsky drew on some of the same sources for her fantastic racial theories. For her and the theosophists, the most ancient surviving transmitter of Lemurian and Atlantean culture were those same Aryans that the Nazis adopted as the ancestors of authentic Germans. Her more bizarre theories had little currency, although they are reflected by Weston in *From Ritual to Romance*. Despite the absence of any real connections, the overlap between theosophical and Nazi versions of world and race history rendered the occult once more as sinister and dangerous as it had seemed to Barruel. But it had changed sides. In the eighteenth century and early nineteenth century, the occult was perceived as seditious, revolutionary, and Jacobin. In the twentieth, it is perceived as retrograde, reactionary, and lunatic.

The Nazi adoption of a sense of history that had currency in occult circles – and virtually nowhere else – attached itself to a reverence for the past that had much greater currency and far more presentable provenance. This reverence was a natural characteristic of the pagan degenerative view of historical process, and it was equally a feature of Christian humanism and perforce of the Renaissance. The common identification of reverence for the past with Romantic nostalgia for a lost innocence is an oversimplification that militates against a proper understanding of modernism and its relations to the political history of this century. Since the passage of time tends to corrupt and degenerate all things, the present can be perfected only by strengthening or restoring its links to the past. Such a view is not idiosyncratic in our culture, nor is it necessarily malign. It is, however, necessarily conservative in the broad sense. Fascism, the occult, Romanticism, modernism, and political conservatism all participate in some version of this view. There are as many different versions, however, as there are periods in history.

By the end of the eighteenth century, Barruel's view that Christianity was the enemy of the revolution and of its leading values – liberty, equality, and fraternity – was unquestioned. An Enlightenment understanding of revolution was a change from an arbitrary or capricious status quo to some superior arrangement rationally selected as superior. An older arrangement could be superior to a more recent one, but no sanctity is attributed to the archaic. The true conservative rejects current arrangements as degradations of some primal state, and seeks to restore that state – a *risorgimento* or rebirth of the old amidst the new. The difference between Poundian – or Nietzschean – and Romantic or aestheticist conservatives is that the latter looked only to a pre-industrial past, whereas the former looked to a pre-rational past in paganism or the pre-Socratics. One consequence of this difference is that there is a confusing overlap between Jacobins, Masons, liberals, utilitarians, aesthetes, occultists, Poundians, Nietzscheans, and Marxists. All are hostile to Christianity simply because it represents the status quo.

In an uncanny anticipation of the Woodstock generation in the Unites States, Nietzsche proleptically singled out the Hashishin, or assassins, as the "order of free spirits *par excellence*" (*Genealogy of Morals*, 3.24). Throughout this century – for Pater, Nietzsche, or Wilde – to be pagan was to be antichristian, and to be antichristian was to be a revolutionary. This little formula is expressed by a clever palindrome that Pound cites in "A Visiting Card" (1973b, 327):

```
A M O R
M     O
O     M
R O M A
```

"Roma" is Rome, the Catholic Church and heir of empire; "amor" is, of course, love, the creed of Christ and Rousseau that was allegedly betrayed by the church. Nietzsche expressed a similar though more Hegelian opposition in his antithetical pair of Apollo and Dionysus. In the 1960s the same ethos was expressed even more directly in the slogan "Make love not war." The Fascists and the Nazis, however, adopted only the continuity with the remote past, retaining – to use Nietzsche's label – Alexandrian hostility to sexual licence and imperial attachment to ecclesiastical institutions. Of course, Fascist and Nazi tolerance of Christian ecclesiastical institutions does not constitute (as is sometimes too easily assumed) adherence to Christianity as a system of values.

Another version of cultural history represents literary and aesthetic modernism as belonging to philosophical modernism; that is, as positivistic, ahistorical, and decontextual. This version was put about by the modernists themselves and has been accepted as just and accurate by postmodern critiques of modernism. So viewed, modernism's entanglements in the violent and passionate political conflicts of the century seem inexplicable except on grounds of moral failure. However, if we understand literary modernism as in fact being antipathetic to the positivism and decontextualism of analytical philosophy, some of the puzzles disappear. Under the analysis offered here, modernism's preoccupation with the modes and mores of the past – with myth, ritual, and mysticism – is no longer anomalous. The attraction of fascism for many modernists, and their friendly relations with the occult, become unsurprising. The moral questions do not go away, but moral failures need not appear so monstrous if we understand how very difficult it was to know just where virtue lay. Even at the end of the century, we are still some way from being capable of a dispassionate assessment of its conflicts.

PSYCHOLOGY AND THE OCCULT

In the nineteenth century and up to the thirties of the twentieth, occult beliefs about contact with spirits, illuminated souls, and divinities seemed at worst goofy and at best a refuge for those whose desire for spirituality was not met by established religions. Eastern mysticism and American spiritualism attracted the interest of such *Kulturträger* as Emerson, Walt Whitman, and William James in the United States; and Balzac, Lamartine, Hugo, Wagner, Heine, and Goethe in Europe.

On the Continent, *Symbolisme* had been the leading literary movement of the late nineteenth century, and it made no effort to disguise its relations with the occult. The pages of *La Renaissance litteraire et artistique* reflect the intimate relations between literary symbolism and occult beliefs and practices in that period. Its pages also reflect the French fascination with American authors, notably Poe and Emerson, whose themes and speculations were seen to be of a piece with the *Symbolistes* and occultists also prominent in the journal (Mercier 1969, 93–102).

Kenneth Cornell's *Symbolist Movement* (1951) is typical of English-language studies of the period in its anxiety to insulate *Symboliste* poetry from any taint of the occult (see esp. 80–1, 107–8). Henri Peyre also is anxious to insulate *Symbolisme* from the occult. While admitting the closeness of contact, he dismisses its relevance to criticism on the unpersuasive grounds that it would be an "impossible task, or almost so" to "determine with precision what Balzac and Nerval might owe to Swedenborgianism, Hugo to talking tables, [or] Rimbaud to certain esoteric books" (Peyre 1980, 102). Such avoidance of the issue is not very satisfactory.

In point of fact, literary and artistic circles in the nineteenth century – as in the twentieth – were not all that devoted to materialism, empiricism, or scepticism. Clearly, few if any were prepared to dismiss out of hand the possibility of unknown psychic phenomena, and many were even prepared to countenance the possiblity of inexplicable physical phenomena. Our century has labelled the former "psychedelia" and confined it to pharmacological inspiration, and the latter is called "parapsychology." Research into both sorts of phenomena has been conducted in some institutions of higher learning in the United States. In short, the climate of opinion has not changed very much in 1990 from what it was in 1890 or 1790.

Some sense of the status of occult speculation and phenomena at the turn of the century can be gathered from the dissertation that C.G. Jung submitted for his medical degree to the University of Zurich in 1902. Its title was "On the Psychology and Pathology of So-called Occult Phenomena." His thesis was a case study of a fifteen-year-old girl who claimed – in the manner of the Fox sisters – to be in communication with ghosts. Although Jung found her claims to be fraudulent, the very fact that a medical faculty would accept such a thesis topic indicates that claims of supernormal psychic capacities were taken seriously by the scientific community of the day. Jung himself, despite catching his subject cheating, remained convinced that some of her communications were not fraudulent and concluded that the unconscious possesses "a receptivity far exceeding that of the conscious mind" (Jung 1977, 71, 83). In his dissertation, in order to illustrate such "heightened unconscious performance" (148) – ecstatic access to deeper or higher psychic realms – Jung cited a passage from *Thus Spake Zarathustra* and placed it beside a passage from Kerner's *Blätter aus Prevorst*, which it closely resembles. Noting that Nietzsche had read Kerner when he was between twelve and fifteen years of age (that is, nearly forty years before), Jung remarked, "If we realize Nietzsche's state of mind at the time when he wrote *Zarathustra*, and the poetic ecstasy that at more than one point verges on the pathological, this abnormal reminiscence will appear more understandable" (87).

About thirty years before Jung submitted his thesis, the Society for Psychical Research was founded (1882) by three Cambridge friends "for the purpose of inquiring into a mass of obscure phenomena which lie at present on the outskirts of our organized knowledge" (*Psychological Review*, 5 Nov. 1882, quoted in Hynes 1968, 459). The society's mandate was not to expose fraud but rather to legitimate authentic "occult" phenomena by discriminating them from mere "tricks." As Samuel Hynes puts it, their motive was "to recover the sense of meaning in the universe" of which Darwin had deprived them. In the event, of course, the society found mostly fraud – most celebratedly in the case of Mme Blavatsky in 1884–5 (Williams 1946, 262–73). Arthur Balfour, William James, and Henri Bergson all served as presidents of the society (Hynes 1968, 139–45), indicating that its interests were far from marginal or discreditable. Other prominent members were Leslie Stephen, John Ruskin, John Addington Symonds, and Charles Dodgson.

The occult served as a resource – and sometimes a refuge – for artists in their struggle with Comte, Spencer, Darwin, and scientific materialism generally. In this century, this refuge has been all the more acutely requited as analytic philosophy has pushed the arts towards the periphery of mainstream culture. No doubt the contempt for the decorative and enjoyable universally expressed by modernist writers and artists is in part a reaction to the reduction of art's function to embellishment or diversion. Literary modernism deployed the principle of textual autonomy and its corollary, authorial impersonality, as a kind of camouflage, for these axioms were paraded as equivalent to analytical philosophy's requirement that knowledge be context-free. However, this strategy had the unfortunate effect that it forbade any appeal to emotional authenticity – a protection against scientific positivism that had served the Romantics and Victorians reasonably well.

Occultism has a ready answer to the problem of art's status within the epistemological tradition, where it has been under assault since Plato. It simply stands Plato on his head and asserts that art is revelatory of a higher reality and truth than mere science or philosophy. Art – like mystical vision – is a gnosis, and the world it "knows" is the noumenal realm, not the mere phenomenal appearance that epistmological philosophy and science "know." Literary symbolism adopted this doctrine with little modification, retaining the essential occultist or esoteric principle that the expression of such a gnosis must be obscure to the uninitiated.

Literary modernism cleverly altered this formula. It retained the obscurity of the *Symbolistes* but justified it on grounds of philosophical relativism, or philosophical perspectivism, rather than on the esoteric grounds of ineffability as *Symbolisme* had done. The argument is clearest in cubism, which abandoned the single point of view, thereby rendering representational painting opaque. Analogously, poetry abandoned the single speaking voice, even for the "mono-logic" lyric, which was assigned a second voice, a "persona" or mask distinct from the author. Modernist narratives affected multiple points of view, confusing chronology, and indeterminate settings – all in the name of modernist relativism.

I must assume that these features of modernist apologetics are familiar to my readers. They have been essentially unaltered since the twenties. Now that philosophical modernism is out of fashion within literary academic circles, literary modernism's camouflage as a mode compatible with empiricism and epistemology has drawn the fire of New Historicists, postmodernists, neo-Marxists, and decon-structors alike. These critiques, are, I think misdirected. Authoritative modernist formulations of the nature of art are closer in provenance and formulation to Evelyn Underhill's characterization of the highest artistic expression as "but symbolic – a desperate attempt to translate the truth of that world into the beauty of this" than they are to Einsteinean relativism or Heisenbergian indeterminacy, despite much prominent testimony to the contrary.

T.S. Eliot's highly influential remarks on literary meaning conform more closely to Underhill's remarks than they do to relativity or quantum physics: "It is a commonplace to observe that the meaning of a poem may wholly escape paraphrase. It is not quite so common-place to observe that the meaning of a poem may be something larger than its author's conscious purpose, and something remote from its origins" ("The Music of Poetry," Eliot [1942] 1975, 110–11). Of course, Underhill was a Christian mystic, not an occultist, even though she was a regular contributor to the *Quest* and her books were reviewed there – albeit criticized for their "narrow concentra-tion" on Christian mystical literature.

This juxtaposition of Eliot and Underhill is not capricious. Eliot owned a well-marked copy of Underhill's *Mysticism: A Study in the Nature and Development of Man's Spiritual Consciousness*, and he copied out the following passage from page 71 (Gordon 1977, 60):

If we would cease, once for all, to regard visions and voices as objective, and be content to see in them forms of symbolic expression, ways in which the subconscious activity of the spiritual self reach the surface-mind, many of the disharmonies noticeable in visionary experience which have teased the devout and delighted the agnostic, would fade away. Visionary experience is – or at least may be – the outward sign of a real experience. It is a picture which the mind constructs, it is true, from raw materials already at its disposal, as the artist constructs his picture with canvas and paint.

Gordon cites this passage but elides "the outward sign of a real experience" and does not include the remark on painters, and she omits the continuation which makes it perfectly clear that Underhill is speaking of mystical experience as analogous to aesthetic experience: "But as the artist's paint and canvas picture is the fruit, not merely of contact between brush and canvas, but also of a more vital contact between his creative genius and visible beauty or truth; so too we may see in vision, where the subject is a mystic, the fruit of a more mysterious contact between the visionary and a transcendental beauty or truth."

Occultism's faith in the capacity of the human soul to apprehend directly the ultimate truth may be seen as a disease of Platonic nativist epistemology, for the latter holds that knowledge arises from within. Occultism would then be the contrary of Aristotelian empirical epistemology, which holds that knowledge arises from without through the agency of sensory experience. The cognitive process that epistemology understands as *learning*, Platonism understands as *remembering*. As we are constantly being reminded these days, philosophical modernism represented the triumph of empiricist epistemology. The birth of modernism cannot be precisely dated, but it was well into its gestation at the time of the publication of Russell and Whitehead's *Principia Mathematica* (1910–13) and was certainly out of the womb by 1922 when Wittgenstein published the *Tractatus Logico Philosophicus*. These works may be taken to represent synecdochically the marginalization for many decades – at least, in the English-speaking world – of the Hegelian or continental phenomenological tradition as represented by Nietzsche, Husserl, and Heidegger.

As a candidate for a Ph.D. in philosophy at Harvard and as a student of Russell, Eliot was a more informed observer of the mainstream current of academic philosophy than any other poet in the history of the language. His Ph.D. dissertation, "Knowledge and Experience in the Philosophy of F.H. Bradley" (completed in 1916), is a fairly typical product of the period in that it deals directly with epistemological questions, drawing on contemporary anthropological as well as philosophical speculation. But despite its very standard and uncontroversial nature as a piece of academic philosophy, the dissertation is not remote from the concerns with a spiritual or noumenal realm that I have found to be ubiquitous in the period.

William Skaff's recent study supports the supposition that Eliot's philosophical and anthropological studies were driven by religious and even mystical impulses, and that all three streams inform his poetry (Skaff 1986, esp. 22–72). Although Skaff makes no mention of the occult, he draws attention to the conflict between empirical and idealist theories of knowledge at the time and to the tendency for the debate to overflow into anthropology and psychology (72–6).

Jeffrey Perl presents an alternate and somewhat idiosyncratic view in *Skepticism and Modern Enmity*. He considers Eliot to be sceptical, but in the manner of a rabbinic, hermeneutic scepticism. Perl explains that in the rabbinic tradition, the text of the Talmud is surrounded by the Midrash – an historical collection of commentaries on it. The "truth" is understood to be embedded in the Talmud, but it can be known only through the "surround" of commentaries articulating distinct and even contradictory interpretations. He calls this combination of text and commentary "abnormal discourse" and classes poetry as a variety of it (Perl 1989, 60–1). Subtle and attractive as Perl's argument is, it seems a little fantastic to reconvert Eliot posthumously from Anglicanism to Judaism. All the same, Perl and I agree that Eliot's "devotion to tradition and convention is not an expression of cultural absolutism, but virtually the opposite: an expression of radical skepticism in regard to any one philosophical perspective" (63). However, scepticism about philosophical positions does not entail scepticism about faith, as Perl seems to assume. Indeed, it was surely Eliot's dissatisfaction with philosophy that led him to religion. He abandoned the search for knowledge and embraced belief.

The arguments that one encounters in occult, mystical, and literary discussion of the issue are fairly easily summarized. One goes as follows: since knowledge is always already available in the mind and since most humans are not enlightened, it must be the case that some obscuring or occluding agency exists, preventing access to it. For the modern occultist, the occluding agency is most commonly the flesh, the body, or – most generally – *hyle*, or matter. In strong forms of nativist epistemology *all* genuine knowledge, all thought, even all perception, is the result of some broaching or surmounting of the hylic veil.

However, in less austere forms of gnostic or insight epistemology, the world of appearances is permitted an heuristic function rather as in Shelley's likening of the hylic veil to a dome of many-coloured glass staining the white radiance of eternity. However, a truly occultist account will add to epistemological nativism an immanentist or pantheist belief whereby everyone – perhaps even every*thing* – has a spark of divinity within, and whereby he or she (or it) may come to "know" that divinity; that is, may participate mystically in the noumenal.

Psychoanalysis, phenomenology, and the occult all privilege the "inward gaze" over the outward look of empirical science. Even though the "object" of the gaze is quite distinct for each of them – being psychological phenomena for psychoanalysis, mental objects for phenomenology, and the noumenal for the occult – it is nonetheless easy enough for the literary imagination to co-opt any or all of them for its own imaginative projects. Surrealism, for example, is a plain and open co-optation of psychoanalytic vocabulary for an occult engagement with the noumenal. Phenomenology is similarly susceptible to a metaphysical turn. Husserl rigorously distinguishes "intelligent insight" – that is, the understanding of the "relations between fact and *eidos*" – from the merely empirical knowledge of fact on the one hand and the purely mystical knowledge of *eidos* on the other (Husserl 1962, 50). He is anxious to insist that "*all* thoughts *partially mystical in nature* and clinging chiefly to the concepts Eidos (Idea) and Essence ... [be] *rigorously excluded*" from phenomenology. However, such an exclusion has proven difficult to maintain among his followers.

The phenomenologist does not deny the possibility of mystical knowledge but merely excludes it from his project. Mystical knowledge is understood as direct knowledge of the "eidetic," independent of any sensory or empirical instantiation of it. For Husserl such knowledge could arise only through direct intuition. But for the mystic it arises in ecstatic experience, and for the occult mystic it may also arise through cultic or ritual practice – initiations, séances, ecstatic dances, and the like. Nineteenth-century aesthetes, symbolists, occultists, and Swedenborgians substituted the arts for ritual. Roman Ingarden, a follower of Husserl, makes essentially the same argument in *The Literary Work of Art*, his first book, but he follows Husserl and insists on the double reference of art to the eidetic and to the sensory or empirical.

Nietzsche's special contribution to the literature was to collapse together these two modes. In *The Birth of Tragedy* he describes the Dionysian aesthetic experience as follows as ecstasy induced by aesthetic performance:

In song and dance man expressed himself as a member of a higher community; he has forgotten how to walk and speak and is on the way toward flying into the air, dancing. His very gestures express enchantment ... He feels himself a god, he himself now walks about enchanted, in ecstasy, like the gods he saw walking in his dreams. He is no longer an artist, he has become a work of art: in these paroxysms of intoxication the artistic power of all nature reveals itself to the highest gratification of the primordial unity. (*Birth of Tragedy*, "Preface to Richard Wagner," s1).

Direct access to the psychic phenomena, however characterized, is called "experience" by all groups. It is always open to doubt, for it cannot be publicly confirmed or tested, precisely because it is insight or gnosis, as opposed to co-gnosis of intersubjective epistemesis. Indirect access through ritual or art ineluctably involves psychology, the arts, anthropology, mythology, and the occult. Since the Freudian revolution, psychology has looked to literature, mythology, and ritual as well as to dreams for testimony on psychic phenomena. Thus, in this century, psychoanalysis, literary scholarship, and the occult all share the same subject matter however much their interests and methods may differ. This overlap of subject produces such organizations as the Society for Psychical Research on the one hand and Jung's Eranos group on the other.

The Eranos group deserves more attention than it has received from intellectual historians. It was founded by Jung in 1935 and met annually to discuss topics of interest to its members, many of whom were religious, literary, and classical scholars and not psychologists. Mircea Eliade joined in 1950. He reports that fellow members at that time were Louis Massignon, Henri Corbin, Gershom Scholem (who was an occasional contribtor to the *Quest*), Walter Otto, and Karl Kerényi (Eliade 1977, xii–xiii). Gaston Bachelard joined in 1954 at the invitation of Henri Corbin, and he tells us that in the discussions, "tout sont animés par la conviction platonicienne en un réalisme primordial de l'image, [et] en un valeur kerygmatique du mythe" – "everything was animated by the Platonic conviction in the primordial reality of the image [and] in the kerygmatic value of myth" (Durand 1976, 12; my translation). This conviction of the "kerygmatic" or annunciatory power of myth is also central to the occult. For them, as for Bachelard, the myth "shows forth" or manifests a knowledge that is inexpressible in any other way. Aestheticism considers the arts to be mythopoeic in Nietzsche's sense that they too are kerygmatic.

Such a view, it hardly needs to be said, is shared by Jung, Northrop Frye, and Freud, even though each of the three would assign different reasons for the ineffability of the insight or wisdom. For Freud, dreams and myths disguise a truth that is too shameful, carrying too much "cathexis," to be plainly expressed. There is nothing "occult" or metaphysical about Freudian mythography. Jung's theory is very little different from occult theories. His collective unconscious is very difficult to discriminate from the *anima mundi*. Both are the repositories of the Platonic archetypes, which are in turn the ultimate source of human thought.

Frye's position is quite different and less coherent. Frye does not make clear what it is that myth and literature announce, but it seems to be the Christian revelation as contained in a Christian typological reading of the Bible and the Christian Gospels. In fact, Frye's ultimate position as developed in *The Great Code* seems very little different from that of eighteenth-century Christian mythographers who sought to derive all world myths from the Bible. He would seem to have been a reincarnation of *Middlemarch's* Casaubon, assuming that all myths participate in the Christian revelation. Frye's advance on Casaubon is that he renounces the Christian mythographers' arrogant presumption that pagan myths were barbarous distortions. Like the theories of Casaubon – and of Creuzer as well – Frye's theory presupposes a single revelation to the world, but he was not a diffusionist. His solution of the problem of diffusion is a little indistinct, but it seems to amount to an appeal, in the manner of Tylor, to a common human nature and environment. But such an explanation of the universality of myth is not very satisfactory for a theory that assserts the kerygmatic nature of myth.

Perhaps the most common thread in all of this is that the object under investigation is understood to be a psychic event, that is to say, inaccessible to empirical investigation, whether the event be considered merely psychological or ontological or noumenal. Even as resolute an empiricist as Freud was susceptible to the innatist sentiment that seems to have been so powerful in the *fin de siècle*. In *The Interpretation of Dreams* he permitted himself to indulge in an archetypal speculation:

We can guess how much to the point is Nietzsche's assertion that in dreams "some primeval relic of humanity is at work which we can now scarcely reach any longer by a direct path"; and we may expect that the analysis of dreams will lead us to a knowledge of man's archaic heritage, of what is psychically innate in him. Dreams and neuroses seem to have preserved more mental antiquities than we could have imagined possible; so that psycho-analysis may claim a high place among the sciences which are concerned with the reconstruction of the earliest and most obscure periods of the beginnings of the human race. (Freud [1900] 1976, 700).

The supposition that Freud assigns to Nietzsche here is, as we have seen, ubiquitous in occultism and is traceable to the religious allegoresis of the ancient world, especially the Neoplatonists. Although

Freud did not go down this road, Jung did, despite Freud's caution that he should avoid such dangerous areas (Jung 1965, 153–5). Nonetheless, Freud continued to regard myths as possessing the same properties as dreams, even though he abandoned the notion of some kind of collective unconscious, world soul, or universal spirit implicit in this early enthusiastic prognosis of psychology's future contribution to anthropology.

To be interested in myth – even in the kerygmatic power of myth – does not make one an occultist. The point I wish to make here is that the occult's preoccupation with the revelatory or kerygmatic character of myth has been far from eccentric during this century, which could fairly be said to have reinvented myth on a Nietzschean ecstatic model. Oddly enough, the occult has generally been less interested in ecstasy than in secret history. Even though the occultist's goal is always to make contact with the divine, he or she also seeks to recover a tradition or "secret doctrine" passed down from high antiquity. The non-occult mystic neither needs nor wants a secret tradition. Evelyn Underhill is typical of the non-occult mystic. She collected revelations in an effort to understand better the ineffable – to approach it more closely – but without any desire to discover some community or society of mystics.

Poets seem to desire a traditional or perennial mode of expression, and hence they are drawn to inventions or discoveries of societies, cabals, and coteries that will maintain the tradition. As a matter of simple pragmatics, the poet needs a special vocabulary or symbolic code in which to express his or her "obscure impulses." Myth has long been ready at hand to meet this need. The names of divinities and stories of theophanies, metamorphoses, and other miracles has been the stock-in-trade of poets from time immemorial. It is little wonder that the modernists took advantage of the compilation of world myths represented in the work of Sir James Frazer, E.B. Tylor, Walter Pater, and Friedrich Nietzsche that was begun in the 1870s and was continued in this century by Jane Harrison, F.M. Cornford, Lévi-Bruhl, Freud, and Jung. As a result, the parallel interests of the occult travelled well in intellectual and aesthetic circles.

REACTION OR REVOLUTION?

I have argued that Barruel's history of a secret Jacobin conspiracy unwittingly invented a secret tradition that turned out to be suitable as evidence of an historical provenance for occultists of the nineteenth and twentieth centuries. One difficulty with this hypothesis is that Barruel's secret tradition was portrayed as Jacobin, atheistic, and revolutionary, and therefore ought to be antipathetic to the Platonism, rationalism, and mysticism of the occult – which, moreover, is justifiably thought to be politically retrograde. Some account must be given of the migration of Barruel's secret conspiracy from atheism and Jacobinism to occultism and conservatism. The atheism is easy to manage, because for Barruel atheism meant any unchristian view, whether scientific materialism or Zoroastrianism. Thus, there is no conflict between atheism and occultism.

Barruel's identification of occultism with revolution remained the standard pairing if Rossetti, Aroux, and Reghellini are any guide, for they all follow Barruel in attaching the occult to revolution and sedition. Even those Cold War cultural movements with an occult component – such as the beats, the Black Mountain poets, and the drug culture – have a self-image as Nietzschean revolutionary free spirits (see Senior 1959).

Nietzsche's equation of Dionysian communal ecstasy with freedom, and of Apollonian subjective rationality with restraint and authority, is the key to the transvaluation of revolution from the overthrow of superstition by reason as it was in Jacobinism to the overthrow of rationality by passion as it has become in this century. In this respect he is followed by Freud and the Freudian neo-Marxist, Herbert Marcuse. Marcuse even repeats a piece of historical fiction traceable to Barruel when he identifies the Albigenses as one of the early libertarian groups oppressed by Christianity:

Equally open was the armed struggle of institutionalized Christianity against the heretics, who tried or allegedly tried to rescue the unsublimated content and the unsublimated objective ... the cruel and organized slaughter of Cathari, Albigensians, Anabaptists, of slaves, peasants, and paupers who revolted under the sign of the cross, the burning of witches and their defenders – this sadistic extermination of the weak suggests that unconscious instinctual forces broke through all the nationality and rationalization. (Marcuse [1955] 1974, 71)

Barruel, of course, was cheering for the opposite team. He calls them a "horde of sectaries," who "under a hundred different and uncouth names, recall to the mind of the reader everything that had been broached by the most direful enemies of morality, government, and the altar, and that had *as yet* appeared in Europe" (Barruel 1797, 2:402). As we shall see in the next chapter, there is no evidence at all to link the Albigenses to Jacobin or liberal principles, any more than there is to link them to Freudian/Marxist theories of transgression. The former linkage is traceable, through a complex chain of repetition and plagiarism, backwards from Marcuse through Denis de Rougemont, Joséphin Péladan, Eugène Aroux, and Gabriele Rossetti to Barruel. That it should still be current amongst the Frankfurt group in New York in 1955 is testimony to the vitality of fiction.

Marcuse not only buys into Barruel's fantasy, but in addition he co-opts Nietzsche to support his own inversion of Freud's cultural theories. Marcuse identifies Nietzsche's eternal return as "the will and vision of an *erotic* attitude toward being for which necessity and fulfilment coincide" (Marcuse [1955] 1974, 122). In Freud, necessity and fulfilment do not coincide, and thereby give rise to a repression that produces civilization. Against Freud's "authoritarian" view, Marcuse mounts a "Gnostic" version of European history very similar to Mead's: "Eros is being absorbed into Logos, and Logos is reason which subdues the instincts. The history of ontology reflects the reality principle which governs the world ever more exclusively: The insights contained in the metaphysical notion of Eros were driven underground. They survived, in eschatological distortion, in many heretic [*sic*] movements, in the hedonistic philosophy" (126). Marcuse's mildly occult theories of history, psyche, and civilization provided aid and comfort to the thoroughly Nietzschean hippie movement in the United States. But the belief in direct access to ultimate knowledge (gnosis) can lead just as readily to authoritarian elitism – as it did with Plato – as to egalitarian freedom. Indeed, nineteenth-century occultists were just as likely to be elitist and antidemocratic as they were to be democratic and egalitarian.

Nietzsche himself – despite the claims of Marcuse and Derrida – believed that egalitarian attitudes and policies were folly. He described the state as

some pack of blond beasts of prey, a conqueror and master race which, organized for war and with the ability to organize, unhesitatingly lays its terrible claws upon a populace perhaps tremendously superior in numbers but still formless and nomad. That is after all how the "state" began on earth: I think that sentimentalism which would have it begin with a "contract" has been disposed of. He who can command, he who is by nature "master," he who is violent in act and bearing – what has he to do with contracts!" (*Genealogy of Morals*, s17)

Remarks like these lend credence to suspicions that Nietzsche had read Gobineau's *Essai sur l'inégalité des races*, although Hegel's theory of master and slave is clearly echoed and is perhaps a sufficient inspiration. This elitism is copiously reflected in modernism. Even the Communists among the modernists – for example, Picasso – could scarcely be described as convinced egalitarians.

One would expect an innatist model of human nature to lead to elitist and authoritarian political postures rather more frequently than to egalitarian and democratic ones. Lockean learning theory seems much more compatible with egalitarian democracy. Even though it is perfectly coherent to suppose that divine wisdom is innately available to everyone while conceding that it is obscured in most by an overlay of antipathetic and false sensory passion and illusion, it is difficult to avoid attributing superiority to those individuals who have actually penetrated the illusion.

There are also institutional grounds for an alliance between occultism and revolutionary sentiment. Because occultism has always perceived itself as a fringe movement, it naturally associates itself with the suppressed – if not so naturally with the oppressed. Occultists seek their co-religionists among those who are the targets of authority, and for most of the history of Christian Europe that authority has been vested in church and crown. Hence, occultism's inherent elitism is commonly tempered by an heretical and republican posture. A parallel instance of the uncertain political career of groups of ideas would be the career of Hegelian philosophy of history. Its progeny includes Marx, the Communists, and the neo-Marxists on the one hand and Nietzsche, the Nazis, and Heidegger on the other.

In much the same way, the totalitarian movements of this century – fascism and bolshevism – could disguise themselves as anti-authoritarian heirs of the French Revolution while simultaneously identifying one another as the greatest threat to liberty, fraternity, and equality. Pound, Wyndham Lewis, D.H. Lawrence, Yeats, and Eliot were prominent modernists who were politically conservative in the sense that they were elitist and that they have been accused – with varying degrees of justification – of being Fascists. It happens that all of these representatives of literary modernism were also friendly to occult or at least mythopoeic theories of art. Of the five, only Lewis and Eliot retained a wide and sceptical distance from the occult revival sweeping Europe and America during their youth and early manhood.

The temptation is to conclude that transcendentalism, mysticism, occultism, and political conservatism are inextricably intertwined, on much the same grounds that others have concluded that modernism and political conservatism are close allied (see John Harrison 1966; Chace 1973; Kazin 1986). A longer historical view, however, indicates just the reverse. Barruel identifies the occult with Jacobinism, with revolution and sedition, with liberty, equality, and fraternity. And as we noted above, Romanticism identified itself with Jacobinism – even though the English Romantics were repelled by the Terror. *Symbolisme* and surrealism both draw on occult and mystical thought, but the *Symbolistes* were typically reactionary and the surrealists typically progressive in political posture.

Occultism in all its varieties assumes that the enlightened individual will inevitably be treated in the same manner as the man who climbs out of the shadows in the parable of the caves in Plato's *Republic*:

Would he not provoke laughter, and would it not be said of him that he had returned from his journey aloft with his eyes ruined and that it was not worth while even to attempt the ascent? And if it were possible to lay hands on and to kill the man who tried to release them and lead them up, would they not kill him? (*Republic*, 7.517)

This scenario of rejection and scorn is repeated time and again in the putative history of enlightened souls. Myths and legends of murder and dismemberment, from Orpheus through Christ, from Mani to Jacques de Molay (implausibly Pound even enrols Mussolini in this canon of theosophical martyrs), are repeatedly encountered as illustrations of the rejection of "higher souls" either by oppressive authority or by the benighted masses. The rejection through scorn and neglect of such historical figures as Swedenborg, Blake, and Blavatsky also fits this rather self-serving scenario. Readers of the polemical writing of early modernism will recognize the same paradigm in the modernist pose of neglected and misunderstood genius. They inherited this pose from the Romantics, of whom they spoke so ill; but the pose itself is founded on Platonic assumptions about the impenetrability and incommunicability of higher knowledge, and hence its accessibility only to "higher souls."

The occult story of secret history assumes that these higher or great souls – called *les Grands Initiés* by Edouard Schuré – leave records of their wisdom in the form of legendary biographies, sermons, and rites. The Christian Gospels and Epistles are fairly typical of these kinds of texts and are often regarded by the occult as a legitimate part of the "tradition." But, of course, the followers of Moses, the Buddha, Mani, Christ, and Mohammed do not properly understand the message passed on by these enlightened souls, according to the occult. The revelation of these higher souls is invariably corrupted or distorted by a worldly priesthood. The task of occult scholarship is to recover the wisdom that survives obscurely and corruptly in religious and philosophical literature. The occultist is capable of doing so in part because the divine spark has flared in the scholar's own soul at one time or another, and in part because of membership in a community of enlightened souls.

Because the revelation is hidden or occluded in rare and little-known texts, occult scholarship is typically antiquarian and archival. It also has a strong hermeneutic component, because every canonical text has a hidden message and belongs to a great intertextual fabric reaching from remotest antiquity to the present. Both notions are given very clear expression by Aldous Huxley, perhaps the most celebrated occultist of the postwar period: "In every age there have been some men and women who chose to fulfil the conditions upon which alone, as a matter of brute empirical fact, such immediate [spiritual] knowledge can be had; and of these a few have left accounts of the Reality they were thus enabled to apprehend and have tried to relate in one comprehensive system of thought, the given facts of this experience" ([1946] 1985, 12). A little later, speaking of the "thought patterns" of "primitives," Huxley endorses the occult double hermeneutic of an exoteric or manifest sense and an esoteric or latent sense as a technique to protect the ineffable from corruption by the profane: "It is highly significant that, among many contemporary primitives, two thought-patterns are found – an exoteric pattern for the unphilosophic many and an esoteric pattern ... for the initiated few" (37). Because the occult does not place great value upon consistency, it is not uncommon to find the same writer stressing the incommunicability of the wisdom while at the same time speaking of the need to hide it in secret codes in order to *protect* it from the profane – or from oppressive authority. The profane are just the masses. But the oppressive authority has a variety of instantiations. The Roman Catholic Church and the papacy – as the heir of empire and leader of the counterrevolution – has been the favourite embodiment of authority for the occult as for the Jacobins, and even for liberalism.

By the late nineteenth century, under Nietzsche's influence, Christianity at large displaced Catholicism as the enemy of liberty. Nietzsche blamed Luther and the Germans for doing Europe out of the harvest of the Renaissance because Luther "restored the church ... at the very moment *when it was vanquished*" (*Ecce Homo*, "The Case of Wagner," s2; Nietzsche's emphasis). Of course, Marx and Comte were also hostile to religion, condemning it as superstition, even though they did not target Christianity exclusively. Nonetheless, at the time that modernism was being born, Nietzscheanism, Marxism, positivism, and occultism all perceived Christianity as a common antagonist – just as occultism, Protestantism, and Jacobinism had all seen Rome as their common antagonist at the end of the eighteenth century. These shared antagonisms have often confused observers of the cultural history of modernism – and not infrequently confused the players themselves.

To some extent occultism, Enlightenment rationalism, and twentieth-century empiricism also share a common vocabulary. All speak of "enlightenment" as the supreme value. And although each means a different thing by the term, they all share the assumption that humans are benighted and need some aid to achieve enlightenment. But no one would permit these conformities to persuade him that Platonism, scholasticism, rationalism, and empiricism are equivalent cognitive systems.

At the same time, I want to draw attention to the propensity for occultism to disguise itself in the clothing of the dominant cognitive system of its day, a propensity aided and abetted by a shared hostility to Christianity. Rationalism, empiricism, and dialectical materialism all regard religion as little more than error and superstition. Christianity is just *our* superstition, and not a particularly vicious or silly one. The occult, however, sees Christianity as a competing revelation, a corrupt or imperfect version of that true revelation of which the occultists are the custodians.

Ezra Pound's reputation has been a beneficiary of a confusion arising from the equation of antichristian sentiment with progressive views in other areas. He has long passed muster as a poet of the age of relativism largely because of his frequent adoption of antichristian postures. It is only recently that scholarship has even noted that he shared the occult interests and beliefs of his mentors, Yeats, Mead, Upward, and Orage. The implications of this connection for an understanding of his life and work are still being evaded.

No one has so far noticed that *The Cantos* is a fairly typical product of occult scholarship in that it presents a history of the adventures of the secret doctrine from earliest times to the present. Pound wrote his epic in the confidence that a new age was about to dawn. Its obscurity, bookishness, interminability, and synopticism are all characteristic of occult works. Such an interpretation of *The Cantos* seems inescapable to me, but it has long been obscured by a misperception of Pound, and of modernism generally, as an expression of the empiricism and positivism of the modern age, when in fact it was an accommodation of the mysticism and occultism of the late nineteenth century to the relativism of the twentieth. Now that postmodernism has highlighted relativism as the *contrary* of the positivism or decontextualism that is central to scientific modernism and political liberalism, it is much easier to see that literary modernism was essentially antipathetic to scientific modernism despite its protestations to the contrary – protestations that were almost certainly perfectly sincere.

Although T.S. Eliot's case is much more complex and delicate than Pound's, his conversion to Christianity was certainly less of a break with his earlier position than it was thought to be. The ironic posture of the early Eliot probably reflects religious anxiety as much as, or more than, the sceptical mockery that it was taken to be. If we re-examine that poetry in the light of the climate of opinion that I have been outlining – which includes not only Blavatsky's theosophy, Mead's Gnosticism, and Myers's psychic phenomena but also Freud's subconscious, Jung's collective unconscious, and Levy-Bruhl's *participation mystique* – we can better understand, I think, its peculiar velleity.

More generally, it may well be that the mood of abulia and paralysis that is so characteristic of high modernism is not so much the ironic and detached mimesis of the moral and intellectual confusion of the age that New Criticism took it to be, as it is an expression of it. My last chapter will undertake an analysis of the formulation of *The Waste Land* under Pound's blue pencil in the light of these considerations.

CHAPTER TWO

The Occult Tradition in The Cantos

TROUBADOURS AND ALBIGENSES

The Abbé Barruel's *Memoirs* were designed to discredit the French Revolution by associating it with disreputable groups and doctrines, which for him were Enlightenment atheism, Rousseauean egalitarianism, and republicanism. In this respect he was scarcely eccentric, even if modern scholarship paints a rather less Whiggish picture of the French Revolution. Barruel concentrated his attack on "atheism," a term which then included any non-Christian belief, whether pantheism, immanentism, or materialistic atheism. A less confusing label for this basket of unchristian beliefs was the "religion of nature," and this is the term Barruel uses most often. His favourite targets are pantheistic or immanentist in doctrine rather than atheistic in the modern sense of scientific materialism. The basic principles common to all varieties of the religion of nature were – according to Barruel – those of the Revolution: liberty, equality and fraternity. His great "find" was that atheism, republicanism, and democracy were the "secret of Masonry" (Barruel 1797–98, 2:289) and that these doctrines had troubled the history of Europe from the earliest Christian times. Barruel's genius, then, was to invent the hypothesis that a single doctrine and political program – Masonry – lay behind all of the subversive movements that had troubled Christian Europe. He revealed that the words of the Master Mason to the initiate are: "My dear brother, the secret of Masonry consists in these words, EQUALITY and LIBERTY; *all men are equal and free; all men are brethren*" (2:289; Barruel's emphasis). These slogans of the revolution were thus revealed as ancient, "atheististic," and heretical.

Masonry's own internal fantasy history – upon which Barruel relied – traces its origin to the masons who built Solomon's temple and claims an underground continuity from that remote time to the present. (For a scholalry attempt to reconstruct the history of Masonry, see Yates 1964 and 1972). In contradiction of this story, Barruel traces Masonry's origin to Mani, the martyred third-century Babylonian reformer of Zoroastrianism and the founder of Manichaeanism. By this move, Barruel is able to link Masonry to heresy, antimonarchism, and revolution at a single stroke:

Attending to the most striking similarities, we have seen the Occult degrees of Masonry founded on the *Bema* of the Manichaeans. It was Manes whom they were to avenge on all Kings, on Kings who had condemned him to be flayed alive and who, according to his doctrines, had only been instituted by the evil spirit; and the word to be recovered was that doctrine itself, to be established on the ruins of Christianity. The Templars, taught by the adepts dispersed throughout Egypt and Palestine, substituted, at their dissolution, their Grand Master Molay for Manes, as the object [i.e., cause] of their vengeance; and the spirit of the mysteries and the allegories remained the same. It is always Kings and Christianity that are to be destroyed, Empires and the Altar to be overturned, in order to re-establish the Liberty and Equality of human nature. (Barruel 1797–98, 2:416–17)

This paragraph pretty well epitomizes both the technique and content of Barruel's *Memoirs* and of the bogus history that descends from them. He takes an obscure story about the execution of Manes (who admittedly was an historical person, like Christ) and treats it as a narrative touchstone by which he can identify followers of Mani. It is apparent to us – as it seems not have been to Barruel – that the story is an analogue of Christ's martyrdom. Mani, like Christ, is unjustly executed by legal authority, that is to say by a king. In strong contrast to Christian acceptance of Christ's death and the willingness to render unto Caesar those things that are Caesar's, Barruel tells us that the followers of Mani are forever after bound to avenge his murder by plotting to murder kings. (This interpretation is the one that Masons themselves put on the murder of Hiram Abiff, chief mason among those constructing Solomon's temple and the first Grand Master.)

There are two observations about Barruel's argument that bear on the secret history that descends from him. The first is the rather obvious one that he identifies heresy and sedition as two faces of the same coin and symmetrically identifies orthodoxy with monarchy.

Of course, Barruel is not the first to make such a link, but his argument that Jacobinism stretched back through the Middle Ages to pre-Christian paganism adds a new dimension to the defence of the status quo. An unanticipated consequence of his attempt to discredit Jacobinism was that revolutionaries were now encouraged to seek legitimating precursors of Danton and Mirabeau in the Middle Ages and antiquity – much as Protestant historians had discovered medieval precursors of Luther and Calvin.

The second observation bears on the hermeneutic technique he uses and applies to historical evidence. His method is based on the principle of analogy or affinity – a standard hermeneutic among modern folklorists, mythographers, and psychoanalysts. Within these disciplines analogy, similarity, resemblance, or correspondence function as identity – sometimes called "identity of form." In this hermeneutic the similar counts as the same. This is an ancient hermeneutic employed by Hellenic mythographers and allegorists, of whom the best known are Plutarch and Porphyry. It was displaced for a long time by the narrower Christian hermeneutic of typology, in which all Old Testament incidents were construed as antetypes of their fulfilment in Christ's life and preaching as recorded in the Gospels. Hellenic allegoresis was revived during the Italian Renaissance.

Barruel applies this hermeneutic to historical documents, thereby producing a history that is a story of a frame of mind, *Weltanschauung*, or tradition, much more than it is an account of events. Barruel, then, not only supplies much of the raw material for the secret history of Europe, but he also adopts a methodology that will permit its almost infinite elaboration. The eccentric and occult history that descends from Barruel adopts his hermeneutic, his reliance on private and unofficial information, his practice of tracing a tradition, and his identification of that tradition with Jacobinism and sedition. But occult history reverses his animus, regarding as oppressed heroes and martyrs those whom Barruel attacked as seditious heretics and revolutionaries. The secret history of Europe becomes the history of the struggle of an oppressed minority culture – typically regarded as morally, spiritually, and aesthetically superior to mainstream culture – against arbitrary authority. After Barruel, even the masonic writers adopt Manes and Jacques de Molay as masonic martyrs.

The strong similarity between the occult reading of European history as a story of an oppressed alternate culture and the hippie, or counterculture, reading of recent history attests to the continuing vitality of Barruel's paradigm within Christian nations, and of its adaptability. It seems equally suitable to the nostalgia of the

Romantics as it is to the epochal pessimism of Barruel, Nietzsche, Yeats, and Lawrence; or to the epochal optimism of Mead, Pound, and Herbert Marcuse. The very successful stage musical, *Jesus Christ Superstar*, clearly exploits the counterculture's image of itself as a morally superior and oppressed underclass, just like the followers of Christ.

The conservative and Catholic Abbé Barruel was blind to the appeal of the paradigm of the underdog in Christian cultures. He was probably unaware of the seventeenth-century English Puritan nar-ratization of secular history as a struggle of the chosen people against oppressive and illegitimate state power, synecdochically represented by Pharoah in the Old Testament and by Caesar in the New.

It is to this story of oppression that Pound appeals in the notorious opening lines of *The Pisan Cantos*, which lament the Italian partisans' lynching of Mussolini and his mistress, Clara Petacci:

> The enormous tragedy of the dream in the peasant's bent shoulders
> Manes! Manes was tanned and stuffed,
> Thus Ben and la Clara *a Milano*
>   by the heels at Milano (canto 84, 425)

The appearance of Mani for the first time this late in Pound's epic is completely puzzling unless one recognizes it as an appeal to the secret history of Europe descending from Barruel, which has ani-mated the poem from the beginning. Here Pound adds Mussolini to the long list of martyrs in the struggle against church and kings, which – according to Barruel – begins with Mani. Later in *The Cantos* (in *Rock-Drill*) Pound also invokes Jacques de Molay, asking, "did Jacques de Molay / know these proportions?" – meaning, of course, the secret proportions of the temple, the great masonic secret, synechdocically standing for all their secrets.

Pound would have read of Molay's role in Nesta Webster, if not elsewhere, for he marked passages in her chapter on the Templars. Although he marked the following passage, he clearly did not adopt Webster's animus towards the Templars, whom she identified as bankers: "The Templars had become the 'international financiers' and 'international capitalists' of their day; had they not been suppressed, all the evils now denounced by Socialists as peculiar to the system they describe as 'Capitalism' – trusts, monopolies, and 'corners' – would in all probability have been inaugurated during the course of the fourteenth century in a far worse form than at the present day" (Webster [1924] 1946, 60). Clearly, Pound rejected Webster's analysis of the suppression of the Templars in favour of the standard masonic and occult understanding of them as suppressed carriers of the wisdom.

It is difficult to say which is most bizarre – Pound's appeal to an unbelievable secret history of Europe or his perception of Mussolini as a martyr in the struggle against arbitrary authority. The extreme oddity of both can be explained only by a long detour through the secret history of Europe and the nineteenth-century occult which adopted it.

I have not found any evidence that Pound ever read Barruel, and I think it unlikely that he did because his habit was to mention in correspondence and published essays whatever he happened to be reading at the time. Nonetheless, there is no doubt that he was familiar with Barruel's argument that traced the Jacobin conspiracy to the Manichaeans by way of a cloud of heresies rampant among those whom Barruel called the "men of the South." Barruel gave the Albigenses or Cathars particular prominence (Barruel, 1979–98, 2:402).

In *Guide to Kulchur* (1938) – a cranky book even for him – Pound continually returns to the topic of secret history, always suggesting that there is indeed a secret but that it is too profound to be plainly uttered. Quarrelling with Luigi Valli (who, like Rossetti, adds Dante to the list of proto-Jacobins) Pound invokes Mani: "'Something' behind it? Certainly 'something' behind it or beyond it. Which the police called 'Manichaean' knowing nothing either of Manes or of anything else" (294–5). Some years earlier – in "Terra Italica" (1931) – Pound had taken issue directly with Barruel's version of the tradition (although without attributing it to Barruel): "The usual accusation against the Albigeois is that they were Manichaeans. This I believe after a long search to be pure bunkumb. The slanderers feared the truth ... The best scholars do not believe there were any Manichaeans left in Europe at the time of the Albigensian Crusade. If there were any in Provence they have at any rate left no trace in troubadour art" (Pound 1973b, 58–9).

Pound's uncertainty about the Manichaeans reflects the uncertainty of the occult generally. Theosophy was very uncomfortable with Mani's intensification of the dualism that was already in Zoroastrianism in the opposition of Ahriman and Ormuzd. Christianity has been less uncomfortable. It revised the Zoroastrian story of a dual creation into the story of Satan's rebellion, which was given canonical form in Milton's *Paradise Lost*. The modern occult is generally hostile to the Manichaean doctrine that the physical universe was created by Ahriman, the spirit of darkness, and to the consequent emphasis on asceticism. Theosophists were not content to reverse Mani's preferences and be "of the devil's party." Mead firmly identified theosophy with Gnosticism but felt compelled to dispute the scholarly belief that Gnosticism derived from Manicheanism. Pound echoed Mead's anti-Manichaean posture during his London years but vacillated later. The issue was a lively one in the period. H.J. Warner, a non-occult student of Albigensianism writing in the 1920s, also argued against the standard identification of Catharism with Manichaeanism (Warner [1922] 1967, 9–18).

Pound's denial of the Manicheanism of the Albigensian heretics seems to have been momentarily forgotten in the opening lines of *The Pisan Cantos*. Perhaps the resemblance of Mani's death to Mussolini's – both of whom were flayed – overrode his opposition to the Manichaean hypothesis. This lapse seems to be an instance of the hermeneutic of resemblance prevailing over analytic content, for a little later, in canto 74, Pound appears to return to his standard denial of the Manichaean origins of the Albigenses (see his remarks in *Guide to Kulchur* cited below). In this passage he is speaking of Scotus Erigina, whose Neoplatonism got him into trouble with the hierarchy, and remarks: "and they dug him up out of sepulture / soi disantly looking for Manichaeans. / Les Albigeois, a problem of history" (Pound 1973a, 429).

In any case, the disagreement between Pound and the theosophists is over details. Both take for granted the general hypothesis that a secret tradition survived from antiquity and that the Albigenses were carriers of that tradition. In "Terra Italica" Pound assigns the tradition an origin of much higher antiquity even than Mani, and this is in conformity with occult opinion at the turn of the century: "On the other hand the cult of Eleusis will explain not only general phenomena but particular beauties in Arnaut Daniel or in Guido Cavalcanti ... I suggest that students trying to understand the poesy of southern Europe from 1050 to 1400 should try to open it with this key" (1973b, 58–9). The "key" is the putative link between the Albigensian heretics and the poets of Provence. More than twenty years ago I pointed out that Pound read the Albigensian Crusade of the thirteenth century as an analogue of the Trojan War (Surette 1971). In a subsequent article I elaborated the historical argument so as to include the supposition of a Barruel-like underground religion. I argued that Pound found this story in the two books by the French occultist Joséphin Péladan which he had reviewed in 1906. However, he went beyond Péladan and traced the tradition to the Eleusinian mysteries, a feature of Pound's world that we shall use to isolate the probable provenance of his views (Surette 1974). I thought at that time – and still thought when I wrote *A Light from Eleusis* (1979) –

that Pound was imitating the "mythological method" of Joyce in his allusions to the Albigensian Crusade, the Manichaeans, and the mysteries of Eleusis. I argued – quite sensibly, I think, even though erroneously – that there was no more reason to suppose that Pound took any of this seriously than there was to suppose that Eliot was an adept of a fertility cult because of the allusions to such cults in *The Waste Land*. In taking this line, I was being faithful to the still prevailing New Critical spirit of textual autonomy, which separated questions of authorial belief rigorously from those purely formal considerations that were the proper concern of the literary scholar.

It is now clear to me that I was mistaken in this assumption. Pound's allusions to the Albigenses in fact appeal to an understanding of the secret history of Europe that was current in London occult circles at the turn of the century. Far from being a mere rhetorical device, this parallel is part of the historical content of the poem. Pound believed the legendary and mythical history contained in *The Cantos* to have the same status as the more empirical history of Italy and America contained in the poem. The evidence for Pound's engagement with the occult is overwhelming, even though it has largely been evaded by the Pound industry. Accounts of Pound's occult contacts and opinions can be found in James Longenbach's *Stone Cottage*, in Demetres Tryphonopoulos's *Celestial Tradition*, and in Peter Makin's *Provence and Pound*. Humphrey Carpenter casually remarks that Pound "regarded himself as a latter-day practitioner" of the cult of amor discussed in "Psychology and Troubadours" in *A Serious Character: The Life of Ezra Pound* (1988, 167), and John Tytell also alludes to Pound's occult connections in *Ezra Pound: The Solitary Volcano* (1987, 56–7, 69–71). The difficulty is not so much to demonstrate the occult provenance and character of Pound's inspiration, but rather to identify and characterize the occult itself so that we can properly assess the pertinence of that inspiration to our understanding and evaluation of his poetry.

This work has not yet been truly begun. Even James Longenbach – despite the unmistakable evidence he gathers in *Stone Cottage* (1988) that Pound fully participated in Yeats's occultism – oddly concludes that modernism as a whole takes only its penchant for deliberate obscurity from the occult, and not its subject matter (92–4). No doubt he reaches this conclusion because he restricts the occult to theurgic or magical interests and fails to recognize as occult the kinds of historical and mystical or esoteric topics and motifs that are put under scrutiny here and are unmistakably reflected in the work of most of the leading modernists – not only in the avowedly occult Yeats, in Pound, and in Lawrence, but also in the genuinely sceptical

Joyce and the Christian Eliot. Even though the ubiquity of the occult as a topic in modernist literature does not establish that the artists in question are themselves occultists or mystics, scholarship needs to know more of the occult if it is to assess the status of occult topics in the literature.

It has become a commonplace of Pound scholarship that the troubadours transmitted some sort of wisdom or insight from high antiquity and that it was passed on, by way of Renaissance Neoplatonism, to the aesthetes and eventually to the modernists. Despite the impression given by Peter Makin and others, scholars of Provençal literature do not endorse this story. Nonetheless, the story is not peculiar to Poundians.

René Nelli, a careful and well-published investigator of this putative tradition, is an enthusiastic promoter of the literature of the troubadours and a proponent of some aspects of the Barruel story. Evryone now agrees that the Albigensian Crusade against the Cathar heresy destroyed the independent civilization of Provence, the *langue d'oc*. The crusade has long been seen as the military conquest of the south by the king of France (Nelli 1972, 13–15). Nelli relies on Pierre Belperron's history of the Cathars and the crusade, but this secular and political reading of the crusade has been standard since Sismondi's history of it. However, Nelli traces Cathar influence to Florence, where Cavalcanti and Dante pass it on to Petrarch (165–73), and argues that it later surfaced in the work of William Blake, Lamartine, and Victor Hugo (189–94). This story is very much in the tradition of the occult history that I hope to elucidate.

Perhaps the best-known modern study which posits a link between the Albigensian Cathars and the troubadours is Denis de Rougemont's *Love and the Western World* (1940). De Rougemont's study has reached a wide audience. It presents much the same version of the story as Pound and Nelli do. Unlike them, he identifies his sources as Péladan and Aroux (78). He argues that the troubadours and the Cathars were adepts of a forbidden "Church of Love." This underground heretical "church" came into Europe from the "East" (82–112) and allegedly survives to the present day in a "tradition" carried on by such poets as Sordello, Cavalcanti, Dante, and Boccaccio, as well as in the Grail literature. (The first three are prominent in Pound's *paideia*.)

Like Aroux, and unlike Pound and the occult, de Rougemont is hostile towards the eroticism of the tradition, which he isolates in one particular myth, Tristan and Isolde, and attacks in its final form in Wagner's opera, *Tristan and Isolde*. He interprets this opera as celebrating eros as a transfiguring force (leading, as he puts it, to *askesis*), which can be fully experienced only in adultery, and as denigrating the restraints of Christian *agape*, or fraternal love, which is fully achieved in matrimony. Clearly, de Rougemont's argument unfolds itself within a Nietzschean reading of a culturally embedded conflict between freedom and restraint. He is anti-Nietzschean, rejecting pagan or Dionysian eros in favour of Christian or Apollonian *agape*, of *askesis* over transubstantiation: "Charitable love, Christian love – which is Agape – appears at last and risen to its full height. It is the expression of being in action. And it is Eros, passionate love, pagan love, that spread through the European world the poison of an idealistic *askesis* – all that Nietzsche lays at the door of Christianity. And it is Eros, not Agape, that glorified our death instinct and sought 'to idealize' it" (Rougemont [1940] 1956, 311).

There is no material difference between de Rougemont's story and Nelli's, despite the fact that Nelli neither cites de Rougemont nor lists him in any of his bibliographies. There are, it is true, important differences of emphasis and detail. Nelli is not a Christian apologist like de Rougemont but is inclined towards esotericism. There is a great deal of overlap between Pound's, de Rougemont's, and Nelli's lists of adepts. De Rougemont omits Blake; but Nelli, like Yeats, includes him. Nelli and de Rougemont both list Poe, Baudelaire, and the *Symbolistes*; but de Rougemont alone adds the surrealists (100–1 and 232). The details are less important than the overriding hypothesis of a link between the troubadours and the Cathars, and they represent a link in a chain of succession reaching back into high antiquity and forward into the present. It is this story that is the touchstone of Barruel's influence.

Barruel himself had precursors. He drew on Martinez de Pasquales, L.C. de Saint Martin, and Adam Weishaupt, all of whom were prerevolutionary occultists who did in fact organize secret societies and who claimed antique origins for their societies. All three attempted to co-opt one another and Freemasonry for their own doctrines and goals, leaving things in an inextricable tangle of claims, counterclaims, historical fabrications, and real historical events. Barruel was content to accept their fantasies (such as the claim of antique origins) when they served his purposes and to reject them when they did not. Whatever the true story of these late Enlightenment secret and occult societies may be, there seems to be good evidence that Barruel's linking of them with antiroyalist and antichristian sentiment is well founded (see Darnton 1968, 33–45).

Given that Barruel's motive was to expose radical political activity in Europe preceding the French Revolution, it is not surprising that modern scholars suggest that he exaggerates (Darnton 1968, 163).

Still, something was going on before the explosion of 1789. Barruel's attribution of the revolution and all earlier upheavals in Europe to a single heretical doctrine is entirely implausible, but its status as the grandfather of modern conspiracy theories is unchallengeable. There were three prominent candidates for organized sedition in France to which Barruel might have turned: the Albigensian Crusade, the suppression of the Templars, and the suppression of the Huguenots. Barruel considers the first two but omits the Huguenots – perhaps out of consideration for the sensitivity of his English hosts. Whatever the reason for his omission, the Huguenots remain outside the tradition. Perhaps they have too few attributes of a mystical and esoteric brotherhood. Barruel's masonic sources, Pasquales, Saint Martin, and Weishaupt, had not claimed the Albigensians as part of their secret history. Barruel's contribution was to add these prominent French heretics and to attach the lot to the Jacobin revolutionaries.

Pound's denial of Barruel's accusation that the Cathars were Manicheans is in conformity with the occult's preference for an origin of much greater antiquity – whether pre-Socratic Greece (Eleusis, Orpheus, Dionysus, Hermes), Egypt (Thoth, Osiris), or India (Hinduism, Buddhism). Mead's version of the story – a version with which Pound was familiar – gave Gnosticism the role of transmitting the wisdom from the pagan world to the Christian. In contrast to Manichaean antithetical dualism, Gnosticism is monistic and palingenetic, considering death to be in reality a second birth, an ascent to what Mead called the "subtle body."

In "The Meaning of Gnosis in Higher Hellenistic Religion" (1913), Mead explains that we have a "spiritual intuitive mind, the human counterpart of that Mind or Divine Monad in which we are to be dowsed or baptised" (683). The "dowsing" or baptism of which he speaks is the exoteric aspect of gnosis, which he describes as "nothing less than the comprehension of the things of the suprasensible world" (680). He goes on to elaborate: "The possession of gnosis means the ability to receive and understand revelation. The true gnostic is one who knows the inner or hidden unveiled revelation and who also understands the outer or published veiled revelation. He is not one who has discovered the truth of himself by his own unaided reflection, but one to whom the disclosures of the inner world are known and become understandable" (680).

In Mead's theosophical story, the illuminated soul belongs to a community of the enlightened. Their gnosis or wisdom is published in an outer (exoteric) form, but its esotric sense is understood only by the enlightened who have been "dowsed" in the Divine Monad, that is, have undergone a palingenetic initiation feebly reflected in

Christian baptism. The gnosis or revelation vouchsafed to the initiate can be spoken of only in veiled terms – often as acquaintance with that "other world" we all enter when we die. In terms of this hermeneutic, mythical accounts of visits to the underworld – such as those of Orpheus, Odysseus, Lazarus, Dante, and the questing knight – are in truth exoteric representations of palingenetic initiations.

The full esoteric sense of such literature is believed to be comprehensible only to "those who know." When Dante describes Aristotle as *il maestro di color che sanno* ("the master of those who know") in *Inferno* 4, occultists understand him to mean "the master of the initiated." And they read the company of philosophers listed by Dante – Socrates, Plato, Democritus, Diogenes, Anaxagoras, Thales, Empedocles, Heraclitus, Zeno, Orpheus, et al. – as a list of enlightened souls.

Rather surprisingly, Mead has nothing to say about the troubadours or Dante. However, other Theosophists of the period – notably Isabel Cooper-Oakley and Jessie Weston – give their attention to the transmission of the esoteric meaning of higher Hellenistic religion from the late classical world to the present, and they find the same provenance for it as Barruel, Rossetti, and Reghellini found for Jacobinism.

The persistence of the Cathars or Albigenses in the story of the tradition depends in part on their natural suitability as victims and, more importantly, on the uncertainty about just what their beliefs were and whence they were derived. Despite Pound's assertions to the contrary, the scholarly consensus has long been that Catharism was essentially Manichaean in doctrine (Mundy 1985, 7–11). However, Jean Duvernoy, in what is recognized as the most authoritative general study of the Cathars (1976 and 1979), has concluded that they were neither Manichaean nor Gnostic in inspiration; they were Origenist (Duvernoy 1976, 359–60). Duvernoy lends no support to the Barruel view of a pagan survival in Catharism. On the other hand, Origen's heresy involved a ritualization of human sexuality, and this aspect of his argument would have been welcomed by Pound and the others who regarded Catharism as a cult of amor.

An even more problematic aspect of the occult reading of the Albigenses is the claim that the troubadours were adepts of the heretical cult. On this point, Duvernoy admits that we know of some troubadours who were indeed Cathars, but he concludes that for the most part they were essentially professional entertainers and were neither allegorical propagandists for the heresy, as the Rossetti-Reghellini argument would have it, nor disseminators of esoteric wisdom, as Cooper-Oakley, Pound, and Weston would have them be

(279). Francis Hueffer comes to essentially the same conclusion in *The Troubadours: A History of Provençal Life and Literature*, a work Pound might well have consulted, since he was under the tutelage of Hueffer's son, Ford Madox Ford, during his Kensington days (see Hueffer [1878] 1977, esp. 232, 254–5).

Duvernoy explicitly rejects Rossetti's theory that the troubadours wrote in a secret code – although he mistakenly attributes the theory to the plagiarist Aroux (Duvernoy 1976, 274). Most damagingly for the occult reading of the heresy, Duvernoy completely rejects the idea that the Cathars themselves, let alone the troubadours, were in any sense mystical, gnostic, or esoteric (269). Duvernoy devotes eleven pages (1979, 335–45) to an assessment of the scholarly and literary survival of Catharism and its attendant history. Of the authors I have identified as the sources of the myth of a pagan survival through the Middle Ages, he mentions only Péladan. He does note that the occult movement picked up the Cathars at the turn of the century, but he relies on the study by E. Barbier (*Les Infiltrations maçonniques dans l'église*, 1910) and misses Barruel, Rossetti, and Aroux (even though he earlier attributes Rossetti's euhemerist arguments to Aroux). That Duvernoy misses these individuals in his survey is, of course, an index of their obscurity, not of his carelessness.

Despite the conclusions of academic historians such as Duvernoy and Mundy, the "rumour" that the troubadours were the heirs and transmitters of an ancient tradition opposed to Catholic orthodoxy and monarchical and aristocratic government persists to this day. It is frequently found in otherwise sound literary scholarship and is ubiquitous in semi-scholarly accounts of the troubadours. No further effort will be made in this discussion to demonstrate the highly questionable character of the putative secret history. Taking the absence of objective evidence for the tradition as established, the following pages will trace its provenance in the quasi-scholarly literature I am calling "occult scholarship."

For a straightforward theosophist like Isabel Cooper-Oakley writing at the turn of the century, there is no question about the mystical nature of the Albigenses. The "philosophical" or "metaphysical" tradition that she sketches is very little different from Barruel's except that it now reaches forward to Blavatskian Theosophy rather than to revolutionary Jacobinism (which is no longer part of the "tradition"):

The doctrines hidden in the secret fraternities have been handed down in regular succession from first to last. We can see that the esoteric teachings in Egypt, in Persia, and in Greece, were kept from the ears of an illiterate multitude precisely because it was known that they could not ... understand the deeper truth of Nature and of God. Hence the secrecy with which these pearls of great price were guarded and handed on with slight modifications into the possession of those grand early Christians, the Gnostics, the so-called heretics; then straight from the Gnostic schools of Syria and Egypt to their successors the Manichaeans, and from these through the Paulicians, Albigenses, Templars and other secret bodies – these occult traditions have been bequeathed to the mystic bodies of our own times. (Cooper-Oakley [1900] 1977, 11)

Although the political dimension of Barruel's conspiracy has disappeared from Cooper-Oakley's account, she retains the essential ingredient of secrecy and cites Aroux copiously to support the importance of the troubadours, Dante, and the Grail literature to the esoteric tradition (103–36).

Cooper-Oakley's assumption that the troubadours were Cathars is plainly derived from Aroux and not from Barruel, who makes no mention of them, the Grail literature, or Dante. We know that Aroux's *Dante hérétique* was plagiarized from Rossetti's *La Beatrice di Dante*, and we therefore have good reason to look to Rossetti as the origin of the link between the troubadours and the Albigenses. The bogus discovery of a connection between a genuine literary tradition and a genuine heresy was virtually a nonce event, the principal agent of which was Gabriele Rossetti. The event has so far entirely escaped the notice of scholarship despite its very considerable progeny in the canonical literature of this century.

DANTE THE HERETIC: ROSSETTI, AROUX, AND VALLI

The story begins with the career of Gabriele Rossetti, the father of Dante Gabriel and Christina Rossetti. The elder Rossetti arrived in England on 24 March 1824, a middle-aged exile from Naples. (He was born in the small town of Vasto on 28 February 1783.) He had written some poems in praise of a constitutional revolt against King Ferdinand of Naples in 1820. When the revolt failed the next year, he found his name on a blacklist. He fled to Malta, where he spent three years and gained the friendship of John Hookham Frere, the English poet and diplomat, who had retired there. He first earned his living in London by giving private lessons in Italian. At the same time he was writing a commentary on Dante's *Commedia*, the first portion of which he published under the title *Commento analitico al inferno* in two volumes (1826, 1827). The derisive reception of this work by the reviewers was to determine the future course of Gabriele's scholarly life and to bring about the importation of the Albigenses into Barruel's secret history. So devastating was the reception of his *Commento* that Rossetti never got beyond the *Purgatorio*, and even the *Purgatorio* commentary was not published until 1967! However, his scholarship gained him the crucial patronage of Charles Lyell, who stuck by him until his death in 1854. Rossetti also made friends in the London Italian community.

It is a curious coincidence that, in April 1826, Rossetti married Frances Polidori, sister of Dr John Polidori. John Polidori was the physician who accompanied Byron on his travels; he was a member of the famous Swiss evenings of 1814 that produced *Frankenstein* and the Byron/Polidori story, *Vampyre*, the prototype for Bram Stoker's *Dracula*. One can hardly fail to recall that *Frankenstein* and *Dracula* are important sources for the popular literature of the occult. However, I do not attach any particular significance to the coincidence. Interest in the occult was a constant if minor current in Europe from at least the Italian quattrocento forward. Dr Frankenstein, for example, learns how to generate life by studying the Kabbala and alchemy and Paracelsus and other medieval theurgic scholars and scientists.

Rossetti's marriage and the arrival of children forced him to find better employment than private teaching. His friends and his qualifications failed to secure him the post of professor of Italian at the newly established University College of the University of London in 1827 – largely because of the unfavourable reception of the *Commento analitico* – but he was able to secure the chair in Italian at King's College, University of London, when it became available in 1831 (Vincent 1936, 16–21). Rossetti now set himself to answer the critics of his *Commento*. In that work he had proposed to "decode" the *Inferno* on euhemeristic principles, assuming that the poem was written in a *gergo* or secret jargon that could be disencrypted if the key could be discovered. Vincent (1936, 72–3) argues that Rossetti was led to do so by his experience as a Mason, an order he joined in 1809 – although he was not very active and did not rise very high (99). In addition to this alleged inclination to secret codes, Rossetti had the further motivation of his own political affiliations, which would presumably foster a wish to make Dante a Ghibelline. This tendency played better in Protestant England than it did in Catholic and Guelph Italy. *Sullo spirito antipapale che produsse la riforma* (1832) was quickly translated into English by Caroline Ward as *Disquisition on the Antipapal Spirit which Produced the Reformation; Its Secret Influence on the Literature of Europe in General and of Italy in Particular* (1834).

This is the the only one of Rossetti's books to be translated into English and is therefore the most influential of them in the English-speaking world. Unaccountably, Akiko Miyake pays little attention to this work in *Ezra Pound and the Mysteries of Love* (1991), and she ignores completely the reception of his work during his lifetime and thereafter, preferring to rely on congruencies, echoes, and affinities between Rossetti's last work, *Il Mistero dell' amor platonico del medio evo*, and Pound's ideas about the "tradition." She does so in the face of the fact that this work was suppressed and untranslated, and was never mentioned by Pound until 1942 when he called for its republication in "A Visiting Card."

The substance of Rossetti's argument in *Sullo spirito* is little different from Barruel's and in fact is derived from Barruel. Rossetti acknowledges him in footnotes, and we have a letter from Lyell recommending Barruel to Rossetti as early as November 1826, just as the *Commento* was being published (Vincent 1936, 99–100). Already in the *Commento* Rossetti had understood Dante's *Commedia* to be a Ghibelline work. Barruel's hypothesis of a continuous history of seditious secret societies linked to Masonry was just what he needed to support the Ghibelline interpretation of the *Commedia* that was so scornfully attacked in reviews of his *Commento*. The only alteration he had to make to Barruel was to substitute Ghibelline sentiment for Jacobinism. In *Sullo spirito*, in the coy manner of one who has discovered a hidden truth, he asks: "Why were the Templars, who were members of the most illustrious families in Europe, sacrificed by hundreds in different countries? Why were the Patarini burned alive in almost every city? History tells us: they belonged to secret societies, and professed doctrines inimical to Rome" (Rossetti 1834, 148).

No doubt the fact that Rossetti was himself a Mason made him all the more willing to accept Barruel's fantasy. He found support in the work of Reghellini da Schio, who not long before had elaborated Barruel's story in *La Maçonnerie considerée comme le résultat des religions égyptiennes, juives, et chrétiennes* (1829). Oddly enough, Reghellini was another Italian exile and Mason. Rossetti draws almost as heavily on Reghellini in *Sullo spirito* as he does on Barruel. Reghellini took Barruel's general thesis and fleshed it out by tracing Masonry to Eleusis, making it the carrier of an ancient religious tradition, which he calls "theosophy" (probably following Fabre d'Olivet and anticipating Mme Blavatsky by half a century). Reghellini tells us: "At the time of the destruction of the Temple at Eleusis by Alaric the Visigoth, in the year 396 of the common era [*"l'ère vulgaire"*, i.e., Anno Domini], the priests who escaped the sword of the barbarians took refuge in Egypt, where they associated themselves with the Gnostics and with the Christian conservers of the Mosaic rites, adding to their number and their knowledge" (Reghellini 1829, 1:289; my translation).

Reghellini's account of the relations between the Greek mysteries of Eleusis and Barruel's Jacobinism is far more circumstantial than anything Rossetti could have found in Barruel but is clearly not independent of it. Barruel only mentions Eleusis in a list, without giving it any prominence. Speaking of the eighteenth-century Illuminists, Barruel wrote: "To follow these instructions faithfully he [the Illuminist initiate] must begin by descanting on the supreme felicity of being versed in sciences which few can approach, of walking in the paths of light while the vulgar are groping in darkness. He must remark that there exist doctrines solely transmitted by secret traditions, because they are above the comprehension of common minds. In proof of his assertions he will cite the *Gymnosophists* in the Indies, the Priests of *Isis* in Egypt, and those of *Eleusis* and the *Pythagorean* school in Greece" (1797–98, 3:51). Rossetti does not pick up the prominence given to the Eleusinian component by Reghellini – as Edouard Schuré and Pound are later to do – but he does repeat it, and he is therefore a possible avenue by means of which it could have entered the London occult circles where Pound picked it up. However, as we shall see below, the weight of evidence points to Friedrich Creuzer as the most probable albeit indirect source for the special prominence that Mead and Pound assigned to Eleusis.

It should perhaps be noted that while there is definitely some overlap between the role of Eleusis in the occult and masonic readings of history and its role in Jungian archetypalism, the latter is quite distinct and much more Creuzerian. The Jungian interest in the Eleusinian mysteries reflects the importance Jung gives to the mother goddess. Of course, it is important for Jung to identify the most archaic forms of the archetypes (see Kerényi 1967), but it is also the case that he read Creuzer's *Symbolik* about 1910 (Jung 1965, 162). Jung's studies are contemporaneous with Pound's. There is no mutual influence of which I am aware, despite affinities between their views and some shared influences.

The Caroline Ward translation of *Sullo spirito* is the only English-language source I have been able to find for the strong link between the Masons, the Cathars, and Eleusis. Rossetti's account of the link falls somewhere between the "one of a series" status of Eleusis in Barruel and the prominence it is given in Reghellini: "Many are the sects, both ancient and modern, of whose final aim we are as ignorant as of the real nature of their veiled mysteries; that we know but very little about the priesthood of Eleusis, or that of Egypt, whose pupils were as innumerable; and that their secret language and their mystic characters still exercise our curiosity. But we assert that these secrets *were* known to a very great number of persons, and that they were faithfully kept for reasons which we have the means of explaining" (Rossetti 1834, 112).

At this point in his development, Rossetti's explanation was a political one. The secrets were seditious rather than mystical, even though maintained by a priesthood. In this euhemeristic version of secret history, the ancient priesthood constituted a sort of parallel government that was interested in the preservation of cultural values, much as the medieval church is credited with preserving Latin culture through the Dark Ages. In order to do so, it was obliged to maintain secrecy *vis-à-vis* the secular authorities. Rossetti is probably following Reghellini here. His explanation also is political and not at all esoteric. Reghellini argues that the members of the sect were revolutionaries who were obliged to conceal their plans and principles out of fear of the authorities; but as masonic revolutionaries, they were also preservers of ancient knowledge.

The most significant departure from Barruel that Rossetti would have found in Reghellini is the inclusion of Dante as a member of a secret and seditious society. In the three volumes and one thousand pages of *La Maçonnerie*, Reghellini speaks of Dante only twice (1:345–6 and 3:48–9), and he makes the same point both times: that Dante was initiated into the secrets of Masonry. But for Reghellini, masonic secrets were those of a society of Jacobin freethinkers, not the secrets of a transcendental realm. Rossetti had decided, independently of Reghellini, that Dante was a freethinking Ghibelline, but Reghellini provided him with independent corroboration of this opinion and extended the putative tradition back towards the ancient wisdom of Eleusis and forward to the poets of the Italian *dolce stil nuovo*.

Despite his credulity as an historian – accepting the most far-fetched analogies and the slightest allusions as evidence for an identity of belief and policy between authors as remote from one another as Homer and St Matthew – Reghellini insists that all of the apparently mystical and esoteric texts he cites are to be understood euhemeristically; that is, as encrypted messages of a secular nature rather than as figurative expressions of the ineffable. For Reghellini, as for Barruel, even the most sublime poem is regarded as an encoded message between lodges of secret societies.

Reghellini extends this hermeneutic principle even to the Gospels. Speaking of Matthew's account of the resurrection of the dead (27:52–3), he argues that "all of this is an allegory; there never were any sorcerers either before or after Circe, and those who are so called did not know how to resurrect an insect. Even the ancients were misled by parables or figurative expressions, but the sense of these lines is clear" (1829, 3:272; my translation). The meaning of all of these stories of resurrection or of visits to the underworld, he tells us, is simply that the people spoken of have been initiated into the secret society of Masonry. Reghellini also applies this strongly euhemeristic allegoresis to Ulysses' descent into Hades, Porphyry's fable of the caves, and even to Dante's great dream poem. Thus, he flatly contradicts the occult reading of these stories as exoteric expressions of initiation.

Although occult students of the tradition – Mead and Cooper-Oakley – consult Barruel, Reghellini, and Rossetti, they reject (or just ignore) their euhemerism. An uninitiated reader of the literature can easily be misled by this conflict between an occult and a political reading of the story. As we shall see below, Pound's dispute with Valli over the latter's reading of Dante's poetry as secret Ghibelline communications is not based – as one would naturally assume – on Pound's scepticism towards Valli's hypothesis that there is a secret message in Dante's poetry. On the contrary, he is disturbed by Valli's assumption that the secret is political rather than metaphysical. Pound wants Dante's poetry to be esoteric and mystical, and is offended at Valli's reading of it as encoded messages between seditious Ghibelline lodges.

It is very difficult when reading Reghellini or Rossetti, or even Barruel, to remember that they understood apparently mystical and occult authors – even clear mystics such as Plotinus and Plotinians or Swedenborg and Swedenborgians – to be men disguising their secret seditious opinions in coded messages passed between lodges. Of course, the euhemerism of Barruel, Reghellini, and Rossetti is no less implausible than the straightforward occult belief that all of these writings contain esoteric wisdom. It is just less occult and mystical. Further confusion is caused because both groups speak of "initiation" but mean very different things by the term. For Rossetti and the other euhemerists, initiation means entry into a secret society; for the occultist, it means entry into higher wisdom, as in the "dowsing" in the Divine Monad described by Mead.

But whether the conspirators are political malcontents or illuminated souls, their secret importance to the history of Europe is much the same for the euhemerists as it is for the theosophists. Rossetti concludes his *Disquisition* with a large general claim, one that became an article of faith in theosophical circles by the late nineteenth century:

The most learned men, and authors of various ages and countries were pupils of this mysterious school, and never losing sight of their one grand object, they were constantly on the alert to bring persons of talent and genius to their way of thinking, and to render them co-operators in their bold projects. There can be no doubt that the present state of civilization in Europe is in great measure an effect of the zeal of this school ... The ungovernable thirst for freedom, and the effervescence of political opinions, which have for long agitated the hearts and minds of men throughout Europe, are but the tardy effects of the slow, but unceasing labours of this ancient school. (Rossetti 1834, 196–7)

Pound's remarks on "secret history" in *Guide to Kulchur* are susceptible of being read as expressing the same sentiment as Rossetti's remarks:

Shallow minds have been in a measure right in their lust for "secret history." I mean they have been dead right to want it, but shallow in their conception of what it was. Secret history is at least twofold. One part consists in the secret corruptions, the personal lusts, avarices etc. that scoundrels keep hidden, another part is the "plus," the constructive urges, a *secretum* because it passes unnoticed or because no human effort can force it on public attention. (Pound 1938, 264)

In the absence of the context I have been generating, one would read this passage as a rejection of secret history, just as one would read Pound's remarks on Luigi Valli as a rejection of allegorical readings of Dante. And it may be that Pound does just mean to reject fantasy histories such as those under scrutiny here. But on this reading it is difficult to account for the recurrent appearance of such historical fantasies in *The Cantos* and in Pound's prose. And the passage is certainly susceptible of an alternative, Rossettian reading.

If we assume that Pound subscribes to some version of secret history, we can read this paragraph as working both sides of the street. On the one hand, Pound endorses the conservative stance of Barruel and Aroux, who see themselves as exposing the sedition of Jacobinism and heresy. (Of course, Pound exposes usurers, not heretics, but the general scenario is much the same.) On the other hand, he also endorses the theosophical hypothesis of a hidden or suppressed tradition that is too subtle to be communicated to the benighted masses but is nonetheless the source of all that is fine and valuable in civilization. Such a view conforms reasonably well to the standard Romantic view that artists are "unacknowledged legislators" in that they formulate – or rather, reformulate – the imagination or "mind-set" of the less sensitive, and it therefore does not attract much comment.

Pound began his epic with a descent, or *nekuia* – with an evocation of the dead, which I compared to a séance. Reghellini tells us that this motif of communication with the dead is an allegory of initiation into Masonry, and he draws particular attention to Odysseus's encounter with Circe and subsequent *nekuia* (1829, 3:267–9). Similarly, Pound gives Odysseus's encounter with Circe great prominence in cantos 39 and 47. My own discussion of Odysseus's role in *The Cantos* in *A Light from Eleusis* (49–66) correctly described, I think, the sense and role of the Circean motif in the poem and identified the proximate sources in Mead's writings. However, I failed then to identify the occult and theosophical nature of Mead's discourse, and I was unaware of the ubiquity of this Odyssean motif in occult literature.

Another pivotal component in my account of the Eleusinian theme in *The Cantos* – which I now recognize as occult and theosophical – was the Cavalcanti canzone, "Donna mi prega" (Surette 1979, 67–79). Pound embeds his translation of the canzone in canto 36. He devoted much effort over a good many years to the translation of this poem. It clearly had special significance for him. Rossetti also singled out this poem, but as an example of a secret message transmitted between chapters of the Ghibelline sect (Rossetti 1834, 99). Of course, Pound's reading is esoteric in contrast to Rossetti's euhemeristic reading. Nonetheless, the poem is one more shared feature between secret history descending from masonic sources through Rossetti by way of Aroux and Péladan to Pound.

When Pound first comes face to face with Rossetti's euhemerist reading of the poem, via Luigi Valli's *Linguaggio segreto* (1928, 1930), he is anxious to reject it: "I do not believe that much, if anything, that Valli says can be applied to the *Donna mi prega*" (Pound 1954, 173). Since this is his response about 1930, when he is working on his final translation of the poem for canto 36, it would seem that he was not familiar with the arguments of Rossetti and Barruel at that time. As it happens, we know that Valli was brought to Pound's attention by Mead. He mentioned *Linguaggio segreto* as a book that would be of interest to Pound in a letter of 11 May 1928 to Olivia Shakespear, Pound's mother-in-law (Elliott 1989, 18). Pound had sent

Mead his translation of "Donna mi prega" through Olivia. The letter is the only evidence I have seen that Pound was still in touch with Mead as late as 1928. Mead was apparently asked to identify any Gnostic elements in the poem, for he confessed that the translation did not call "up any distinct Gnostic associations." Clearly, Pound was not following Mead slavishly; but, equally clearly, he valued the old theosophist's opinion of his translation of this esoteric poem.

Valli clearly identifies his debt to Rossetti (and to Giovanni Pascoli, who argued at about the same time as Rossetti, but independently of him, that Dante was a Ghibelline). However, Pound makes no mention of either Rossetti or Pascoli in his critique. Nor does he respond to Valli's dismissal of Péladan – an author whom he knew and might be expected to defend (Valli 1928, 1:19). Nonetheless, Valli's work obviously made a big impression on Pound. He is still exercised enough about Valli six years later to bring him up for critical attention in a letter to his Paris friend William Bird (unpublished, 18 March 1934). And he is scathing about Valli in *Guide to Kulchur*, written three years later still: "Luigi Valli's *Linguaggio Segreto* oughtn't to mislead any reader of judgement. The lack of proof in his arguments, the non sequiturs and failures to see other alternatives might even serve as a lesson to cranks and faddists. Some kind of line to hang one's facts on is better than no line at all" (221).

Pound's preoccupation with Valli puzzled me for a long time. It seemed clear enough that Valli's arguments were crankish, so why should Pound bother himself with them? It was not until I realized that Valli's euhemerist interpretation of the secret tradition was more threatening to Pound than the mainstream dismissal of the tradition altogether that I could understand his response to Valli. This motive is clear from his second reply to Valli in *Guide to Kulchur*: "Says Valli all these poets were Ghibelline. That seems to be provable assertion, while the rest of his, Valli's wanderings in search of a secret language (for Dante, Guido, and the rest of them) are, at mildest estimate, unconvincing. 'Something' behind it? Certainly 'something' behind it or beyond it. Which the police call 'Manichaean' knowing nothing either of Manes or of anything else" (294–5). In short, Pound wants an esoteric mystery, not a political secret; a society of illuminated souls, not a cabal of zealots.

Rossetti, on the other hand, is not mentioned at all by Pound until "A Visiting Card" (1942), where, *à propos* of nothing at all, he calls for a new edition of *Il Mistero dell' amor platonico*. It is highly unlikely that, at the time, Pound knew anything more than the title of Rossetti's last and largest work, because although printed, it had never been published. After it had been printed (in 1840), Rossetti's friend and the dedicatee of the work, Charles Lyell, persuaded him not to publish it. Most copies were destroyed, but some survived, permitting an Italian reprint house to publish it by offset in 1982.

We have good reason to believe that Pound was ignorant of Rossetti's work until after his arrest and indictment, because of the happy accident that he met Gabriele Rossetti's granddaughter, Olivia Agresti, in 1937 and maintained an epistolary friendship with her until her death. At the time they became acquainted, Olivia Agresti was a journalist. Pound came into contact with her through his economic and political activities. Agresti approached Pound, seeking assistance in generating Italian propaganda for an American audience. Apart from promoting Italian interests, they shared an interest in economic theory.

Their correspondence does not touch upon poetry and religious history until very late. As late as May 1949, Agresti confesses that she has never read any of Pound's poetry and that she has known only his economic ideas (15 May 1949, Yale Coll. Za Pound fol. Aa-al 1937–59). As a result, Signora Agresti's illustrious grandfather is not mentioned in their correspondence until February 1956, when in response to a reading of her sister's (Helen Agneli) book on the Pre-Raphaelites, Pound asks her whether it was her grandfather or great-grandfather who wrote *Il Mistero* and whether it was the mother or grandmother who burned the remaining copies (1 Feb. 1956, Yale Coll.). Her answer has not survived, but she later tells him – apparently explaining why she cannot send him a copy – that she has sold her copy of *Il Mistero*. (Indeed, Pound seems to have helped arrange the sale through John Alden; see the letter to Agresti of 26 Sept. 1948, Doolittle-Pearson corresp., Yale Coll.) In place of it, she sent him one of her two remaining copies of *La Beatrice di Dante*, the work that Aroux had plagiarized and that was published in its entirety only in 1935 (24 Sept. 1956, Yale Coll.). Pound received the book from Agresti in December 1956. He set to work reading it at once, and fired off more queries to her (6 and 7 Dec. 1956, Yale Coll.).

It is apparent from this correspondence that Pound was ignorant of Gabriele Rossetti's work during his Kensington years when he adopted for his epic the very secret history that Rossetti had largely been instrumental in formulating. I brought this correspondence to Akiko Miyake's attention in 1989, when her *Ezra Pound and the Mysteries of Love* had already been accepted by Duke. Instead of altering her argument for Pound's dependence on Rossetti, she rather fancifully construed his remark "Interested to see he hooks D[ante] to Swedenborg, as I have done for 50 years" (letter of 7 Dec. 1956, Pound-Agresti, Yale Coll.) as testimony that Pound had read Rossetti fifty years earlier – that is, in 1906 (Miyake 1991, 226–7)! The remark obviously refers to Pound's long-standing interest in Swedenborg – one that goes back to his Pennsylvania days – and not to a reading of Rossetti in 1906 (see Tryphonopoulos 1991, esp. 12–13).

Pound did not need direct knowledge of Barruel, Rossetti, or even Aroux, because the notion of a secret and seditious underground society had become current and standard in London and Paris occult circles as early as 1900. Pound's testimony to his ignorance of Rossetti strengthens the hypothesis that he derived his esoteric knowledge from occult circles in London (and perhaps Paris). There is no doubt about his contact with members of the London occult. Paris is a different matter. We know that he had read Péladan (who had read Rossetti) and that he met Erik Satie (who had been part of the Péladan circle). For the rest, we are not well informed on Pound's activities in Paris for the two years or so that he lived there (1920–22).

Presumably, because Dante was his point of departure, Rossetti was far more interested in recruiting poets into his secret society than either Reghellini or Mead were. Rossetti adds Cavalcanti, Boccaccio, Petrarch, and Chaucer as well as Dante to a secret society that had originally included only troubadour poets. He also argued that the lives of the troubadours were to be understood esoterically as accounts of initiation into the secret society, the society he called *fedeli d'amore*. One of the *vidae* he so interprets is that of Pierre Vidal, one that Pound returns to several times and that will be examined in the next chapter.

On the whole, Rossetti follows Reghellini's euhemeristic line, but in his later work he constantly alludes to the Greek mysteries of Eleusis, to Pythagoras, and to Plato. The "Ragionamento secondo" of *La Beatrice di Dante*, for example, traces Dante's "lingua mysterioso" to Egypt by way of Plato, and Pythagoras (Rossetti 1935, 59). The mystery is couched in erotic language characterized by Plato's *Symposium*, Dante's *Vita nuova*, and Petrarch's sonnets, and it was, he claims, widespread in Italy and especially in Tuscany in Dante's time. However, he insists that the erotic language was not to be taken literally, but merely as an allegorical expression of a philosophy. Pythagoreanism was not itself to be understood as an erotic cult, but rather as a society dedicated to wisdom (*scienzia*) with grades. For Rossetti, the meanings of the myths and rites were symbolic for the neophyte, and philosophical or metaphysical for the contemplative grade of the "epopt" or "illuminati" (58–9). But after having described the nature of Pythagorean wisdom as handed down to the Italians, he tells us in the next section that they jealously guarded their secrets (*arcano*), and he goes on to confess that he is ignorant of them himself:

"What their doctrines were I do not know, because they were never revealed, but I do know that they were innumerable and that they were the most illustrious, the most gifted, and the most talented of the nation; from the illustrious effect we can judge the loftiness of the cause" (Rossetti 1935, 80; my translation).

It is very difficult to know how to take these apparently contrary tendencies in Rossetti. Much of the time he appears to be resolutely euhemeristic, but the next moment he may be hinting at incommunicable mysteries. Elsewhere in *La Beatrice* he cites authorities on Eleusinian and Mithraic initiations and asserts that they are palingenetic initiations without registering any scepticism about the efficacy of these rites (26–9). He sums up his account of *La Vita nuova* with a clearly occult interpretation: "*La Vita Nuova* of Dante is a network of mystical numbers which expound the *palingenesis* or *regeneration* or *initiation* into the mysteries of the Middle Ages, which come down from a remote epoch. The poet takes on the character of the *reborn [palingenio]* or the *regenerated*, or the *initiate*, or the *newborn*, or the *renewed [neo-fito]*; a symbolic death is placed between the two symbolic lives, the *old* and the *new*, from which issues *the mystical life*" (Rossetti 1935, 140; my translation, Rossetti's emphasis).

The occultists also speak of rebirth and believe that initiates literally enter a higher plane of being and knowledge through the experience of palingenesis. It is difficult to see how such mystical and esoteric convictions can be reconciled with Rossetti's earlier euhemeristic position. It may well be that he simply slips into the ethos of whatever source he is relying on at any particular place in the text. When he begins to read Petrarch and Ficino, he becomes more mystical than when he is reading Reghellini or Sismondi. When he is reading Swedenborg, he becomes more occult, and when he relies on Reghellini, he becomes euhemeristic once again.

Certainly, one finds a very similar flightiness and even shiftiness in Pound's prose, and perhaps for the same reason. Both Pound and Rossetti were educated men whose scholarship was eccentric and compulsive. Both read widely and both distrusted standard scholarly authorities. They preferred obscure sources, and both continued to discover new sources almost randomly over a lifetime of obsessive reading. Rossetti had a clear hypothesis to be demonstrated: that Dante's Ghibelline politics were encrypted in his poetry. Pound's goal and motive is less clear. I am suggesting that his studies were driven by the need to establish the "tradition" which his epic represented and whose imminent triumph it celebrated.

Rossetti found support for his argument first in Barruel and then in Reghellini. Both sources led him into a labyrinth of pagan mysteries – notably Gnosticism, Manichaeanism, Mithraism, Pythagoreanism, Eleusinian mysteries, and Hermeticism. There is no doubt that these mystery religions existed, and we have some bona fide documentation of their practices and beliefs. But Barruel, Reghellini, and Rossetti all started from the assumption that the record is encrypted. Once such a radical hermeneutical assumption is entered into, it is very difficult to extricate oneself from it and quite impossible to rule out any connection, filiation, or identification that human ingenuity can generate.

Although Barruel and Reghellini were primarily interested in identifying the persistence of a secret society of "free thinkers" from the Middle Ages up to the French Revolution, their motives were not the same. Barruel sought to expose and discredit the seditious conspiracy of Freemasonry. Reghellini wished to celebrate the antiquity of the revolutionary ardour still surviving in nineteenth-century Freemasonry. Rossetti's contribution was to inject Dante – together with his literary predecessors and followers – into this "tradition." His intention – at least, initially – was to demystify Dante, Cavalcanti, and the troubadour *vidae* by providing a clear and euhemeristic disencrypting of them. In the event, however, he came to attach Dante and the others to a galaxy of speculation that was even darker and more mystical than the Christian Neoplatonism to which Dante and the Tuscan poets were undoubtedly exposed.

Rossetti's opinions on the nature of the mystery he so diligently tracked down is less important to my story than the fact that he propagated the secret history of Europe and gave it a literary bent. Except for the *Commento* and the *Disquisition*, Rossetti's own writing was not much circulated. His ideas, and those of Barruel and Reghellini, were transmitted primarily by the plagiarist and Catholic apologist Eugène Aroux and by the occultist Joséphin Péladan. Of his later, more metaphysical argument, only the "Ragionamento primo" of *La Beatrice* was published during his lifetime. Apart from his family and friends, and perhaps a few diligent readers in the British Museum, only Eugène Aroux knew Rossetti's later position. Despite these difficulties, Rossetti's theories have proven to have an extraordinary staying power. As we have seen, they live on in the work of de Rougemont and René Nelli, as well as in Jessie Weston and Ezra Pound.

Rossetti's inexorable progress from the rather mild theories about Dante's Ghibelline sentiments in the *Commento* of 1826 to the far more sweeping and even mystical theories of the suppressed *Mistero dell' amor platonico* fourteen years later is echoed by Pound's progress into more and more radical postures over his long career. Because he had the misfortune of living in an age even more violent and politically volatile than Rossetti's, Pound's radicalization led him into greater evil and greater personal misfortune. In *Guide to Kulchur* (1938), we find Pound repeating the substance of Rossetti's assessment of the Italian *dolce stil nuovo* writers:

Civilization went on. I reiterate that the cultural level is the determinant. Civilization had been in Italy. It had hung on in Provence and the Exarchate after Romulus Augustulus.

A conspiracy of intelligence outlasted the hash of the political map. Avicenna, Scotus Erigena in Provence, Grosseteste in Lincoln, the Sorbonne, fat faced Frankie Petrarch, Gemisto, the splendour of the xvth century, Valla, the over-boomed Pico, the florentine collectors and conservers. (263)

Although the details are somewhat different, the general argument for a conspiracy of intelligence is the same, and there is plenty of overlap between Pound's list and Rossetti's, in particular Avicenna, Petrarch, Valla, and Pico. Pound scholars (including myself) have typically read such accounts of a privileged tradition as hyperbolic and "poetic." In the face of their close approximation to views current in circles that Pound frequented, it is difficult to "save the appearances" by maintaining that Pound is speaking of undifferentiated intelligence rather than of some self-perpetuating group or society.

Even though Dante is missing from this particular list, Pound includes him in the "tradition" elsewhere in *Guide to Kulchur:*

Real knowledge does NOT fall off the page into one's stomach. Allow, in my case thirty years, thereabout, for a process which I do not yet call finished, the process of gradually comprehending why Dante Alighieri named certain writers. Sordello he might also have touched in spoken tradition. Cunizza, white-haired in the House of the Cavalcanti, Dante, small guttersnipe, or small boy hearing the talk in his father's kitchen or, later, from Guido, of beauty incarnate, or, if the beauty can by any possibility be brought into doubt, at least and with utter certainty, charm and imperial bearing, grace that stopped not an instant in sweeping over the most violent authority of her time and, from the known fact, that vigour which is a grace in itself. (107–8)

The very interminability of the last sentence attests to the agglutinative nature of occult scholarship, based as it is on discovered affinities, coincidences, and contiguities. Pound, far more than his predecessors, is a sucker for contiguity. Dante's connection with the Cavalcanti family is more than enough to tie him to Cunizza da

Romano, the mistress of Sordello. In her old age, she took shelter in the Cavalcanti home and there wrote a will in which she freed her slaves. In *Guide to Kulchur*, Pound is essentially repeating what he had written eight years earlier in the final version of canto 6 and in canto 29.

JOSÉPHIN PÉLADAN AND THE SECRET TRADITION

It has long been recognized that Pound endorsed a view of European history which supposes that some individuals or groups – some "conspiracy of intelligence" – maintained a special knowledge or wisdom in the face of official scorn, neglect, and persecution. This view is not that strikingly odd for a modernist, since modernism as a movement was distinctly elitist. However much they differed in other respects, modernist art, music, and letters were all "difficult," austere, and remote. Like Yeats's Maude Gonne in "No Second Troy," modern art was always "high and solitary and most stern." Modernism legitimized this cognitive elitism by an implied, and occasionally an explicit, analogy with modern science. Occultism is similarly elitist and is similarly prone to point to science as an analogously elite activity. Because of these fortuitous and motivated congruencies between modern science, aesthetic modernism, and the occult, it is all too easy to misconstrue the apologetics that surround the latter two.

In the case of Pound, there is good reason to believe that the inspiration for his elitism, exclusivity, and obscurity was neither the arcane obscurity of Einsteinian relativity nor Planck's quantum physics, but rather the esotericism of the occult. The congruence of opinion between the occult and various other contemporaneous intellectual and cultural tendencies and interests, in particular between the historical fantasies of Barruel and Rossetti and those of Ezra Pound, is far more circumstantial, and more compelling, but has received less attention than the putative congruencies between scientific "relativism" and aesthetic modernism. In the case of Pound, scholarship has by and large avoided discussion of the historical fantasy contained in *The Cantos* – either out of embarrassment at its eccentricity or out of fear and loathing of its occult provenance.

Some studies – notably my own *Light from Eleusis* and those of Miyake and Tryphonopoulos – give the occult material careful consideration, but none have attached the historical content of the poem to the Barruel-Rossetti secret history. The most recent work to address the historical content of *The Cantos* is Lawrence Rainey's very careful study of the Malatesta group, *Ezra Pound and the Monument of*

Culture. Rainey acknowledges Pound's commitment to "an historio-graphical matrix" linking the pagan and Christian worlds by way of the troubadours but attributes it narrowly to his reading of J.H. Smith, *The Troubadours at Home*, an 1899 study which Pound read in 1912 and which attached May Day festivals to the worship of Venus (Rainey 1991, 39–41). Rainey recognizes Pound's commitment to the same picture of the transmission of a secret knowledge from high antiquity, but concentrated as he is on minute details of that trans-mission, he misses the occult and masonic provenance of it. While his work is more careful and more reliable than Miyake's, he fails to perceive the occult components of the Malatesta group that Miyake examines – notably, the importance of Gemisto Plethon and his role in the transmission of Greek wisdom which interleaves Pound's treat-ment of Malatesta's career (Miyake 1991, esp. 66–85).

It is not surprising that the story of occult scholarship that we have been surveying has never been told. It is a romance, an intricate and tangled story of chance encounters, unexpected denouements, and even "divine interventions." Set in obscure backwoods and featuring unkempt and scarcely civilized players, it is unlikely to enhance Pound's always problematic reputation. But familiarity with it will permit a more truthful and accurate portrait of his career than the naturalistic *Bildungsroman*, which is the standard story. Insofar as Hugh Kenner's placement of Pound at the centre of modernism in *The Pound Era* is justifiable, a revision of his career will involve a revision of our view of modernism itself.

In the hands of Barruel, Reghellini, and Rossetti, the secret history of Europe remained largely a secular history. They painted a picture of secret societies communicating in secret codes and conspiring against the authorities. Pound is unequivocal in his rejection of this euhemeristic picture and is scarcely less unequivocal in his endor-sation of the theosophical picture of these same societies as guardians of an esoteric wisdom. The esoteric version of secret history dominate the theosophical circles of Kensington in which Pound moved from 1909 until about 1920. Yeats, Orage, Upward, Mead, and Weston all endorsed the theosophical story of an ineffable wisdom surviving from great antiquity. However, everyone had a slightly different story about how that wisdom was transmitted, and even though they all agreed that the wisdom was ineffable, they nonetheless quarrelled about its nature. It may seem inconsistent to quarrel over the nature of a truth all agree to be ineffable, but occultists took their disagree-ments seriously. The fact that they disagreed provides apologists with convenient remarks – by Pound or Yeats – disassociating themselves from one or another occult belief or practice.

I believe that it was just because Pound believed himself to be in the vanguard of a new age that he set out to write an epic poem, a poem that he claimed would "include history." The new age would be an efflorescence of that wisdom which lies dormant in the world much of the time but which periodically bursts forth in spurts of creativity – as in Provence, Rimini, Florence, and (briefly) in Massachusetts. Pound's epic would be a history of that wisdom and a herald of its imminent efflorescence.

In conformity with the views that Rossetti expressed on Dante's *Vita nuova*, occult Kensington believed that one attained wisdom through a palingenetic experience. As Mead put it, "According to the belief of the mystae, gnosis was operated by means of an essential transformation or transmutation leading to transfiguration. There was first of all a 'passing out through oneself,' a mystical death, and finally a rebirth into the nature of a spiritual being or of a god. Indeed it is indubitable that in the inner circles of the mystae the chief interest was in this apotheosis of transfiguration effected through gnosis or the vision of God" (Mead 1913, 685–6).

Pound's outline of his proposed epic in the oft-quoted letter to Homer Pound of 11 April 1927 describes just such a theosophical palingenesis, or death and rebirth leading to revelation, together with its secular or historical analogues:

A. A. Live man goes down into world of Dead
C. B. The "repeat in history"
B. C. The "magic moment" or moment of metamorphosis, bust thru from quotidien into "divine or permanent world." Gods, etc. (Pound 1951, 285)

Everyone has noticed that this schema accounts for *The Cantos* beginning with a translation of the *nekuia*, or summoning of the dead, from *Odyssey* 11. For my own part, I made much of that "descent" being preceded in the Odyssean story by a sexual encounter with the witch-goddess Circe (Surette 1979, 57–66). Everyone has also noted that *The Cantos* are sprinkled with stories of metamorphoses and theophanies. It has less often been noted that it is these latter that are repeated in history – according to the pattern of letters: A. A.; C. B.; and B. C. The descent is not repeated – indeed, the *nekuia* is not, properly speaking, a descent at all.

As I argued above, *The Cantos* were initially conceived as a kind of séance in which the poet is the medium and the reader the witness. As in a séance, dead souls pass before us, speak to us, and are overheard by us. They do not appear in neat chronological order, but anachronistically and capriciously. In a séance, the dead are relatives or friends, but the dead who appear in *The Cantos* are wise rulers, great artists, and a few villains. *The Pisan Cantos* are much more like a séance, for they are dominated by Pound's recollection of friends – both dead and absent – and even contain a few apparitions, for example (in Pound 1973a):

> But on the high cliff Alcmene,
>   Dryas, Hamadryas ac Heliades
>   flowered branch and sleeve moving
>   Dirce et Izotta e che fu chiamata Primavera
>   in the timeless air
>
> that they suddenly stand in my room here
> between me and the olive tree
>   or nel clivo ed al triedro? (canto 76, 452)

The Cantos as we have them do not neatly fulfil the *nekuia* or séance formula, but it remains the only embracing structural principle possessed by this enormous poem. Pound hoped that he could trace in his poem an irregular recurrence of divine efflorescence in the past and – most particularly – in the present. The present, of course, is a moving location; the "present" of *The Cantos*, that is; the time of composition, turned out to be a half-century long. These periodic efflorescences were to be recovered by the poem for "use" in the efflorescence we call modernism. It is in this sense that *The Cantos* were to be an epic "including" history.

The Cantos as we have them move through such moments: the age of the troubadours, Renaissance Italy, revolutionary America, and the present. Each age has its own particular wisdom and manner of expression: for Dante and the troubadours it was poetry and music; for Renaissance Italy, painting, sculpture, and architecture; for revolutionary America, political and economic insight; and for the present, it was science, Douglasite economics, and technology. Unlike Dante's ascent from a world of damned souls, through purgatorial souls to a heaven of beatified souls, Pound's poem would reveal the pattern hidden in the steel dust of historical event. Its *Paradiso* would be a recognition of the pattern, a revelation. As Pound puts it in a late fragment

> again is all "paradiso"
>   a nice quiet paradise
>   over the shambles,
>   and some climbing

         before the take-off.
to "see again,"
the verb is "see," not "walk on"
i.e. it coheres all right
         even if my notes do not cohere. (canto 116, 796–7)

In other words, Paradise is a state, not a place. It is a sort of refuge from the mire and blood (the "shambles") of the world but is neither a cure for it nor truly outside or transcendent of it. The magnetic forces that were to organize the chaos and produce the revelation Pound found in the wisdom and insight of occult Kensington. That historical wisdom derived largely from Barruel and his strange progeny.

The account of *The Cantos* as an articulation of a theosophical understanding of history fits the poem reasonably from its 1915 false start up to *The Fifth Decad of Cantos XLII-LI* (published in 1937). *The Fifth Decad* began to celebrate modern Italy; however, World War II had not been foreseen by Pound. It caused him to tread water, since he could not celebrate a new order in the midst of the violent disorder of the war. Unfortunately, he did not stop turning out cantos but published a further twenty, *Cantos LII-LXXI*, only three years after *The Fifth Decad*. These cantos are known as the Chinese and Adams cantos and – as I pointed out in *A Light from Eleusis* – are perfunctory redactions from single sources, quite unlike earlier and subsequent sections.

Before the collapse of the Axis powers in 1945, Pound had written two cantos in Italian, presumably as part of the next proposed section. These suppressed cantos have only recently been republished. If they represent a contribution to a new section, they reveal that he would have dealt directly with the hostilities of the war, and very much from the partisan perspective of Fascist Italy. Canto 73 celebrates the heroism of a Romagnese girl who lures a Canadian troop into a minefield at the cost of her own life. It is attached to earlier cantos by its location at Rimini, the site of Malatesta's Tempio (which was destroyed by Allied bombardment). Rainey has shown that the incident was a fabrication of the Italian press, which Pound uncritically accepted (Rainey 1991, 212–17 and app. 3). Canto 72 is a conversation with the recently deceased Filippo Marinetti. In addition to being a return to the séance paradigm, it is a similar expression of Italian jingoistic patriotism.

But events overwhelmed Pound's program, and instead of a section on the destruction of Italy, we have *The Pisan Cantos*, a lament for a world he had thought was about to be born but which was now reduced to a city in the mind. Yet the failure of *The Cantos* to fulfil its own program should not be allowed to block inquiry into the nature and provenance of that program. The very fact that the project was conceived, undertaken, critically acclaimed, and remains the object of scholarly industry is an important datum in the history of modernism.

We have brought our account of the secret history of Europe to the point where Jacobinism has been traced back through Dante, the troubadours, the Albigenses, the Gnostics, and Hellenic paganism to Eleusis. But we know that Pound did not read Rossetti until the 1950s, and we have no reason to believe that he ever read Barruel or Reghellini. Unless he just picked the idea out of the air – as he might well have done in Kensington – he must have found it in some other source. As it happens, we have a definite candidate as a source – Joséphin Péladan's *Secret des troubadours*, one of two Péladan works Pound reviewed in 1906:

If one studies the hidden meaning of medieval literature, the Renaissance no longer appears to be a sudden resurrection of the ancient world.

Neoplatonism had already penetrated our [i.e., French] tales of adventure, and when it showed itself openly under the Medicis it was because they assured it effective protection against the Roman Inquisition.

Gemisto Plethon and Marsilio Ficino are the official teachers of old Albigensianism, as Dante is its prodigious Homer.

Fiction and history correspond with a striking similarity on this subject: do not the knights Templar represent in reality the Grail Knights, and does not Monsalvat have a real name, Montségur? (Péladan 1906, 44–6; my translation)

This passage pretty well sums up Pound's historical fantasy, including the importance of Malatesta in it, for Malatesta was so impressed by Gemisto Plethon, who came from Byzantium to Florence in 1438 (canto 8, 31, and canto 26, 123), that he brought Plethon's remains back from his campaign in Greece and buried them in the Tempio.

Pound's connection with Péladan (1858–1918) has been well recognized since my 1974 article and has been independently remarked upon by Peter Makin (1978) and Massimo Bacigalupo (1980), as well as being noted in my own book of 1979. However, neither the quantity nor quality of comment on Péladan's role has been adequate, for it has not been understood that he was merely transmitting Barruel's and Rossetti's secret history. Bacigalupo (1980), for example, misrepresents the contents of *Le Secret* when he claims that Péladan links the troubadours with Eleusis (21–2). No such connection is drawn either in *Le Secret des troubadours* or in *Origine et esthétique de la tragédie*, the other book Pound examined in the same review. Indeed, I was troubled by Péladan's failure to draw the connection (Surette 1979, 36–7). Peter Makin (1978) is even more perfunctory than Bacigalupo, suggesting that "Péladan perhaps gave him [Pound] the idea of an esotericism and a sect" (242). Unlike Baciagalupo, Makin does mention Rossetti, but he has nothing to say about this work, and he confuses Rossetti *père* with Rossetti *fils*, identifying the author of *Il Mistero dell' amor platonico* as D.G. Rossetti (242–3).

As it turns out, Péladan is a principal avenue for the supposition of a strong link between the troubadours and the Cathars – a link that has survived to the present day as a well-attested historical fact, despite its spurious provenance. Péladan does not seem to have persuaded Pound in 1906, for his review is sceptical about this hypothesis. But before examining Pound's response to the secret church argument when he first encounters it, I want to explore how Péladan came to adopt it.

Reghellini and Rossetti's inclusion of Dante in the hypothesized secret society encouraged their readers to draw the inference that Dante's troubadour predecessors were also either Ghibellines or Cathars, or both. Reghellini does not develop this implication, and Rossetti only does so in the suppressed *Il Mistero*. Péladan, by contrast, is explicit on this point – as the title of his book would suggest. Speaking of the Cathars he wrote, "The heretics, then, became troubadours in Provence, and "trouvères" in the north, *guillari*, men of joy in Italy, *minnesingers* in Germany, *scaldes* in Norway, minstrels in Welsh countries" (Péladan 1906, 54; my translation). In other words, the medieval poets were heretics; they were propagandists for the mystical underground church hypothesized by Barruel, Reghellini, and Rossetti. Péladan, in contrast to his predecessors, gives a thoroughly esoteric reading of the tradition and places the troubadours firmly within it.

Rather inconsistently, Péladan retains euhemeristic elements in his study, despite his postulate of an esoteric sect, and repeats the extreme hermeneutical flights required by Barruel's euhemerism: "In the provençal religion marriage meant obedience to Roman orthodoxy, and love meant adherence to the Occitane doctrine; such is the first key to all the love literature" (Péladan 1906, 67; my translation). Pound ignored these euhemeristic tendencies in Péladan, but he retained the schematic opposition between Rome and amor that lies behind Péladan's remark and is expressed by the clever palindrome already cited:

```
A M O R
M     O
O     M
R O M A
```

The two books Pound reviewed were written in 1905 and 1906. At that time Péladan was nearly fifty years old and was well past the notoriety he had enjoyed in *fin de siècle* Paris as the organizer of the Salons de la Rose-Croix with Antoine de La Rochefoucauld. When Péladan first arrived in Paris in 1883, he was already deeply involved in occultism and magic, practices he shared with his father and elder brother. He became the champion and impresario of the symbolist painters Félicien Rops, Puvis de Chavannes, and Gustave Moreau. Pincus-Witten describes Paris of the time as being alive with occult publications and exhibitions. Emond Bailly, Chacornac, Dorbon, Chamuel were all bookshop publishers specializing in occult works. Stanislaus de Guaïta, Péladan, Huysmans, Villiers de l'Isle-Adam, Jules Bois, Elémir Bourges, Paul Adam, Oswald Wirth, Edouard Schuré, Papus (Dr Gérard Encausse), and Eliphas Lévi (l'Abbé Constant) were all active and prominent in a Parisian ambience where the line between poet and mage was thinner than it has ever been before or since in Europe (Pincus-Witten 1976, 58).

Pound presumably knew little if anything of *fin de siècle* Paris when in 1906 he picked up the two Péladan books in the "nervy little bookshop of E. Sansot, which lucky wanderers will fall upon in the rue St André des Arts 'on the other side of the river'" (Pound 1906, 54). He was a fresh American M.A. in Romance languages touring Europe on fellowship money from the University of Pennsylvania (Stock 1970, 28–9). As an undergraduate he had read Yogi Ramacharaka and Balzac's *Séraphita* (Doolittle 1979, 45–6; French and Materer 1982, 11).

In *Séraphita* Pound would have found a capsule presentation of Swedenborgian philosophy embedded in the story of a love triangle between an enlightened and angelic seventeen-year-old androgyne (Séraphita/Séraphitus), a young girl (Minna), and a mature young man (Wilfrid). Both mortals fall in love with the androgyne, each supposing him/her to be a him or a her. They are both disappointed when Séraphita/Séraphitus ascends into the empyrean. The novel also contains passages articulating Balzac's understanding of Swedenborgianism. Séraphita explains that poets, philosophers, and men of action are all submerged in he who prays: "The Poet expresses, the Wise Man meditates, the Just Man acts; but he who places himself on the margins of the Divine Works prays; and his prayer is at once word, thought, and action. Yes, his prayers enclose everything, they contain everything, they complete nature for you, disclosing to you spirit and action" (Balzac [1835] 1950, 567; my translation). This description of the nature and power of Swedenborgian prayer, if applied to poetry, would justify an epic project like *The Cantos*, for they are posited upon a presumption that poetry can "go into action" and affect the course of history. The idea behind Séraphita's assertion is of a kind of mental magnetism or force. The same idea is found in the Ramacharaka book that Pound and Hilda Doolittle read at about the same time.

Ramacharaka's "yogi" philosophy is much like that still current in North America, involving physical exercises to achieve superior mental powers. There are features of Ramacharaka's thought that are found in Pound's mature aesthetic, in particular, Ramacharaka's theory of communication charged with "Prana":

The man of strong will sending forth a vigorous, positive thought uncon-
sciously (or consciously if he understand the subject) sends with it a supply
of Prana, or magnetism, proportioned to the force or energy with which the
thought is propelled. A thought sent forth when one is laboring under a
strong emotion is likewise heavily charged with magnetism. Thoughts so
charged, are often sent like a bullet to the mark, instead of drifting along
slowly like an ordinary thought emanation. (Ramacharaka 1903, 131)

Sentiments such as these can, admittedly, be found elsewhere. Nonetheless, their similarity to Pound's theory of the image and his under-
standing of *direction voluntatis* is striking (see Sosnowski 1991 for an exploration of the Swedenborgian contribution to Imagism).

During the same period referred to by Hilda Doolittle, Pound wrote to W.C. Williams in a clearly occult vein, incidentally alluding to his reading of Swedenborg:

I am interested in art and extacy [sic] –, extacy which I would define as the
sensation of the soul in ascent, art as the expression and sole means of
transmuting, of passing on that extacy to others.

Religion I have defined as "Another of those numerous failures resulting
from an attempt to popularize art." By which I mean that it is only now and
then that religion rises to the dignity of art, or from another angle. That art
includes only so much of religion as is factive, potent exalting.

Swedenborg has called a certain thing "the angelic language" by the way
I will send you certain things out of Swedenborg that will save me much
preface. It will take a week or two for me to get at them. This "angelic
language" I choose to interpret into "artistic Utterance." (Letter headed "Oct

24 '07, Milligan Place Crawfordsville," in Yale Collection, "Pound to William Carlos Williams 1907–1958")

Such interests were not particularly eccentric in the early decades when the mystical works of the *Symbolistes* were very much in vogue. However, in the light of Pound's subsequent career, it is difficult to reject these sentiments as juvenile preoccupations soon outgrown. (For a discussion of Pound's debt to Swedenborg, see Tryphono-poulos 1991 and Sosnowski 1991.)

No doubt these interests would have rendered Pound sympathetic to the mystical turn Péladan wished to give troubadour poetry: "In 'Le Secret' the derivation of Don Quixote, and the distinctions between that bedraggled hero of La Mancha and Parsifal, are sound and brilliant. Parsifal is the idealist triumphant, the seeker of the Sanc-Graal in enthusiasm. Don Quixote – Cervantes's self in many ways – is the idealist vanquished, the seeker in disappointment" (Pound 1906, 54). That Pound should have called this mixture of Wagnerism and the secret tradition – a mixture already standard in occult circles by 1906 – "brilliant" is a good indication that he encountered it here for the first time. Attractive as he finds it, Pound expresses scholarly scepticism about the role Péladan assigned to the troubadours that is very much at odds with his later acceptance of it: "But Péladan invades the realm of uncertainty when he fills in the gap between these two with four centuries of troubadours singing allegories in praise of a mystic extra-church philosophy or religion, practiced by the Albigenses, and the cause of the Church's crusade against them" (54).

We have no record of Pound's change of heart about the Péladan hypothesis, but there can be no doubt that it took place. I do not know what Pound did with his copy of *Le Secret des troubadours*, but he did ask his father to send *Origine et esthétique de la tragédie* to him (in a letter of 20 July 1909, Yale Coll.). Perhaps he had brought his copy of *Le Secret* with him to England. At any rate, when he returned briefly to London from a lengthy holiday in Italy during the early spring of 1910 before his return to America, he spoke to D.H. Lawrence of his desire to write "an account of the mystic cult of love – the dionysian rites and so on – from earliest days to the present." He was fearful that no publisher in England would touch it (Boulton 1979, 165–6).

Shortly after he returned to London, early in 1911, Pound met Mead, and at the Kensington Town Hall meetings of the Quest Society he found an outlet for his proposed history of the mystic cult of love, first publishing in Mead's *Quest* in 1912. In this essay, written six years after his review of the Péladan books, Pound is fully committed to the esoteric reading of the troubadour poets. (The essay is now found as chapter 5 of *The Spirit of Romance*, an addition to the original 1910 Dent edition.)

Although we have no record outlining Pound's change of heart, the dates suggest very strongly that it was brought about by his exposure to Kensington and its occult ambience – an ambience that has been almost entirely neglected by Pound's biographers. An instance of almost deliberate neglect is revealed in the unpublished correspondence between Pound and Patricia Hutchins, which led her to write *Ezra Pound's Kensington*. In this correspondence (1953–59) Pound stressed the importance of Mead and the Quest Society to his Kensington years, but Hutchins ignored Mead and the Quest Society in the published book – much to Pound's irritation: "I put a LOT of work telling you KENSINGTON, its inhabitants to which you paid not the least bloody damn bit of attention" (letter 159, 15 June [1959], Patricia Hutchins Coll. British Museum, Add. 57725).

Pound's letters to Hutchins are somewhat cryptic, but no. 19 (30 Oct. [1953]) is of interest for the galaxy of persons and interests it mentions. He is responding to Hutchins's query about the lecture he gave in the town hall (the 1912 "Psychology and Troubadours"):

GRS Mead, quest society / I wonder if any survivors, mostly generation before mine / for lecture etc / was it Town Hall (must hv/been) can't think where else was space. name forgotten. The heroic feminist came first, as I recall, and that made link with "The New Freewoman" H.S.W., Rebecca, D. Marsden ... Lecture, I suppose Town Hall / some where about there. Hulme lectured, possibly Wyndham at least he WAS there on some occasion, I think he lectured. And what is now "Psychology and Troubadours" in new edn. Spirit of Romance.

H.S.W. is doubtless Harriet Shaw Weaver, publisher of the *New Freewoman*, later the *Egoist*. Rebecca is probably Rebecca West, and D. Marsden would be Dora Marsden. Wyndham is, of course, Wyndham Lewis. Pound, Lewis, and T.E. Hulme all delivered lectures at the Quest Society meetings on 22 January 1914 (Levenson 1984, 75). Pound's most recent biographer, Humphrey Carpenter, misconstrues the list as one containing possible amorous interests for the young Pound, and he is puzzled to find rather mature women amongst them (Carpenter 1988, 336–7). But, of course, these are just members of the circle in which Pound moved, and the no-longer-young women are simply members of his literary and occult circle.

Even though Pound's memory of events – which in 1953 were forty years and more in the past – had faded, he put great emphasis on

Mead's Quest Society lectures in the Kensington Town Hall. Hutchins does not even mention Mead or the Quest Society in her book; nor do they receive any attention from Pound's other biographers. Yet the letters Pound wrote to his parents at the time evince a very lively interest in Mead. (They are in Yale's Pound archive). He first mentions Mead in a letter of 17 September 1912, where he reports having spent the evening with Mead, who invited him to give a lecture to the Quest Society. Mead is described in a December letter as "rather interesting," and again in February 1912 as "about as interesting – along his own line – as anyone I meet." In a March letter, Pound gives an account of a Mead lecture on "Heirotheos" and quibbles about the attractiveness of doctrines of reincarnation. He remarks in a letter of 5 November 1912 that Mead's lectures are beginning that evening, and again, in a letter of 3 December, that he is going out to Mead's lecture "as usual."

There are a few more references to Mead and his society's lectures in Pound's correspondence of the period (see Pound 1984 and 1988). But by 1914, Orage and the *New Age*, Wyndham Lewis, and W.B. Yeats had pretty well replaced Mead and his circle in Pound's life. However, we must not forget that Yeats, Hulme, Lewis, and Olivia and Dorothy Shakespear also attended the Mead lectures, and that Dorothy was still corresponding with Mead in the 1930s. The strongest evidence of Pound's indebtedness to Mead is in the nature of *The Cantos* and in his responses to Hutchins's queries forty years later (but see also Surette 1979; Tryphonopoulos 1992).

Once we have established that Pound was in contact with Mead and other occult thinkers such as Swedenborg, Yeats, Orage, and Upward, it is not difficult to document his engagement in the occult speculation of Kensington in his poetry and prose. At least, it would not be difficult if those texts were not already well known and differently interpreted. A comparison of a few passages from canto 1 of "Three Cantos" (as they appeared in *Poetry* for June 1917) with some of Mead's remarks makes their occult and theosophical provenance apparent. In this way we can gain some sense of Pound's absorption in the "dark wood" of Kensington.

As originally conceived, Pound's epic (which remained incomplete and untitled at his death) was to be a kind of spiritual journey freely moving through time and space, or – as I have suggested – a séance:

> Ghosts move about me
> Patched with histories ....
> I walk Verona. (I am here in England.)
> I see Can Grande. (Can see whom you will.)

....

As well begin here. Began our Catullus:

....

And the place is full of spirits.
Not *lemures*, not dark and shadowy ghosts,
But the ancient living, wood-white,
Smooth as the inner bark, and firm of aspect,
And all agleam with colors – no not agleam
But colored like the lake and like the olive leaves,
Glaukopos, clothed like the poppies, wearing golden greaves,
Light on the air.
Are they Etruscan gods?
Sun-fed we dwell there (we in England now);
It's your way of talk, we can be where we will be,
Sirmio serves my will better than your Asolo
Which I have never seen. (*Poetry*, June 1917, 114–16)

The "you" throughout is Robert Browning, to whom the poem is addressed. Catullus was a native of Verona, where Sordello lived in the thirteenth century, hence the focus on that city in these lines. Glaukopos is an epithet of Athena, variously translated as "grey-eyed" or "green-eyed," but for Pound it probably means light that "blinks like an owl." He gets this idea from Upward, who claims that the blinking is also a property of olive leaves, which have a shiny side and a dull side (see Bush 1976, 94ff). Sirmio is Sirmione, an Italian resort town that Pound visited in 1910 and was still invoking in *The Pisan Cantos* (see cantos 76 and 78, Pound 1973a, 458, 478).

This playful opening has been completely abandoned, but the poem it promises is not so very different from the poem we have. Both move freely through time and space, and even between the hylic, or material, world of the senses and the spiritual or noumenal world of the mind. All readers have taken these lines figuratively, as is normal and proper, for they describe a rhetorical structure, invoking Browning's *Sordello* as a model. However, the possibility of movement through time and space, and even between the quotidian and astral, is something that Pound's Kensington friends took quite literally and practised in séances. Longenbach's account of Pound's winters with Yeats at Stone Cottage have left no doubt of Pound's friendliness to such notions (Longenbach 1988).

In *The Gnosis of the Mind* (1906) Mead looks forward to the imminent dawn of the new age and also speaks of the possibility of moving in both space and time:

We are living in the twentieth century; we do not want to return to the modes of thought of two thousand years ago; we can create a new Gnosis that will interpret the facts of present-day science and philosophy and religion.

I too await the dawn of the New Age; but I doubt that the Gnosis of the New Age will be new. Certainly it will be set forth in new forms, for the forms can be infinite. The Gnosis itself is not conditioned by space and time; it is we who are conditioned by these modes of manifestation. He who is reborn into the Gnosis becomes, as I have heard, the Lord of time and space, and passes from man into the state of Super-man and Christ, or Daimon and God ... Indeed ... the very essence of the Gnosis is the faith that man can transcend the limits of the duality that makes him man, and become a consciously divine being. (45–6)

Miyake does not discuss Mead, but she nonetheless concludes that Pound imagined himself to be such a "Lord of time" on the model of Gabriele Rossetti's *fedeli d'amore* and Plotinus (Miyake 1991, 220). While I am not persuaded that he went so far in megalomania, it is clear that *The Cantos* are intended to instantiate an awareness or knowledge that transcends "space limits and time limits" – although in a different manner than Pound once thought the Image could do. Also, early poems – notably "Und Drang" from *Canzoni* (1911) and "The Flame," excerpted from it for *Personae* (1926) – echo Mead's doctrine of reincarnation. They also attribute esoteric wisdom to Provence, echoing the historical fantasy Pound first encountered in Péladan.

Those cantos written while Pound was detained in St Elizabeth's (*Rock-Drill*, *Thrones*, and *Drafts and Fragments*) turn to vision and magic in a manner reminiscent of the so-called Ur Cantos. He reintroduces the Restoration magus, John Heydon (who had originally appeared in "Canto Three" of 1917 but did survive early revisions). He and the Hellenic magus, Apollonius of Tyana, are presented in the late cantos as magi who engage in magical feats such as metempsychosis and vision. Writing to Virginia Cazort in 1955, Pound associates Apollonius with Mead, even though he remarks that Mead's "notes" (that is, Mead's short study *Apollonius of Tyana*, 1901) are "no substitute for Philostratus" (11 April [1955], HRC Austin).

Writing for a more committed and sophisticated audience than he had in mind for theosophical primers like *The Gnosis of the Mind* just cited, Mead describes wisdom as a "spiritual consciousness ... initiated by an illumination, generally set forth in terms of vision, but of a vital intelligible nature" (Mead 1913, 684). Pound echoes this more "platonic" and mystical account of gnosis towards the end of the 1917 "Canto One" in a what appears to be a pastiche of artistic visions:

> And shall I claim
> Confuse my own phantastikon
> Or say the filmy shell that circumscribes me
> Contains the actual sun;
> confuse the thing I see
> With actual gods behind me?
> Are they gods behind me?
> How many worlds we have! If Botticelli
> Brings her ashore on that great cockle-shell –
> ....
> Oh, we have worlds enough, and brave *décors*,
> And from these like we guess a soul for man
> And build him full of aery populations. (Pound 1990, 234)

These lines reflect the occult belief that the individual is a little cosmos, a Leibnizean monad infinitely repeated in the cosmos. As Mead puts it, "The whole theory of attainment [i.e., of salvation through revelation] is conditioned by the fact that man in body, soul, and mind was a world in himself – a little world, it is true ... but a world for all that – a monad" (Mead 1906, 33). Pound echoed this belief in "Psychology and Troubadours": "It is an ancient hypothesis that the little cosmos 'corresponds' to the greater, that man has in him both 'sun' and 'moon'" (Pound [1929] 1953, 94).

Ronald Bush argues that these early cantos express the speculative thought of Allen Upward – especially as expressed in *The New Word* (1908) and *The Divine Mystery* (1913). Such an approach takes one a considerable way towards a better understanding of the first beginnings of *The Cantos*. However, Bush does not recognize that Upward's psychological theories belong to the general occult belief that there are superior souls – such as Séraphita or Mejnour – living amongst ordinary mortals. Pound had expressed his belief in a society of superior souls as early as the 1912 Quest Society lecture – before either of the Upward books appeared: "One must consider that the types which joined these cults survived, in Provence, and survive today – priests, maenads and the rest – though there is in our society no provision for them" (Pound [1929] 1953, 95).

Pound's heavily marked copy of *The New Word* is in the archive of the Humanities Research Center at Austin, Texas. Among the passages he has marked is the following one on the "whirl-swirl" – the vortex, or funnel that is reported in many mystic visions of the other world. It was adapted by Pound and Lewis for their Vorticist movement, and by Yeats for his historical system. Yeats calls it a "gyre." Upward's book, published in 1908, is contemporaneous with both. His "whirl-swirl" is, he says, "no longer a mere word":

It is a magic crystal, and by looking into it, you will see wonderful meanings come and go. It will change colour like an opal while you gaze, reflecting the thoughts in your own mind. It is a most chameleon-like ball. It has this deeper magic that it will show you, not only the thoughts you knew about before, but other thoughts you did not know of, old, drowned thoughts, hereditary thoughts; it will awaken the slumbering ancestral ghosts that haunt the brain; you will remember things you used to know and feel long, long ago. (198)

Pound marked only the first three sentences, but the whole passage seems to have stuck in his mind. It is surely the failure of *The Cantos* to become such a whirl-swirl that is lamented in the famous lines from canto 116 (Pound 1973a, 795–6):

> I have brought the great ball of crystal;
> who can lift it?
> Can you enter the great acorn of light?
> But the beauty is not the madness
> Tho' my errors and wrecks lie about me.
> And I am not a demigod,
> I cannot make it cohere.

These lines are not, however, a confession of failure; rather, they are an effort to stipulate just what a successful Poundian *paradiso* would be. It would be a revelation, rather like Upward's "whirl-swirl," as opposed to a Dantean or Swedenborgian idealization of earth:

> but about that terzo
> third heaven,
> that Venere,
> again is all "paradiso"
> a nice quiet paradise
> over the shambles,
> and some climbing
> before the take-off,
> to "see again,"

the verb is "see," not "walk on"
i.e. it coheres all right
           even if my notes do not cohere. (796–7)

Jung's "Septem Sermones ad Mortuos" is a text contemporary with *The New Word*, Vorticism, and Yeats's formulation of *A Vision*. But even though written and printed in 1913, it could not have been a source for Pound because it was not publicly available until 1965. The sermons develop much the same conceptions of the soul and of knowledge. Jung attributes his theory to Gnosticism, a religion he knew from the same sources available to Mead – primarily patristic condemnations. Although the sermons are Jung's own composition, he attributes them to the Gnostic writer Basilides: "Because we are parts of the pleroma, the pleroma is also in us. Even in the smallest point is the pleroma endless, eternal, and entire, since small and great are qualities which are contained in it. It is that nothingness which is everywhere whole and continuous" (Jung 1965, 379; "pleroma" is Jung's name for infinity, thought of as both a fullness and an emptiness). Jung's sermons attest to the ubiquity of such ideas in Europe early in this century, just as his cautious withholding of them until Amiela Jaffé persuaded him to print them as an appendix to his autobiography, *Memories, Dreams, Reflections*, attests to their disreputability.

Somewhat earlier than either Pound or Jung, Péladan underwent a conversion experience that he says changed his life. It took place in July 1888, at Bayreuth, in the company of "the Wagnerian mystic" William Ritter and after three hearings of *Parsifal*. At that moment, and all at once, he says that he had the idea of the Rosy-Cross, the Temple, and the Grail (Péladan [1894] 1981, xii). Péladan's story of a sudden illumination or epiphany is more or less formulaic within the occult movement. All the same, the attribution of his inspiration to a hearing of *Parsifal* underlines the pivotal role of Wagnerism in the history of the modern occult.

In point of fact, Péladan's "illumination" had begun much earlier than the trip to Bayreuth. He had grown up in an occult household. Both his father and elder brother were actively involved in occult studies (Pincus-Witten, 1976, 9–28). It is only his conversion to Wagnerism and Rosicrucianism that dates from 1888. After the Bayreuth visit, Péladan, Stanislaus de Guaïta, and Papus founded the short-lived Ordre kabbalistique de la Rose-Croix. By 1890, Péladan had split with Guaïta and Papus, objecting to the antipapal posture of his fellow Rosicrucians (Pincus-Witten 1976, 71). He formed his own order, the Rose-Croix catholique. Two years later, with the help of

Antoine de La Rochefoucauld, he organized the Salons de la Rose-Croix (1892–96). These salons announced that the purpose of the art they exhibited was "to restore the cult of the IDEAL" through the depiction of beauty and on the basis of tradition. By the mid-1890s, Péladan had adopted the title Sar and had taken to calling himself by the name of the Assyrian god Mérodack (the name he had given to the hero of his novel series *Le Vice suprême*). He dressed like a stage magician and wore a full Assyrian-style beard. (Even though Péladan remains very little known to English-language scholars, the literature on him is quite extensive. See Praz 1970, esp. 330–41; Cornell 1951; Pincus-Witten 1976; Bertholet 1952–58; Doyon 1946; and Webb 1974, esp. 153–85.)

Some idea of the nature of Péladan's imagination and of the tolerance of the time for theurgic nonsense can be gleaned from the dedication to his Wagner book, *Le Théâtre complet de Wagner* (1894). Addressed to Judith Gautier (the daughter of Théophile Gautier and an intimate correspondent with Wagner), the dedication includes an account of a Brittany night in 1889 that he, Judith Gautier, and the printer Poirel experienced. Judith left the cottage and returned with three "relics" of the deceased Wagner – a hank of white hair, some dried bread, and a bundle of letters:

Those hairs had covered the sublime head which conceived the Tetralogy, that piece of bread, the master had brought to his mouth at the banquet of Parsifal, those letters in French were all from the hand that had written Tristan.

In a loud voice, with sustained emotion, I read those evocative pages of the most beautiful reality that a woman had ever dreamed; and this was truly a beautiful evocation of the dead, an unforgettable night; the dawn poked her livid face through the windows before we returned from our ecstasy. (vi–vii; my translation)

That Péladan would preface a book he hoped to sell to Wagnerians with such an account, and involve his dedicatee in such a bizarre event, suggests that even hard-core occultism was tolerated by the artistic community in the 1890s. The anecdote is a clear case of a séancelike evocation of the famous composer, deceased six years earlier.

Péladan is of particular interest for the troubadour-Albigensian link because we can follow his conversion from an initial scepticism to unqualified endorsation, as we cannot with Pound. Péladan encountered the Rossetti theory just prior to his conversion to Wagnerism, for he discusses it in a long introduction to Clemence Couve's

French translation of D.G. Rossetti's *House of Life*, published in 1887. There Péladan presents Dante as a *fidèle d'amour* and traces the cult of amor to Plato's *Symposium*, arguing that Plato's Diotima is the antetype of Beatrice (Péladan 1887, ix–xii). He traces the descent of Platonic thought from Plato himself down to Dante, and in so doing assesses the theories of Gabriele Rossetti (from whom he got all of his information).

However, before he comes to his critique of the elder Rossetti's *Disquisition sullo spirito antipapale*, Péladan turns his attention to the troudabours. His account is conventional and very unlike the one Pound encountered in *Le Secret des troubadours*, written nearly twenty years later. He points out that the troubadours were the "masters of the Italians" and that they learned their lore from the Arabs (xix), who had preserved Platonism after it had disappeared from the West following the collapse of the Roman Empire. The troubadours, he says, bridged the gap from the eighth century to the thirteenth. In these remarks, as in his identification of the Crusaders as the carriers of Platonism from Islam to Provence, he appears to be following Barruel and Reghellini. Like these authors, Péladan denies that the troubadours were in any sense mystical or Neoplatonic. Indeed, his position in 1887 is essentially the same as that of the current authority, Jean Duvernoy, cited earlier: "One finds lots of passion in Provençal poetry but no trace of metaphysics or of the mysticism of love. For the psychologist, the languorous troubadour is nothing more than a roué, and there is no great distance between Provençal sensuousness and that of the Regency" (Péladan 1887, xx–xxi; my translation).

After a long consideration of Gabriele Rossetti's works, Péladan returns to the troubadours and restates his exclusion of them from the Platonic tradition, which begins only with the Italians of the *dolce stil nuovo*: "I think I have shown that if the Provençal poets were never anything but sensualists, the Italians gave feminine traits to metaphysical entities" (xlvii; my translation). Thus, even though Péladan is very friendly to Rossetti's mystical tradition in 1887, he excludes the troubadours from it and attributes any metaphysical content that medieval poetry may have had exclusively to their Italian followers. Clearly, there was some movement in Péladan's position between 1887 and 1906 when he published *Le Secret des troubadours*.

Péladan devotes eleven pages of his introduction in *La Maison de vie* to a discussion of Gabriele Rossetti's contention in the *Disquisition sullo spirito antipapale* that Dante was a Ghibelline. Not surprisingly, since Péladan regarded himself as a good Catholic, he concludes that Rossetti is wrong to read the tradition as being exclusively political rather than "mystical," and equally wrong to regard it as heretical:

Certainly, the imposing erudition of the author lends an interest and an appearance of consistency to his theories; but only one part is true, even though undeveloped. The great truths spoken by the initiators of such people as Orpheus, Moses, the Hebrew prophets, and Plato have come down to the poets and mystical thinkers of our time: these truths, which Mr Rossetti represents without understanding them, agree with the Roman teaching, since no one has found in Dante, Petrarch, or Boccaccio, in the middle of their vituperations against the clergy, a single attack on dogma. (Péladan 1887, xxxiii–iv; my translation)

Péladan based his discussion of Rossetti's theories primarily on the *Disquisition*, but he does mention *Il Mistero dell' amor platonico* and devotes three paragraphs to an assessment of this five-volume work. Nothing he says is of any great interest, but it is odd that he should have known of *Il Mistero*, for, although printed in 1840, except for fifty copies retained by Rossetti, the edition was destroyed (see Giannantonio's introduction, Rossetti 1967, xxxvi–vii). It is unlikely that Péladan could have seen a copy.

Rossetti did send twenty copies to Italy and two to Germany (Vincent 1936, 27). Eugène Aroux also had a copy, and he discusses *Il Mistero* in *Dante hérétique* (436–7). Péladan was not above commenting on a work he had not read, but it is surprising that he had even heard of *Il Mistero* unless he had read Aroux. It is possible that he had not read either the *Disquisition* or *Il Mistero*, but knew only Aroux's *Dante hérétique* (1854). But although Aroux incorrectly gives the date of *Il Mistero* as 1842 (436), Péladan gives the correct date, 1840 (xxxii). The only mention of Aroux that I have found in Péladan's writing is in *Le Secret des troubadours* (1906) and it is just a mention – although it does link Rossetti and Aroux: "Some, Rossetti, the father of the Pre-Raphaelite painter, and Arnoux [*sic*], a little-known scholar, have perceived what a dream of justice, of charity, and of beauty was conceived in the South and from there has spread throughout the world, enchanting men's imaginations" (70; my translation).

Whatever his knowledge of Rossetti, Péladan's shift from hostility towards the Rossetti thesis in 1887 to enthusiastic endorsation of it in 1906 mirrors Pound's own conversion from scepticism to belief. I argued in *A Light from Eleusis* that the notion of the idealist vanquished elaborated by Péladan in *Le Secret des troubadours* was an important inspiration for similar figures in *The Cantos*. Pound's prototype is Sigismondo Malatesta, but the type is found everywhere in the poem. The paradigm is even applied to Benito Mussolini – in a spectacular case of fiction dominating fact. Although I still stand behind this reading of the poem, in hindsight I believe that I exaggerated Péladan's role in my earlier account.

I gave Péladan such prominence because I was unable to find anywhere else the whole story of a suppressed and persecuted society made up of avatars of wisdom and beauty and stretching back from the Renaissance through the troubadours to Eleusis (Surette 1979, 40–1). When one recognizes that Péladan was just one voice in a babble of occult and mystical speculators and revisers of history – even though an important one for the role of the troubadours – the mystery is lifted. None of this would carry much conviction if we did not have independent evidence of Pound's engagement with occult or theosophical speculation through Yeats, Mead, Orage, and Upward.

Pound, of course, works his own "changes" on the Rossetti-Reghellini hypothesis. In "Psychology and Troubadours" he paraphrases Richard of St Victor – "by naming over all the most beautiful things we know we may draw back upon the mind some vestige of the heavenly splendor" – then claims that the troubadours had, as it were, a shortcut to revelation in their cult of amor: "I suggest that the troubadour, either more indolent or more logical, progresses from correlating all these details for purpose of comparison, and lumps the matter. The Lady contains the catalogue, is more complete. She serves as a sort of *mantram*" (Pound [1929] 1953, 96–7).

POUND'S ESOTERIC EROTICISM

Péladan insists that the troubadours "were priests or pastors much less susceptible to feminine charms than the orthodox priests" (1906, 69). However, for Pound the eroticism of the troubadours was not figurative but literal: "The problem in so far as it concerns Provence, is simply this: Did this 'chivalric love,' this exotic, take on mediumistic properties? Stimulated by the colour or quality of emotions, did that 'colour' take on forms interpretive of the divine order? Did it lead to an 'exteriorization of the sensibility,' and interpretation of the cosmos by feeling?" (Pound [1929] 1953, 94). This reading of the erotic aspects of Gnosticism and the troubadours is plainly contrary to Mead's purely symbolic understanding – as I pointed out in *A Light from Eleusis* (62–3). Mead would have regarded Pound's literal understanding of the steamy Gnostic myths and accounts of erotic rituals as depraved: "The mysteries of sex were explained in the adyta of the ancient temples; and naturally enough the attempt to get behind the great passion of mankind was fraught with the greatest peril. A knowledge of the mystery led many to asceticism; a mere curious prying into the matter led to abuse. Illumination, seership, and spiritual knowledge, were the reward of the pure in body and mind; sexual excess and depravity punished the prying of the unfit" (Mead 1900, 184).

An earlier version of Pound's mystical eroticism can be found in "Piere Vidal Old," a very early poem first published in *Exultations* (1909) before the Kensington ambience could have had much influence on him. Not only does he invent a nighttime tryst between the troubadour Vidal and his lady, la Loba of Penautier, but he describes it in terms that bring together love, death, and valour in a manner that might have made Virgil blush. La Loba approaches Vidal through the dark forest dressed in a green "mantel" made of flimsy mousse-line "wherethrough her white form fought." There were no words spoken, for "Hot is such love and silent, / Silent as fate is ... / Stark, keen, triumphant, till it plays at death." Vidal, of course, is not silent, for this is a poem of reminiscence. He expostulates, "God! she was white then, splendid as some tomb." Not content with comparing her to a tomb, Vidal continues: "Half-sheathed, then naked from its saffron sheath / Drew full this dagger that doth tremble here." We do not learn why he draws his dagger, for "Just then she woke and mocked the less keen blade ... Was there such flesh made ever and unmade!"

Péladan discusses the same Provençal *vida* – in which no tryst is mentioned – in *Le Secret des troubadours*. In contrast to Pound, he gives it a thoroughly euhemeristic interpretation, devoid of either mystical or erotic dimensions: "This story of a garlanded wolf translates as follows: The parish of Penautier belongs to the orthodox side. Vidal took on a Roman disguise; the heretics believed that he was a heretic and manhandled him until he revealed his heresy" (66–7; my translation). Clearly, Pound did not get his interpretation of Pierre Vidal's *vida* from Péladan. Indeed, it seems that the particular erotic interpretation Pound gives to the esoteric tradition that he found in various scholarly holes and corners is very much his own. Interestingly enough, Rossetti also gives an interpretation of the Vidal story. His version is less euhemeristic than Péladan's but has no hint of the erotic mysticism of Pound's version: "If we would perfectly understand the meaning of Pier Vidal's singular costume, we must see how the sect figured itself. To show how it was inwardly at war, and outwardly at peace with the object of its satire, it represented itself at the beginning of its works, covered with a wolf's skin, full of eyes and ears to denote vigilance; and from its mouth appeared the motto *Favete linguis*, that is: Take heed of my words" (Rossetti 1834, 171).

Although Péladan and Mead suppress the obviously erotic component of the legend, the mixture of green maidens and hoary forest men, of passion and death, of violation and mutilation, penetration and revelation that Pound finds in the legend is not at all rare in nineteenth-century literature. They are the stuff of romance. Much the same collection can be found, for example, in William Morris's *Wood beyond the World*, a work published just sixteen years before Pound's poem and much admired by Yeats. *Symboliste* painting and poetry is replete with rather similar admixtures of eros and thanatos. Péladan's own novels are steamy with sexuality, death, and mysticism. The fascination of Wilde and Beardsley with Salomé and John the Baptist are further cases in point, as is the tremendous vogue of Wagnerian *liebestod*.

Eroticism – even a mystical eroticism such as Pound's – is not something that one can profitably trace to some particular intellectual or emotional source. However, Mead and his circle were certainly not the source. Mead was hostile to all varieties of eroticism – whether phallocentric and mystical like Pound's, voluptuary like Remy de Gourmont's, bisexual like Aleister Crowley's, or ecstatic like D.H. Lawrence's. Mead maintained this hostility in the face of the inescapably erotic nature of the mystical, cultic, and mythographic literature which he studied. Mead's group is of one voice in insisting that the eroticism of occult and mystical literature is symbolic and is not to be taken literally. Pound was entirely out of step with the prevailing prudishness of Kensington.

In his Quest Society lecture Pound expressed his phallocentrism in terms native to occultism and mysticism:

There are at least two paths – I do not say that they lead to the same place – the one ascetic, the other for want of a better term "chivalric." In the first the monk or whoever he may be, develops, at infinite trouble and expense, the secondary pole within himself, produces his charged surface which registers the beauties, celestial or otherwise, by "contemplation." In the second, which I must say seems more in accord with "mens sana in corpore sano" the charged surface is produced between the predominant natural poles of two human mechanisms. ([1929] 1953, 94)

Nine years later, Pound committed himself to print once again on this subject in his extraordinary "Postscript" to his translation of Remy de Gourmont's *The Natural Philosophy of Love*. Richard Sieburth, in his excellent discussion of Pound's relation with Remy de Gourmont (1978) does not touch on the topics that I discuss. Sieburth regards de Gourmont as a "learned humanist" and an "elegant sceptic" (3–4) and quite fails to see the sexual fantasist and sensualist that Pound found in the author of *The Natural Philosophy of Love*. In his "Postcript," Pound's sexual speculations are formulated as a biological theory, drawing on de Gourmont's fantastic eroticization of J.H. Fabre's entomological observations.

De Gourmont's main source appears to have been Fabre's *Souvenirs entomologiques*. At least that is the only work by Fabre that he mentions. He describes Fabre as "the man who, since Réamur has penetrated furthest into the intimacy of insects, and whose work is veritably the creator, perhaps without his having suspected it, of the general psychology of animals" (Gourmont [1922] 1950, 69). Fabre's works are difficult to come by, but it is unlikely that he interpreted the philoprogenitive instinct as a Nietzschean "will to power" issuing in the genital morphology of insects and animals as de Gourmont does. No doubt de Gourmont is admitting as much in his remark that Fabre perhaps did not suspect that he had created a general psychology of animals.

Undeterred by his own ignorance of Fabre's work, Pound enrols the biologist in his always growing and idiosyncratic canon of enlightened thinkers. After 1921 he almost invariably links Fabre with Frazer as the two essential sources of "contemporary clear thinking" (Pound 1954, 32, 85, 343, 395). He even engages in a dispute with Eliot over the importance of Fabre in the 1930s (Lindberg 1987, 108), despite being innocent of any direct knowledge of Fabre's works. Jean-Henri Casimir Fabre (1825–1915) received his doctorate in biology in 1855. He never held a university position but was consulted by Louis Pasteur in 1863 on the problem of diseases of silkworms. He published a great deal, mostly of a popular nature, for in his later years he earned his living by his pen. His best-known work is the nine-volume *Souvenirs entomologiques* (1879–1907). Fabre is a reasonable candidate for a Poundian hero, for he got into difficulty with ecclesiastical authorities for contradicting Genesis in his teaching at a college. His anti-Darwinian insistence on a pre-Bergsonian *élan vital* also qualified him as a Poundian hero, alongside the more famous Lamarckian, Louis Agassiz, whom Pound also praised. It also caused his reputation to go into eclipse after the Second Empire. Hence, Fabre was a bit of a martyr, both to Catholic conservatism and to progressive materialism. Nonetheless, he was made a member of the Academy of Sciences on 11 July 1887, at the age of seventy-one.

A Cartesian, Fabre argued for an absolute break between the animal and human, and thought the Darwinian mechanism of natural selection inadequate to account for human evolution. Although he attributed insect behaviour to innate instinctual capacities, I have been unable to find any support in Fabre for de Gourmont's Gnostic understanding of the philoprogenitive instinct – an understanding Pound was predisposed to find attractive. Fabre merely provides de

Gourmont with illustrations of the great variety of genital morphology and sexual behaviour in the insect world.

Whereas de Gourmont goes wildly beyond Fabre in *The Natural Philosophy of Love*, Pound goes still further in his postscript, taking off from de Gourmont's remark, "There could be, perhaps some correlation between complete and deep copulation and cerebral development." Pound's biology is embarrassingly uninformed but should be faced as an example of his effort to find a scientific basis for occult beliefs he already held: "It is more than likely that the brain itself, is, in origin and development, only a sort of great clot of genital fluid held in suspense or reserve ... This hypothesis ... would explain the enormous content of the brain as a maker or presenter of images" (Pound 1958, 203). He goes on to speculate that more intelligent species discharge less seminal fluid in ejaculation than the less intelligent. The retained seminal fluid, of course, enlarges the brain.

This pseudoscience is, I think, much harder to take seriously than the mystical eroticism of "Psychology and Troubadours." It is also blatantly and offensively sexist. Women don't have seminal fluid and spermatozoa to withhold, and therefore they can have only "the accumulation of hereditary aptitudes," the "useful gestures," and "the perfections." Man, on the other hand, produces "the 'inventions,' the new gestures, the extravagance, the wild shots, the impractical, merely because in him occurs the new up-jut, the new bathing of the cerebral tissues in the residuum, in *la mousse* of the life sap" (Pound [1929] 1953, 204).

Richard Sieburth sees little of the occult in de Gourmont in his study of de Gourmont's influence on Pound, but his list of ideas shared by de Gourmont and Pound fits comfortably into an occult ambience: "All of these terms, clarity (*claritas*), process (*tao*), and liquid light (*e lo soleils plovil*; iv/15;19), in conjunction – chthonic, sexual forces joined with love, lustre, and fluidity – form an epiphanic ideogram absolutely central to the *Cantos*" (Sieburth 1978, 135).

It is possible to concede that Pound, de Gourmont, Agassiz, and Fabre formed common cause with one another and with the occult in their hostility to Darwinism. But there is no justification for Pound's assignment of great importance to Fabre's work. Fabre was not an important biologist. Nor was he an occultist. He was not even an animist or immanentist, but merely a Cartesian vitalist. He was important primarily as a scientific journalist, the French Isaac Asimov of biology.

It is embarrassing that Pound should have been attracted by such absurd speculation as de Gourmont's, but he was not alone in assigning extraordinary psychic or even metaphysical power to sexuality and to the erotic. Once again we can turn to the contemporaneous "Sermones ad Mortuos" of Jung for an independent but similar version of a sexual theory of inspiration. The similarity is hardly astonishing, for Jung's and Pound's sources are the same Gnostic texts (Jung 1965, 200–1). It is striking that two men of such divergent backgrounds – an American occultist and poet, and a Swiss medical doctor and psychologist – should be drawing on such obscure and steamy sources. Perhaps the most remarkable coincidence is that both became such successful public figures in their own spheres in spite of – or perhaps because of – such apparently "unscientific" views.

Jung tells us that "the world of the gods is made manifest in spirituality and in sexuality." Spirituality is "womanlike and therefore we call it MATER COELESTIS." Sexuality is "manlike, and therefore we call it PHALLOS" (Jung 1965, sermo 5, 386–7). For Jung, the essence of Gnosticism is self-contradiction, the logical *via negativa*. Consequently, we learn in the next sermon that the female has two aspects: "The daemon of sexuality approacheth our soul as a serpent. It is half human and appeareth as thought-desire. The daemon of spirituality descendeth into our soul as the white bird. It is half human and appeareth as desire-thought." The serpent, we learn, "is a whore. She wantoneth with the devil and with evil spirits," while "the white bird is a half-celestial soul of man. He bideth with the Mother, from time to time descending." "He is chaste and solitary, a messenger of the Mother" (sermo 6, 388). Jung's account should be compared to Mead's handling of the Gnostic legend of Simon Magus and Helen of Tyre, to which Pound ([1929] 1953, 91, note) refers admiringly (see Surette 1979, 60–6).

Jung's terminology is Neoplatonic and even Christian – though the theology is neither – and his theory is cosmological and theological, in contrast to the biological and psychological theory of Pound and de Gourmont. It is not a little ironic that a major poet should articulate (and promulgate) a biological and psychological theory of intellectual creativity while a major psychological theorist should develop (and conceal) a cosmological and theological myth accounting for human personality. Such incidents suggest that the cognitive scene in which the modernist drama was staged was stranger than scholarship has so far imagined.

It is worth noting that a major part of Jung's quarrel with Freud – at least, according to Jung's account – was over the nature and function of human sexuality:

Freud, I concluded, must be so profoundly affected by the power of Eros that he actually wished to elevate it into a dogma – *aere perennius* – like a religious numen ... To be sure, he did not do this too loudly; instead he suspected *me* of wanting to be a prophet. He made his tragic claim and demolished it at the same time. That is how people usually behave with numinosities, and rightly so, for in one respect they are true, in another untrue. Numinous experience elevates and humiliates simultaneously. If Freud had given somewhat more consideration to the psychological truth that sexuality is numinous – both a god and a devil – he would not have remained bound within the confines of a biological concept. (Jung 1965, 154)

This assessment of Freud, spoken to Amiela Jaffé in 1957 or 1958, reflects in somewhat more sober language the understanding of sexuality which Jung developed forty years earlier in the "Sermones ad Mortuos": "The world of the gods is made manifest in spirituality, and in sexuality. The celestial ones appear in spirituality, the earthly in sexuality" (Jung 1965, 386).

Compare "The Flame" from *Canzoni*, a volume published just a year earlier than the lecture "Psychology and Troubadours." The poem is a somewhat veiled description of what "Provence knew." The refrain is "'Tis not a game that plays at mates and mating." The "it" is never identified, but clearly the referent is love making. The point of the poem is to assert that the flame of love is a window on the noumenal:

'Tis not a game that plays at mates and mating,
Provence knew;
'Tis not a game of barter, lands and houses,
Provence knew.
We who are wise beyond your dream of wisdom,
Drink our immortal moments; we "pass through."
. . . .
... man doth pass the net of days and hours
Where time is shrivelled down to time's seed corn
We of the Ever-living, in that light
Meet through our veils and whisper, and of love. (Pound 1990, 64)

In conformity with these sentiments, Pound claims in "Psychology and Troubadours" that sex is "of a double function," and he castigates those who "find the source of illumination, or of religious experience, centred solely in the philo-progenitive instinct" ([1929] 1953, 94).

The phallocentrism of de Gourmont and Pound puts them thoroughly out of step with mainstream occult attitudes, which are distinctly gynocentric – either privileging the female or celebrating androgyny. Jung, too, wished to bring the goddess back into religion in order to balance the patriarchalism of the Christian tradition. He not only accuses Freud of patriarchalism but, on the promulgation of the doctrine of Mary's Assumption in 1950, he congratulated the Catholic Church for finally receiving "the Mother of God and the Bride of Christ" into the "divine thalamus" (Jung 1965, 201–2).

Mead and Schuré are similarly gynocentric. They follow Creuzer in privileging Eleusis specifically because of its *theacentric* nature. Eleusis is also very important to Jungians, and for the same reason. For his part, Péladan celebrates the androgyne in his fiction. Another instance of this gynocentric tendency of the occult is found in Bulwer-Lytton's 1871 novel, *The Coming Race*. He there describes a race living in an underground world as representative of the next evolutionary stage of homo sapiens. Amongst this advanced race, the women are physically and intellectually superior to the men and fly with artificial wings at maturity. Bulwer-Lytton's female "angels" invoke Louis Agassiz as an early prophet of their psychobiological beliefs, but Fabre is not mentioned. George Bernard Shaw claimed that *The Coming Race* had a formative influence on his own conception of the Superman, which – despite his Nietzscheanism – was also gynocentric. Balzac's Séraphita/Séraphitus is pointedly androgynous and rejects the merely physical love of both of his/her admirers – the *ingénue* Minna and the mature, rather Byronic, Wilfrid.

Pound's extreme phallocentrism was very much out of step with the gynocentrism dominant in the theosophical circles he frequented. No doubt he was pleased to find "scientific" support in de Gourmont for a belief he had already formulated – that sexual copulation was somehow a ritual and revelatory act. At the end of the "Postscript," he invokes this theory to explain the religious history that he has learned from occult Kensington: "The mystics have sought the gleam in the tavern, Helen of Tyre, priestesses in the temple of Venus, in Indian temples, stray priestesses in the streets, un-uprootable custom, and probably with a basis of sanity." He clarifies his point in a typical Poundian manner by citing a tag from Propertius, *Ingenium nobis ipsa puella fecit* ("Our genius is made by just this girl"). From this sentiment derives "the whole of the xiith century love cult, and Dante's metaphysics a little to one side" (Pound 1958, 213–14).

Pound recruits de Gourmont, then, to provide a biological and scientific explanation for the esoteric erotic "tradition." That Pound should wish to find a scientific or materialistic explanation certainly sets him apart him from mainstream occultists. Mead and Weston both subscribed to the Blavatskian version of biological history, succinctly expressed in the "Preliminary Notes" to *The Secret Doctrine:*

As regards the evolution of mankind, the Secret Doctrine postulates three new propositions, which stand in direct antagonism to modern science as well as to current religious dogmas: it teaches (a) the simultaneous evolution of seven human groups on seven different portions of our globe; (b) the birth of the *astral*, before the *physical* body: the former being a model for the latter; and (c) that man, in this round, preceded every mammalian – the anthropoids included – in the animal kingdom. (Blavatsky [1888] 1963, 1)

Authorities for this view cited by Blavatsky are Genesis (appropriately reinterpreted), the *Divine Pimander* of Hermes, the *Zohar*, and the Egyptian *Book of the Dead* (1–3). At least Pound had enough strength of mind to avoid being tainted by these truly far-out Blavatskian fantasies.

Bizarre as Blavatsky's world and racial history are, they belong recognizably to the same tradition as that whose lineaments we have traced above and in which Swedenborg, Blake, and Yeats also participated. Yeats's *Vision*, as an historical fantasy, clearly belongs to this stream of revealed history. Yeats, of course, had studied Blake and Swedenborg to prepare his edition of Blake in collaboration with Edwin Ellis, and therefore was very familiar with both. The year in which he began *A Vision* was also a year in which he and Pound were engaged in collaborative occult research at Stone Cottage. They were reading Swedenborg as well as other occult texts.

Pound's adoption of the Barruel/Rossetti secret history and of de Gourmont's silly biological theory might count as keeping his head, when one considers the ambience in which the ambitious young poet moved between 1909 and 1917. To men like Yeats and Pound, who were scientifically illiterate, occult physical theories – which were essentially just ancient pre-Aristotelian monism – probably seemed no more mystical than Mme Curie's radiation, Einsteinian relativity, Planck's quantum theory, Freud's subconscious, or Bergson's *élan vital*. Indeed, in many cases they seem to have thought that all of these descriptions of the nature of reality were interchangeable. Mrs Mather's 1926 preface to a new edition of her husband's translation of *The Kabbalah Unveiled* reflects this occult understanding of the scientific revolution contemporaneous with literary modernism:

Since the year 1887, when the first edition of the *Qabalah Unveiled* appeared, the whole attitude of the thinking world has changed considerably towards occult philosophy and science. The gigantic strides made by science since the end of the last century, the staggering facts disclosed by its practical demonstrations, simultaneously with the development of the great occult movement, must strike all thoughtful people as the evidence of some imminent change in the evolution of this planet. Material science would appear to be spiritualizing itself and occult science to be materializing itself. If not clasping hands, they are certainly making tentative attempts in that direction. The Ancient Wisdom, the Sacred Books taught ... that Matter and Spirit are only opposite poles of the same universal substance. (vii–viii)

(Moina Mathers was the sister of Henri Bergson, but the French vitalist never approved of his brother-in-law's speculations.)

The ubiquity and acceptability of such views is attested to by Edmund Wilson's very similar views, as expressed in his influential *Axel's Castle*, a work published only a few years later:

This new language may actually have the effect of revolutionising our ideas of syntax, as modern philosophy seems to be tending to discard the notion of cause and effect. It is evidently working, like modern scientific theory, toward a totally new conception of reality. This conception, as we find it to-day in much Symbolist literature seems, it is true, rather formidably complicated and sometimes even rather mystical ... And the result may be, not, as Valéry predicts, an infinite specialisation and divergence of the sciences and arts, but their finally falling all into one system. (Wilson [1931] 1984, 234)

Once one is familiar with this "occult" view of physics and the cosmos, it is difficult to avoid the conclusion that it animates the original "Canto One," and perhaps *The Cantos* themselves. Certainly it permits a rereading of the puzzling canto 23, where Pound juxtaposes the Plotinians, Psellos, and Gemisto Plethon with M. Curie and other metonyms of science. In canto 8 (Pound 1973a, 31), we heard Gemisto Plethon complaining of the Italians during the conference at Ferrara where Malatesta and Cosimo first encountered his Neoplatonism. Then, in canto 23:

> "Et omniformis," Psellos, "omnis
> "Intellectus est." God's fire. Gemisto:
> "Never with this religion
> "Will you make men of the greeks.
> "But build wall across Peloponesus
> "And organize, and ...
> > damn these Eyetalian barbarians."
> And Novvy's ship went down in the tempest
> Or at least they chucked the books overboard. (107)

(The elision is Pound's. The Latin translates: "All intellect is omniform." "Novvy" is Novella Malatesta, Sigismundo's brother.)

This passage is followed, after a space, by metonyms of Cartesianism, a comment on its inadequacy, and of the technological products of modern science, concluding with an anecdotal metonym of the discovery of radiation:

> How dissolve Irol in sugar ... Houille blanche,
> Auto-chenille, destroy all bacteria in the kidney,
> Invention-d'entités-plus-ou-moins-abstrait-
> en-nombres-égal-aux-choses-à-expliquer ...
>   La Science ne peut pas y consister. "J'ai
> Obtenu une brulure" M. Curie, or some other scientist
> "Qui m'a coûté six mois de guérison."
>   and continued his experiments.
> Tropismes! "We believe the attraction is chemical." (107)

These lines are too cryptic to be glossed with confidence, but the juxtaposition of the French metaphoric terms for hydroelectricity and the bulldozer ("houille blanche" and "auto-chenille") with a comment in French that science does not consist of the invention of abstract entities more or less equal to things would appear to prepare us for the judgment that these are merely "tropes" or figures for a deeper understanding, such as that expressed in the Greek wisdom represented in the following lines, which invoke the descent of Apollo, the sun god, and then of Hercules and Odysseus: "With the sun in a golden cup / and going toward the low fords of ocean." This is followed by a Greek passage, which translates as "The sun, Hyperion's child, stepped down into his golden bowl and then after crossing." Pound then inserts a Latin phrase, *ima vadis noctis obscurae* ("the lowest depths of darkest night"), which is what the sun "crosses." The next line, "Seeking doubtless the sex in bread-moulds," places modern science in the midst of these archaic explorations in dark regions. By way of some Greek etymology out of Liddel and Scott worthy of Heidegger, we learn that "helios" is related to "ali-otrephès," meaning "sea-reared." The point would seem to relate to Plethon's derivation of everything from water, and "talking of Poseidon" in canto 8. In any event, this fanciful etymology surrounds the sentence, "The idiot Odysseus furrowed the sand," which refers to his digging of a trench for the blood of the black sheep as described in the first canto. This blood summons the dead to him at edge of ocean. Hence, the canto continues, "down into, / descended, to the end that, beyond ocean, / pass through, traverse."

The point would seem to be that Odysseus's descent is esoterically equivalent to the diurnal death and rebirth of the sun. The following Greek passage describes the "stream of ocean rejoining his wife and dear children in the depth of black night, while the son of Zeus

(Heracles) entered the laurel shaded grove." Pound follows this with English lines that equate the archaic stories with Dante's medieval epic. The point of it all would seem to be that the discoveries of the Neoplatonists, of science, and of mythical heroes should be understood as coming under the same occult description. They all amount to recognitions of a universe alive, a world immanent with spirit. To put it another way, everything is intellect. Matter is merely a thick manifestation of mind, or of the *nous*, which is the beginning and end of all matter as well as of all form.

Coupled with the Plotinian belief that the universe is a unity, a Mind, is the theosophical belief in the possibility of contact with the noumenal. The dominant formulation of this contact for the occult is palingenesis, and this is commonly represented as a descent and resurrection, as it is here in the circuit of Hyperion. An alternative representation is the sacred marriage, or *hieros gamos*, in which one returns to the astral realm by the same route as one left it: a woman's vagina. Pound reads Odysseus's sexual encounter with Circe as such an *hieros gamos*. In cantos 39 and 47 the revelation accompanies the act of copulation, in contrast to the *Odyssey* itself in which Odysseus must journey to the river of Ocean and perform the *nekuia* before he achieves illumination. (For a discussion of the *hieros gamos* in *The Cantos*, see Surette 1979, 57–66, 207–23.)

The occult and palingenetic ambience of canto 23 can perhaps best be illustrated by interpreting the next lines in the passage under examination in the light of some passages from Mead that appear to be relevant. The canto continues:

Precisely, the selv' oscura
And in the morning, in the Phrygian head-sack
Barefoot, dumping sand from their boat
'Yperionides! (108)

The reference to Dante's "dark forest" in this context is clearly emblematic of Dante's own descent, and particularly of its commencement in the confusion of life. Dante's journey poem is to be read in terms of the palingenetic paradigm. It is a journey towards wisdom on the model of those already alluded to in the preceding lines. The Phrygian head-sack is an attribute of Mithra, mentioned by Mead in his pamphlet *The Mysteries of Mithra* (1907) in a description of a tableau of Mithra *Petrogenes*:

There is a great tree with leafy branches extending to the top of the picture. Before it is standing a young man, quite naked, except for his Phrygian cap.

He is cutting from the tree a branch covered with leaves and fruit. The spark becomes active in the vegetable kingdom on earth; it plants there a branch from the tree of life.

Often in this same scene is seen a figure in an oriental tunic half issuing from the leafage of the tree, while another figure blows or breathes straight in his face. This is evidently a different incident in the cycle of experience, and the two scenes were sometimes depicted apart. It seems clearly to represent the passage from the vegetable to the animal kingdom, and the inbreathing of the second spark, the breath of lives, the animal soul. The naked first spark is half clothed by the second. (81–2)

Although Pound's scene does not correspond closely to Mead's, it can nonetheless be illuminated by it. Pound's "'Yperionides" is an erroneous transliteration of *Alios d'uperionidas*, cited earlier in the passage in the Greek alphabet. It translates as "Hyperion's child"; that is, Apollo, the sun. Terrell glosses the passage in the *Companion* as an account of the rising of the sun, aided by the dumping of sand from the sun's boat. However, Pound's reference to the Phrygian head-sack suggests that the setting and rising of the sun is to be understood esoterically as the death and rebirth of the soul – an interpretation at least hinted at by the earlier mention of "M. Curie," the co-discoverer with Mme Curie, of radiation, that "subtle body" or emanation of matter. If Pound meant merely to describe the daily round of the sun, he has been unusually obscure and eclectic even for him. Moreover, if we accept the pertinence of Mead's account of Mithraic transmigration of souls, the lines immediately following make more sense:

> And the rose grown while I slept,
> And the strings shaken with music,
> Capriped, the loose twigs under foot;
> We here on the hill, with the olives. (108)

In the light of the Mead passage, these items can be read as emblems of the incarnation of souls; that is, of their transmigration from the astral or etheric plane to the material or hylic plane, the first birth.

The whole passage concerning Hyperion and invoking Odysseus begins with the lines, "With the sun in a golden cup / and going toward the low fords of ocean" (107). We are not told who or what is "with the sun." In the light of Mead's discussion of Mithra, it might well be Mithra himself, rather than either the reader or the author – although Mithra is, like Christ and all the gods in occult doctrine, a representative of man, a divine man. In Mead's account of a Greek Mithraic frieze, the last scene "depicts the Departure of Mithra, in the Chariot of the Sun, towards the Region of the West, represented by the figure of Ocean. It is the *consummatum est*; He goes unto His own" (Mead 1907, 89). It is just possible that Pound is recollecting this passage in canto 74 when he echoes the Latin phrase from the conclusion of the Catholic mass – *Consummatum est* ("It is achieved") – which Mead employs here. However, Pound has the phrase as it occurs in the mass – *Est consummatum, Ite* – where its simply means "It is finished, you may go."

Mead's reading of the frieze renders Hercules' departure an apotheosis, a reading that makes sense of the allusions in canto 23. This esoteric reading of canto 23 is supported by canto 47, where the Mithraic bull is invoked in a passage that makes sense only in a Mithraic reading:

> Moth is called over mountain
> The bull runs blind on the sword, *naturans*
> To the cave art thou called, Odysseus,
> By Molü hast thou respite for a little
> By Molü art thou freed from the one bed
> > that thou may'st return to another. (237)

As in canto 23, these lines make sense as the expression of the *anima mundi* or life force guiding insects, animals, and men to their respective destinies – in all cases through the agency of philoprogenitive instincts. The "cave" is the womb, through which men pass to a higher birth.

Canto 47 represents Odysseus's conquest of Circe. The moly given him by Hermes protects him from a merely physical or hylic passion, which is allegorically represented by his men being turned into swine. In the *Odyssey* his conquest of Circe precedes the voyage to the River of Ocean where the *nekuia* is performed. In canto 47 the *nekuia* and the sexual copulation seem to be folded together:

> The light has entered the cave. Io! Io!
> The light has gone down into the cave,
> Splendour on splendour!
> By prong have I entered these hills:
> That the grass grow from my body,
> That I hear the roots speaking together. (238)

The great obscurity of this canto is much alleviated by Mead's prosaic explanation of some Mithraic scenes:

These scenes in which Mithra grasps the horns of the Bull, seem to signify the marriage of what might be called an atom of the mental nature with an atom of the passional nature. There is struggle, there is conquest, and finally there is death prior to resurrection.

The passional nature is converted, led back by the initiate into the cave, in the depth of his own substance, there to be slain – "the lamb slain from the foundation of the world" – and from its blood will spring up the plants and trees of life, and it will give corn with which to feed the hungry with the bread of life. (Mead 1907, 86)

Although Pound's version of apotheosis in cantos 23 and 47 (canto 39 belongs in this set as well) is not just a poetic version of Mead's interpretation of a series of Greek Mithraic tableaux, these deeply obscure cantos make much more sense if they are read as representations of metempsychosis, transfiguration, and apotheosis along the lines indicated by Mead's commentaries. To read them in this way transforms apparently wilful obscurity into an elaborate variation on traditional occult themes.

CHAPTER THREE

Nietzsche, Wagner, and Myth

THE *ZEITGEIST:* SCEPTICISM AND RELATIVISM

The topic of this chapter – Nietzsche, Wagner, and myth – is too vast even for a single book. Nonetheless some effort must be made to place Pound and modernism in the context of these two colossal figures and their impact on the study of myth. Nietzsche and Wagner have received far less attention from literary scholars than one would expect, even though the ubiquity of their influence on literature is widely granted. David S. Thatcher's *Nietzsche in England 1890–1914* (1970) is the best study of Nietzsche's influence on the artistic and political scene, although it is seldom cited by literary scholars. Jeffrey Perl ascribes a Nietzschean historical paradigm to modernism in *The Tradition of Return* (1984) but does not discuss Nietzsche's direct influence on modernists (225–35). Wagner's influence is assessed in Stoddard Martin's *Wagner to "The Waste Land"* (1982), which documents Wagnerian references and allusions in the works and letters of literary figures – notably Yeats, Lawrence, and Eliot. Martin does not include Pound in his study, and Thatcher erroneously concludes that Pound was little influenced by Nietzsche (160).

Myth is a topic that has long been a favourite for literary criticism. However, studies of myth in literature of the modern period have tended to be thematic or stylistic, paying little attention to the origins and variety of theories of myth. Literary scholarship has tended to attribute the efflorescence of literary interest in myth to Frazerian anthropology rather than to Wagner, Nietzsche, and the occult, despite many indications that these sources are probable and suitable. Kenneth Cornell's authoritative remarks on the matter set the tone of scholarly dismissal of the occult:

Symbolism, in its search for the soul of things, in its constant preoccupation with the mysterious, seems to have affinities with the mystic traditions begun with Swedenborg, Catherine Théot, Montfaucon de Villars, J.-B. Boyer, Martinez Pasqualis, brought to the threshold of the nineteenth century with Saint-Martin, and continued in such works as Gérard de Nerval's *Les Illuminés* or Balzac's *Séraphita*. But in 1889, despite the example of Verlaine, mysticism seems only a secondary and vague influence in symbolist poetry. The concept of the oriental religions had entered much more profoundly into the poetry of Leconte de Lisle and his Parnassian followers, for in the symbolists are usually present only the symbols of the liturgy, the exterior trappings of religion.

On the other hand, poetry in 1889 among the symbolists is almost entirely a reflection of the mind, the repudiation of realities ... Living and sensory impression are only the pretext of the dream, and it is this, perhaps more than questions of form or outloook on life, which gives the maturing movement its character. (Cornell 1951, 80–1)

The purpose of this chapter is to present a case for the continued and lively influence of the occult by exploring the role that Edouard Schuré and Joséphin Péladan played in formulating Wagnerian and Nietzschean notions and of transmitting them to *Symbolisme*, and thence to Yeats, Pound, and Eliot.

In addition to *Nietzsche in England*, two single author studies of his influence have recently appeared: a scholarly study of Yeats's knowledge of Nietzsche by Frances Oppel, *Mask and Tragedy* (1987), and an exploration of affinities between Pound and Nietzsche by Kathryne Lindberg, *Reading Pound Reading Nietzsche* (1987). None of these studies explore the role that the occult played in the transmission of Wagnerian and Nietzschean ideas. Thatcher is a partial exception to this rule, for in his chapter on Orage he acknowledges the occult provenance of much of Orage's thought. However, he is silent on Yeats's occultism in the chapter on Yeats.

There is no single and undisputed standard version of the literary history of modernism, nor even any one or two studies that could uncontroversially represent the range of approved versions. In the absence of any standard authority, it seems reasonable to take two prominent and divergent versions as representative of the range of scholarly opinion. The two most influential general studies are, I think, Hugh Kenner's *The Pound Era* (1971) and David Perkins's *A History of Modern Poetry* (1976). Kenner's study could fairly be regarded as an "inside" view of modernism in that it adopts a modernist or impressionistic methodology. Perkins's study, on the other hand, is "disinterested" and "scholarly" or philological in method.

Kenner's study brilliantly enacts the *Symboliste* principles of correspondence, affinity, and serendipitous coincidence, but he says next to nothing of Wagner, Nietzsche, and the occult whence these techniques are derived. His most extended comment on these topics is probably the following discovery of coincidences:

They were born within a six-year span: Joyce and Lewis, 1882; Williams, 1883; Pound, 1885; Eliot, 1888. (And Picasso, for that matter, 1881, and Stravinsky, 1882.) And how remote those dates seem! The lanes of London were still scavenged by municipal goats. *Marius the Epicurean* was published in the year of Ezra Pound's birth. Browning and Ruskin were active. Wagner was but two years dead, Jesse James but three.

When those men were children the *Symbolistes* were active, so their heritage included those dark worlds, that succulent craftsmanship, in which urbanized post-Romanticism sought satiety. (Kenner 1971, 551)

Perkins, more cautious and circumstantial than Kenner, gives the question of the occult brief attention. He calls the mix of symbolism, aestheticism, and impressionism out of which modernism grew "ars victrix" and disposes of occultism and esotericism in a few sentences. (The "he" in the first sentence is the aesthete.)

He presented without criticism the ugly, morbid, perverse, pathological, neurasthenic, self-destructive, and the like, and he found in them a deeper reality and a strange new beauty, as is suggested in Baudelaire's title, *Les Fleurs du Mal*. The Symbolist of the nineties returned, often by way of German or English Romanticism, to Neoplatonic philosophy, Rosicrucianism, Alchemy, Jakob Boehme, Giordano Bruno, and occult lore of every kind ... Symbolism expressed a religious feeling or hope, and though the distinction between symbolism and mysticism was well understood, the two modes of quasi-religious experience were often presented in the same writer, so that in practice "symbolic" and "mystical" tended to become interchangeable epithets. Impressionism, on the other hand, presupposed scepticism and relativism. (Perkins 1976, 33)

Kenner cleverly links modernism to *Symbolisme* by way of Jesse James and municipal goats. Perkins, in contrast, explicitly identifies the occult component of *Symbolisme* but isolates modernism from it on grounds that the former is "symbolic" and "mystical" while the latter is sceptical and relativist.

Perkins's comfortable isolation of modernism from the morass of symbolism and mysticism by means of a putative "scepticism and relativism" is worth pursuing for a moment. The two principles are merely invoked as the unchallengeable touchstones of impressionism, a *Weltanschauung* that Perkins takes to be the immediate precursor of modernism. Taken together it would seem fair to say that scepticism and relativism have been the touchstone of enlightened humanism in this century. It is not, however, entirely clear that they are much honoured in modernism. Indeed, the current controversy between the postmodern and modernism is precisely on the degree to which modernists were orthodox in their adherence to these touchstones of intellectual respectability. Either the modernists were good sceptical relativists as their defenders maintain, or they were credulous absolutists and fellow travellers of other credulous absolutists such as the Fascists, Nazis, Christians, or occultists as their postmodern detractors maintain.

Another case in point is the study of modernism by James Longenbach, *Modernist Poetics in History* (1987). Longenbach argues for the centrality to modernism of a school of opinion that he describes as "visionary" and "sceptical." The "theorists" of this visionary scepticism are, he says, Wilhelm Dilthey, Jacob Burckhardt, Benedetto Croce, and R.G. Collingwood; its literary figures are Walter Pater, T.S. Eliot, and Ezra Pound. All of them are said to look to the past for solutions and to be opposed to "positivism" and "historicism" (Longenbach 1987, 10–22). Longenbach's attribution of such a philosophical posture to a Christian theologian like Dilthey and to Christian thinkers like Burckhardt, Croce, and Collingwood is symptomatic of the prestige of scepticism.

Surely it is not scepticism that his thinkers share so much as a religious sensibility – a feature of their thought that Longenbach chooses to disguise under the term "visionary." Eliot's Christianity is no more in doubt than Dilthey's. Pater and Pound, however, need some other designation. The one I have suggested for Pound (and Yeats) is "occult." Longenbach himself – both in *Modernist Poetics* and in *Stone Cottage* – continually comes up against evidence of the occult provenance of Pound's ideas on religion and history. His invariable response is to skirt them, covering these embarrassing items by alluding indistinctly to "esoteric sources" or "medieval mysticism" (Longenbach 1987, 23–4, 55–61). Because it is very difficult to pair scepticism with occultism, Longenbach must constantly close his eyes to the evidence thrust before them if he is to maintain Pound's status as a sceptic. For example, when he cites a passage in which Pound appeals to the authority of Pater and Swedenborg, Longenbach discusses the Paterian passages that would support Pound's appeal but passes over the Swedenborg reference in silence (55). Lawrence S. Rainey, in his very fine recent study of the Malatesta cantos, follows

Longenbach in this evasion and speaks of a "secular spirituality" sought by Malatesta and Isotta (Rainey 1991, 219).

Perkins accurately represents received opinion in his reliance on the "well understood" distinction between symbolism and mysticism. But as the discussion in the previous chapters indicates, this "well understood" distinction is an artifact of literary apologetics. It is, I think, quite impossible to draw a clean line between the symbolism of Yeats or the imagism of Pound and their respective occult interests. Such a line can, I think, be drawn in the cases of Joyce and Stevens with respect to the occult, but to say that it is well understood is to say far too much. And while Eliot's brush with occult topics can be isolated within his career, it is highly doubtful that his mysticism can be so cleanly isolated (for Eliot, see Gordon 1977; Skaff 1986, 20–43). Certainly, Perkins does not bother to articulate the distinction – any more than he explains the putative dependence of impressionism on scepticism and relativism.

Although scepticism and relativism are undoubtedly the two definitional dogmas of modern enlightened academic humanism, it is far from obvious that they are the guiding principles of modernism. Certainly, it is difficult to understand how impressionism depends on such principles unless we argue that subjective perspectivism is derived from them. Presumably, the argument would go something as follows. Impressionism as an aesthetic movement is contiguous with aestheticism in that both, to use a Jakobsonian term, "privilege" internal, subjective, and psychological *experience* over external, objective, and phenomenal *event*. The aesthete does so on the grounds that the external, phenomenal world is chaotic, coarse, and delusive in comparison with the order, subtlety, and clarity of internal experience. The impressionist puts most of his polemical weight on the "discovery" that the world we experience is a *construct*, fabricated by each of us out of disparate phenomenal clues, and therefore it is "relative" and idiosyncratic for each of us and must be taken with a sceptical grain of salt.

So described, Perkins's unarticulated distinction between a premodern aestheticism and modern impressionism seems to hold up very well, for the aesthete credulously grants some intrinsic superiority to the internal over the external, to the subjective over the merely factual, to the subtle over the coarse, and so forth. He or she offends relativism by hierarchizing at all, and offends scepticism by hierarchizing varieties of *knowledge*. The true sceptical relativist – in contrast to the aesthete – would never be dogmatic and would be even less likely to succumb to the "absolutism" of the mystic's or occultist's claim to knowledge of absolute reality.

But if we look at the conduct of self-confessed impressionists such as Ford Madox Ford and Joseph Conrad, we find that they did in fact claim a superior truth value for their "renderings" of the world and therefore cannot be considered to be either relativist or sceptics – at least, not in the postmodern or Nietzschean sense. Impressionism has much more in common with Husserlian phenomenology in that it would seem to hold that the internal mental principles governing the *construction* of the perceptions are objective, absolute, and transcendent. It is true that phenomenology – like aestheticism and Nietzscheanism – is sceptical and relativist *vis-à-vis* scientific claims to knowledge, but it is idealist and metaphysical with respect to its own claims to unmediated knowledge of the epistemé, if not of the noumenal. Modernism belongs to the same family of thought.

If we turn to the political sphere, scepticism and relativism seem to line up appropriately in opposition to the naïve credulity on which demagoguery depends and, on the other hand, to the absolutism on which monarchy and dictatorship depend. These postures are thus on the side of Rousseau and revolution, and are ranged against the reactionary views of such as Barruel and Aroux. Jacobinism and revolution, then, are ranged on the side of the modern and the enlightened, just where liberal humanism would wish them to be. Unfortunately, neither Jacobinism nor communism are in fact sceptical or relativistic ideologies. Both appeal to absolute and universal principles of social justice. Communism, insofar as it is a philosophy of dialectical materialism adhering to historical determinism, can hardly count as sceptical and relative.

Scepticism and relativism work more satisfactorily as touchstones in the discrimination between the Comtean, Spencerian, and Darwinian faith in historical meliorism on the one hand, and the more "realistic" pessimism of Nietzsche and modernism on the other. Scholarship has identified historical optimism with Romanticism as firmly as we identify happy endings with sentimentalism. However, secret history – or metahistorical schemata such as those of Vico, Yeats, Spengler, or Chamberlain, discussed above – will serve just as well as Nietzschean scepticism to account for modernism's contempt for belief in progress. And modernist credulity when confronted with conspiracy theories or metahistorical patterns is well attested.

The "ahistoricism" of modernism has often been illustrated by Pound's remark that "all ages are contemporaneous" ([1929] 1935, 8). But such achronology in fact reflects a metahistorical attitude that regards history as the playing out of a story. That same story has its "ages," all of which are instantiated somewhere in the world at any given moment. Pound's *Cantos* amply support such an interpretation.

Bernstein's argument that *The Cantos* do not express either an ahistorical or a cyclical view of historical process (1980, 107–10) is, I think, correct. However, it remains the case that the "repeat in history" enacted in the poem requires some metahistorical apparatus if it is to have any meaning at all. History is *real* for Pound and is irreversible, but not irredeemable. As it turned out, history was not redeemed by the Axis powers as they – and, alas, Pound too – dreamed it could be, hence *The Pisan Cantos* begin with an invocation of the "city in the mind, indestructible."

Central to positive ahistoricism is the affirmation that "science" or knowledge is uniform for all times, cultures, and peoples. Of course, this affirmation entails a denial of the historicist assumption that human knowledge is context specific. But – unlike Platonism, phenomenology, and the occult – positivism also holds that human knowledge is experientially derived and cumulative – once again entailing a denial of Platonism, phenomenology, and the occult for which knowledge is innate and given.

Eliot domesticated positivistic ahistoricism for literature in the essay "Tradition and Individual Talent" (1917). He modified the doctrine in three ways: firstly, he confined the uniformity to the "mind of Europe" as opposed to all of humanity; secondly, he coyly appealed to the old historicist notion of *Zeitgeist*; and thirdly, he cast doubt on the assumption of cumulative advance: "The poet must be very conscious of the main current, which does not at all flow invariably through the most distinguished reputations. He must be quite aware of the obvious fact that art never improves ... He must be aware that the mind of Europe ... is a mind which changes, and that this change is a development which abandons nothing *en route* ... That this development, refinement perhaps, complication certainly, is not, from the point of view of the artist, any improvement" (Eliot 1951, 16).

The utility of Perkins's touchstones is even more questionable when we turn to the natural sciences. We might assume that scepticism and relativism are properties of scientific materialism. Insofar as scepticism and relativism are the contrary of superstition and dogmatism, such an equation is fair enough. Bertrand Russell is a paradigmatic instance of one who was a champion of scientific materialism and a vigorous critic of religious superstition. Karl Popper, another scientific materialist, has been equally indomitable in the struggle against political ideology and dogmatism. But neither Russell nor Popper is a sceptical relativist. Popper, indeed, is as fiercely opposed to relativism as Russell is to superstition. Both men are clearly positivists in the broad Comtean sense as opposed to relativists. Surely, materialism and positivism are the leading characteristics of late-nineteenth- and early-twentieth-century academic culture, not relativism and scepticism – still less "visionary scepticism." What is true is that literary modernism and academic humanism have both set themselves against the dominance of positivist sociology and scientific materialism by adopting the weaponry of psychology, mysticism, and philosophy.

On the other hand, it is playing rather fast and loose with the term to count Pater and James as sceptics because of their rejection of Christianity, as Perkins and Longenbach appear to do; and it is thoroughly misleading to describe the credulous Yeats as a sceptic. It is true that all of the modernists except Eliot are sceptical with respect to Christianity, but most of them are credulous with respect to spiritual, visionary, or mystical doctrines and beliefs. Indeed, the fuss that criticism has made about Eliot's conversion would suggest that it is Christianity, not spirituality or metaphysical credulity, that scholars abhor.

This negative attitude towards Christianity seems to be the touchstone for scepticism for Perkins and Longenbach. Longenbach, for example, rates Pound as more sceptical than Eliot (1987, 22). Since Longenbach is very familiar with Pound's involvement in occult speculation, this ranking is difficult to understand unless Eliot's conversion to Anglicanism counts as a deeper descent into superstition than Pound's persistent "paganism." I cannot imagine that Longenbach thinks Artemis and Aphrodite more presentable divinities than Christ. But I do not know what other construction could be put on such a remark. Perhaps he cannot imagine that a poet's paganism needs to be taken seriously; it is no threat to the dominance of scepticism and relativism. Christianity, by contrast, is still a powerful force and hence attracts fear and loathing.

At a little higher level of discussion it is sometimes supposed that even if natural scientists are themselves inclined to positivism and dogmatism, modern theoretical physics confirms sceptical relativism. One often hears Einstein's relativism, Planck's quantum physics, and the Heisenberg uncertainty principle invoked as evidence that science itself concedes that positive knowledge is not possible. Of course, these principled limits on the accuracy and fineness of information in no way support sceptical relativism of the appropriate type. On the contrary, they define the practical limits of *empirical* knowledge, and do so without questioning empirical and Lockean theories of knowledge at all. Such principled limits to knowledge make no sense in a philosophy like Schopenhauer's or Nietzsche's where *all* supposed knowledge is mere delusion. True philosophical scepticism and relativism deny the possibility *in principle* of what Richard Rorty calls "incorrigible" knowledge; that is, absolute, unrelativized or nonperspectival knowledge (Rorty 1979, esp. 88–98). Nelson Goodman goes so far as to claim that "there are many realities, if any." Such radical relativism – although based on nominalism – fits well with monistic psychologism. However, it is not at all supported by modern physics, which remains resolutely realist despite its reluctance to indulge in descriptions of material reality. Relativism is no more supported by modern science than monism is supported by the Einsteinian equivalence between matter and energy.

On the contrary, modern physical scientific research is designed to "discover" the facts, to discover – in the early Wittgenstein's language – "what is the case" (Wittgenstein 1922, para. 2) independently of angle of view, interest, bias, distortion, ignorance, limited comprehension, and so forth. Philosophical modernism is committed to the achievement of "context-free" knowledge – the very contrary of relativism or scepticism. The controversial reception of T.S. Kuhn's explanation of the social nature of scientific revolutions is a case in point. His argument is attacked by many philosophers of science just because it is perceived to be relativistic and historicist (Kuhn 1977, 34–51). As we have seen, Kuhn's "relativism" is derived from cultural relativist theories long domesticated in literary hermeneutics. Literary modernism also adopted hermeneutic cultural relativism and deployed that relativism against analytical philosophy's decontextualism. But such relativism is not the natural ally of scepticism. On the contrary, it supposes that there are many roads to truth. In this respect, hermeneutic relativism is very friendly to the eclecticism characteristic of the occult and of literary postmodernism.

Literary modernism itself adopted some protective decontextual colouring with the doctrine of textual autonomy, which holds that the only context relevant to the meaning of a work of art is the work itself. Thus, the work is context-free in the sense that its meaning cannot be limited by its author's intentions, hopes, or desires, or even by the cultural or intellectual milieu out of which it grew. This latter exclusion discriminates literary modernism from the hermeneutical historicism of Dilthey and Schleiermacher, which held that the scholar could bridge the gulf between himself and the distant – either temporally or culturally distant – cognitive universe of the text he studied. Literary modernism perceived Dilthey's hermeneutic historicism as romantic and relativistic, in contrast to its own positive practice, which rendered the text an unmediated absolute. Ironically, postmodernism critiques accept modernism's self-assessment on this point – to its discredit as a failure of relativism and scepticism.

It is not particularly germane to this discussion, but I cannot refrain from observing that New Criticism squared the hermeneutic circle by also insisting that the sense of each word in the context-free text was itself context-dependent, deriving its particular sense from its "surround," which "warped" poetic sense away from the merely "scientific" or "referential" sense otherwise attached to these lexical items.

The provenance of sceptical relativism in this century is not amongst scientific materialists, nor is it amongst antimaterialistic hermeneuts and idealists such as Wilhelm Dilthey, Walter Pater, Benedetto Croce, and R.G. Collingwood, where Longenbach places it. Nor is it in the philosophy of Lord Russell and Karl Popper, or in the science of Albert Einstein and Max Planck – where New Criticism implied that it could be found. Modern – and postmodern – sceptical relativism derives principally from Friedrich Nietzsche, for whom scientific materialism is just one more dogma to be overturned by an all-embracing scepticism. Nietzsche's antipathy for science coupled with an hostility towards Christianity made him the darling of the credulous and dogmatic occult in the nineteenth and early twentieth century. His more recent adoption as the avatar of the postmodern has created rich opportunity for a misreading of his role in modernism.

The systematic confusion of the supposedly sceptical implications of modern physics with aesthetic modernism has made it difficult for literary scholarship to confront the facts squarely. Received opinion to the contrary, Pound did not abandon the aestheticism of his early London years in favour of an authentically modern sceptical relativism. On the contrary, he carried forward these juvenile preoccupations as the agent and engine of a stylistic transformation in English letters. The modernist, allusive, discontinuous, and obscure style introduced by Joyce and imitated by Pound and Eliot made it possible for Pound to retain his mystical eroticism while presenting himself in avant-garde circles as an avatar of scepticism and relativism.

NIETZSCHE AND THE THEORY OF MYTH

Long neglected by students of literary modernism, Nietzsche is now celebrated by postmodernism as the discoverer of the deconstructive *aperçu* that the world and everything within it is a text and therefore must be, and can *only* be, interpreted (Nehemas 1985, 3–5; Derrida 1979). Such an hermeneutic imperative can be seen as the corollary of sceptical relativism – a leading postulate of postmodernism, as it is alleged to be of modernism, and of authentic Nietzschean provenance: "This pair, science and the ascetic ideal, both rest on the same foundation – I have already indicated it: on the same overestimation of truth (more exactly: on the same belief that truth is inestimable and cannot be criticized). Therefore they are *necessarily* allies, so that if they are to be fought they can only be fought and called into question together. A depreciation of the ascetic ideal unavoidably involves a depreciation of science: one must keep one's eyes open to this fact" (*Genealogy of Morals*, 3.25).

The agenda of deconstruction and postmodernism is admirably adumbrated in this paragraph. The "ascetic ideal" to which Nietzsche refers is Christianity – still a force to be reckoned with in 1887. Jacques Derrida's ingenious enfolding of science and Christianity together within the ideology he calls "logocentrism" is very much within the spirit of this passage. Derrida's logocentrism would seem to overlap considerably with Nietzsche's *bête noir*, variously labelled "Apollonian," "will to truth," or "Socratism." Derrida argues that logocentrism has controlled *"the history of* (the only) *metaphysics*, which has, in spite of all differences, not only from Plato to Hegel (even including Leibniz) but also beyond these apparent limits, from the pre-Socratics to Heidegger, always assigned the origin of truth in general to the logos: the history of truth, of the truth of truth, has always been – except for a metaphysical diversion that we shall have to explain – the debasement of writing, and its repression outside "full" speech" (1976, 3; Derrida's emphasis).

This passage – and postmodern thought generally – clearly reflects Hegelian philosophy of history. However, in this "new historicism" as it is often called, the historical pattern seems to be an almost Manichean psychomachia, a struggle between a repressive force – Apollonian, Socratic, subjective, capitalist, statist, or logocentric – and a liberating energy – Dionysian, holistic, Communist, anarchist. The scene of this struggle is mind-sets, language, ideology, and theory. Since the new historicism is resolutely anti-empirical, the presumption is that events are determined by the ideas or theories to which individuals or groups subscribe. In effect, the theory inverts Marxist historiography of base and superstructure by making the superstructure (ideology) determine the base (material conditions, especially of industrial production and its ownership).

At the turn of the century Nietzsche was perceived as a liberator from religion and the prophet of the coming of the Superman (see Thatcher 1970, esp. 27–9). The postmodern Nietzsche is a liberator from empirical science, and the prophet of the untrammelled free spirit, in short, the Nietzsche of Heidegger and Derrida (Nehemas 1985, 16–17). Although, as any Nietzschean knows, there are as many

Nietzsches as there are readers of Nietzsche, there are only two that are important to my story. These two can be characterized by three texts: *The Birth of Tragedy* (1872), *Thus Spake Zarathustra* (1884), and *On the Genealogy of Morals* (1887). In particular, I want to consider these texts as they were read by Schuré, Péladan, and Orage.

The first Nietzsche, the Wagnerian celebrator of myth and ancient wisdom, is frequently forgotten these days. Even Stoddard Martin considers him essentially an anti-Wagnerian, even though he knows very well that Nietzsche first achieved notice as an enthusiastic Wagnerian (Martin 1982, esp. 1–18). But Nietzsche never escaped Wagner and Wagnerism, as Roger Hollinrake notes in his 1982 study of the relations between the two (16). The second Nietzsche is the nihilistic sceptic and relativist who calls for the triumph of an elite over the undeserving masses. It is this second Nietzsche – filtered through such readers as Freud and Max Weber – that Allan Bloom identifies as the source of contemporary American relativism and scepticism (Bloom 1987, 141–56). Bloom, indeed, casually remarks that Nietzsche had his "greatest direct influence on artists, most notably, of course, Ezra Pound" (149), and says not another word about Pound in the entire book. I doubt that Bloom knows much about Pound, but he is correct to identify the mocking, elitist Nietzsche in Pound – even though he is wrong to characterize the influence as direct.

The readers of Nietzsche with whom Pound was in closest contact were Yeats and Orage. Yeats read *Thus Spake Zarathustra* in 1902 and proceeded to read *The Case of Wagner*, *Nietzsche contra Wagner*, *The Twilight of the Idols*, *The Antichrist*, *On the Genealogy of Morals*, and *Thus Spake Zarathustra* again in 1903. He did not read *The Birth of Tragedy* until 1904, and then only in excerpted passages (Oppel 1987, 1). Orage's first two books were a study of Nietzsche and a brief anthology of Nietzschean aphorisms. He, too, ignores the Wagnerian Nietzsche and instead presents him as the celebrator of the blond beast and as a precursor of the Superman. Yeats and Orage, themselves occultists, read Nietzsche as a fellow occultist (Thatcher 1970, 139–40, 219).

Yeats and Orage were crucial influences on Pound during his Kensington years as well as important voices in the London literary scene. Yeats was by no means entirely sympathetic to modernism (which he tended to identify with realism). Nonetheless, his influence on the young Ezra Pound – from their first meeting in 1910 until at least Yeats's visit to Rapallo in 1927 – contributed significantly to the formulation of modernism. Orage's influence was less direct, but his editorship of the *New Age* from 1908 until his departure for New York in 1922 gave him a prominent role in the development of modernism, particularly through his influence on Ezra Pound's career and politics.

The *New Age* was Pound's principal outlet for prose during his London years, and it was read by almost everyone in London avant-garde circles. Although in 1920 Eliot confessed to Sidney Schiff that he never read it (Eliot 1988, 405), apparently he reformed, for he contributed to the memorials published in the *New English Weekly* on Orage's death in 1934, describing him as "the best literary critic of that time" (15 Nov., 100). In a characteristic paroxysm of caution, Eliot withdrew the praise at his next opportunity – in the next "Commentary" section of *Criterion* (Jan. 1935, 260–4), where he described himself as an avid reader of the *New English Weekly*, the journal Orage founded on his return to England in 1933. Incidentally, Orage immediately opened the pages of the *New English Weekly* to Pound, even though he did not share Pound's admiration for Mussolini and they had not been in touch for a decade.

Kathryne Lindberg's study of Pound's relation to Nietzsche, *Reading Pound Reading Nietzsche* (1987), makes no effort to discover what Pound might have known of Nietzsche or how he could have learned it, but instead offers a free-standing examination of the affinities between Pound and Nietzsche. She explicitly turns away from "close encounters of an intertextual kind" and devotes her attention to "the instability and figural energy of language that Pound and Nietzsche stressed in modern art and/or criticism" (13). In short, Lindberg applies a Nietzschean hermeneutic to Pound and finds Nietzschean components in his work. The affinities between the two authors apparently demonstrate that they both transmit or embody some *Zeitgeist*, or permanent wisdom. In short, Lindberg's study unwittingly participates in the Hermetic technique of the historical fabulists that was examined in the last chapter.

Affinities and coincidences, however striking and persuasive, are not in my view sufficient justification for the interpretation of one text in terms of another. Tempting as such an approach is, I have done my best to resist it. An example of a tempting coincidence is that Nietzsche wrote *Thus Spake Zarathustra* while vacationing in Rapallo, an Italian resort village where Pound lived from about 1922 until his arrest in 1945. It is tempting to guess that Pound moved to Rapallo in homage to Nietzsche. But, in fact, Pound did not learn about Nietzsche's residence in Rapallo until he had lived there for some time, as we know from the letter of 14 April 1936 to Joseph Darling Ibbotson: "Nietzsche was here, tho I didn't know it till I had been here for a long time" (Mondolfo and Hurley 1979, 34). He probably learned of it from Yeats, for when Yeats visited him at

Rapallo in 1927, they visited the hotel where Nietzsche had stayed (Oppel 1987, 234).

A less hypothetical example of the disjunction between an affinity study and an historical one is Lindberg's casual reference to the *New Age* as "A.R. Orage's little magazine for popularizing Nietzsche and other continental fads" (Lindberg 1987, 10). She does not follow this up with an analysis of Orage's two books on Nietzsche or with a chronological consideration of Pound's contributions to the journal, but simply continues an "intertextual" comparison of Nietzschean and Poundian postures. Lindberg does suggest that Pound, Nietzsche, and Wagner should be thought of as belonging to the same cultural spectrum, speculating that one might be able to "trace a line of deflected influence from Nietzsche and Wagner through French Symbolism to Pound" (12). Indeed, one can trace such a line, but through the occult rather than through *Symbolisme*. However, she merely mentions the possibility and then airily dismisses it, since it would, she says, "read like a pedant's dream, a hermeneut's nightmare, or a typical interpretation of the meaning of any of Pound's Cantos" (12).

The nihilistic Nietzsche, the prophet of the Superman, was identified by the Allies with German nationalism during World War I. But this aspect of him had already been absorbed by Yeats, Orage, and George Bernard Shaw. Orage, in fact, was a member of the Fabian Society. Shaw was one of the anonymous "angels" who bankrolled his purchase of the *New Age* in 1907. Shaw also contributed to memoirs in the *New English Weekly* on the occasion of Orage's death. He reported there that he "put down £500 ... to found a weekly magazine to be called *The New Age*" (*New English Weekly*, 15 Nov. 1934, 99; see also Thatcher 1970, 94–114).

The question of Nietzsche's relation to nazism is a difficult one, especially given Pound's Fascist sympathies. Certainly, Nietzsche is often regarded as the progenitor of nazism, and there is no doubt that many prominent Nazis greatly admired him – including Heidegger. His defenders point out that he was not anti-Semitic and that he was implacably opposed to the idea of the German Reich. It is true that he was not anti-Semitic, but he was not always hostile to German nationalism. The Wagnerian Nietzsche of *The Birth of Tragedy* reveals himself as a proud and even jingoistic veteran of the Franco-Prussian war. Moreover, Nietzsche does, in his later work, praise the assassins as the "order of free spirits *par excellence*" and credits them with having "obtained a hint of that symbol and watchword reserved for the highest ranks alone as their *secretum*: 'Nothing is true, everything is permitted'" (*Genealogy of Morals*, 3.24). Whatever one may wish to say about Nietzsche's subtle meaning in this remark, there can be little doubt that it was seized upon by the Nazis as their watchword. Alfred Bäumler's 1931 study, *Nietzsche der Philosoph und Politiker*, prospectively canonized him as a Nazi saint (Nietzsche 1967, 148 n.2).

When Pound arrived in London in 1909 – and even in 1915 when he began to write his epic of the new age – the dark future of Europe was still unknown and unimagined. Even the Great War had not (in 1915) become the monstrosity that it was destined to be. The great bloody battles of the Somme and Passchendaele were still in the future, and Nietzsche's prophecy for the next two centuries in the penultimate section of the *Genealogy of Morals* could not have had the terrible resonance for his readers then that it now has for us:

Christianity *as morality* must now perish, too: we stand on the threshold of *this* event ... What meaning would *our* whole being possess if it were not this, that in us the will to truth becomes conscious of itself as a *problem*?

As the will to truth thus gains self-consciousness – there can be no doubt of that – morality will gradually *perish* now: this is the great spectacle in a hundred acts reserved for the next two centuries in Europe – the most terrible, most questionable, and perhaps also the most hopeful of all spectacles. (3.27)

It is not possible to demonstrate that Pound had read the *Genealogy of Morals*. The Levy complete English translation of Nietzsche's works was just beginning to appear in 1909. However, the full eighteen volumes were available by 1911, early enough for Pound to have read Nietzsche if he had wished, though there is no indication that he ever did. However, he need not have done so, for London was redolent with the spirit of Nietzsche. Shaw, Edwin Ellis, Yeats, and Orage were all deeply influenced by Nietzsche (for Ellis, see Thatcher 1970, 105–13).

Yeats shared Nietzsche's apocalyptic perception that he stood at the end of an era. For Yeats it was the two-thousand-year-old Christian era, whose baptismal rite ("the ceremony of innocence") he imagined being drowned in the onset of a new era symbolized by a "rough beast":

Things fall apart; the centre cannot hold;
Mere anarchy is loosed upon the world,
The blood-dimmed tide is loosed, and everywhere

The ceremony of innocence is drowned;
The best lack all conviction, while the worst
Are full of passionate intensity.

.... but now I know
That twenty centuries of stony sleep
Were vexed to nightmare by a rocking cradle,
And what rough beast, its hour come round at last,
Slouches towards Bethlehem to be born?
            ("The Second Coming," Yeats 1958, 210)

Yeats's "rough beast," although distinct from Nietzsche's Antichrist
and "man of the future," owes as much to him as to occult sources:
"This man of the future, who will redeem us not only from the
hitherto reigning ideal but also from that which was bound to grow
out of it, the great nausea, the will to nothingness, nihilism; this bell-
stroke of noon and of the great decision that liberates the will again
and restores its goal to earth and his hope to man; this Antichrist
and antinihilist; this victor over God and nothingness – *he must come
one day*" (*Genealogy of Morals*, s24).

As we noted above, Yeats began reading Nietzsche towards the
end of 1902 or very early in 1903, and he maintained a lively interest
in him for the rest of his life (Thatcher 1970, 139–41; Oppel 1987, 42,
234). Yeats derived some of his apocalyptic imagery from Nietzsche
(Oppel 1987, 49–52), and the formulation of apocalyptic history that
he attributes to his astral teachers probably has a more secular source
in Nietzsche.

Of course, apocalyptic anticipation gripped the end of the nineteenth century and was not a Nietzschean invention. On this point
– as on so many others – he participated in a wider European *angst*
(or *Drang*) that was expressed as early as Matthew Arnold's "Dover
Beach," an *angst* shared by Mead, MacGregor Mathers, the Wagnerians, and the whole occult world. Nor were apocalyptic fears and
hopes confined to the aesthetic and occult fringes of the culture.
Fabians, Marxists, and nihilists also laboured to give birth to a new
age. Generally speaking, the occult and the socialists eagerly anticipated the dawning of the new age while the orthodox and the
Bloomsbury liberals feared it. In this respect, Eliot belongs with
Bloomsbury despite his disapproval of their sexual proclivities and
their unchristian spirituality.

The spirit of apocalyptics, or at least epochalism, infuses modern
and postmodern thinking alike. The latter welcomes and celebrates
the end of "Socratism," of the "will to truth," or of "logocentrism,"

because all of these are understood as ideologies of cognitive dogmatism whose political expression is called Alexandrianism by Nietzsche and imperialism by Marx, and is identified with European economic, political, and intellectual hegemony by the postmodern. Although modernism did not share postmodernism's antipathy to empire, it did share its fear and loathing of Socratism, if that is understood as a reliance on logical inquiry. In this respect, Yeats followed Blake more obviously than Nietzsche in his targeting of Locke, Newton, and industrialism instead of Socrates, Alexander, and empire:

FRAGMENTS

I

Locke sang into a swoon
The Garden died;
God took the spinning-jenny
Out of his side.

II

Where got I that truth?
Out of a medium's mouth,
Out of nothing it came,
Out the forest loam,
Out of dark night where lay
The crowns of Nineveh.

    (Yeats 1958, 240–1)

Scholarship's focus on the "critical" dimensions of modernist art – on its dismantling of the "old" artistic canons and practices – has systematically occluded modernism's participation in such apocalyptic and eschatological sentiments. It has been necessary to suppress this aspect of modernism because the four horsemen of the anticipated apocalypse actually arrived in a brutal historical event – the convulsion of Europe which began in 1914 (or perhaps 1870) – and which we still cannot be sure has definitively concluded. The phenomenon of postmodernism – which can be understood as a Marxist-inspired revision of Nietzschean relativism – is now forcing a reassessment of modernism's relation to communism, fascism, and nazism. Unfortunately, the reassessment is taking place mostly within a simplistic dualist schema inherited from the thirties, which sets left against right, communism against fascism, as Manichean opposites. In a notable exception to this simplisitic schema, Jeffrey Perl discusses the issue in terms of what he calls an "axiological crisis" arising from the postmodern rejection of "the concept of a hierarchy of value … in the name of democracy" (Perl 1984, 275). I think he is right when he observes that both Pound and his critics "may have fallen victim to the Hegelian presumption that … 'all aspects of a culture can be traced back to one key cause of which they are the manifestations'" (278), although the presumption seems more characteristic of Nietzsche than of Hegel. In any event, it is a historicist or metahistorical notion entirely at home in the intellectual milieu of modernism.

Such a duple schema does not map very well onto the alignment of literary modernists, none of whom were Communists, and of whom only Pound was a Fascist, although Wyndham Lewis was notoriously sympathetic to the Nazis in the early going. Yeats, Lawrence, Joyce, and Eliot are a different matter. Largely because they were clearly not Communists, they remain under recurrent suspicion. It is my hope that this survey of the ideological landscape of the period will help to clear up some of the ambiguities concerning the political affiliation of modernism caused by a too vigorous application of a simple dual good-guy/bad-guy schema.

Yeats wrote "The Second Coming" in 1919 – *after* the horrors of the trenches. Ten years earlier, Pound had celebrated war and violence in "Sestina: Altaforte":

> The man who fears war and squats opposing
> My words for stour, hath no blood of crimson
> But is fit only to rot in womanish peace
> Far from where worth's won and the swords clash
> For the death of such sluts I go rejoicing;
> Yea, I fill all the air with my music.

Pound's celebration of violence as masculine, and his characterization of its object as womanish, is very much in tune with Nietzsche's similar violent misogyny as expressed in *Genealogy* s7: "War is another matter. I am warlike by nature. Attacking is one of my instincts." And he goes on to excoriate "womanish" weakness: "The *aggressive* pathos belongs to weakness. Woman, for example, is vengeful: that is due to her weakness, as much as is her susceptibility to the distress of others." Later in *Genealogy* Nietzsche points to

the ever-increasing spiritualization and "deification" of cruelty which permeates the entire history of higher culture (and in a significant sense actually constitutes it). In any event, it is not long since princely weddings and public festivals of the more magnificent kind were unthinkable without executions, torturings, or perhaps an auto-da-fé, and no noble household was without creatures upon whom one could heedlessly vent one's malice and cruel jokes ... To see others suffer does one good, to make others suffer even more; this is a hard saying but an ancient, mighty, human, all-too-human principle ... Without cruelty there is no festival. (2.6)

Neither Pound nor Yeats go quite as far as this towards the complete rejection of a despised, "bleeding-heart" Christian *caritas*, but Artemis's "compleynt" against pity in canto 30 reflects Nietzsche's replacement of morality by pathology, and of pity by "hygiene." For Nietzsche, pity was a negative virtue denying the life-giving power of will and was antipathetic to the vigorous brutality of pagan myth (see *Genealogy*, 3.13–18). Canto 30 reflects all of these features:

> Compleynt, compleynt I heard upon a day,
> Artemis singing, Artemis, Artemis
> Against Pity lifted her wail:
> Pity causeth the forests to fail,
> Pity slayeth my nymphs,
> Pity spareth so many an evil thing. (Pound 1973a, 147)

For Nietzsche and Pound, pity is synechdochic for Christianity. It is Christianity that has slain Artemis's nymphs and thereby sickened the forests they magically tended. (Similar sentiments can be found today in polemics against environmental exploitation which attribute our rape of nature to the ideology of human stewardship elaborated in Genesis as opposed to the immanentism of shamanistic religions for whom nature is sacred.)

We have no direct evidence that Pound admired either Nietzsche or Wagner. The most extensive remark on Nietzsche that I have been able to find is a stanza in "Redondillas, or Something of that Sort," a poem withdrawn from *Canzoni*, which suspects that Nietzsche was the "one modern Christian" and in which Pound confesses, "I never have read him except in English selections" (King 1970, 217). The selections he is most likely to have read are Orage's two works and Thomas Common's anthology. Pound's library does not currently contain any of these. Yeats used the Common anthology, but he borrowed John Quinn's copy during his first American tour and did not own a copy.

Apart from this fugitive remark, what little Pound has to say of Nietzsche is negative or ambivalent – as in "Mauberley":

Mildness, amid the neo-Nietzschean clatter,
His sense of graduations,
Quite out of place amid
Resistance to current exacerbations. (1990, 199)

It is difficult to be confident of what Pound has in mind here. If we read Mauberley to represent the aesthete whom Pound had been and now is no longer, then "neo-Nietzschean clatter" can be understood to be that which Pound now embraces. On the other hand, it is difficult to ignore the negative connotations of a word like "clatter" when applied to intellectual discourse.

I have found only three other references to Nietzsche. They all link Nietzsche to Shaw and are essentially equivalent: "Mr James Joyce and the Modern Stage" (1916) and "Le Prix Nobel" (1924), both found in Forrest Read's *Pound/Joyce*; and "How to Read" (1929) in *Literary Essays*. The 1916 remark is as follows: "So we have Shaw; that is to say, Ibsen with the sombre reality taken out, a little Nietzsche put in to enliven things, and a technique of dialogue superadded from Wilde" (Read 1967, 51). The other occurrences repeat the same point with slight modification. Since three of the four are penned between 1916 and 1919, it is reasonable to assume that Pound had in mind the boom in Nietzsche that followed the appearance of the Levy edition and the end of World War I. Nietzsche's apocalyptic prophecies had taken on new relevance – and even urgency – in the light of the horrors of trench warfare, of the Bolshevik revolution, and the redrawing of the map of Europe by the Peace of Versailles.

Although the passage from "Redondillas" is the only direct evidence I have been able to find that Pound had read any of Nietzsche's works, he echoes Nietzschean sentiments frequently enough for Allan Bloom to identify him as an undoubted Nietzschean. Even if Pound read little in Nietzsche, he could easily have picked up lots of his ideas and attitudes from Yeats and Orage. Even before he became a close associate of these two Nietzscheans, he had encountered Nietzschean cultural analysis in Péladan's *Origine et esthétique de la tragédie*. Another source is Max Nordau's *Degeneration*, which Pound read late in 1912. He wrote to Dorothy Shakespear that Nordau was as stupid as de Maupassant was intelligent – "or rather his conclusions are fairly sound, but his reasons for 'em are idiotic. If he had sense enough to dogmatize, he might pass for a sage" (Pound 1984, 171).

Nordau's argument is that virtually all of the art of the nineteenth century – Pre-Raphaelitism, Wagnerism, *Symbolisme*, aestheticism, naturalism, and realism, and especially Nietzscheanism – are the product of hysteria and mania. He includes Péladan in his net but is much kinder to Péladan than to Rossetti (Dante Gabriel), Wagner, Ibsen, or Zola. That Pound should have agreed with his conclusions is remarkable in itself. On Nietzsche, Nordau wrote: "The 'bullies' gratefully recognise themselves in Nietzsche's 'over-man,' and Nietzsche's so-called 'philosophy' is in reality the philosophy of 'bullying.' His doctrine shows how Bismarck's system is mirrored in the brain of a maniac. Nietzsche could not have come to the front and succeeded in any but the Bismarckian and post-Bismarckian era. He would, doubtless, have been delirious at whatever period he might have lived; but his insanity would not have assumed the special colour and tendency now perceptible in it" (Nordau [1895] 1913, 470). It is striking that Pound should have been so ambivalent about Nordau – particularly just at the time he had written "Patria Mia," a very Nietzschean analysis of America (New Age, 5 Sept. – 14 Nov. 1912).

It is similarly difficult to get a "fix" on Pound's attitude towards Wagner. We are fortunate in having a compendious collection of Pound's music criticism compiled by Murray Schafer, which permits an easy survey of Pound's remarks on Wagner. Wagner's name turns up on twenty-six different occasions, the first in 1912 and the last in 1938. Most of the comments are noncommittal and reflect no attitude of hostility towards this great Nietzschean figure and Teutonic prophet. However, there are two very negative notices, both appearing in the New Age, the first in 1918 and the second in 1919. I suspect that they are inspired more by wartime anti-German feeling than by any judgment based on general aesthetic principles.

Having reported on Rosing's singing of Wagner several times before without any negative remarks about the composer, Pound leaps on him with both feet in the 27 January 1918 New Age review. The remark is worth citing at length, for it demonstrates that Pound was familiar with a fair bit of the Wagner canon:

It is all very well to say the Wagner sounded dull because one was more familiar with it, but there is simply no interest in the melodic line of the notes for the seventeen words beginning "Donne lui donc si Dieu, etc." The composer has used the same set of effects in his Lohengrin, in the "Rêves" which followed and in Tannhäuser, usual intervals, patches lacking in interest, composer so little absorbed in his subject and so intent on being the colossus that he does not keep his hand on the tools. Wagner's "position" is in part due to the xixth century lust for great figures; its domination by rhetoric. (Schafer 1977, 109)

Similar sentiments are expressed in the 1919 remark, but never again in notices more remote from the passions of the Great War. On the other hand, it must be admitted that Pound's pro-German sentiments in the forties do not produce enthusiastic assessments of Wagner's music.

Of course, Pound ought to have been hostile to Wagner on aesthetic grounds. Pound's aesthetic was committed to detail and precision – to small, exquisite effects. He speaks always of the line, the contour, the sculpted edge, and the like. Wagner, by contrast, was committed to the grand, the large effect, the dramatic, and the heroic. However, the "logic" of aesthetic opinion is not sufficient grounds upon which to posit an hostility that is otherwise poorly attested. The whole thrust of this study is against such ideologically driven *a priori* judgments. It is certainly the case that many of Pound's cultural and historical attitudes come to him from sources deeply imbued with Wagnerian provenance. This datum must be placed in the balance on the other side from scattered negative remarks on Wagnerism and an aesthetic which could be considered antipathetic to Wagner's.

Thus, even if Pound's assessment of Wagner and Nietzsche was strongly negative, he nonetheless imbibed Wagnerism and Nietzscheanism at second and third hand. Their greatest influence on him began around 1912, long before fascism or nazism appeared either as ideologies or as political movements. Mussolini's march on Rome initiated the *era fascista* in 1922, Hitler's *Mein Kampf* was published in 1925, and Rosenberg's *Der Mythus des 20. Jahrhundert* in 1930. Pound encountered Nietzsche and Wagner within the ambience of the occult rather than of nazism.

Granting the mercurial nature of Nietzscheanism, there are still some constants in his thought, and one of them is the perception that art and vision are in touch with the noumenal. The competing disciplines – science, scholarship, theology, and even philosophy – are deemed to be Apollonian and "Socratic." They are seen to traffic in illusion, in power, in ideological hegemony, and in oppression. The political counterpart of Socratism is Alexandrianism. Nietzsche in his later thought, like postmodernism, draws the relativistic corollary: if the fictional and factitious mode of art is the supreme mode of knowledge, there can be no truth, but only various fictions or perspectives.

In *The Birth of Tragedy*, Nietzsche sounded much more like a proponent of Perennial Philosophy or a theosophist. And that is what one would expect, given the provenance of his early thought in Wagner, Creuzer, and Schopenhauer. All three deny the possibility of reasoning one's way to truth and affirm a higher reality, the knowledge of which is vouchsafed only in revelation or mystic gnosis:

To our humiliation *and* exaltation, one thing above all must be clear to us. The entire comedy of art is neither performed for our betterment or education nor are we the true authors of this art world. On the contrary we may assume that we are merely images and artistic projections for the true author, and that we have our highest dignity in our significance as works of art – for it is only as an *aesthetic phenomenon* that existence and the world are eternally *justified* ... Only insofar as the genius in the act of artistic creation coalesces with this primordial artist of the world, does he know anything of the eternal essence of art; for in this state he is, in a marvellous manner, like the weird image of the fairy tale which can turn its eyes at will and behold itself; he is at once subject and object, at once poet, actor, and spectator. (*Birth of Tragedy*, s5)

This Wagnerian (almost Hindu) Nietzsche was warmly received by the aesthetic sensibility schooled in Pater, Wilde, and Emerson that was then dominant in Britain and America. That it should do so is not so very surprising, for the roots of the early Nietzsche in German idealism and Christian pietism (Nietzsche 1961, 27–9) are shared by Pater and Wilde, and Pater shares a Creuzerian input via K.O. Müller. The Eastern mysticism that Nietzsche found in Schopenhauer, and the late Herderian *volkisch* Romanticism he found in Wagner, are also features of the Emersonian and Whitmanian *paideuma* very familiar to Pound as to every educated American of the period. Moreover, Nietzsche himself was an admiring reader of Emerson, as well as of Shelley (Nietzsche 1974, translator's introduction to "Gay Science," 7–13).

So far as the *literary* history of Modernism is concerned, the impact of the mystical, mythic, and nonsceptical Nietzsche – the Wagnerian Nietzsche – was felt primarily in the vogue for mythopoeia. The practice of mythopoeia has been thought to be almost definitional for literary modernism but, as I argued above, has been misattributed to the influence of Sir James Frazer, even though the aura of sanctity with which literary modernism, Jungianism, and myth criticism surround myth is not found in Frazer. It *is* found in Creuzer, in Nietzsche, and in Wagner.

Although the importance of Schelling and Coleridge for the modernist conception of myth cannot be discounted, their influence was systematically occluded in order to preserve the isolation of modernism from Romanticism – an isolation that was an important element in modernist polemical rhetoric. The same mythopoeic tradition contributed importantly to Freud's psychoanalytic theories, but Freud was vigilantly hostile to all forms of mysticism and transcendentalism. As is well known, he broke with Jung on precisely this point.

Without doubt *The Birth of Tragedy* is the most influential theoretical formulation of Wagnerian mythopoeia. As it happened, its publication in 1872 coincided with an efflorescence of interest in myth quite independent of any Nietzschean, Wagnerian, or occult influence. An important component of this effloresence was E.B. Tylor's landmark study, *Primitive Culture* (1871). Tylor's study was resolutely positivistic in motive as in method. Nietzsche targeted the Alexandrian techniques of Tylor and Frazer (though he never mentioned them so far as I know) as just those which his "genuine" scholarship must overcome. "Our whole modern world," he wrote "is entangled in the net of Alexandrian culture. It proposes as its ideal the theoretical man equipped with the greatest forces of knowledge, and labouring in the service of science, whose archetype and progenitor is Socrates" (*Birth of Tragedy*, s18). He defines Socratism as the nefarious creed "whose supreme law reads roughly as follows: 'To be beautiful everything must be intelligible.' That law is said to be the corollary of the Socratic dictum, 'Knowledge is virtue'" (s12).

Such sentiments naturally found a ready audience among the occult. And as we have seen, they were adopted by the supposed Frazerian, Jane Harrison, who described herself in the preface to the second edition of *Themis* as a "disciple of Nietzsche." Her remarks in the preface to the first edition (1911) certainly bear her out, while at the same time bringing Henri Bergson and William James – prominent members of the Society for Psychical Research – into what we might regard as the Nietzschean vortex:

When four years ago I read his [Bergson's] *L'Evolution Créatrice*, I saw dimly at first, but with ever increasing clearness, how deep was the gulf between Dionysos the mystery-god and that Olympos he might never really enter. I knew the reason of my own profound discontent. I saw in a word that Dionysos with every other mystery-god, was an instinctive attempt to express what Professor Bergson calls *durée*, that life which is one, indivisible and yet ceaselessly changing. I saw on the other hand that the Olympians, amid all their atmosphere of romance and all their redeeming vices, were really creations of what Professor William James called "monarchical deism." Such deities are not an instinctive expression, but a late and conscious representation, a work of analysis, of reflection and intelligence. (xii)

Harrison, and her fellow Cambridge anthropologist F.M. Cornford followed Nietzsche's lead and sought the irrational and mystical in myth where Nietzsche said it was to be found. Cornford's belief that in myth one could find the expression of "the unity of all life, the kinship of all living things" (Guthrie 1967, viii) echoes Nietzsche's remark in *The Birth of Tragedy* that "myth wants to be experienced vividly as a unique example of a universality and truth that gaze into the infinite" (s17). Nietzsche's, Harrison's, and Cornford's interest in myth as a repository of divine revelation is entirely in conformity with the theosophists and entirely out of step with the positivistic motivations of Tylor and Frazer. Nietzsche's pious reverence for myth cannot be doubted: "He who recalls the immediate consequences of this restlessly progressing spirit of science will realize at once that *myth* was annihilated by it, and that because of this annihilation, poetry was driven like a homeless being from her natural ideal soil" (*Birth of Tragedy*, s17; Nietzsche's emphasis).

Despite what might be a latent esotericism, Harrison and Cornford maintained that they were carrying forward the positive inquiry into religion and myth begun by Tylor and Frazer. Harrison even lists a set of positivistic interpretive principles as her own "heresies" – that is, revisionist views – which had come to be accepted as "ortho-doxies" by the date of the preface to the second edition of *Themis*, (1925). There are four of them: "that gods and religious ideas gen-erally reflect the social activities of the worshipper; that the food-supply is of primary importance for religion; that the *daimon* precedes the full-blown god; that the Great Mother is prior to the masculine divinities" (ix). Only the third and fourth of these sound at all "occult" or "mystical," and only if we take her to be speaking literally of *daimons*, gods, and goddesses.

The deflections of Romanticism achieved by *The Birth of Tragedy* located the imaginative impulse in the historical past, rather than in the personal past where Romanticism had placed it, and articulated a new corporate myth of the Fall by placing it within secular history – at the very beginning of Western history. For Nietzsche, the fall from grace occurs with Socrates, who introduced the "dialectical desire for knowledge and the optimism of science" (s17). This Socratic ethos Nietzsche believed inimical both to music and to myth.

For clarity, we should remind ourselves that at this early stage of his career, Nietzsche did not set the Dionysian against the Apollonian in permanent Manichean opposition. Rather, they were antithetical players in an Hegelian dialectic. Dionysus was described as the god of ecstasy and transport, and hence of music, while Apollo was described as the god of conscious illusion, and hence of poetry and sculpture. Nietzsche's argument is that these two antithetical divinities produced the synthesis of the tragic drama, which combined music, dance, poetry, and spectacle. In *The Birth of Tragedy* death and evil were attached to Socratic culture and Alexandrian politics rather than to Apollonian religion, as was later the case.

Jane Harrison understood Nietzsche's fundamental perception to be that myth belongs to the history of prophecy. Competing formulations attached myth to political history (masonic and secret history) or to the history of religion (Creuzer and Renan) or to literary history (philology) or to the history of natural science (Tylor), or even to the history of philosophy (the later Nietzsche). The history of prophecy must be understood as a history of revelation. Myth on this view cannot be reduced – either to superstition or to political ideology, and still less to linguistic corruption (as Max Müller argues). On this view, religions are regarded as merely the etiolated and ossified remnants of a revelation that is eternally available to prophets, visionaries, ecstatics, and artists. Such a view was held by some Romantic poets as well, notably William Blake.

Nietzsche found a special case of this view – that all world myths are exoteric formulations of a single universal revelation – in Creuzer's *Symbolik und Mythologie* (1810–12) and in K.O. Müller's *Die Dorier*, a revisionist application of Creuzer. Nietzsche is an important conduit for these Creuzerian ideas to *Symbolisme*, aestheticism, archaeology, and anthropology. Modern mythopoeia is the heir of this tradition whose history is both complex and largely unexamined. We have already brought Ernest Renan to bear witness to the importance of Creuzer to the study of myth. Let me quote again from his 1853 review of Guigniaut's translation of *Symbolik und Mythologie*:

It was like a revelation, a grand lesson, to see, for the first time, united in a scientific pantheon, all the gods of humanity – Indian, Egyptian, Persian, Phoenician, Etruscan, Greek, Roman. The sustained elevation, the religious and profound tone, the perception of the higher destinies of humanity, which breathe throughout this book, announced that a great revolution had been accomplished, and that to an irreligious age – because it was exclusively analytic – there was about to succeed a better school, reconciled by synthesis, with human nature in its entirety. The Neo-platonist spirit of Plotinus, of Porphyry and of Proculs seemed to revive in that grand and philosophical manner of hearing a doctor in Christian theology proclaim that paganism could supply the most profound needs of the mind, and to grant an amnesty to those intelligences which, at the last hour, sought to revive in their bosoms those deities which had almost fled from them. (9–10)

None of Creuzer's followers adopted either of his leading hypotheses – that the Christian revelation fulfilled all previous myths, and that myths were deliberate concoctions of a priestly caste so as to convey divine truth in a veiled form to an ignorant and crass populace. Creuzer was still a child of the Enlightenment and saw himself as describing the *progress* of religion through a slow advance in the capacity of ordinary people to receive directly a revelation that had been preserved in the secret codes of mythology from antiquity by a priestly caste. Christianity represented for him the latest stage of religious history where the divine revelation was open to all. In effect, although the great reviver of pagan myth, he was, after all, an early contributor to the demythologization of religion.

Thus, despite his own theories and motivations, Creuzer has to be credited with reviving the *religious* relevance and sanctity of the pagan revelation that the Christian Fathers had attributed to the Devil. Theosophy entirely agreed with Creuzer's hypothesis of a single revelation, and also with his exoteric/esoteric hermeneutic, as did Yeats. In his edition of Blake, Yeats succinctly articulates the occult understanding of myth and revelation:

The religions of all nations are derived from each nation's different reception of the poetic genius which is everywhere called the Spirit of Prophesy. This poetic genius or central mood in all things is that which creates all by affinity – worlds no less than religions and philosophies. First, a bodiless mood, and then a surging thought, and last a thing. This triad is universal in mysticism, and corresponds to Father, Son, and Holy Spirit. In Swedenborg it is divided under the names celestial, spiritual, and natural degrees; in the Kabala as Neschamah, Ruach and Nesphesch, or universal, particular and concrete life. In Theosophical mysticism we hear of the triple logos – the unmanifest eternal, the manifest eternal, and the manifest temporal; and in Blake we will discover it under many names, and trace the histories of the many symbolic rulers who govern its various subdivisions. (Yeats and Ellis 1893, 1:241)

As this remark makes clear, the synopticism of the occult was far more vigorous and hegemonic than anything scholarship would countenance. Archaeologists, philologists, and religious historians, such as K.O. Müller, Nietzsche, Renan, and Mircea Eliade, discarded the single revelation hypothesis and the exoteric/esoteric herme-neutic, but accepted the perception that myths belong to the history of religion rather than to political, linguistic, literary, scientific, or tribal history, as the positivistic heirs of the Enlightenment tended to argue. In reclaiming the myths of the pagan world for historians of religion, Creuzer also made them available for visionary poets. Unlike Blake, Walt Whitman, and even Yeats, Pound was not obliged to invent his own myths; he could merely adopt, and where necessary adapt, the pagan myths that were now resanctified and relieved of the curse that Wordsworth had placed upon the Augustan decorative reliance on them.

Nietzsche, then, is not the fountainhead of the "modern" understanding of myth as a symbolic revelation, as mythopoeia. Friedrich Creuzer preceded him by more than fifty years. In addition to arguing that myths were the religious texts of the Greeks, Creuzer maintained that the myths were concocted by alien (he thought Egyptian) priests to make their advanced religion palatable to the native Pelasgians of the Peloponnesus. K.O. Müller altered the latter argument slightly by proposing in *Die Dorier* that Apollo was an alien god brought to Greece by the Dorians, thereby displacing the chthonic and ecstatic gods of the Dorians. Müller's revision of Creuzer led Nietzsche to his famous bifurcation of the Greek revelation into an ecstatic Dionysian cult and a rational Apollonian cult, and also inspired his epochal understanding of European history as a series of intellectual and political hegemonies.

Creuzer's *Symbolik* was a source book for the nineteenth-century occult, much as Frazer's *Golden Bough* was for Eliot, Pound, and the other modernists. His work even contributed to Blavatsky's Theosophy. Alexander Wilder, an American occultist who contributed importantly to Blavatsky's *Isis Unveiled*, was an enthusiastic reader of Creuzer (Williams 1946, 123–5). Carl Jung reports discovering Creuzer in about 1909 and reading him "with feverish interest" (Jung 1961, 162). Wagner knew Creuzer's *Symbolik* from his school days and set Nietzsche to read him and K.O. Müller as research for *The Birth of Tragedy*. Wagner still had a copy of *Symbolik* in his library on his death (Westernhagen 1978, 1:20, 2:411–12). Edouard Schuré read Creuzer in Guigniaut's translation in his youth and remembered its impact in his autobiography: "In the end, the myth of the two Great Goddesses [the Eleusinian divinities, Demeter and Persephone] were for me a marvellous symbol of the human soul, of its descent into the lower world, and of its resurrection into the bosom of the heavenly light" (Schuré 1928, 23; my translation).

In contrast to Schuré and Mead, Nietzsche rejects Creuzer's synoptic Christianity and takes from Creuzer only the resacralization of myth and the bifurcation of Greek religion into chthonic and celestial components. Creuzer also distinguised two types of revelation – intuitive and discursive. The intuitive was manifest in symbol, myth, icon (i.e., picture), and number (i.e., music), and was most fully developed in the Eleusinian rites. The discursive type was manifest in prophecy and science, and was most fully developed in the Delphic oracle and in philosophy (Münch 1976, 78–9; Andler 1958, 1:403–9). Although this division is not quite Nietzsche's, it achieves a similar bifurcation of the Greek *paideia* into an imaginative or intuitive realm and a rational or scientific one. Müller's attribution of the mythic to the indigenous Pelasgians, and of the prophetic and scientific to the invading Hellenes and their god Apollo, is much closer to Nietzsche's pair of Dionysian ecstasy and Apollonian illusion.

The idea most firmly identified with *The Birth of Tragedy* – that Greek myth represents the survival of an ancient and primitive relig- ious awareness or wisdom, and that this wisdom was unhappily supplanted by philosophy – is taken from Creuzer (Andler 1958, 1:405). Nietzsche's claim that Wagner's musical drama could restore this ancient wisdom comes, of course, from Wagner himself. Nietzsche's later sceptical messianism of *Thus Spake Zarathustra* remains Creuzerian in important respects, but – like Wagner and unlike Creuzer – is thoroughly millenarian and future-oriented, with hints of katabatic and palingenetic cultic provenance, as the closing paragraph of part 1 indicates:

And this is the great noontide: it is when man stands at the middle of this course between animal and Superman and celebrates his journey to the evening as his highest hope: for it is the journey to a new morning.

Then man, going under, will bless himself; for he will be going over to Superman; and the sun of his knowledge will stand at noontide.

"All gods are dead: now we want the Superman to live" – let this be our last will one day at the great noontide! (Nietzsche's emphasis)

Nietzsche's distinction between Apollo and Dionysus derives from Müller's refinement of Creuzer in *Die Dorier* to the effect that Apollo was brought to Greece by the Hellenic invaders and largely sup- planted the chthonic Pelasgian, except for its survival at Eleusis. Müller, explicitly correcting Creuzer, sought to preserve the ration- ality of the Greeks and hence their status as the *fons et erigo* of Enlightenment culture. Nietzsche – more faithful to Creuzer than to Müller – identified Apollonian rationality with the beginnings of Socratism and hence with the loss of a primeval revelation or wisdom (Andler 1958, 2:403–15). Creuzer's impact on Nietzsche was neither shallow nor short-lived. It is still reflected in *Zarathustra* (Andler 1958, 1:415; Janz 1978, 1:316, 2:230).

Creuzer contributed to the development of the Romantic theory of the symbol. He understood it as a sign that participates somehow in that which it signifies, and is therefore revelatory. As Münch puts it, "Since the link between the sign and signified is 'original and divine,' the symbol is by far the first of the figures or images. Thus, philology also reveals an important characteristic of the symbol: it reveals instantly the truth that it expresses. According to this new definition: 'Every sign or word which, confirming the truth of a revelation or a dogma, gives immediately a complete certainty is also a *symbolon'"* (Münch 1976, 79; my translation). For Creuzer, these "natural" signs and myths were fixed and unalterable. In this respect, he conforms to the cryptological hermeneutic of the Hellenic period as practised by Plutarch and the Neoplatonists. He argued that the priestly caste preserved encrypted texts and protected them from corruption by the profane, and added to Hellenic cryptology the Romantic principle of metaphoric resemblance. Creuzer's understanding of symbol was much more occult than that of his English Romantic contemporaries – Coleridge, Keats, and Shelley – who understood symbols as essentially *figures*; that is, metaphors and similes freely invented by poets and comprehensible to all.

Creuzer, more Hegelian than Kantian, believed that early men were closer to God and possessed "a power of sensing and understanding everything in a 'magnetic' manner" of which "popular mythology is only a pale disguise" (Guigniaut 1825, 3:835, 833; my translation). Guigniaut, Creuzer's French interpreter and translator, finds this claim too strong and dissociates himself from it; but, of course, it is not too strong for his occult readers, who echo Creuzer's belief that "the gods themselves have formed the first formulas for the worship of men with their own powerful hands, they themselves were the founders of their own cults; they descended onto the earth to instruct mortals" (Guigniaut 1825, 1:11; my translation).

Pound's understanding of symbol as conveyed to his fiancé Dorothy Shakespear in a letter written at Stone Cottage, 14 January 1914, is similar to Creuzer's. Dorothy had spoken in a previous letter of studying *Symbolisme*. Pound asks if she means "real symbolism" and lists Cabala, which he characterizes as the "genesis of symbols," "picture language," or "the aesthetic (symbology) symbolism of Villiers de l'Isle Adam ... that Arthur Symons wrote a book about." Pound goes on, in an even more Creuzerian manner, to complain of dictionaries of symbols as "immoral" because a superficial knowledge of the meaning of symbols weakens "the power of receiving an energized symbol" (Pound 1984).

It is very probable, however, that Pound's view is informed more by Swedenborg than by Creuzer, for he and Yeats were reading Swedenborg that winter at Coleman Hatch. Yeats's essay "Swedenborg,

Mediums, and the Desolate Places" registers his attempt to consolidate Swedenborg, Blake, spiritualism, theosophy, and the Japanese Noh drama, which he and Pound were translating into a single theory of visionary symbolism. He begins with Swedenborg's account of the after-death experience. The soul then "lives a life so like that of the world that it may not even believe that it has died, for 'when what is spiritual touches and sees what is spiritual the effect is the same as when what is natural touches what is natural'" (Yeats [1938] 1961, 6).

It is Yeats's explanation for this phenomenon that accounts for the power of symbol. He tells us that "this earth-resembling life is the creation of the image-making power of the mind, plucked naked from the body, and mainly of the images of the memory." These images constitute a kind of purgatory in that they "draw forth all the past, and make us live again all our transgressions." But, eventually, "another impulse comes and goes," which could be characterized as paradisal. It is, he says, "a preparation for the spiritual abyss, for out of the celestial world, immediately beyond the world of form, fall certain seeds as it were that exfoliate through us into forms, elaborate scenes, buildings, alterations of form that are related by 'correspondence' or 'signature' to celestial incomprehensible realities" (6–7). This "descent" of celestial forms into the mind of the "ascending" soul after death is the paradigm for vision and the explanation of the esoteric symbol.

"Canto One," written at the same time as Yeats's essay, promises a poem written out of just such visionary experience:

I have but smelt this life, a whiff of it –
The box of scented wood
Recalls cathedrals. And shall I claim:
Confuse my own phantastikon,
Or say the filmy shell that circumscribes me
Contains the actual sun;
                              confuse the thing I see
With actual gods behind me? (Pound 1990, 234)

It is not entirely clear if the questions are rhetorical or are genuine expressions of uncertainty. This unclarity reflects an endemic ambivalence towards the occult materials with which Pound was working in his poetry of this period. But despite that ambivalence, this Swedenborgian understanding of the *au delà* and its manifestation through the symolizing capacity of art is consistent throughout Pound's career. It stands behind these lines in the *The Pisan Cantos*, which follow a bleaker question: "Nux animae? / is there a blacker or was it merely San Juan with a belly ache writing ad posteros / in short shall we look for a deeper or is this the bottom?" St John of the Cross's vision stands synecdochically for all dark nights of the soul, that bleak time of despair that necessarily precedes beatific vision – although not necessarily followed by such vision. Pound's vision in *The Pisan Cantos* is just such a memorious catalogue of all the past as Yeats described in 1914:

> Le Paradis n'est pas artificiel
>   but spezzato apparently
>   it exists only in fragments unexpected excellent sausage,
>   the smell of mint, for example,
>   Ladro the night cat;
> at Nemi waited on the slope above the lake sunken in the pocket of hills
> awaiting decision from the old lunch cabin built out over the shingle,
> Zarathustra, now desuete
> to Jupiter and to Hermes where now is the castellaro
>   no vestige save in the air
> in stone is no imprint and the grey walls of no era. (canto 74, 438)

"Le Paradis n'est pas artificiel" – through its allusion to Baudelaire's famous study of the inspirational power of hashish, *Les Paradis artificiel* – denies that vision is merely a product of pharmacological stimulus; instead, it is "broken" (*spezzato*) and embedded in the world in a Swedenborgian manner. Nemi is a recollection of Frazer's *Golden Bough*, which explains that the priest of Artemis at Nemi must keep a constant vigil "with drawn sword," – as Pound has it in canto 77 (467) – because he will be succeeded by his murderer. The old gods, Zarathustra, Jupiter, and Hermes have left us. We have only the broken castles (*castellaro*) and other "grey walls" to remind us.

The French phrase is repeated six times in *The Pisan Cantos*. The next two are close together in canto 76 (460): "Le Paradis n'est pas artificiel / States of mind are inexplicable to us." And "Le paradis n'est pas artificiel, / l'enfer non plus." Pound cites the phrase twice in canto 87 (468), juxtaposing it with invocations of Aphrodite (as Cythera) and of Cadmus's sowing of the dragon's teeth that grew out of the earth as men – a reference to katabasis, or descent and resurrection, a motif worked pretty hard in subsequent cantos. The final appearance of the phrase (canto 83, 528–9) links it to Yeats in a cryptic allusion to his theories of symbol:

> Le Paradis n'est pas artificiel
> and Uncle William dawdling around Notre Dame

in search of whatever
            paused to admire the symbol
with Notre Dame standing inside it
Whereas in St Etienne
            or why not Dei Miracoli:
mermaids, that carving.

Pound scholiasts all read these lines as indicative of Pound's rejection of Yeatsian vague symbolism in favour of a more hard, clear, imagistic rhetoric. However, the passage occurs in a canto celebrating church architecture as an authentic manifestation of vision. There is no warrant for supposing that Yeats is being mocked, except for that puzzling "whereas." It is not entirely clear in canto 83 just what Yeats was admiring, but fortunately Pound returns to the recollection in canto 113 (788–9):

That the body is inside the soul –
            the lifting and folding brightness
            the darkness shattered,
                  the fragment.
That Yeats noted the symbol over that portico
                              (Paris).

The "symbol" is the statue of the Virgin Mary over the door of the church. Notre Dame stands "inside" the symbol esoterically. The symbol is "outside" because it is the soul, the essence, not the matter, or accident. Mead and theosophy believed that "the body is inside the soul" and not the other way round as dualistic Christianity believes. Pound inscribes this perception in canto 83 in a tag from Scotus Erigena: "lux enim / ignis est accidens" ("light is an attribute of fire"). The esoteric meaning is that it is the power or energy that is fundamental, not the manifest appearance. The symbol is the power itself, not its manifestation. Hence, Notre Dame stands "inside" the Virgin's effigy, for it is she, not the church, that is authentic and essential.

A passage in Upward's *New Word* (1914) that is heavily underlined in Pound's copy at the Humanities Research Center in Austin confirms such a reading. Upward cites the famous lines from Shelley's Adonais," "Life, like a dome of many-coloured glass / Stains the white radiance of eternity," and comments:

So does the stained-glass window of the church debar our vision of the sun; so is the Winged Figure it reveals, a false likeness of the Man Outside. Until that is learnt, nothing is truly learnt about God.

God is the right name of that Figure of the painted window, a Figure made by men's hands, however honourably and beautifully; and whosoever confounds it with That of which it is the symbol is the heretic of the True Church.

It is not the business of the Idealist to break the painted window, but rather to make it. (236)

(Pound has marked the last two paragraphs but not the first.) The "painted window" stands metonymically for the work of art. It transforms the appearance on the ordinary man outside the window into a winged figure. That "false likeness," the Figure produced by the window, is God, "a Figure made by men's hands." But instead of iconaclastically abjuring this man-made God – as Nietzsche does – Upward asserts that it is the business of "the Idealist" to make such illusions, "symbols" not to be confounded with "that of which it is the symbol."

Obviously, these ideas about the *au delà* and about symbol have a provenance so tangled that no single study can disentangle it. Nonetheless, it is worth pursuing the career of Creuzer's symbolic and cryptological theory of the meaning of pagan symbol and myth. (Born in 1771, he died in 1858.) Even though his fame did not cross the channel (*Symbolik* has never been translated into English), his influence reached Pater through K.O. Müller, and Nietzsche conveyed it to a later generation of English readers. Such modern students of myth and religion as Mircea Eliade and the Jungian, Karl Kerényi, are his heirs. The bolder Joseph Campbell's theory of the monomyth is very much a revision in the light of ethnological information of Creuzer's main hypothesis that a single divine revelation was disseminated throughout the world. Campbell does not acknowledge his filiation with Creuzer, but he does acknowledge Wilhelm Wundt, Creuzer's successor at Heidelberg (Campbell 1976, 16; Münch 1976, 16); (for Creuzer's influence on French literary figures, see Sohnle 1972).

Andler's summary of Creuzer's basic ideas reveals sharply their similarity to the occult version of religious history that we have been sketching, except that it assigns to the priesthood what the occult would assign to initiates: "The *Symbolik* of Creuzer argues that the history of all literatures is completely dominated by priestly castes. All literary emotion derives from sacred experience. All literary forms derive from rituals where this experience is gathered and by means of which it is propagated. Only the priesthood is intellectually creative. It invents and maintains the symbols that conceal a gnosis, that is to say, a knowledge of the final secrets of the birth of the gods and of the world. In the beginning priests were kings" (Andler 1958, 1:404; my translation). In Pound's version of this story, artists replace both priests and initiates. Like Creuzer's priests, the artistic community is intellectually creative, inventing the symbols and images out of which religions, cultures, and civilizations are crafted by lesser mortals.

Of course, the metaphysical or noumenal approach to myth divides into a number of distinct streams according to the approach adopted and the focus selected. Creuzerians accord a special status to Eleusis and tend to adopt a cryptological hermeneutic of symbolic icon or image. There is an occult linguistic line of mythography as well, descending from Fabre d'Olivet, a contemporary of Creuzer's. The Wagnerians focus on the Grail literature and music. The Nietzscheans and Wagnerians overlap. Dionysius and ecstasy are the touchstones of the Nietzscheans. With the exception of Mead, the Blavatskians are not much interested in myth but – reflecting their spiritualist origin – focus on psychic phenomena. This rainbow character of myth studies makes it possible to affirm or deny almost any affiliation of views imaginable.

Pound certainly has no interest in Blavatskian phenomena or in Wagnerian/Dionysian ecstasy. But he does adopt Creuzer's privileging of Eleusis, and also a Creuzerian cryptological hermeneutic. Although he adopts Rossetti's theory of a secret medieval tradition filtered through Péladan's Wagnerian reading of Rossetti, Pound adopts very little from Wagner. Pound's enthusiasm for the Chinese ideogram is directly attributable to Fenollosa, but he was exposed to Fabrean linguistic theories through Allen Upward – especially through *The New Word*, a work Pound read carefully and much admired. It was Upward who introduced Pound to Chinese language and literature, as Pound indicates in a letter to his mother of October 1913: "You'll find Giles 'Hist. of Chinese Literature' a very interesting book. Upward has sort of started me off in that direction. I have also embarked on a French translation of Confucius and Mencius" (Yale Coll. Mss 43, box 52, folder 1955).

Schuré, himself a Fabrean as well as a Creuzerian, had no doubt about the occult nature of Wagner's operas and his cultural theory. Schuré did not avoid the labels "occult" or "theosophical" in *Le Drame musicale* (the work upon which French Wagnerians depended for their knowledge of Wagner's thought and libretti): "Who could deny the transcendentally occult and theosophical character of the ideas that Wagner drew from a profound study of mythology and from his superior intuitive genius? These ideas are so much more remarkable in that they are opposed to the philosophy of Schopenhauer, which

Wagner had adopted as a speculative thinker ... For occult science and theosophy, there is nothing remarkable in such a pairing" (Schuré [1876] 1886, 83; my translation).

Synopticism has been an endemic characteristic of myth studies since the beginning with Euhemerus and Strabo – whether these studies were positivistic like Frazer's and Tylor's, psychological like Freud's and Jung's, literary like Northrop Frye's, anthropoligical like Lévy-Bruhl's and Lévi-Strauss's, or noumenal like Mircea Eliade's and Joseph Campbell's. Creuzer was neither idiosyncratic nor original in this respect. His diffusionism, his cryptological hermeneutic, and his Christianity were less acceptable features to those who followed him.

His Christianity manifested itself in the hypothesis of a single revelation traceable through Egyptian and Persian myths of soteria (that is, salvation through enlightenment), in Pelasgian (Eleusinian) and Mithraic palingenetic rites, and in the Christian Gospel story of redemption through Christ's death and rebirth (Christ's palingenesis) – a surrogate initiation for all humankind. Eleusis represented for Creuzer the highest development of pagan religious thought and practice, and he regarded it as a precursor of Christianity, whose rite of baptism preserved pagan palingenetic rites. And even though a committed Lutheran, Creuzer was sympathetic to Catholic Mariolatry as a survival of Eleusinian Demeter worship.

Nietzsche does not share Creuzer's admiration for Eleusis as the summation of pagan religion, perhaps because Creuzer assigned Eleusis the role of precursor of Christianity. Nietzsche, in contrast, reflects the implacable hostility towards Christianity of his first mentor, Arthur Schopenhauer. He replaces the Eleusinian rites with tragedy as the summation of the Greek *paideia* and assigns the origin of tragedy to the Dionysian as Aristotle did, rather than to the Eleusinian festivals as Creuzer did.

Pater reflects Creuzer's privileging of Eleusis in *Greek Studies* ([1895] 1910), devoting a chapter to the Eleusinian mysteries. Like Creuzer, he equates Demeter with Mary, as "our Lady of Sorrows, the *mater dolorosa* of the ancient world" (114). Pater did not read Creuzer (who has never been translated into English, as was mentioned above), but he did read K.O. Müller in translation. He follows Müller's Lessing-inspired choice of sculpture and the worship of Apollo as the ultimate expression of Greek genius, rather than Creuzer's choice of Eleusis and painting, or Nietzsche's choice of tragedy and music (187–269). Still, Pater's conclusion to the chapter on Eleusis could have come straight out of Creuzer and his struggle with his indefatigable euhemerist critic Johann Heinrich Voss:

The myth of Demeter and Persephone, then, illustrates the power of the Greek religion as a religion of pure ideas – of conceptions, which having no link on historical fact, yet, because they arose naturally out of the spirit of man, and embodied, in adequate symbols, his deepest thoughts concerning the conditions of his physical and spiritual life, maintained their hold through many changes, and are still not without a solemnising power even for the modern mind ... they may be a pledge to us ... of Greek religious poetry in general, of the poetry of all religions. (151)

If we try to trace the resacralization of pagan mythology to Nietz-sche – as is commonly done – the appearance of almost identical ideas in Pater at about the same time is puzzling and must be assigned to ideas "in the air," or to some *Zeitgeist*. Even though there undoubtedly was a great appetite for noumenal, metaphysical, or mystical insights within the aesthetic community at the turn of the century, appetites are not automatically satisfied. We can understand the phenomenon of modernism much better if we can discover just what intellectual food and drink met that appetite. The table was set not just with Nietzsche and Blake, but also with Creuzer, Sweden-borg, Blavatsky, Wagner, and many others. Pound was "grazing" at the banquet from his undergraduate years until in old age and ill health he ceased reading and writing.

When we recognize that Pound received ideas and attitudes similar to Nietzsche's from his reading of Balzac and Swedenborg back in Pennsylvania, and that he got Nietzsche second hand in London from Yeats, Mead, Upward, and Orage, the affinity of his prose and poetry with Nietzsche is hardly surprising. It is also important to recognize that Pound's involvement in occult mythography is far less eccentric than those who fear it – or those who celebrate it – imagine. Of course, the ubiquity of folly does not render it wisdom, but an individual's participation in a folly that is shared by many does not require recourse to pathology as an explanation.

Mead knew Continental philology well and was familiar with both Creuzer and Müller. Although he rarely cites Creuzer, he accepts the Creuzerian thesis, and he adumbrates it admirably in an endnote to "Notes on the Eleusinian Mysteries" (1898):

The earlier forms of the mystery-cultus were invariably attached to the most ancient form of religion known to the people of the land; the Eleusinia were no exception to this rule and though they underwent numerous modifications and partial blendings with other great mystery-cults, such as the Orphic, Bacchic, and perhaps even Isaic, they can be traced back to Graeco-Pelasgic forms, and so back to the pre-historic period, thousands of years B.C., of which the sole surviving tradition is preserved in the *Critias*, and the *Timaeus* of Plato, concerning the Atlantis legend. (147)

As the authority for these remarks, Mead refers not to Creuzer but to François Lenormant and J.D. Guigniaut. Lenormant was a French archaeologist, and Guigniaut was Creuzer's French translator. Rather oddly, Mead includes Creuzer's *Symbolik* in the bibliographical note at the end of the piece and comments (inaccurately): "Creuzer was a Doctor in Theology of the Roman Church and found symbolism everywhere." Mead adds a note claiming that Creuzer was "violently attacked by J.H. Voss, a zealous Protestant in an *Anti-Symbolik*."

Voss did indeed attack Creuzer, but as a translator of Homer, not as a Protestant. The long-running dispute between the two men was hermeneutic, not religious. Indeed, the dispute was the same as that between Pound and Valli. Voss insisted, on euhemeristic and Straboistic grounds, that pagan myths were merely allegories and were not symbolic carriers of esoteric and metaphysical truths as Creuzer argued – and as Mead also believed (Münch 1976, 111). However, Mead's understanding of Eleusis owes more to Gnosticism and theosophy than it does to Creuzer.

Péladan clearly reflects Creuzerian ideas, which he could have found in Edouard Schuré, whose work he certainly knew, or in Guigniaut's translation of *Symbolik*. Pound, then, need not ever have read any of Nietzsche to have imbibed the leading idea of *The Birth of Tragedy* that pre-Socratic Greek myth preserves a genuine archaic wisdom occluded by Socratism and its heir, Christianity.

However, Nietzsche did write *The Birth of Tragedy* and thereby reintroduced into the late nineteenth century an Hegelian dialectical version of Creuzer's symbolic reading of myth expressed in terms of sexual copulation. The opening sentences of *The Birth of Tragedy* set both its "argument" and its tone: "We shall have gained much for the science of aesthetics, once we perceive not merely by logical inference, but with the immediate certainty of vision, that the continuous development of art is bound up with the *Apollonian* and *Dionysian* duality – just as procreation depends on the duality of the sexes, involving perpetual strife with only periodically intervening reconciliations" (S1). It should be noted that, for Nietzsche, both Apollo and Dionysus are "art deities." The art of Apollo is sculpture (a detail he gets from Müller), and that of Dionysus is music (this detail is explicitly derived from Schopenhauer). "These two different tendencies," we are told, "run parallel to each other ... and continually incite each other to new and more powerful births." Eventually, "by a metaphysical miracle of the Hellenic 'will,' they appear coupled with each other, and through this coupling ultimately generate an equally Dionysian and Apollonian form of art – Attic tragedy" (s1). It is this account of the origin of tragedy that represents Nietzsche's original contribution to German classical philology. Niether then nor subsequently has it been well received by classical philologists.

Mead would have recognized Nietzsche's remarks as Gnostic. Mead, for example, wrote in *The Gnosis of the Mind* (1906): "In this Religion of the Mind there is no opposition of the heart and head. It is not a cult of intellect alone, it is not a cult of emotion alone; it is the Path of Devotion and Gnosis inseparably united, the true Sacred Marriage of Soul and Mind, of Life and Light, the ineffable union of God the Mother and God the Father in the Divine Man, the Logos, the Alone-Begotten of the Mystery of Mysteries, the All and One – Ineffability and Effability eternally in simultaneous Act and Passion" (14). Mead's prose is flabbier, his imagery more careless and conventional – but still copulative – and his point fuzzier. No doubt Nietzsche would have brushed aside such remarks as of no interest if he had come across them. My point is not that Nietzsche's discourse can be reduced to the level of Mead's theosophy, but rather that Nietzsche and Mead share a mind-set in which cognitive, religious, and cultural phenomena belong to a single realm and are described in terms of human sexuality: of attraction, coupling, pregnancy, and birth. That paradigm was shared by Nietzsche, Mead, Yeats, Remy de Gourmont, and Pound. Their disagreements – which were many – were fought out within this paradigm of a single European (or Aryan) revelation expressible in the dialectic of sexual procreative behaviour.

The copulative and palingenetic representations of initiation and revelation ubiquitous in Hermetic and Neoplatonic texts is strongly reflected in Nietzsche: "The *tragic* myth is to be understood only as a symbolization of Dionysian wisdom through Apollonian artifices. The myth leads the world of phenomena to its limits where it denies itself and seeks to flee back again into the womb of the true and only reality, where it then seems to commence its metaphysical swansong" (*Birth of Tragedy*, s22). By "myth" Nietzsche means the story or fable, an entity distinct from the inarticulate and nearly immaterial Dionysian music, as well as from the "Apollonian artifices" of dramatic representation. Although now standard in literary criticism, this understanding of myth as a symbolic story is an invention of the German *Aufklärung* – especially of Schiller, to whom both Creuzer and Nietzsche are indebted. *The Birth of Tragedy* and *Symbolik* played large, but distinct, roles in establishing that sense of myth. In the passage cited above, Nietzsche is labouring to establish just this honorific sense of "myth" and to assign this sense to the stories told in Greek tragedy. Nietzsche has revised Creuzer and Schiller along Hegelian lines by aligning myth – the narrative component of tragedy – with the high arts of sculpture and epic.

Creuzer had *contrasted* "primitive" myth and lyric to "advanced" sculpture and epic, but he inverted Enlightenment prejudices by making myth the primary art, albeit an arbitrary invention of a priestly class. Nietzsche is more Hegelian. He aligns myth and the language arts, along with dream and sculpture, as "material" arts in contrast to the "spiritual" art of music. Sculpture is seen to emphasizes materiality, while the epic attaches itself to the state and to the status quo. Music is Dionysian: passionate, spiritual, unsocial, and metaphysical. Although his argument is Hegelian, he cites Hegel's arch enemy, Schopenhauer, to press home the metaphysical nature of music (*Birth of Tragedy*, s16).

Myth is given the mediatory role that Creuzer assigns to it as symbol. It bridges the gap between material illusion (spectacle) and noumenal reality – most closely approached by music. The four characterizations of the Apollonian thus can be arranged hierarchically from the most material and fixed (sculpture) to the least material and most plastic (dream), with the poetry of the state (epic) and the poetry of religion (myth) disposed between them. The motivation of Nietzsche's analysis of Greek tragedy is to demonstrate the great superiority of Wagnerian musical drama over Italian opera and the theatre. Its superiority rests on the displacement of secular story with symbolic mythical story.

Nietzsche derives tragedy from the union of an intuitive, chthonic, and Dionysian impulse with a conscious, celestial, and Apollonian impulse. What emerges is the union of the three Apollonian representational modes – spectacle (sculpture), narrative (myth), and theatrical illusion (dream) – with Dionysian representational modes, music and dance:

In the total effect of tragedy, the Dionysian predominates once again. Tragedy closes with a sound which could never come from the realm of Apollonian art. And thus the Apollonian illusion reveals itself as what it really is – the veiling during the performance of the tragedy of the real Dionysian effect; but the latter is so powerful that it ends by forcing the Apollonian drama itself into a sphere where it begins to speak with Dionysian wisdom and even denies itself and its Apollonian visibility. Thus the intricate relation of the Apollonian and the Dionysian in tragedy may really be symbolized by a fraternal union of the two deities: Dionysus speaks the language of Apollo;

and Apollo, finally the language of Dionysus; and so the highest goal of tragedy and of all art is attained. (*Birth of Tragedy*, s21)

It is a little difficult to be sure what all of this means, but it seems to belong to the same realm of discourse that we have encountered in Mead and Yeats. Nietzsche's theory is more clearly ecstatic, however, than either of Pound's friends. Nietzsche imagines that the audience of the Greek drama fell into an ecstatic state and experienced a collective hallucination. For this reason he counts the stage spectacle as dream. But he is very obscure on the question of dream and hallucination. The following is as clear a brief passage as I can find: "We must understand Greek tragedy as the Dionysian chorus which ever anew discharges itself in an Apollonian world of images ... In several successive discharges this primal ground of tragedy radiates this vision of the drama which is by all means a dream apparition and to that extent epic in nature" (*Birth of Tragedy*, s8).

In effect, Nietzsche ratchets German thought about the rational and the intuitive up a notch. Lessing had identified the intuitive with the iconic, particularly with sculpture. Schelling identified the intuitive with the symbolic, whose model was poetry, a less material art than sculpture and painting, but still "concrete" in its referentiality. Nietzsche retreats one step further into the ineffable by assigning music the role that his predecessors had assigned to the visual arts or the language arts. His genius was to focus on the drama where iconic objects (actors, costumes, masks, and properties) combined with abstract symbolic objects (words) and abstract "sensual" objects (rhythm and pitch, that is, music). Nietzsche attached all of this to Wagner's musical drama, where the mundane purpose of the words and spectacle is to hold the sensitive soul down from a possibly fatal ecstasy: "I must appeal only to those who, immediately related to music, have in it, as it were, their motherly womb, and are related to things almost exclusively through unconscious musical relations. To these genuine musicians I direct the question whether they can imagine a human being who would be able to perceive the third act of *Tristan and Isolde*, without any aid of word and image, purely as a tremendous symphonic movement, without exploring in a spasmodic unharnessing of all the wings of the soul?" (*Birth of Tragedy*, s21). (Nietzsche's lapse into the imagery of copulation even here in this sublime moment seems almost pathological.)

Before turning to the Nietzschean and Wagnerian impact on European aestheticism and thence on literary modernism, it is instructive to turn once again to a leading modern theorist of myth, Carl Jung. Jung studied at Basel, where Nietzsche had taught and where there were still some professors "who had known Nietzsche personally and were able to retail all sorts of unflattering titbits about him" (Jung 1965, 101). Jung "was held back" from reading Nietzsche "by a secret fear that I might perhaps be like him." The similarity that Jung feared was that Nietzsche, like Jung himself, had perhaps had "inner experiences, insights which he had unfortunately been tempted to talk about." Nonetheless, Jung did read *Thoughts Out of Season* and *Thus Spake Zarathustra* and – as with his later reading of Creuzer – was "carried away by enthusiasm" (102). Like Creuzer and the theosophists, Jung believed in a single revelation, a single tradition of gnosis. He called it the *Aurea Catena*, the "Golden Chain," and thought that it "existed from the beginnings of philosophical alchemy and Gnosticism down to Nietzsche's *Zarathustra*. Unpopular, ambiguous, and dangerous, it is a voyage of discovery to the other pole of the world" (189). Although Jung's occultism is far more explicit than anything in Nietzsche, it was not fully revealed until the publication of his autobiography in 1965. Jung's influence on the literary world has been to perpetuate and even intensify the Creuzer-Nietzsche-Wagner perception of myth as the expression of a universal wisdom older, deeper, and darker than the merely rational and conscious mind could possibly fathom.

A recent symptom of the persistence of this tradition within literary scholarship is James Olney's *The Rhizome and the Flower: The Perennial Philosophy, Yeats and Jung* (1980). Olney acknowledges that Jung was ignorant of Yeats and that Yeats knew little of Jung (4–6), but he nonetheless produces a long study demonstrating "the similarities between Yeatsian poetics and Jungian psychology and ... that Perennial Philosophy that in ancient Greece spoke the language of the Pre-Socratics, Plato, and Platonism" (ix). Olney's "ahistorical" sense of the tradition is shared by Nietzsche and Jung – neither of whom locate the wisdom or gnosis in a specific historical tradition traceable in texts, rituals, or stories as the occult does. The avoidance of the historical fantasies of Barruel et al. by Nietzsche and Jung makes them much less open to contradiction than the masonic and occult fantasists. Nonetheless, this "ahistoricism" can blind one to boring historical information. Olney, for example, misses the data that Jung and Yeats were both enthusiastic readers of Nietzsche, that Nietzsche, Mead, and Jung all read Creuzer, and that Pater read K.O. Müller. Obviously, Creuzerian ideas reached Yeats through Pater as well as through Nietzsche and Mead. To trace this filiation, however, undermines the confirmatory force of a discovered identity of opinion or expression widely dispersed in the culture, a confirmation upon which the occult typically relies.

In "Psychology and Troubadours" – the most theosophical of all his works – Pound combined the Creuzerian hypothesis of a single, universal revelation with the occult notion of a secret tradition, in a much-cited but little-understood passage:

I believe in a sort of permanent basis in humanity, that is to say, I believe that Greek myth arose when someone having passed through delightful psychic experience tried to communicate it to others and found it necessary to screen himself from persecution. Speaking aesthetically, the myths are explications of mood: you may stop there or you may probe deeper. Certain it is that these myths are only intelligible in a vivid and glittering sense to those people to whom they occur. I know, I mean, one man who understands Persephone and Demeter, and one who understands the Laurel, and another who has, I should say, met Artemis. These things are for them *real*. (Pound [1929] 1953, 92)

Pound scholiasts have tended to interpret this passage as a meta-phorical, hyperbolic, or playful account of the literary imagination. But in the theosophical context in which they were pronounced, Pound's remarks could not have been understood as anything but a version of the Creuzer/Wagner/Nietzsche understanding of myth as a compendium of divine revelations. The added condition that the revelation be disguised in an exoteric form in order to avoid perse-cution is one of the two main doxologies in those circles – the secret history one of Barruel, Reghellini, and Rossetti.

Jung is just as confident as Creuzer, Blavatsky, Mead, Yeats, Pound, Campbell, Huxley, and Olney that there is a *single* tradition of wisdom or gnosis:

If for a moment we put away all European rationalism and transport ourselves into the clear mountain air of that solitary plateau, which drops off on one side into the broad continental prairies and on the other into the Pacific Ocean; if we also set aside our intimate knowledge of the world and exchange it for a horizon that seems immeasurable, and an ignorance of what lies beyond it, we will begin to achieve an inner comprehension of the Pueblo Indian's point of view. "All life comes from the mountain" is immediately convincing to him, and he is equally certain that he lives upon the roof of an immeasurable world, closest to God … The holiness of mountains, the revelation of Yahweh upon Sinai, the inspiration that Nietzsche was vouch-safed in the Engadine [that is, *Thus Spake Zarathustra*] – all speak the same language. (Jung 1965, 252–3)

EDOUARD SCHURÉ'S WAGNER

The occultist who first adopted Nietzschean ideas is Edouard Schuré, who is also the man who introduced Wagnerian musical drama to a wide French audience with his study *Le Drame musicale*, which was published in 1876, just four years after Nietzsche's *Birth of Tragedy*. There was a brief Wagner vogue in France following the performance of *Tannhäuser* in Paris in 1861, which prompted Baudelaire's "Richard Wagner et Tannhäuser à Paris" (Martin 1982, 3). Martin credits Catulle Mendès and Edouard Dujardin with being the prime movers of the French Wagnerian craze in the 1880s and completely misses Schuré (3–4, 8). Dujardin was the founder of *La Revue Wagnérienne*. Mendès published two influential articles on Wagner in that journal in 1885. But these events are nine years after the apperance of Schuré's book.

Schuré had obviously read *The Birth of Tragedy* before or during the composition of *Le Drame musicale*, but we know that he had read Creuzer long before. Moreover, he had seniority on Nietzsche as a Wagner enthusiast, having met Wagner in 1865, three years before Nietzsche did (Schuré 1904, 134; Hollinrake 1982, 123) and four years before Catulle Mendès, his wife Judith Gautier, and le Comte Villiers de l'Isle-Adam made their famous pilgrimage to Wagner (Martin 1982, 3–4). As it happens, Nietzsche met Wagner in the same year that Péladan made his pilgrimage to Bayreuth in the company of William Ritter – 1888 (Péladan [1894] 1981, xii). Péladan seems not to have been favoured with an introduction to Wagner, but he, too, wrote a Wagner book, *Le Théâtre complet de Wagner* (1894).

Schuré was about the same age as Nietzsche. (He was born in 1841; Nietzsche, in 1844.) Before his Wagner book, Schuré had made a reputation for himself with another musical study, *Histoire du lied* (1867), a work praised by Gaston Paris. Schuré's success as a music critic was not dependent on his occultism, but he made no effort to hide his occult views. Indeed, there was no reason to do so in *fin de siècle* France.

The most successful of Schure's many publications was *Les Grandes Initiés* (1889). It articulates the Creuzerian hypothesis of a single religious inspiration surviving from high antiquity and adds Fabre d'Olivet's hypothesis that the revelation is transmitted in the inspiration of "Higher" or Divine men. *Les Grands Initiés* was in its ninety-third edition in 1927, the last imprint during Schuré's life; it is still being reprinted in France today. Among its influential admirers were Stéphane Mallarmé and Paul Sérusier. Arthur Symons, who spent some months in Paris every year from 1889 to 1899, must have known of it, but he does not refer to it in anything I have read. However, the same or similar speculation can be found in Mead, Blavatsky, Creuzer, and Nietzsche. It is more important as a symptom of standard occult historiography of the period than as a likely source for any English-language author.

An instance of a feature shared among the occult and occuring in Nietzsche is the Higher Man. Schuré derives it from Fabre d'Olivet, but it is found in Balzac in a Swedenborgian form and in Bulwer-Lytton in a more fanciful quasi-Darwinian form. As we have seen, at about the same time as Schuré's study, Shaw and Yeats were both expressing Nietzschean versions of the Superman. Nietzsche himself may have derived it from Emerson, a reader of Swedenborg. A little later Upward and Orage were promulgating the idea of the Superman or Divine Man for a different audience. At about the same time, Maurice Bucke advanced his occult adaptation of Darwinian evolution to the requirements of a Higher Man. Nietzsche's Superman is a unique individual whose coming will change the world. By contrast, the occult Higher Man is always amongst us. He has been manifest in history by such figures as Dionysus, Orpheus, Buddha, and Christ. The Nietzschean Superman is much more like a Messiah: "You solitaries of today, you who have seceded from society, you shall one day be a people: from you, who have chosen out yourselves, shall a chosen people spring – and from this chosen people, the Superman" (*Zarathustra*, "Of the Bestowing Virtue," s2).

It is likely that Schuré was the avenue by which Creuzerian – and perhaps Wagnerian – ideas reached Péladan, for De Guaïta, an associate of Péladan's in the Ordre de la Rose-Croix, read Schuré's study and even wrote to him expressing his admiration for it (Schuré 1928, 223–5). In any event, *Origine et esthétique de la tragédie*, the second of the two books Pound reviewed in 1906, echoes Schuré and Nietzsche. Schuré's understanding of Wagner and myth was thus available to Pound as early as 1906 and may well have helped to formulate his theories of myth and cultural history. Schuré's "two principal ideas" were "the continuity of inspiration in world history, and the plurality of the soul's existences before and after this terrestrial life" (1928, 220). The first idea is shared by Creuzer and the occult. The second, reincarnation, is an ubiquitous – although by no means universal – belief within occultism, no doubt deriving from Hinduism. Both ideas are also found in the Blavatskian theosophy of Mead, Yeats, and Orage.

Schuré's *Drame musicale*, like *The Birth of Tragedy*, is dedicated to Wagner. Both books were written to explain and boost Wagner's new musical drama, and both men knew the composer, although Nietzsche was much closer to him than Schuré ever was. Indeed, *The Birth of Tragedy* might well be considered as a collaboration between Wagner and the young Nietzsche (see Andler 1958, 1:398ff; Nietzsche 1922, 35–8). Nietzsche's initial response to Wagner was not so different from that of the mystical Schuré and the French Wagnerians: "What I like about Wagner," Nietzsche wrote in 1868, "is what I like about Schopenhauer: the ethical air, the Faustian fragrance, cross, death, and tomb, etc." (Nietzsche 1967, note on p. 120).

Schuré follows Creuzer's valorization of myth and Wagner's attachment of the mythpoeic to music. "Whence comes," he asks, "the irresistible attraction which the primitive myth exercises over the poet's imagination?" The answer is that it comes from a "hidden correspondence between this kind of poetry and the genius of music" (Schuré 1876, 334). Schuré also praises Wagner for his choice of mythical material from the legends and myths of postclassical Europe: a sailor's legend in *The Flying Dutchman*, a German medieval legend in *Tannhäuser*, Celtic legends in *Lohengrin* and *Tristan*, and Nordic epic in the *Nibelung* (333). Schuré omits the Grail legend drawn upon in *Parsifal* only because that opera was still in the future in 1876, being first performed in 1882.

Nietzsche broke with Wagner before the efflorescence of Wagnerianism in France, leaving the field, as it were, to Schuré. The split came in 1878 when Wagner sent the libretto of *Parsifal* to Nietzsche and when Nietzsche sent Wagner a copy of *Human, All-Too-Human*. Nietzsche was disgusted with what he considered to be the Christian piety of *Parsifal*, and Wagner was offended at what he considered the Enlightenment scepticism of *Human, All-Too-Human*. Wagner attacked Nietzsche in the *Bayreuth Blätter*, and Nietzsche replied with *The Case of Wagner* (1888) (see Nietzsche 1967, 149; Hollinrake 1982, 123–4, 253).

Nietzsche's attack on Wagner in *The Case of Wagner* pretty well sets the tone for the modernist rejection of Wagnerian art as vague and bombastic. It also – rather surprisingly – anticipates Eliot's assessment of the modern world in his 1921 review of *Ulysses*. In the preface to *The Case of Wagner*, Nietzsche sarcastically characterizes Wagner as "a guide more initiated, a more eloquent prophet" of "the labyrinth of the modern soul" than any other artist whatever. Just because of his immersion in modernity, Nietzsche claims, "Wagner was unable to create from a totality; he had no choice, he had to make patchwork, 'motifs,' gestures, formulas, doing things double and even a hundredfold" (*Case of Wagner*, s10). In his attack on Wagner, Nietzsche is sitting on both sides of the fence as well as on the fence. For the Wagnerians, he is the theorist of the transcendence of art. For religious historians like Underhill and Cornford, he is the theorist of the transcendence of myth. For sceptics like Shaw, he is the prophet of scepticism and relativism.

Eliot seems not to have been much interested in Nietzsche. He did write a brief review of *The Philosophy of Nietzsche* by A. Wolf in 1915. The review is rather dismissive of Nietzsche, who is described as "one of those writers whose philosophy evaporates when detached from its literary qualities, and whose literature owes its charm not alone to the personality and wisdom of the man, but to a claim to scientific truth" (Eliot 1975, 426). This is hardly a flattering assessment, but neither is it very circumstantial.

While preparing for his Ph.D. examinations in philosophy, Eliot wrote to his mother (18 Nov. 1915) that he was "reading some of Nietzsche's works which I had not read before, and which I ought to read anyhow before my examinations" (Eliot 1988, 120). He does not reveal, anywhere else that I have found, which works he read or what he thought of them. There are a few other scattered references to Nietzsche – none of which indicate admiration; but neither do they indicate very strong antipathy. In "The Stoicism of Seneca" he describes Nietzsche as "the most conspicuous modern instance of cheering oneself up" (Eliot 1951, 132).

It seems unlikely that Eliot was influenced in this by Nietzsche; nonetheless, he does place all modern artists in much the same difficulty as that in which Nietzsche placed Wagner when he described contemporary history as "an immense panorama of futility and anarchy." He also praised Joyce for having discovered the mythical method – with the aid of psychology, Yeats, and Sir James Frazer. This method, Eliot mused, was a "step toward making the modern world possible for art" (Eliot 1975, 177–8). We are not accustomed to thinking of Joyce's art as Wagnerian, but the technique Eliot praises was hailed first in France by the Wagnerian, Edouard Dujardin, who – unlike Eliot – may very well have construed it as an application of Wagnerian mythopoeia and leitmotif to fiction.

In *The Case of Wagner*, Nietzsche vigorously disassociated himself from Wagner, and consequently from *The Birth of Tragedy*. He attributed all of his erstwhile Creuzerian "vagueness" to Wagner and the German soul:

Let us remember that Wagner was young at the time Hegel and Schelling seduced men's spirits; that he guessed, that he grasped with his very hands the only thing the Germans take seriously – "the idea," which is to say, something that is obscure, uncertain, full of intimations; that among Germans clarity is an objection, logic a refutation ... Hegel is a *taste*. And not merely a German but a European taste. A taste Wagner comprehended – to which he felt equal – which he immortalized. He merely applied it to music – he invented a style for himself charged with "infinite meaning" – he became the *heir of Hegel*. Music as "idea." (*Case of Wagner*, s10)

It is striking that Nietzsche substitutes Schelling for Creuzer, and Hegel for Schopenhauer. Creuzer and Schopenhauer are well known to be the proximate influences on Wagner, as well as on Nietzsche in *The Birth of Tragedy* – rather more than Schelling and Hegel. Nietzsche first read Schopenhauer in 1865, before he met Wagner and while he was still an undergraduate. Wagner had read him ten years earlier. According to Hollinrake (1982), it was their common admiration for Schopenhauer that drew the eminent composer and the young philologist together (61–2).

In the "Postcript" to *The Case of Wagner*, the author of *Thus Spake Zarathustra* and *The Genealogy of Morals* inveighs against Wagner's obscurity and decadence: "There is nothing weary, nothing decrepit, nothing fatal and hostile to life in matters of the spirit that his art does not secretly safeguard; it is the blackest obscurantism that he conceals in the ideal's shrouds of light. He flatters every nihilistic (Buddhistic) instinct and disguises it in music; he flatters everything Christian, every religious expression of decadence." These late estimates of Wagner by Nietzsche are the ones that have prevailed in avant-garde circles in this century. But these very circles retained a belief in the profundity of myth, now detached from Wagner, Nietzsche, Creuzer, and Schopenhauer, and patched it improbably onto Frazer. The Creuzerian legacy was first Gallicized in the poetry of Mallarmé, Rimbaud, and the *Symbolistes* – the very same influences that formulated the early poetry of T.S. Eliot. It was then Anglicized through a motivated misreading of Frazer's positivistic history of European religious superstition. Yeats, Pound, and Eliot read Frazer's study of myth as evidence of the continuity of the human soul with its archaic past, rather than as an account of the institutionalization of primitive superstition in political and religious institutions – which is what it plainly is. Paterian aestheticism in England and Emersonian transcendentalism in America were necessary to the success of such a program, which otherwise would have borne its occult provenance plainly on its face.

This said, it remains true that it is still not possible to arrive at a definitive assessment of the nature and extent of Wagner's influence on modernism. Wagner's reputation and influence – like Nietzsche's – became entangled in the progress of mystical German nationalism. The taboos against discussion of Wagner and Nietzsche were especially strong during the postwar period when literary modernism was being absorbed and civilized by the academy. An index of the resurgence of these taboos was the reissue of Max Nordau's *Degeneration* by Heinemann in 1913. The first English edition of 1895 had gone through eight printings before the year was out, but the vogue did not last. Thatcher (1970) says that Nordau's polemic damaged the English reception of Nietzsche for two generations (27–34). It is really only in the last three decades that Foucault, Derrida, and

DeMan have rehabilitated Nietzsche's reputation from its tainting by Nordau's criticism and then by the Nazis' adoption of Nietzsche as their philosopher. They have achieved this by attaching him to dialectical materialism. Wagner, however, still labours under the censures that Nietzsche applied to him – at least, so far as literary modernists are concerned.

In 1876, when Schuré's study, *Le Drame musicale*, was published, France was still recovering from the shock of her defeat at the hands of the Prussians. Mussolini, Hitler, and Franco were far in the future, but German nationalism and French patriotism had begun the confrontation that was to dominate the next seventy-five years of European history. Arguably, the anti-Alexandrian and Wagnerian Nietzsche of 1873 was as important a player in the ensuing confrontation as was the *echt* Alexandrian, Karl Marx. At least, he would be considered so if we were to construe those seventy-five years as the confrontation of the French Enlightenment rationalism with German Romantic idealism. Nietzsche – himself a proud veteran of the Franco-Prussian war – presented Wagner as the voice of the new German Reich (see "Attempt at Self Criticism" the 1886 preface to *Birth of Tragedy*, both in Nietzsche 1967).

However, it was Schuré, not Nietzsche, who informed the French about Wagner. Schuré's Wagner is not jingoistic like Nietzsche's. The latter calls upon Wagner to renovate and purify the "German spirit through the fire magic of music" (*Birth of Tragedy*, s20). Schuré's Wagner was perceived by the *Symbolistes* as a prophet of the new age, rather than as the harbinger of a Teutonic military, political, and cultural conquest of Europe. Wagner's attachment to Nietzsche's Teutonic "blond beast" gained currency in France and England only after 1893 with the publication of *Degeneration*, Nordau's unrestrained attack on Nietzsche and on the whole of nineteenth-century art. Interestingly, one of the earliest publishing ventures of Orage's journal was to reprint Shaw's essay of 1895, "On the Sanity of Art," as a small book (in 1908). The reissue of Shaw's rebuttal of Nordau did not have the desired effect, for *Degeneration* was reissued by Heinemann in 1913 (Thatcher 1970, 27–34).

Schuré's *Drame musicale* held the field in France as *the* Wagner book for almost twenty years prior to Nordau's attack. It contained a detailed discussion of each of Wagner's operas extant in 1876 as well as a Creuzerian cultural history and assessments of Nietzsche's still untranslated *Birth of Tragedy*. Following Creuzer, Schuré saw Greek tragedy as the expression of a "profound enthusiasm, the sacred awe of the old cults, and the sublime breath of the Mysteries [which was] the regenerator of the dithyrambic choir" (Schuré [1876] 1886, 318;

all quotations from Schuré are my translations from the original French). Greek theatre he described as "the efflorescence of a whole religion, the masterpiece of an harmonious civilization," in contrast to Shakespearean tragedy, which he saw as the "great flowering of the individual, his expansion in every direction" (323). In Greek tragedy "the human world emerged from the divine," while in Shakespearean tragedy "humanity was liberated to itself" (324). The former was the "ideal drama of myth," while the latter was the "drama of historical reality" (325).

Schuré's praise of Wagner – for the genius to find common stories, legends, and myths and to raise them to the level of high art comparable to Greek tragedy – is independent of Nietzsche: "The special genius of Richard Wagner consists in stripping the myth of the foreign coverings in which it has been successively reclothed by literature or the Church, and grasping it just when it surfaces from the imagination of the people with the imposing and inevitable character of a natural growth. Thus it retains its primitive grandeur, its original tincture; at the same time it knows how to appropriate the passions and feelings which are our own, because they are eternal, and subordinates it all to a philosophical idea" (334).

This galaxy of Creuzerian, occultist, Wagnerian, and Nietzschean speculation about myth and poetry enforces upon us the recognition that modernism cannot be characterized as secular and sceptical. However, this picture has been painted before. Early observers, such as Edmund Wilson in *Axel's Castle*, understood early modernism to be the heir of *Symbolisme* – as Yeats himself understood it. But this view was displaced by one in which the modernists presented themselves as sceptical relativists implacably hostile to the credulity and "romantic" mysticism of their immediate predecessors.

The central document in this story is *The Waste Land*. Both theoretically and stylistically, *The Waste Land* can be said to have formulated modernist poetry, but it did so through a deliberate misreading of the poem, and one that was perpetrated by its first reader, Ezra Pound. *The Waste Land*'s success was almost an accident, because it was read – and, indeed, advertised – as a technical achievement making poetry possible in an age of Nietzschean scepticism – without gods or sacred myths. That is to say, it was received as an expression of the peculiar moral and ethical impasse in which Europe found itself in the wake of World War I. The impasse was occasioned as much (if not more) by the loss of faith in progress as by the often-cited death of God. *The Waste Land* caught the postwar mood just right. Its mixture of *Symboliste* and Wagnerian religiosity with Nietzschean scepticism caught the mood of disillusionment felt by the generation that had come of age to be slaughtered in the trenches.

But one could just as reasonably read *The Waste Land* as the product of the half-century of resacralization of non-Christian mythology that preceded it. This alternative reading need not render the poem a credulous or occult document, but it would produce a poem more elegiac than satiric, more despairing than scornful, more mystical than sceptical. Instead of being seen as a sardonic celebration of Nietzschean relativism and scepticism, it would be seen as a lament for a lost certainty and dogma.

It has been difficult to detach modernism from relativism and scepticism, because of a well-founded scholarly phobia of the occult. Even though modernist preoccupation with myth has been impossible to ignore, "occultophobia" has dictated that it be attributed to academic anthropology, in particular to the positivism of Sir James Frazer, rather than to his more "metaphysical" successors, Jane Harrison and F.M. Cornford. The earlier, Continental view that Frazer displaced, represented by Creuzer and Renan, has been entirely ignored, as have the views of the occult, even though these are represented by Mead, Upward, Orage and Weston – all of whom were known to Yeats, Pound, and Eliot. The Wagnerian and occult inspiration for the resacralization of myth has largely been ignored by literary scholarship. Even Nietzsche's prominent and universally acknowledged role in the process has been slighted by scholarly construal of the "mythical method" as a rhetorical strategy.

Perhaps the phobia would not be so strong if literary scholarship was not so thoroughly committed to the historicism and organicism that has dominated European cultural theory since the late Enlightenment. If ideas come in the form of undecomposable unities variously labelled – as, for example, *Weltanschauungen*, *Zeitgeist*, paradigm, or "mind-set" – then it is intolerable to suggest that modernism has some affinities with the occult. It is intolerable because if one holds an organic theory of culture, such a suggestion must either elevate the occult or discredit modernism. And, in fact, scholarly attention to links between modernism and the occult has tended either to legitimize the occult or to debunk modernism.* However, if

---

* Examples of the former are too numerous to list, but Peter Makin's *Provence and Pound* is an example of such an approach applied to Pound. Kathleen Raine is a well-published occult reader of Yeats and Blake.

Debunking studies are much rarer. Cautious suggestions of possible filiations such as those found in John Senior's, *Way Down and Out* or Edward Hynes's *Edwardian Turn of Mind* are more common. Indignant exposés – such as Chace's *Political Identities of Ezra Pound and T.S. Eliot*, Bacigalupo's *Formèd Trace*, or Casillo's *Genealogy of Demons* – concentrate on errors of political ideology rather than metaphysical errors.

we suppose that an individual's beliefs, motives, and plans are a polyglot collection of capriciously acquired attitudes, opinions, and hopes, then we can permit silly ideas to co-exist with profound ones in the same author or *oeuvre*. At least, we would be able to if we agreed that such hierarchization of ideas were in principle possible.

The modernists and their nineteenth-century predecessors had no fear of hierarchization. Creuzer, Schuré, and Péladan all saw Catholic Christianity as the legitimate heir of a single divine revelation. In contrast, Nietzsche, who also believed in a single revelation, was unreservedly hostile towards Christianity. He tied Christianity to systematic science, and hence to Socratism. He has been followed in this equation by postmodernism, but not by modernism. Theosophists, together with Pater, Underhill, and Cornford, fell between these two extremes. Sharing Nietzsche's hostility to empirical science, they nonetheless did not equate science with Socratism (which is essentially equivalent to Heidegger's "ontotheology" or Derrida's "logocentrism"). Nor did they equate Socratism with Christianity – an equation that would have seemed as bizarre to them as to the modernists. However, there was a widespread tendency to equate Christianity with authority, dogma, and repression, and to equate Socratism with individualism, sceptical inquiry, and oppression. It is only very recently – with the rise of philosophical relativism – that Nietzsche's attachment of Christianity to science has been taken up in the English-speaking world. (For the equation of Christianity with science, see Derrida 1976. For the rise of philosophical relativism, see Rorty 1979. Rorty acknowledges his own Heideggerian inspiration but does not invoke Nietzsche. For a discussion of Nietzsche's relevance to current American relativism, see Nehemas 1985.)

Modernism's precursors, the aesthetes, shared Nietzsche's hostility towards science, but their attitude towards Christianity was more scornful than hostile, and they did not share Nietzsche's scepticism (except in the narrow sense that they were irreligious). Nietzschean sceptical relativism – that is, the view that all versions, all theories, and all descriptions are equally valid or invalid – was for them a problem to be confronted rather than an opportunity to be embraced. In fact, it would not be too much of a distortion to define aestheticism as the application to secular works of art of the piety that had been traditionally reserved for religious rituals and artifacts.

Scientific materialism was the principal antagonist of the aesthetes. Even though they were typically hostile towards Christianity, they were far from equating Christianity with science as Nietzsche and his followers tended to do. Science itself – particularly the new social sciences descending from Comte, Marx, and Weber, which took religion and myth as part of their subject – maintained the Enlightenment scorn of religion as nothing more than superstition. For these reasons it is inappropriate to take scepticism about Christianity or hostility towards it as a touchstone of scepticism – as many students of the period have done. Positivists, empiricists, Nietzscheans, aesthetes, and many occultists were indeed antichristian, but each had very different reasons for hostility. (Of course, Marxists, Jews, Muslims, Hindus, Confucians, and Zoroastrians also are sceptical, and occasionally hostile, towards Christianity.)

The aesthetes and the occult regarded Christianity as a rival and degenerate claimant to revelation – much as any rival religion would do. Nietzsche regarded Christianity and science as equivalent and misguided seekers after a nonexistent truth, and he prophesied their displacement. Empirical scientists and materialist philosophy reject all religion as false superstition, but they are hardly sceptical, for they maintain a faith in objective truth and in the identification of error.

Nietzscheanism straddles the divide. Yeats, Orage, and Weston regarded Nietzsche as a champion of Dionysian ecstasy and revelation, and hence as a fellow occultist. As we have seen, the anthropologist Jane Harrison concurred and saw Nietzsche as legitimizing myth as a repository of genuine religious revelation. Shaw, in contrast, read Nietzsche much as the postmodern does – as the champion of sceptical doubt and the herald of the end of religion and metaphysics. On this last point, the credulous occult and the sceptical Shaw are in agreement; both endorse Nietzsche's proclamation of the final liberation of mankind from the shackles forged by the prospect of an eternal reward or the search for an objective truth, both of which he exposes as vanities of human wishes.

This heteroclite family of opinions helps, I think, to account for the enthusiastic reception of The Waste Land, as well as for the excessive anger and disgust among Waste Land boosters when Eliot abandoned the "Nietzschean" ethos of relativism and scepticism that had been ascribed to the poem. To the Nietzschean readers of The Waste Land, Eliot's conversion to Anglicanism seemed a particularly weak and cowardly capitulation to a romantic Drang for a rational and orderly cosmos, and the betrayal of an heroic Nietzschean angst in the face of an absurd cosmos.

PÉLADAN'S WAGNER

The secret history stemming from Barruel, Masonry, and the occult also finds its way into The Waste Land. It comes directly and explicitly through Weston's study of the Grail legend. If it is true, as I maintain, that *The Cantos* were originally designed to articulate secret, occult history, then it is plausible to suppose that Eliot sought Pound's assistance with *The Waste Land* just because he knew of his familiarity with the occult material upon which he (Eliot) had drawn in his sardonic mini-epic. We know that Pound understood Eliot to have succeeded where he had so far failed. He returned the typescript with the remark, "Complimenti you bitch. I am wracked by the seven jealousies, and cogitating an excuse for always exuding my deformative secretions in my own stuff, and never getting an outline" (Pound 1951, 234).

What we know about the famous collaboration is that Pound was very impressed by the typescript that Eliot sent him and, correlatively, that Eliot was receptive to Pound's suggestions and criticisms. The standard story is that Eliot sought, and Pound offered, stylistic and rhetorical assistance. I want to consider the possibility that the collaboration was driven more by Eliot's concern about the *content* of the poem, in particular its use of Wagnerian and occult materials representative of an encounter with death and the other world, but also the Grail materials suggestive of a pagan cult surviving in medieval Europe. This argument will be vigorously resisted by most of my readers. Let me then first turn back to the occult background in order to discover which aspects of it might have come to bear on the collaboration.

Schuré seems to have been ignorant of the secret history that Pound encountered in Péladan, but he may nonetheless have played a role in Péladan's adoption of it. We have seen that Péladan was sceptical about the Rossetti hypothesis in his introduction to the translation of D.G. Rossetti's *House of Life* (1887). This scepticism is replaced nineteen years later by a complete endorsation of it in *Le Sécret des troubadours* (1906), which was one of the books Pound reviewed and which sketches out the Barruel/Rossetti hypothesis of a secret religion, which Péladan calls *fidèle d'amour*, translating Rossetti's *fedeli d'amore*.

Péladan attributed his conversion to Wagnerism to his 1888 visit to Bayreuth (Péladan [1895] 1981, xii), thereby attaching himself to Wagnerism in its ascendency. In the other book Pound reviewed, *Origine et esthétique de la tragédie*, Péladan follows Schuré and Creuzer rather than Nietzsche, for he identifies the Eleusinian rather than the Dionysian rites as the origin of tragedy. Schuré's disagreement with Nietzsche is clear from the following remarks in *Précurseurs et révolté* – as is his esoteric reading of Eleusis and tragedy: "If there is a weak point in his essay [*The Birth of Tragedy*], otherwise so remarkable, it is that he did not illuminate Greek tragedy by the Eleusinian mysteries and that he confused the dismembered Dionysus of the earthly life with the Liberator of the heavenly life, and he [mistakenly] understood the descent into the elements as the mystical union of the regenerated and revived soul with the divine spirit" (Schuré 1904, 136–7; my translation). Pound was much more impressed by *Origine et esthétique de la Tragédie* than by *Le Secret*. He repeats the attribution of an Eleusinian origin for tragedy without comment, which suggests that in 1906 he was unfamiliar with the competing Nietzschean version of the story: "Péladan's "Origine et Esthétique de la Tragédie (1905) is ... apparently sound, and brim full of clear views on the drama from its Greek beginnings in the Mysteries of Eleusis to the point in literature where Sancho Panza takes unto himself the functions of the chorus of Euripides" (Pound 1906, 54).

Péladan also follows Schuré in defending the Virgin Mary against Nietzsche's attacks on the "Christian Demeter" (Péladan [1895] 1981, 10). And on the same page he gives an esoteric interpretation of Persephone as "the soul that has tasted the fatal seed and must descend into Hades in order to be reborn" (my translation). As we have seen, this esoteric reading of the mysteries is shared by Mead and was standard in theosophical and occult circles of the time. Péladan's most probable source is Schuré. Pursuing this esoteric and un-Nietzschean interpretation, Péladan identifies Dionysus with physical life and Apollo with transcendent life, and argues that the function of the Greek tragedy was to express the Eleusinian secret in an exoteric form. He goes to great lengths to present the Creuzerian argument for the persistence of the Eleusinian wisdom in Christianity – particularly the survival of Demeter in the Virgin Mary. Far from sharing Nietzsche's antipathy for Christianity, Péladan follows Creuzer and Schuré in identifying Catholic Christianity as the legitimate heir of ancient esoteric wisdom. Pound remains throughout his career ambivalent about Christianity, being sometimes implacably hostile and sometimes friendly. This ambivalence reflects the tensions produced by the conflicting antichristian Nietzschean and prochristian Creuzerian legacy in the occult.

These tensions are also there in Péladan's *Origine*, for while chapter 1, "Le Mystère d'Eleusis," is clearly Creuzerian, chapter 2, "La Religion et le théâtre," is equally clearly Nietzschean and – uncharacteristically – explicitly acknowledges its Nietzschean provenance. Péladan cites Henri Albert's French translation – sometimes with and sometimes without acknowledgement (see Péladan 1905b, 56–8, 61–2). Pound's review does not indicate that he was familiar with either the Creuzerian or the Nietzschean account of the origin of tragedy.

Certainly, Pound could not have sorted out the Nietzschean elements from the occult ones in 1906 – assuming that he would have wished to do so. For example, there is no Nietzschean warrant for the following symbolic and Creuzerian assessment of the function of Greek tragedy:

It takes a great effort for us to conceive of tragedy as other than affective and aesthetic; archaeology, like exegesis, hesitates to recognize ideas under such beautiful forms. What else? This incomparable art is not content with beauty; it proposes for itself another end. *The tragic poet not only spoke religiously and was so understood; but above that he embodied a secret doctrine beneath an orthodox surface and thus satisfied the crowd and the artists. This accumulation of distinct purposes, the purpose of art, of devotion, and of initiation were so ideally combined that the most routine of spectators could not be scandalized, and the most sceptical of moderns cannot believe themselves to be in the presence of nothing more than a literary work; this prodigious mixture of the rules of art, of state religion and of the most liberal esotericism,* this triplet of elements confounds our habits, disorients our presuppositions and, to say the truth, seems unbelievable to us. (Péladan 1905b, 42–3; my emphasis)

Although somewhat garbled by the confusion of euhemerist motives with Creuzerian symbolic motives and occult esoteric motives, this account demonstrably derives from a Creuzerian reading of myth and religion. As is clear in Münch's excellent – if rather scornful – summary (1976, 8), "he thought he had discovered in the Bible and in the Ancients traces of a single and common symbolic language, which had served, he thought, as a kind of esperanto in images, but an esperanto known to all and understood by all" (that is, by all the initiates).

There is little reason to suppose that Pound read Péladan with great care and understanding in 1906. But we know that he did read these two books and that he subsequently found very much the same ideas and postures in Kensington when he arrived there. We also know that these same ideas are manifest in *The Cantos* from their earliest beginnings in the 1917 "Three Cantos" to the last fragments published in 1968. The conclusion that Pound participated in such a galaxy of occult speculation for his entire career is inescapable, even though it has long been evaded.

The occult's esoteric reading of Eleusis is plainly illustrated by Mead's 1898 article, "Notes on the Eleusinian Mysteries." Mead cites a famous passage by Plutarch in which the initiates' experiences are likened to the after-death experience, and then comments:

Plutarch is here evidently referring to certain experiences out of the body, in which the soul of the candidate penetrated various regions or states of the unseen world, traversing their various "elements," encountering their powers, and passing by the denizens. This he did with consciousness, and knowledge, and help, so that the terrors of death were for ever removed. But prior to such real initiation, the candidate ... had to submit to and successfully pass a long probation, and a number of natural and in some cases artificial tests to prove his courage and character. The uninitiated, at death, had and have to pass through the same realms, and ignorance of their nature, accentuated in our own times by the soul-deadening doctrine of an eternal hell, creates difficulties and terrors which for the most part are entirely needless. (157)

It is difficult to find such bald expressions of occult illumination as this. It is unlikely that Pound ever read this Mead article, but he was certainly familiar with Mead's understanding of after-death experience. For him, as for Mead, "Eleusis" was a code for mystical illumination on the model here outlined.

A recognition of the occult provenance of *The Cantos* will doubtless prove of considerable interpretive utility if accepted. Canto 4, for example, contains a pastiche of stories of sexual transgression of women by men – in each case leading to death. All of these stories can be read as analogues of the Creuzerian and occult reading of Eleusis that Pound first encountered in Péladan. The conclusion of the canto with the hierogamy of Danaë and Zeus, and an invocation of the Virgin Mary as represented in a procession and a painting, also lends itself to an Eleusinian interpretation. The title of the painting, "Madonna in Hortulo" ("The Virgin Mary in a Garden"), underlines the Virgin's affinity with Demeter.

The violent sexual encounters are the following: Actaeon's dismemberment by Artemis's dogs; the feeding of Itys to his father Tereus by his wife Procne and her ravished sister Philomela; the medieval legend of Cabestan's murder by his lover's husband (who serves Cabestan's cooked heart to her), and the love-crazed Pierre Vidal's wolf-disguise which results in his being mauled by his lover's dogs. These violent stories are quite suitable as analogues of what Schuré calls "the dismembered Dionysus of the earthly life," while the hierogamic tales of Danaë and Mary are suitable as examples of the contrasting "Liberator of the heavenly life."

Canto 4 has been so copiously annotated and commented upon that the weight of commentary cannot be displaced by these brief observations. However, if we read the stories in the light of Péladan's and Schuré's esoteric reading of the Eleusinian myths, we have an interpretive paradigm that resolves hermeneutic puzzles that have so far resisted any consensual resolution. In Creuzer, Schuré, Péladan, and Mead we find such tales of dismemberment and theophagy – myths and legends, ancient and modern – given a fairly standard esoteric interpretation as tales of encounters with the divine or the noumenal. More specifically, the mixture of ancient pagan myth with "modern" Christian legend found in canto 4 is just what Schuré identified as Wagner's great contribution to the handling of myth. It has also long been considered the hallmark of literary modernism in English. In canto 4, tales of dismemberment and theophagy are juxtaposed with allusions to two hierogamies and two brides of gods and mothers of "heroes": Danaë, bride of Zeus and mother of Perseus; and Mary, bride of God and mother of Christ. Canto 4 also juxtaposes light and water with the allusions to the goddesses – a recurrent juxtaposition in The Cantos. If we read all of this in the light of the understanding of Eleusis found in Péladan, we can interpret the canto as representing a descent of the soul into the dolorous realm of Persephone, followed by a bright epopteia, or "manifestation," which accompanies an hieros gamos, or divine marriage.

Of course, Pound does not follow his occult precursors faithfully. Here he is guilty of confusing "the descent into the elements" with "the mystical union of the regenerated and revived soul with the divine spirit," just as Schuré complains above of Nietzsche. Pound is at odds here with Schuré (of whom he was probably ignorant), as well as with Mead (whose position he knew very well), and was at one with Nietzsche (although probably ignorant of the fact).

As is almost always the case with The Cantos, one can find the same paradigm elsewhere – most strikingly in canto 92 (Pound 1973a, 619) where he invokes Danaë once again and juxtaposes her with Anubis (the Egyptian Cerberus), with Aphrodite (through the epithet ex aquis nata, "water-born"), and with Mary ("Coeli Regina") among a cloud of other allusions that fit the paradigm – including Mont Ségur, the last Albigensian stronghold, which Pound took to be a temple to the sun god: "Mt Ségur, sacred to Helios" (574).

Canto 92 is further interesting in that it begins with a passage that readily yields an esoteric interpretation along occult or Creuzerian lines. An esoteric reading of the Persephone myth runs roughly as follows: Persephone's gathering of flowers symbolizes the discarnate (unborn) soul's seduction by earthly (hylic) beauties. Pluto's rape of Persephone symbolizes the soul's embodiment at conception. Her consumption of a pomegranate seed in the underworld (symbolizing the material world) symbolizes the soul's condemnation to mortality through corruption by matter (*hyle*). Once corrupted, the soul can return to its heavenly home only for temporary sojourns (symbolized by spring and summer) and must periodically return to this vale of tears in recurrent reincarnations (symbolized by fall and winter).

Pound probably did not ascribe to this particular interpretation of the myth. Unlike Schuré and most of the occult, who believed in reincarnation, Pound was not attracted to the Hindu doctrine (see the account of his response to the death of Margaret Cravens: Pound 1988, 124, 142). He preferred the palingenetic model in which the soul's return to the *au delà* is a unique and permanent event, perhaps best understood as a deification (as in Ovidian metamorphosis) or an ascension like Balzac's Séraphita – or like Apollonius, who walked "under the larches of Paradise" but did not get there "by ditch-digging and sheep's guts" (canto 94, Pound 1973a, 638). Still another version of ascent is the esoteric reading of Odysseus's rescue from the storm by the sea-nymph Leucothea. Leucothea is his psycho-pomp – as Beatrice is Dante's in the *Paradiso*. Pound closes *Rock-Drill* with this incident (canto 95):

> That the wave crashed, whirling the raft, then
> Tearing the oar from his hand,
> > > broke mast and yard-arm
> And he was drawn down under wave,
> > The wind tossing,
> Notus, Boreas,
> > > as it were thistle-down.
> Then Leucothea had pity,
> > > "mortal once
> Who is now a sea-god ... " (647)

The quotation closes with some imperfect Greek from *Odyssey* 5 (ll. 344–5) which translates as "try to reach Phaecia." The standard eso-teric interpretation of this incident is of the soul's ascension. This reading is reinforced by the detail that Leucothea herself – as Pound has it – was "mortal once" but is now a "sea-god."

The esoteric understanding of birth is that it represents the soul's descent into this world. Naturally, incarnate souls long to be reborn from this "vale of tears." These sentiments make sense of the opening of canto 92:

> And from this Mount were blown
> > seed
> and that every plant hath its seed

so will the weasel eat rue,
and the swallows nip celandine
and as engraven on gold, to be unity
but duality, brass
and trine to mercurial
shall a tetrad be silver
with the smoke of nutmeg and frankincense
and from this a sea-change? (618)

On an esoteric reading, these seeds are souls, and the hoped-for
"sea-change" is palingenesis, or "backward birth," into the higher
realm of being from which we descended at conception. The descent
from golden unity to silver quaternity through a brazen duality and
a mercurial trinity is a bit of alchemy that I cannot decipher, but the
general point of a descending spiritual metempsychosis exoterically
represented by botanical and metallurgical vehicles is not obscure.
Pound is apparently appealing to an esoteric hierarchy of plants and
animals which is analogous to Jung's *Aurea Catena* but of which I am
ignorant.

However, I can gloss some of the imagery, much of which is taken
from John Heydon's *Holy Guide*, a work Pound first read with Yeats
during the winters they spent together at Stone Cottage. Heydon
was a Restoration occultist. He had nothing to say about Eleusis or
transfiguration. His works were mostly plagiarized – principally from
Sir Thomas Browne's *Religio Medici* and Plutarch's *Isis and Osiris*. He
also borrowed copiously from alchemical sources. (Surette 1979, 264–
5; Baumann, "Secretary of Nature, J. Heydon," in Hesse 1969). The
"sea-change" is always palingenetic in *The Cantos* – as in the passage
cited from canto 95, or canto 4, or in canto 20. The ultimate source
of such a reading of "sea-change" is Porphyry's account of metempsychosis in his commentary on "The Cave of the Nymphs," but it
is ubiquitous in the occult.

Péladan says very little about mystical death and rebirth in the
works Pound read, so he could not have been the source of Pound's
palingenetic and soteriological poetry. Mead is a far more likely
source. Mead discusses palingenesis in many places; one discussion
Pound may have read is found in a brief article in the *Quest* of July
1913, just a few months after Pound's "Psychology and Troubadours"
had appeared in the same journal. He is explaining the "doctrine of
spiritual union or 'sacred marriage,'" the *hieros gamos*. It was, he says,
"regarded as the birth of a new creature. It was this substantial
transmutation into a spiritual being that made gnosis possible and
bestowed the power of divine vision, by means of the unitary sense

of the intelligence. The new consciousness was conceived as the result of the impregnation of the inner self, so they phrased it, by the rays, emanations, effluxes or influences of the divine splendour. In an ethical sense, these seeds were, as we have seen, virtue, self-control, devotion, and in general the choir of the virtues" (Mead 1913, 686). Pound prefers *choroi nymphari* to choirs of virtues, but the community of imaginative realm between this passage and those from *The Cantos* is evident.

An understanding of the relationship between the imaginative world of *The Cantos* and that of the Creuzer/Nietzsche/Wagner nexus on the one hand and the occult on the other is essential for a successful interpretation of *The Cantos*. It permits an interpretation that accounts for all of the features of the poem and not just those we approve, such as the lyric; or those we deplore, such as the political; or those that bemuse us, such as the economic; or those that bore us, such as the historical. More generally, Pound's occultism accounts for the peculiarly intractable rhetoric of the poem – a feature to be expected of an esoteric poem whose sense is darkly manifest in an exoteric surface, impenetrable to the uninitiated. The supposition of an occult provenance and purpose for *The Cantos* also explains the overweening ambition that led Pound to attempt an epic of the modern age.

Through an understanding of the provenance of modernism under examination here, we can better understand the stresses and tensions the movement had to undergo in order to present itself as sceptical and relativist without abandoning its credulous and rationalist roots. In this light, Joyce's *Ulysses* and Eliot's *Waste Land* can be seen as evasions of the more extreme occultist/symbolist mind-sets that surrounded them. To put it another way, the obscurity of Pound's *Cantos* is the result of a commitment to esotericism, a practice of their *Symboliste* predecessors that licensed the obscurity of the paradigmatic modernist works, *Ulysses* and *The Waste Land*.

Joyce's "mythical method" is an adaptation and secularization of the mystical symbolism of the *Symbolistes*. Joyce replaces the esoteric sense by a merely allusive and metonymic sense. The "hidden" sense of *Ulysses* is simply the network of allusions to the *Odyssey*, to Irish and European history, to Christian liturgy, to philosophy, and to a few other open or exoteric realms. Joyce in fact is closer to Creuzer than to the occult, for *Ulysses* is a self-consciously encrypted text just as Creuzer believed ancient myths to be. In contrast, *Symbolisme*, the occult, and Pound insisted that the esoteric sense was not just encrypted but was ineffable – a gnosis accessible only to the enlightened.

Neither *The Waste Land* nor *The Cantos* has the ironic detachment from its traditional material that is characteristic of Joyce's work. *The Waste Land* is quite Wagnerian, retaining a sense of sublime awe in the face of its mythical and religious material. Eliot not only alludes to Wagnerian opera, but the poem invokes the Wagnerian topos of *liebestod*. In addition, its rhetoric of resonance and repetition is highly reminiscent of Wagner's technique of *leitmotif*. Nonetheless, *The Waste Land* is not an occult-inspired work like *The Cantos*.

Let me return to a consideration of the occult nature of *The Cantos* for a moment. Most Pound scholiasts consider discussion of his occultism to be an allegation and seek counter-evidence. For example, the equivalence between Demeter and the Virgin Mary in cantos 4 and 91 discussed above can be challenged by an unpublished letter in the Yale Collection cited by Terrell in the *Companion* (1981, 1984). Pound is explaining the following lines to his father:

> "Saave!"
> Procession, – "Et Sa'ave, sa'ave, sa'ave Regina!" –
> Moves like a worm, in the crowd.

His comment on the passage does not support the admiring equivalence between the Virgin ("Regina") and Demeter that I have found in Schuré and Péladan: "This worm of the procession had three large antennae, and I hope to develop the motive later ... No merely medieval but black central African superstition and voodoo energy squalling infant, general murk and epileptic religious hog wash with chief totem magnificently swung over whole" (my elision; spelling normalized). If this remark is accepted as an authoritative interpretation of the passage, then it would seem clear that the passage expresses a positivistic critique of Catholic superstition and is not a celebration of its Creuzerian role as a transmitter of a mystic wisdom as I have interpreted it. The letter is undated, but Terrell places it in 1919, two years after the first publication of canto 4. Five years before that Pound wrote in Mead's journal, the *Quest*, the following:

The rise of Mariolatry, its pagan lineage, the romance of it, find modes of expression which verge over-easily into the speech and casuistry of Our Lady of Cyprus, as we may see in Arnaut, as we see so splendidly in Guido's "Una figura della donna miae." And there is the consummation of it all in Dante's glorification of Beatrice. There is the inexplicable address to the lady in the masculine. There is the final evolution of Amor by Guido and Dante, a new and paganish god, neither Erôs nor an angel of the Talmud. (Pound [1929] 1953, 91–2)

This remark is embedded in a discussion that is deeply committed to the occultist psychology that Pound learned from Mead (see Surette 1979, esp. 60–3) and is diametrically opposed to the attitude towards "superstition and voodoo energy" expressed in the 1919 letter to his parents. The only salient difference between this passage and my interpretation of canto 4 is that Pound equates the Virgin Mary with Aphrodite, by the phrase "Our Lady of Cyprus," instead of Demeter.

I have no neat explanation of the apparent contradiction, but two factors are worth consideration. Most generally, Pound – like Nietzsche – is far from consistent in his views and judgments, as anyone who pays attention to dates can easily demonstrate. We have seen that the severity of his hostility towards Wagner varied with the rise and fall of political passions. Secondly, and more specifically, it may well be that in 1919 Pound was drawing away from the occultism that he had so thoroughly imbibed since his undergraduate years. That the hostility to Wagner is of much the same date as the letter to Homer Pound lends some credence to this view.

We know that Pound had adopted Major Douglas's Social Credit theories by this time (Surette 1983). And "Hugh Selwyn Mauberley," also 1919–20, is commonly read as a rejection of his early symbolist or occult career. Pound referred to it as a "farewell to London" and might better have called it a farewell to Kensington. Another possibility (suggested to me by my colleague Stephen Adams) is that Pound may have wished to shield his New England father from any fear that his son was soft on Catholicism. Whatever the correct explanation for the apparent contradiction between the 1919 Pound and the 1912 and 1917 Pound, the evidence of The Cantos is massively and overwhelmingly in favour of the persistence of occult themes and topoi in Pound's work.

On the same point, it is worth repeating the observation that occultists were typically hostile to Christianity as a rival, institutionalized, and adulterated religion. Pound may be reflecting this prejudice in the letter – as he certainly does elsewhere. Pound was exposed to Nietzschean hostility towards Christianity through Orage, his editor at the New Age. Orage's influence on Pound was certainly in the ascendant in 1919, for it was just then that Orage had adopted Major Douglas's economic theories and virtually turned over his magazine and his own pen to the promotion of Social Credit. Pound had earlier picked up some Nietzschean ideas from Orage. They are manifest in Patria Mia, a series of essays on America, first published from September to June 1913 in the New Age and thus contemporaneous with "Psychology and Troubadours."

NIETZSCHE AND ORAGE

A.R. Orage, another prominent London theosophist, played a much more public role in the history of literary modernism than Mead did. Born on 22 January 1873 in Fenstanton, Orage was twelve years Pound's senior. While a young teacher in Leeds, he became an active member of the Leeds branch of Blavatsky's Theosophical Society. His closest friends at Leeds were Holbrook Jackson and Arthur J. Penty – also theosophists. The former introduced Orage to Nietzsche and the latter introduced him to socialism and economics. The three friends founded the Leeds Arts Club and organized lectures on religious, philosophical, social, and economic subjects. (The account of Orage's biography is based on Surette 1983, Mairet 1936, Thatcher 1970, and Finlay 1972.)

Penty was the first of the three to depart for London, where he established handicraft workshops as part of a Ruskinian craft movement. Orage and Jackson followed him in 1905. They were active in the foundation of the Fabian Arts Group in that same year. Two years later (in May 1907) Orage and Jackson purchased a failing magazine with money donated by the prominent Fabian, George Bernard Shaw, and by a wealthy theosophist, Lewis Wallace – who later contributed as "M.B. Oxon." (Selver 1959; Webb 1980). This magazine was the *New Age*, which had been founded thirteen years earlier by Frederic A. Atkins. Before the year was out, Jackson had withdrawn from the magazine and Orage was left in charge.

F.S. Flint introduced Pound to Orage, but these two were by no means the only literary figures of note associated with the magazine. The *New Age* was also T.E. Hulme's primary outlet. After Hulme's death in the trenches, Orage asked F.S. Flint to edit the manuscript material Hulme had left with him. When Flint declined, Orage picked the young Herbert Read for the task. Read successfully created the extraordinary reputation that Hulme still enjoys and that has reflected on him as well. Edwin Muir was another *New Age* alumnus. Muir became a regular contributor after he moved to London in 1919, but he had been publishing in the journal as Edward Moore since May 1913. Although the *New Age* was not exclusively an occult journal like the *Quest*, Orage found magazine space for occultists such as Philip Mairet, Ouspensky, and his intimate friend Beatrice Hastings.

Even before the purchase of the *New Age* in 1907, Orage had written two books on religious and philosophical subjects: *Friedrich Nietzsche: The Dionysian Spirit of the Age* (1906) and *Consciousness: Animal, Human, and Divine* (1907). Both were based on lectures he had delivered at the Leeds Theosophical Society. In addition, he published a selection of Nietzsche's aphorisms, *Nietzsche in Outline and Aphorism* (1907). In contrast to the *Quest*, the *New Age* was a journal of radical or avant-garde political, economic, and cultural opinion – gradually moving across the political chart from left to right. Pound joined the stable of *New Age* contributors in late 1911. He and Orage were at that time poles apart in both style and interests, so far as one can judge by their writing. In fact, Beatrice Hastings claims that "Orage ... said, so late as Oct. 1913, nearly two years after Pound's debut: Mr Pound's style is a paste of colloquy, slang journalism and pedantry. Of culture in Nietzsche's sense of the word, it bears no sign" (Hastings 1936, 7).

Beatrice Hastings was Orage's companion from 1907 to 1914, but Orage dropped her and later married Jessie Dwight, whom he met during his years in New York (1923–32). Among Hastings's works are *Defence of Madame Blavatsky*, vol. 1 (Worthing, Sussex: The Hastings Press 1937) – volume 2 never appeared – and *Our Own Business* from the same press in 1938. It is clear from her memoir that she was an occultist – and from *Defence of Madame Blavatsky* that she was a theosophist. She accuses Orage of sorcery and links him with the notorious Aleister Crowley: "I first met Orage at a theosophical lecture he gave in 1906, when on a visit to London from Leeds. Afterwards in the smoking room I rallied him on his perverse loquacity (of the which I later detected every trick). A year or so after, when Aphrodite had amused herself at our expense, I found in his rooms a collection of works on sorcery. Up to this time, Orage's intimate friend was not Mr Holbrook Jackson, who thought he was, but Mr Aleister Crowley" (Hastings 1936, 19). Although Ms Hastings's memoir must be handled with some caution, it is telling that she should attempt character assassination by the charge of sorcery. Only an occultist would choose such a charge. The occult believed in magical powers but regarded their use for material purposes to be sinful. Aleister Crowley claimed to have such powers and was widely criticized in occult circles for the exercise of them. Sudden deaths were often attributed by the occult to sorcery.

Since Orage continued to publish Pound for the entire period of his editorship of the *New Age* and also welcomed him to the pages of the *New English Weekly* (which he founded on his return to London 1932), we must suppose that Pound acquired some "Nietzschean" culture. To learn what this is we need only turn to Orage's *Friedrich Nietzsche: The Dionysian Spirit of the Age* (1906):

Every organism, whether an individual, a people, or a race, belongs either to an ascending or a descending current. And its morality, art, form of society, instincts, and in fact its whole mode of manifestation, depend on whether it belongs to one or the other order of being. The primary characteristic of the ascending life is the consciousness of inexhaustible power. The individual or people behind which the flowing tide of life-force moves is creative, generous, reckless, enthusiastic, prodigal, passionate: its virtues, be it observed, are Dionysian. Its will-to-power is vigorous; in energy it finds delight. And the moral code of such a people will reflect faithfully the people's power.

But the prevailing characteristic of the descending life is the consciousness of *declining* power. The individual or people in whom the life-force is ebbing instinctively husband their resources. They are preservative rather than creative, niggardly, careful, fearful of passion and excess, calculating and moderate. And, in turn, their code of morality faithfully reflects their will. (50–1)

Pound reflects these Nietzschean sentiments in *Patria Mia*, which was first published as a double series of articles in the *New Age* in 1911 and 1912 (see Pound 1962):

I see also a sign in the surging crowd on Seventh Avenue (New York). A crowd pagan as ever imperial Rome was, eager, careless, with an animal vigour unlike that of any European crowd that I have ever looked at. (13)

And the city itself about him, Manhattan! Has it not buildings that are Egyptian in their contempt of the unit? For that is the spirit of the Pyramids. The Egyptian monarch despised the individual slave as effectively as the American despises the individual dollar. (14)

Pound also reflects Nietzsche's rather silly views on climate in his effort to make the United States of America fulfil the role Nietzsche assigned Germany at the end of the *Birth of Tragedy*:

It is certain that the climate has about as much to do with the characteristics of a people as has their ethnology. And especially if the race is mongrel, one stock neutralizing the forces of the other, the climate takes up its lordship and decrees the nature of the people resulting ... The most apparent effect of the American climate is the American Morale. Especially in matters of sex all concepts of right depend upon the nerves, which depend on the sun, on the wind, the dryness or dampness of the air. (12)

Since Nietzsche's views on race and climate are among his less well known beliefs (another is his conviction that Bacon wrote Shakespeare's plays), some illustration of them might be helpful. In

Genealogy of Morals (3.17) he observes, "In certain parts of the earth a *feeling of physiological inhibition* is almost bound to seize on large masses of people ... The pessimism of the nineteenth century is essentially the result of an absurdly precipitate mixing of classes ... [and such a feeling may arise from] a race introduced into a climate for which its powers of adaptation are inadequate." Nietzsche's transvaluation of values has survived better than his views on climate and eugenics. But this more admired aspect of his is only weakly reflected in *Patria Mia* – in such remarks as "The awakening comes when men decide that certain laws need no longer be stuck to" (56). Nietzsche wrote that the awakening requires "a *critique* of moral values, *the value of these values themselves must first be called in question* (*Genealogy*, Preface, 6).

These racist ideas were endemic in Europe from the Enlightenment on. Jacques Barzun traces the idea of the dependence of racial characteristics on geography and climate to Montesquieu (Barzun 1965, esp. 52). Artur de Gobineau elaborated a racist understanding of history based on these notions in *Essai sur l'inégalité des races humains* (1853). This work's influence on modern European racism has been much noted. The particular idea of the suitability of a "race" to a climate is specifically Gobiniste. Nietzsche's sister reports that she read Gobineau's *Essai* to him and that he was much impressed (Barzun 1965, 62–3).

Perhaps it is such views that Pound meant to designate by the phrase "neo-Nietzschean clatter" in "Hugh Selwyn Mauberley," a fuss and vigour for which Mauberley's mildness was "quite out of place." The figure of Mauberley might be understood as a portrait of the characteristics of the "descending life." He is conservative, niggardly, careful, fearful of passion and excess, calculating, and moderate. Mauberley probably represents the rather precious crowd of preening superior consciousnesses amongst whom Pound had been pleased to number himself during his London years. A sample of that earlier preening is Pound's review of Upward's *The Divine Mystery*: "He thinks, *il pense*. He is intelligent. Good God! is it not a marvel that in the age of Cadbury and Northcliffe, and the 'Atlantic Monthly' and the present 'English Review,' etc., etc., ad nauseam, is it not an overwhelming wonder that a thinking sentient being should still inhabit this planet and be allowed to publish a book!!" (*New Freewoman*, 15 Sept. 1913, 207).

From his very earliest association with A.J. Penty in Leeds, Orage maintained an interest in economics alongside his occult interests. Indeed, one can perceive economic metaphors in his characterization of the "ascending life" as generous and prodigal, while the "descending life" is husbanding and niggardly. Except for the ten-year period when he was a Gurdjieffian, Orage maintained these two interests actively. Gurdjieff was an Armenian guru and the inventor of the technique of encounter groups. His London missionaries were the Russian, P.D. Ouspensky (brought to London in August 1921 by Lady Rothermere), and the Yugoslav, M.M. Cosmoi. (Orage "Englished" Cosmoi's byline, called "World Affairs," in the *New Age*.) Orage left London in 1922 to join the Gurdjieffian "institute" at Fontainebleau in the old priory building which Gurdjieff had purchased and continued to call Le Prieuré. Orage remained there until December 1923 when he sailed to New York as a Gurdjieffian missionary.

Orage returned to Fontainebleau for several visits to fulfil his assignment to translate Gurdjieff's *Beelzebub's Tales to His Grandson* – a task he never finished. But he remained head of the movement in New York until 1931 when he broke with Gurdjieff (Welch 1982, 44, 120). Orage returned to London and in April 1932 founded the *New English Weekly* as a Social Credit journal. He immediately opened its pages to his old London friend Ezra Pound, with whom he had kept in touch (Welch 1982, 62). George Russell, G.K. Chesterton, G.B. Shaw, C.H. Douglas, T.S. Eliot, and Pound all contributed to the memoir in the *New English Weekly* on Orage's sudden death (5 Nov. 1934).

In his memoir for Eliot's *Criterion*, Pound denied an "interest in Orage's mysticism." But he did not raise the question in his contribution to the *New English Weekly* "In Memoriam." Instead, he spoke exclusively of Social Credit. However, Orage did not meet Douglas until 1917, a good six years after their association had been cemented. Nor did Pound begin to address economic issues until late in 1917 (Surette 1983). The evidence of *Patria Mia*, "Psychology and Troubadours," and the early cantos gives the lie to this disclaimer – at least, if we lump Orage's Nietzscheanism with his theosophy, as I think we must. There are also scattered biographical details, such as Pound's visit to Le Prieuré and the sampling of Gurdjieff's cooking (Pound 1938, 112).

Certainly, Nietzsche's peculiar sexual and sexist notions are given considerable prominence in Orage's *Nietzsche in Outline and Aphorism* (1907, 41–51), and we have seen that Pound maintains similar views in the "Postscript" to his translation of de Gourmont's *Natural Philosophy of Love*. The "Postscript" was written after Pound's conversion to Social Credit and his apparent turn away from occult Kensington, marked by the Mauberley sequence (1921). But clearly this "turn" does not take him very far from the pseudo-science, vitalism, and Nietzscheanism of which he had drunk so deeply. Indeed, Nietzsche's definition of virtue from *Beyond Good and Evil* as it appears in Orage's *Nietzsche in Outline and Aphorism* is a more plausible source for de Gourmont's outrageous biological speculations than anything I can find in Fabre: "The instinctive desire to pour out life and not to preserve or amass life; the will to spend and not to acquire, the virtue of liberality, courage, gaiety, strength, the sense of inexhaustible powers, the atmosphere of an original fount and source of life, the spirit of self-giving, of prodigality, of ecstasy, of careless rapture in action, of spontaneity" (Orage 1907, 109).

This passage also helps to explain why Orage and Pound so eagerly embraced Social Credit. Douglas's theory was an underconsumptionist one; that is, one that privileges expenditure over saving as the engine of wealth creation. Economic theories can be bifurcated into two broad types: scarcity economics, which is mainstream and includes Marxist economics; and underconsumptionism, which is heretical. Orthodox economics argues that we must save and husband our resources carefully so that the resulting surplus will permit some individuals the leisure to oversee and organize collective activities and hence permit economic, cultural, and social betterment. The underconsumptionist argument contradicts this orthodox view and holds that prosperity depends upon the rapid and profligate dispersal of resources rather than on their selfish hoarding. On this view, expenditure on monumental and artistic activities is not only culturally valuable but also promotes general well-being. For this reason, and because underconsumptionism privileges the aristocratic virtues of magnanimity and display, it tends to appeal to the artistic temperament. Scarcity economics – as has frequently been observed both before and since Nietzsche – privileges the bourgeois virtues of parsimony and caution, and appeals to the acquisitive temperament.

Every mainstream variety of general economic theory since Adam Smith has rejected underconsumptionism. A partial exception to this rule is John Maynard Keynes, whose general theory is a sophisticated and moderated variety of underconsumptionism. Keynes has been expunged from orthodox economic theory since the 1970s when the phenomenon of "stagflation" discredited underconsumptionism once again. After long study, I have concluded that Pound never fully understood the economic theories he espoused. He picked economic postures and theories that fitted comfortably into his occultist-Nietzschean views. For example, he championed the bullionism of John Adams even though this economic "theory" is the very antipathy of

Social Credit. All that Adams and Social Credit have in common is an antipathy to banks. But such a trivial agreement was enough for Pound when he was writing the Adams cantos in the 1940s.

In the light of our exploration of the galaxy of mythographic, occult, and aesthetic theory, it is worth pointing out that the most influential underconsumptionist in England prior to John Maynard Keynes was John Ruskin, whose *Unto This Last* is based on an underconsumptionist argument. This work is a central document in English socialism, particularly that variety of socialism espoused by English artists such as William Morris. And, of course, Ruskin is a central figure in English aestheticism (Surette 1983; 1986).

Social Credit, which was an underconsumptionist theory, was developed under Pound's nose in the offices of the *New Age.* Major Douglas came to Orage with a rough idea about prices and costs that he had formulated while managing the Royal Aircraft Works at Farnborough. At the time, Orage was pushing the Guild Socialist ideas of S.G. Hobson, but Guild Socialism was being taken away from him by G.D.H. Cole, who admired Hobson's ideas for social and economic organization but was not enamoured of Orage and his dreamy crowd. Douglas was a godsend for Orage and a revelation for Pound, who had paid scant attention to Hobson's Guild Socialism or the Fabianism that preceded it in Orage's enthusiasms. Social Credit, however, quickly converted Pound – presumably because it admirably fitted the Nietzschean principle of excess that Pound had imbibed from Orage. Pound memorializes his *New Age* office experiences in canto 46 ("the "fuzzy bloke" is Pound and "the major" is Douglas):

> Seventeen
> Years on this case, nineteen years, ninety years
> on this case
> An' the fuzzy bloke sez (legs no pants ever wd. fit) "IF
> that is so, any government worth a damn can
> pay dividends?"
> The major chewed it a bit and sez: "Y–es, eh ...
> You mean instead of collectin' taxes?"
> "Instead of collecting taxes." That office? (1973a, 231)

Social Credit economic theory revealed the secret springs of political and military history in much the way that the Rossetti/occult thesis revealed the secret dynamic of cultural history. In both cases there existed a wisdom, gnosis, or knowledge possessed by a privileged few, unknown to the many, and suppressed or occluded by a corrupt and venal conspiracy of several. Pound had the opportunity to observe at first hand the political and academic establishment's rejection of Social Credit, a theory that he, Orage, and Douglas were convinced provided simple and clear solutions to the business cycle, to poverty, and to international conflict.

In the case of the subtle and ineffable wisdom of higher things, one could expect such a rejection of the revelation. For this reason, the Higher Souls were careful to express their esoteric wisdom in exoteric or disguised forms. But despite his strong tendency to regard himself as a superior person, Pound seems to have been uncomfortable with such doctrines, and he accommodated himself to them by formulating non-elitist theories of obscurity, such as the "doctrine of the image." Imagism – although by no means a uniquely Poundian achievement – is surely the greatest democratization of gnosis that has ever been attempted. Be that as it may, Douglasite economics was not a higher wisdom, and it should have been communicable to anyone willing to listen – at least so Pound and the Social Crediters believed. Alas, hardly anyone took the lesson.

The failure of Social Credit to sweep all before it had devastating consequences for Pound's personal life that are familiar to everyone, and also greatly altered the nature of his epic poem. Pound's political career cannot be assessed here (see Surette 1988 and 1989–90; Redman 1991). The point I want to make is that although Social Credit was a deflection from Pound's occult interests, it was not a departure from them. He encountered it within the occult circles in which he moved; and, moreover, Social Credit, with its insistence on a simple cognitive solution to economic problems, participated in the occult mind-set, which tended to *a priorism* and had little patience with the slow process of empirical inquiry.

The argument goes something like this: just as wisdom is everywhere available and is earned by grace, not by study, so economic prosperity and justice are naturally available and are not earned by labour so much as by the grace of harmonious relations with the cosmos. Social Credit revealed how this harmony could be achieved on the economic front. Just as the noumenal revelation is obscured by passion, superstition, and sensuality, so economic bounty is denied us by greed, ignorance, and prudery. In this view, both ignorance and poverty are the automatic consequences of a failure that is at once moral and intellectual.

Pound expresses this simplistic analysis in many places. It is the main theme of *Guide to Kulchur* (1938):

We know that these causes [of historical events] were economic and moral; we know that at whichever end we begin we will, if clear headed and thorough, work out to the other.

We know that there is one enemy, ever-busy obscuring our terms; ever muddling and muddying terminologies, ever trotting out minor issues to obscure the main and the basic, ever prattling of short range causation for the sake of, or with the result of, obscuring the truth. Captans annonam etc. (that is to say hogging the harvest, aiding the hoggers and so forth). (31)

A theory that ignorance and misery are the consequences of moral and intellectual failure is very liable to lead its adherents into socially regressive postures. Whatever morality may be, one cannot have morality without the possibility of choice. Hence, ignorance and misery must for some reason be chosen by the ignorant and the miserable. That they should do so would seem inexplicable unless we suppose some fundamental degeneracy in those who so choose. If the degeneracy is simply cowardice, then it makes sense to preach to the mob and enjoin them to rise up, for they have nothing to lose but their chains. However, it is equally plausible to argue – as Gobineau and the Nazis did – that the degeneracy is racial; or – as Nietzsche argued – that it is eugenic, the consequence of a mismatch of "blood" and climate. In such cases, only massive "social engineering" such as the Nazis' "final solution" can resolve the problem of ignorance and misery.

Of course, the most influential application of the principle of degeneracy was in Max Nordau's virulently anti-Nietzschean work, *Degeneracy*. Apart from Nietzsche, Nordau's targets were the same as Pound's culture heroes, so they are on opposite sides of that fence. However, Pound, Nietzsche, and Nordau all share the metahistorical theory that negative cultural phenomena are best understood as the result of pathology. Healthy societies, cultures, and individuals produce healthy politics, economies, science, and art. Sick societies, cultures, and individuals produce degenerate politics, economies, science, and art.

Pound himself has fostered the story that his conversion to Social Credit transformed him from an apathetic aesthete like Mauberley to an *engagé* and hard-nosed modernist. There is some truth to this story, even though it is plainly an oversimplification. No doubt Pound's economic awakening caused the 1917 beginning on *The Cantos* to be abortive. The poem projected in the Ur Cantos could not have absorbed with any ease the raw history that Pound's economic story required. On the other hand, the embracing "myth" or story of the poem remained the secret and occult history of Europe, a history of a carefully hidden albeit widely published wisdom, an esoteric revelation hidden in texts understood by the uninitiated only exoterically.

Yeats seems to have understood Pound's epic in this way. As we noted earlier, he attached "A Packet for Ezra Pound" as a kind of preface to the revised, 1938 edition of *A Vision*, and some of the revision of *A Vision* (Yeats's own universal history) as well as the writing of "A Packet" was undertaken in Rapallo, where Yeats and his wife had taken a flat in the autumn of 1928, having been charmed by the town during an earlier visit there with the Pounds. Pound and Yeats must have discussed Pound's epic, for Yeats describes its structure – whether a rhetorical or a substantive structure is not entirely clear – in the "packet." He also offers Pound some public advice, drawing on his experience as a senator of the Irish Free State: "Neither you nor I, nor any other of our excitable profession, can match those old lawyers, old bankers, old business men, who, because all habit and memory, have begun to govern the world ... You and I ... are as much out of place as would be the first composers of sea-shanties in an age of steam. Whenever I stood up to speak, no matter how long I had pondered my words ... I was ashamed until shame turned at last, even if I spoke but a few words ... into physical pain" (Yeats [1938] 1961, 27).

Clearly, Yeats was troubled by the political turn that Pound's poem was taking, and he warned him in a rather gentle but very public way. It is unlikely that Yeats would have been troubled by the particular direction that Pound's political sympathies were taking. There was little in Mussolini's fascism, except perhaps for bombast, that would have bothered the elderly Yeats. It is more likely that he understood his own limitations – and those of poets generally. In Yeats's view, Pound's error was to place his own judgment about contemporary events in competition with the "old lawyers, old bankers, and old business men." Yeats believed – and the event has proven him correct – that uncanny poets like himself and Pound could only appear as fools or worse in competition with such canny judges. Alas, Pound did not heed the warning of his old mentor.

Instead, he replied, some ten years later, with some of the occultism and Nietzscheanism he had learned from Mead and Yeats: "Two mystic states can be dissociated: the ecstatic beneficent-and-benevolent, contemplation of the divine love, the divine splendour with goodwill toward others. And the bestial, namely the fanatical, the man on fire with God and anxious to stick his snotty nose into other men's business or reprove his neighbour for having a set of tropisms different from that of the fanatic's or for having the courage to live more greatly and openly" (Pound 1938). Yeats would have endorsed Pound's pronouncement on mystic states. But he had seen in 1928 that Pound was becoming a fanatic, sticking his nose into matters he did not understand. Pound did not listen in 1928, and he was even more persuaded of his own wisdom in 1937 when he rendered the preceding judgment in his own Baedeker of Western history, *Guide to Kulchur*.

CHAPTER FOUR

Pound's Editing
of The Waste Land

JESSIE WESTON
AND THEOSOPHY

In the preceding chapters we have surveyed a galaxy of texts and authors that came together in the poetic program of Ezra Pound to produce an unexampled work in *The Cantos*. It has not been possible to do much more than indicate some ways in which Pound's epic manifests its occult provenance by pointing to occult motifs, themes, and topics in a few isolated instances. A full-dress demonstration of the occult nature of *The Cantos* is quite within reach but could not be accommodated within this study without extending it well beyond reasonable length. Even though it does not properly identify the provenance of these views, my earlier study, *A Light from Eleusis*, articulates the congruence between the world of secret history and occult wisdom and the world generated in Pound's *Cantos*. These relations are further explored in Demetres Tryphonopoulos's work (1989; 1992).

Pound's indebtedness to Yeats, Orage, and Upward has been widely noted even if the occult nature of the debt has been evaded. But except for *A Light from Eleusis* and the recent work of Tryphonopoulos, Mead has largely been ignored – partly because Pound gave him little notice or credit. Because of Pound's reticence, it is difficult to assess just what role Mead played in his intellectual and social life. Dorothy, for example, wrote to Pound in Paris on Bloomsday of 1912: "The Meads here [at her parents' house] at tea yesterday: they both have so much, & such pleasant, personality. I expect you are seeing the Hamadryad [Hilda Doolittle]? Give her my best love – Tell her Mead says Centaurs can't have existed 'in the flesh' because if so by now we should have found skeletons" (Pound 1984, 114). The bizarre application of negative empirical evidence in the remark on centaurs is characteristic of Mead's mind-set. Pound picks on the same attributes in his affectionate mention of Mead in *Guide to Kulchur*, where he relates an anecdote in which Blavatsky tells Mead that another globe was attached to the Earth at the North Pole. Pound remarks, "Mead years after was looking for a meaning and did not suspect the old lady of pulling his leg" (Pound 1938, 225–6).

Beside the credulity and hard-core occultism of Mead and Yeats, Pound's occult tendencies seem sceptical and balanced. It is largely by virtue of such contrasts that he has managed to pass muster as a good sceptic and relativist despite the very clearly mystical and occult cast of so much of what he has written. His scepticism about ghosts and poltergeists and his lack of interest in séances and other occult phenomena have been taken as evidence of his scepticism, despite the counterindication of his talk of divinities and revelation in prose and verse, as in the following remark: "What remains, and remains undeniable to and by the most hardened objectivist, is that a great number of men have had certain kinds of emotion and, *magari*, of ecstasy. They have left indelible records of ideas born of, or conjoined with, this ecstasy" (Pound 1938, 225). These remarks are unmistakably theosophical but have passed muster as all sorts of things, including oxymoronic evasions like Rainey's "secular spirituality" (Rainey 1991, 219).

Pound's mother-in-law, Olivia Shakespear, was herself a habituée of London occult circles. An intimate friend of Yeats and a social friend of the Meads, she was the co-author with Florence Farr of two occult plays – *The Beloved of Hathor* and *The Shrine of the Golden Hawk* – and was a close friend of Yeats's wife, Georgie Hyde-Lees. She also wrote a mainly feminist but mildly occult and quite readable novel, *Uncle Hilary* (London: Methuen 1910). Olivia Shakespear's literary career, minor as it was, brings to one's attention the very strong ties between feminism and the occult in late-Victorian and Edwardian London.

These ties are even stronger in the career of Annie Besant. She was a prominent feminist before she succeeded Colonel Olcott as the leader of the Theosophical Society. An ex-lover of G.B. Shaw (who, like Florence Farr, was another devotee of strange lore), she was an occasional guest of George and Charlotte Shaw during her theosophical years (Dunbar 1963, 249). Charlotte Shaw herself was keenly interested in occult "research" and retained the services of the astrologer Isabelle M. Pagan for at least fifteen years (from 1914 to 1929). It would seem that Besant's presidency of the Theosophical Society did not render her socially unacceptable – at least, not for the Shaws (Charlotte Shaw Papers, British Museum, Add. 56491 and 56492).

In an ambience where the president of the Theosophical Society could be received socially at the home of the most prominent dramatist in England, Pound's participation in the Kensington meetings of the Quest Society was not an especially odd event. As noted above, Wyndham Lewis and T.E. Hulme also gave lectures at those meetings and attended them with some regularity. Nor did Orage's overt theosophy prevent Shaw from financing the *New Age* or from contributing a memorial essay to the *New English Weekly* on the occasion of Orage's death – in the rather surprising company of the mystical George Russell and the Anglican T.S. Eliot.

Shaw's friend was Orage's co-editor, Holbrook Jackson, but they had some common ground – notably their mutual enthusiasm for Nietszche. Indeed, the first pamphlet publication of Jackson and Orage was Shaw's *Sanity of Art: An Exposure of the Current Nonsense about Artists Being Degenerate*. This was Shaw's response to Nordau. It was originally published in Benjamin Tucker's American journal, *Liberty*, in 1895. Orage and Jackson reissued it in 1908. In his preface, Shaw immodestly claims that the "brisk and quick sale" of *The Sanity of Art* resulted in the disappearance of *Degeneration* from public view. However, he admits this phenomenon may have been "a mere coincidence – that the *Degeneration* boom was exhausted at that moment; but I naturally prefer to believe that Mr Tucker and I slew it" (Shaw 1908, 8).

Although we have only the scantiest information about the Quest Society lectures, it is worth reminding ourselves who attended and spoke at them. The names one would expect are all there: A.E. Waite, Fiona Macleod, W.B. Yeats, and Rabindranath Tagore. Other contributors were Ernest Rhys, Denis Saurat, John Masefield, Arthur Symons, Evelyn Underhill, Robert Eisler, Gershom Scholem, Martin Buber, and Jessie Weston. This last set is much more of a mixed bag. Martin Buber, Gershom Scholem, and Robert Eisler were all Jewish scholars of religion. Buber and Scholem are well known, the former as the pre-eminent modern scholar of Hasidism, and the latter as the leading modern scholar of Kabbala. Eisler's bent was as an historian of religion in the school of Ernest Renan. His reputation has gone into eclipse with that of Renan. Ernest Rhys, John Masefield, and Arthur Symons were individuals of solid literary reputation, the last a close friend of Yeats and a formative influence on the undergraduate Eliot. Evelyn Underhill we know as a mystic and scholar of mysticism who also was read by the undergradute Eliot. Denis Saurat was a professor of French literature at the University of London, a friend of Orage, and a student of relations between literature and the occult.

The name on this list of most particular interest to the history of literary modernism is Jessie Weston. Her mere appearance as a regular contributor to the *Quest* is not sufficient to mark her as an occultist. However, even a cursory examination of her publications does mark her as both an occultist and a theosophist – albeit a Mead loyalist and therefore in schism with the Theosophical Society from 1909. She acknowledges her indebtedness to Mead in *From Ritual to Romance* (1920):

Finally, a casual reference, in Anrich's work on the Mysteries to the *Naassene Document*, caused me to apply to Mr G.R.S. Mead, of whose knowledge of the mysterious border-land between Christianity and Paganism, and willingness to place that knowledge at the disposal of others, I had, for some years past, had pleasant experience. Mr Mead referred me to his own translation and analysis of the text in question, and there, to my satisfaction, I found, not only the final link that completed the chain of evolution from Pagan Mystery to Christian Ceremonial, but also proof of that wider significance I was beginning to apprehend. The problem involved was not one of Folk-lore, not even one of Literature, but of Comparative Religion in its widest sense. (viii)

That she also acknowledges a debt to Sir James Frazer, Franz Cumont, and Jane Harrison, and thanks Professor von Schroeder for help rendered during the Bayreuth festival of 1911, indicates the degree to which theosophical, scholarly, and Wagnerian circles interconnected.

As I have observed above, scholarly ignorance of theosophy and the occult has led Eliot scholars and folklorists alike to accept *From Ritual to Romance* as a standard folkloric study belonging to the Frazer school. Margaret Reid, for example, cites Weston frequently as a standard authority in her study of the Grail legend. However, she finds the handling of Grail motifs by John Cowper Powys and Eliot questionable (Reid [1938] 1961, esp. 149–57). Any careful reading of Weston's study will reveal that it is not a standard anthropological study; rather, it is a tracing of an occult tradition that has secretly maintained itself from remotest antiquity. Weston's little book brings together most of the threads that we have been following in previous chapters. Her only misses are the troubadours, Dante, and the *dolce stil nuovo*.

The occult hypothesis of a wisdom secretly maintained from remote antiquity by societies and enlightened individuals is also the central hypothesis of *From Ritual to Romance* – and, indeed, of all her other studies of medieval legend. Weston's particular interest is inspired by Wagner, for it is the Grail legends of the Arthurian cycle understood as transmitters of the wisdom disguised in Christian garb. The interesting question for literary history, however, is why Eliot chose this rather eccentric work as an interpretive device for *The Waste Land*. It may be – as scholarship has tacitly assumed – that the theosophical and Wagnerian provenance of *From Ritual to Romance* is not truly relevant to an understanding of *The Waste Land*. The question is a literary historical one rather than a strictly hermeneutic one, for a better understanding of the ambience that generated *The Waste Land* may very well not produce an interpretation of the poem that is otherwise unavailable. Certainly, New Critical doctrines have discouraged scholarship from asking questions about historical context for most of the period of *The Waste Land*'s critical reception. Indeed, Eliot's little epic stands as the paradigmatic case of a text for which context is held to be not only irrelevant to its interpretation but positively impertinent, if not downright impious.

The reader should be warned that the following discussion flouts the New Critical axiom of textual autonomy, as well as the deconstructive axiom of readerly pre-eminence, and it may therefore appear tangential to many readers. This is an exercise in literary history; that is, an effort to recontextualize *The Waste Land* within the occult ambience which we have been surveying and which heretofore has not received scholarly attention.

We must begin with an assessment of the notice taken of *From Ritual to Romance* by Eliot criticism. The theosophical provenance of Weston's book was in fact noticed in a review, but none of the early critics of *The Waste Land* – whether admiring, judicious, or dismissive – picked up on F.L. Lucas's observation (*New Statesman*, 3 Nov. 1923) that "Miss Weston is clearly a theosophist, and Mr Eliot's poem might be a theosophical tract. The sick king and the waste land symbolise, we gather, the sick soul and the desolation of this material life." Lucas had taken the trouble to read Weston's "interesting, though credulous work" but found that "even when thus instructed and with a feeling of virtuous research the reader returns to the attack, the difficulties are but begun" (Grant 1982, 196). In the end, Lucas dismisses the poem as a failure – thus guaranteeing that his review would be ignored by subsequent scholarship.

Among the earliest and most influential assessments of Weston's relevance to *The Waste Land* was F.O. Matthiessen's. Like Lucas, he found the Weston book to be unhelpful, but on very different grounds. Matthiessen judged *From Ritual to Romance* to be redundant to the autonomous self-sufficient affectivity of the printed text on the New Critical grounds of textual autonomy. He questioned

whether Miss Weston's valuable study has enabled me to feel the poem more intensely. For nearly everything of importance from her book that is apposite to an appreciation of *The Waste Land*, particularly her central emphasis on the analogous way by which various myths express the mysteries of sex and religion, has been incorporated into the structure of the poem itself, or into Eliot's Notes. Unlike many sections of Pound's *Cantos*, *The Waste Land* does not require recourse to the poet's reading in order to become comprehensible. Its structure is pre-eminently self-contained. (Matthiessen [1935] 1958, 50)

Matthiessen's praise of *The Waste Land*'s autonomy in contrast to the bookishness of *The Cantos* is symptomatic of early scholarship's felt need to isolate Eliot's canonized achievement from Pound's obviously similar but failed effort.

Cleanth Brooks, in a 1939 essay, refers to Weston exclusively for elucidation of what he calls "the basic symbol used, that of the waste land" and the equivalence operative between physical and spiritual sterility (64). Twenty years later, Hugh Kenner cites Ezra Pound himself to the effect that Weston's book is of extremely marginal relevance: "For the rest, I saw the poem in typescript, and I did not see the notes till 6 or 8 months afterward; and they have not increased my enjoyment of the poem one atom. The poem seems to me an emotional unit ... I have not read Miss Weston's *Ritual to Romance*, and do not at present intend to" (Kenner 1959, 151–2). Since Pound was the original editor of *The Waste Land*, his testimony carries peculiar authority. However, we shall see that his editing of the poem tended to remove its reliance on the Weston material – as if to disguise the esoteric inspiration of the poem. If, in fact, Pound's role was to "clean up" the poem's esotericism, we may be justified in taking this disclaimer with a grain of salt. Kenner himself later alters his own position and argues that Eliot intends to parody the Weston argument (Kenner 1971, 109–10, 437–44).

The mainstream critical consensus, then, has underplayed Weston's relevance to the poem even in the face of Eliot's headnote. We should have that note clearly in mind:

Not only the title, but the plan and a good deal of the incidental symbolism of the poem were suggested by Miss Jessie L. Weston's book on the Grail legend: *From Ritual to Romance* (Macmillan). Indeed, so deeply am I indebted, Miss Weston's book will elucidate the difficulties of the poem much better than my notes can do; and I recommend it (apart from the great interest of the book itself) to any who think such elucidation of the poem worth the trouble. To another work of anthropology I am indebted in general, one which has influenced our generation profoundly; I mean *The Golden Bough*; I have used especially the two volumes *Adonis Attis Osiris*. Anyone who is acquainted with these works will immediately recognize in the poem certain references to vegetation ceremonies. (Eliot 1971, 146)*

This note has been rather a problem for those who wish to argue that the Weston book is a red herring. However, critical avoidance of Weston eventually received the support of Eliot himself, for he recanted the generous acknowledgement of his debt to Weston – thirty-two years after the event: "It was just, no doubt, that I should pay my tribute to the work of Miss Jessie Weston; but I regret having sent so many enquirers off on a wild goose chase after Tarot cards and the Holy Grail" ("The Frontiers of Criticism," 1956, in Eliot 1961, 122). Thus, Eliot himself joined the consensual dismissal of *From Ritual to Romance*, apparently agreeing with Matthiessen, Brooks, and Kenner that his original recommendation was, after all, misleading.

The whole affair is rather puzzling. Of course, it is complicated by the fact that *The Waste Land* is a monument of literary modernism. This monument and others have been insulated from their rather unseemly provenance by the New Critical doctrine of aesthetic autonomy. The doctrine requires the rejection of influence and permits the rejection even of the authority of the author himself. With *The Waste Land*, we have a poem that is, more or less, co-authored, and both "authors" deny the relevance of a source that one of them first recommended to his readers. This ambivalence is mirrored by critics who deny the importance of the alleged source yet employ selected components of it in critical interpretations.

If we add to this mix the fact that scholarly attention was drawn to the occult provenance of Weston's study once again nearly thirty years ago, the affair becomes even stranger. In the little-noticed *The Way Down and Out: The Occult in Symbolist Literature* (1959), John Senior pointed out the true nature of Weston's book. It was, he said, a book

---

* All citations of *The Waste Land* are from the facsimile edition of 1971. Note that Eliot incorrectly identifies the publisher as Macmillan rather than Cambridge. This error is corrected in *Collected Poems*.

  I don't want to put too much stress on this point, but it is worth noting that in contradiction of the scholarly consensus descending from Brooks, Eliot attributes the vegetation ceremony elements to Frazer rather than to Weston.

whose burden is that the medieval grail stories are based upon the rituals of a lost religion which once covered Europe, the Near East, and even Asia, if not Atlantis and Lemuria – in a word, the burden is the "secret doctrine." And the myths which clothe the doctrine, according to Miss Weston, are occult. The grail legend is one more rendering of the mysteries; its meaning, she says, is identical, exoterically, with the story of Osiris or Christ.

And when we discover from her footnotes that Miss Weston relies heavily on W.B. Yeats, Arthur Waite, and G.R.S. Meade [sic], we should be tempted to suggest more than a suspicion of occultism, and openly declare Miss Weston a member of the occult laity, if not an initiate. This is not to say that Eliot is as close to occultism as Miss Weston – her book was a source, not the poem. (176–7).

We shall shortly see that Senior's estimate of *From Ritual to Romance* is accurate, but the remarkable thing about his "exposure" of Weston is that it has been completely without consequence for criticism of *The Waste Land*. Even the flurry of reassessment that followed publication of Valerie Eliot's facsimile edition of the poem fails to take notice of Senior's observations. Senior himself has not pursued his discovery, and he backs away from it even in the 1959 study in which it appeared.

A lesson can be taken from the misfire of Senior's discovery. *The Waste Land* is a text of such importance and sanctity that it must be protected from any suggestions that it is less than it has been seen to be. Like other classics, it has able defenders and apologists. For whatever reason, Senior's revelation suffered the same fate as the so-called homosexual theory, which drew attention to Eliot's relationship with Jean Verdenal (see Miller 1977).

An "occult theory" of the poem would doubtless suffer the same fate if it were put forward. So far as I can determine, no one has yet put forward such a theory, although some hints and suggestions have been made. The closest thing to an occult reading that I have been able to find is in an interesting article by Tom Gibbons (1972). Gibbons presents a persuasive argument that Eliot's source for the tarot material was not Weston but the occultist A.E. Waite: "Two main points seem to me to emerge from all this [Gibbon's precedent discussion]. The first is that Eliot appears to have known considerably more about occult literature than he admitted to in his notes to *The Waste Land*. The second is that the Tarot cards appear to play a much more important part in the meaning and organization of *The Waste Land* than is generally allowed" (564). Gibbons does not make anything of Weston's occult connections, but Grover Smith, in his most recent discussion of *The Waste Land* – apparently following Gibbons

– does acknowledge Weston's occult provenance. However, he does not pursue the question (Smith 1983, 88–97).

I have no evidence that Eliot was interested in the occult speculation that so clearly seized his fellow expatriate, Ezra Pound. However, he could not have been ignorant of those occultists who were the constant subject of gossip in the newspapers of the day. His inclusion of the fortune teller Mme Sosostris in *The Waste Land* is good evidence that he was at least aware of the vogue of fortune telling in polite society. Nor is it plausible that he would have been unaware of Pound's engagement with the occult. Certainly he knew that Pound was a close associate of Yeats and Orage, both of whom he knew to be occultists. Nor could he have been ignorant of the occult interests of Dorothy Pound's mother, Olivia Shakespear, and her famous friend, Florence Farr. Given the ubiquity of occultists and mystics in London and Paris at that time, it seems unlikely that Eliot could have failed to notice the occult nature of Weston's book.

Certainly, he was aware of Orage's occultism. In his obituary commentary on Orage (*Criterion*, Jan. 1935, 260–4) he alludes to Orage's "preoccupation with certain forms of mysticism" and says that he deprecates "that tendency in Orage." But he goes on to remark, "Perhaps my own attitude is suggestive of the reformed drunkard's abhorrence of intemperance." Presumably, Eliot is referring to his own attraction to Christian mystical writing. Eliot and Orage met just after Eliot had completed *The Waste Land* – in July 1922. He liked Orage (Eliot 1988, 550) but could not have seen much of him, because Orage shortly joined Gurdjieff at Fontainebleau.

It is possible that Eliot submitted his long poem to Pound's scrutiny specifically because he knew Pound to have some competence in occult theories and beliefs. If so, he would have been seeking guidance on the thematic coherence and perspicuity of the poem as much as, or more than, on its rhetorical structure, which has been the long-standing assumption of critical commentary. He was uncertain about the poem just because of his unfamiliarity with the Wagnerian and occult materials he self-consciously employed, which he knew were more familiar to Pound.

Everything we know about Eliot's philosophical and religious affiliations would suggest that he would have been deeply sceptical about the theosophical and Swedenborgian ideas with which Pound had been "dabbling" since his undergraduate days. But by the same token, his career makes it clear that he would not have been contemptuous of the mystical and metaphysical speculation of the occult. The occult's commitment to the reality of the noumenal and of its relevance to human life would naturally attract rather than repel Eliot, whose spirituality cannot be doubted. His subsequent decision to commit to orthodox Christianity clearly separates him from the occult movement, but it does not erase a common ground of interest.

As we have seen, the Christian mystic, Evelyn Underhill, was a regular contributor to Mead's journal. It is true that the reviews of her work in the *Quest* show that the theosophists thought her Christian "prejudices" to be restrictive and narrowing, but the fact that Mead published her work, as well as that of Buber, Scholem, and Eisler, shows the tolerance of the "mystical" community for divergence of opinion. Because of this tolerance, it is not necessary to argue that Eliot invested any belief either in Weston's occultism or in her historical argument for a secret theosophical cult exoterically expressed in the Grail legend. The claim that Eliot borrowed a story and a secret history of whose occult provenance he was aware is not different in character from the long-standing claim that he borrowed fertility cult elements. No one has ever supposed that Eliot believed that royal impotence could cause crop failure. No more need we suppose that he believed in the existence of a secret mystery tradition, or that he accepted Weston's account of it as involving an initiation into the double mystery of life and death. What I do claim is that the original version of *The Waste Land* incorporated them as elements of its theme and, further, that Pound's editing removed much of the occult and in so doing contributed to the poem's obscurity – and to its success.

Jessie Weston's occultist beliefs, attitudes, and scholarly program are not difficult to document despite a dearth of information about her. *From Ritual to Romance* was the only one of her books published with a regular academic press and was therefore a little more cautious than the others. *The Quest of the Holy Grail*, an earlier work, clearly reveals her occultist predilections:

It is not also without interest, or significance, that readers of romances, unacquainted with the Grail literature in general but familiar with "occult" tradition and practice, should invariably detect this [initiation] element in the story. More than once I have lent a translation of the *Gawain* Grail adventures to friends whom I had reason to believe were familiar with such subjects; invariably the result has been the same – the book has been returned with the remark: "this is the story of an initiation, told from the outside." (Weston [1913] 1964, 96)

Earlier in the same book Weston shows her occult colours quite plainly in a comment reminiscent of Pound's claim, in "Psychology and Troubadours," that he knew a man who "understood Persephone and Demeter, and one who understands the laurel":

No inconsiderable part of the information at my disposal depended upon personal testimony, the testimony of those who knew of the continued existence of such a ritual, and had actually been initiated into its mysteries – and for such evidence the student of the letter has little respect. He worships the written word; for the oral, living, tradition from which the word derives force and vitality he has little use. Therefore the written word had to be found. It has taken me some nine or ten years longer to complete the evidence, but the chain is at last linked up, and we can now prove by printed texts the parallels existing between each and every feature of the Grail story and the recorded symbolism of the Mystery cults. (4–5)

Readers of *The Cantos* will recognize "sagetrieb" or the "oral tradition" as identical to Weston's "oral, living tradition": "That is Sagetrieb, / that is tradition" (canto 95, Pound 1973a, 605). Like Weston, Pound devoted his entire career to finding written corroboration of the "living tradition" which he believed himself to be perpetuating. *The Cantos* are a ransacking of the written record, seeking the "gists and piths" which only the initiate, or enlightened one, can recognize as pieces of the puzzle. Pound seems to have believed, or hoped, that a collection of a sufficient number of such fragments would lead to the enlightenment of his readers – perhaps even to illumination or revelation.

This notion of a broken or fragmented tradition is evoked in Mead's title, *Fragments of a Faith Forgotten* (anticipating the phrase at the close of *The Waste Land*: "These fragments I have shored against my ruins"). Dorothy Pound was reading Mead's big work in 1912, and she complained that it took a lot of space in her suitcase as she packed (letter of 21 Sept. 1912, Pound 1984, 160). Pound also recalls the phrase at the beginning of the Malatesta cantos:

These fragments you have shelved (shored).
"Slut!" "Bitch!" Truth and Calliope
Slanging each other sous les lauriers. (canto 8, 28)

Pound distinguishes his epic project, inspired by Calliope, from Eliot's mere expression of truth – that the "tradition" is fragmented and has been "shelved" by him. The story of Malatesta is of one who attempts to unshelve and reintegrate the tradition – but it is a tragic tale of failure.

Weston and Pound – like Rossetti, Creuzer, and Mead – were diggers in the midden heap of the past, confident that they could separate wisdom from superstition, revelation from barbarism, and quality from kitsch. Eliot had no such confidence when he wrote *The Waste Land*. All the same, it grows out of the enterprise to recover the past – just as *Ulysses* does.

ELIOT AND TRADITION

Eliot certainly did not share the occultists' confidence that they could separate gold from dross in the world's cultural residue. On the contrary, he feared that the unity of European culture – of Christendom – had been broken and that, like Humpty Dumpty, it could not be put back together again. In this, Eliot was hardly idiosyncratic. The sentiment was widely shared throughout the latter half of the nineteenth century and had been variously expressed by Arnold and Pater long before Eliot. Like his Victorian predecessors, Eliot found himself in a cultural milieu dominated by optimism for the future. However, the modern optimism was founded on a sense of apocalyptics rather than progess. The occult, the Comteans, and the social Darwinians all agreed that a new age was being born. They differed radically in their views of the difficulty of the parturition.

The fragments collected in *The Waste Land* are only "shored against" the ruins of Europe, and – contrary to the occult faith – they do not yield a unity esoterically hidden in familiar texts. Indeed, read from this perspective, part of the point of the poem is its denial of the synopticism of Creuzer and the occult. It equally rejects occult faith in an imminent rebirth of an antique culture – envisioned as a return of Eleusis by Creuzer, Schuré, and Pound; as a return to Dionysian ecstasy in Wagnerian opera by the early Nietzsche; and as a turn of the Platonic year by Yeats.

Psychoanalysis similarly argued that all of humanity shared a universal psychic structure that generated culture and civilization. As we have seen, Jung and Freud drew on some of the same sources as the occult. Jung's collective unconscious is quite explicitly derived from the Neoplatonic world soul. Both are the repository of the cognitive and imaginative contents of the human mind. The mind draws from them as a bucket from a well. For Freud, the universal character of the psyche had a sociobiological basis in the inherent opposition between the impersonal life force of the Id, the personality of the Ego, and the communal pressures of the Super Ego shared by all humans. His theory required the further – and apparently unfounded – feature of a universal prohibition of incest. As noted above, both Jung and Freud employed the same exegetical technique as the occult in order to reveal the hidden universal character of apparently highly variegated cultural artifacts.

Of course, I do not claim that Freudian and Jungian psychology are reducible to occultism. My point, rather, is to draw attention to the widespread pressure during the period under study to find some grounds for universality in cultural phenomena. This pressure manifested itself in every branch of study addressing culture and was naturally drawn to the synopticism of the Hellenic period. Indeed, "culture" was a relatively new object of scholarly investigation. The nineteenth century had begun to explore – under the pressure of European exposure to alien cultures – the nature, sources, purpose, methods, and means of *culture*, which now, for the first time, was seen as an arbitrary creation of human ingenuity rather than the natural growth of soil, climate, and race as Herder, Vico, Gobineau, and Nietzsche had imagined.

The origin of the social sciences, whose special subject is human culture, is usually placed in the eighteenth century – either with Giambattista Vico or Jean Jacques Rousseau. Although "culture" as an object of study was a creation of the Enlightenment, its articulation was a preoccupation of the Romantics – of Blake, Schelling, Wordsworth, Coleridge, and Goethe, not to mention Hegel and Schopenhauer. Nietzschean nihilism was an almost inevitable consequence of asking questions about the legitimacy of cultural values in the wake of the loss of faith. Nietzsche was one of the first to "call into question" the legitimacy of European culture – whether defined as Christendom, rationality, or empiricist realism. Creuzer and the Romantics had only questioned its priority. Despite the occasional appearance of Frazer's *Golden Bough* in this company, it must be recognized that Frazer's work was not part of this questioning. It was neither nihilistic nor sceptical. On the contrary, it was very positivistic and tended to explain myths and religions as superstition, as failed applications of human reason to intractable problems such as birth, death, and authority.

The occult had a nonsceptical, nonpositivistic answer to the problem of cultural relativism. Its first modern expression is found in Giambattista Vico. As an Enlightenment thinker, Vico had a simple and coherent theory of cultural universality (even though he regarded cultures as human artifacts – an idiosyncratic opinion in that age):

Uniform ideas originating among entire peoples unknown to each other must have a common ground of truth. This axiom is a great principle which establishes the common sense of the human race as the criterion taught to

the nations by divine providence to define what is certain in the natural law
of the gentes ... Thence issues the mental dictionary for assigning origins
to all the diverse articulated languages. It is by means of this dictionary that
the ideal eternal history is conceived which gives us the histories in time of
all nations. (Vico [1744] 1961, 22)

The Platonic mental dictionary to which Vico appeals in this passage
has been revived in this century by the linguist Noam Chomsky, but
in the high modernist period it had no currency at all in academic
circles. It survived only on the margins, in occult literary circles,
until it gained some respectability in Jung's psychologization of it in
his archetypalism.

Similarly, the notion that the ideal had a history of contact with
the world – a story of the "intersections of time with eternity" –
survived only on the margins, where it had been transformed into
secret history, metahistory, or deterministic historicism. Eliot's philosophical training effectively inoculated him against innatist archetypalism. Pound – like Yeats – was less well "buffered" against the
corrosive effects of occult and mystical speculation, proving vulnerable to belief in secret histories.

On the other hand, neither Pound nor Eliot were protected by their
education from those theories of culture that measured an individual's humanity by his or her "level" of culture. At the beginning of
this century, the problem of culture for Americans was to achieve
the "level" already attained in Europe. Americans had been persuaded by Emerson, Whitman, Thoreau, and Henry James that they,
as Americans, had no culture. No doubt, such a lack encouraged
adoption of the postulate that no one *had* culture and that the business of life was the acquisition of culture, a view not remote from
the occult belief that life was a vale of soul-*making*.

Pound and Eliot, like so many Jamesian protagonists, went to
Europe where "culture" supposedly lay awaiting acquisition. Alas,
when they arrived they found European culture in crisis. Unlike
Jamesian heroes and heroines, they were not troubled by the moral
laxity and hypocrisy of European Svengalis. They knew about that
danger from reading Henry James and were prepared to risk it – or
even, in Pound's case, to wallow in it. What they were less prepared
for was the sad fact that the Europeans had lost faith in their own
culture. The Americans were, in short, ill prepared for the Nietzschean scepticism that was stalking the souls of Europeans. Having
travelled to Europe in order to imbibe high culture, they were little
inclined to abandon the belief in cultural progress – whether a Hegelian progress of spirit or a Romantic recovery of authentic origins.

The Europeans themselves were hesitant to embrace the Nietz-schean revelation. Locke, Voltaire, Rousseau, Kant, Hegel, Schelling, Creuzer, Schopenhauer, Wagner, Gobineau, Marx, Freud, Jung, Husserl, and Heidegger – for all their great differences – shared a faith in the universality of Western (or Aryan) culture values. Americans, I believe, are less alarmed by cultural relativism than Europeans are. The United States, after all, was founded on the Enlightenment belief that cultures are artifacts of human reason and therefore share the universality of rationality itself. If this were not so, the process of assimilation called the "melting pot" could not take place. On culture-specific theories, only a mongrel culture could arise from the mixture of the world's races and peoples in America.

Americans grow up in the conviction that their nation is daily engaged in culture-creation, accepting all the various fabrics of world cultures and sewing them into a crazy quilt of homely but robust beauty. Although Pound never articulated such a view, it seems that his *Cantos* were designed to be the literary equivalent of the American melting pot – a patchwork of the best of all cultures and nations stitched into a single magnificent quilt. The Europeans, by contrast, feared that the doctrine of cultural universality was too susceptible to be captured by jingoism. European experience with universal culture has not been a happy one. It has typically taken the form of an imperium – whether Alexandrian, Roman (both the military/political and the ecclesiastical variety), Napoleonic, or Hitlerian. Pound early recognized the equivalence of empire and universal culture, but he was not alarmed by it: "All the fine dreams of empire, of a universal empire, Rome, the imperium restored, and so on, came to little. The dream, nevertheless, had its value, it set a model for-mulation, a model of orderly procedure, and it was used as a spur through every awakening from the eighth century to the sixteenth. Yet it came to no sort of civic reality, either in the high sheriffage of Charles the Great, or in its atavistic parody under Napoleon" (Pound 1962, 49).

British modernists, like the Europeans generally, can be divided into those who believed in cultural universality – either on a Spen-cerean-Darwinian model of gradual evolution or on an Hegelian-Marxian model of violent revolution – and those who rejected cultural universality and withdrew into insular nationalism. Bloomsbury belonged to the latter camp, remaining resolutely English. *A Passage to India* is more a meditation on Kipling's perception that cultural diversity was something fundamental and insurmountable, that East was East and West was West, than it is a prose filling out of Whitman's more relativistic poem. Virginia Woolf's novels are even more anti-universal, insisting upon the personal and incommunicable – as well as upon the ineffectual but somehow transcendent nature of artistic revelation, a revelation that in her work is a metonym for culture.

Joseph Conrad – who, as a Pole, was cautious about the imperium – generates the darkness and evil in *Heart of Darkness* out of the fear that there is after all a fundamental kinship between Europeans and the black Africans and their "unspeakable rites": "It was unearthly, and the men were – No, they were not inhuman. Well, you know, that was the worst of it – this suspicion of their not being inhuman. It would come slowly to one. They howled and leaped, and spun, and made horrid faces; but what thrilled you was just the thought of their humanity – like yours – the thought of your remote kinship with this wild and passionate uproar" (Conrad [1902] 1973, 51). Conrad is a transitional figure on the question of universality. For him the possibility of European kinship with the African "savages" is frightening and alarming. He has Marlowe stand before the unified human soul in fear and trembling, and not at all with Nietzsche's ecstatic joy. Where Nietzsche finds that there is no truth and that everything is permitted, Conrad finds a frightening truth before which the man of character must stand firm: "The mind of man is capable of anything – because everything is in it, all the past as well as all the future. What was there after all? Joy, fear, sorrow, devotion, valour, rage – who can tell? – but truth – truth stripped of its cloak of time. Let the fool gape and shudder – the man knows, and can look on without a wink. But he must be as much of a man as these on the shore. He must meet that truth with his own true stuff – with his own inborn strength" (52).

As an Irish artist, Joyce was perhaps the most sensitive of all to the imperial aspect of a theory of cultural universality. He responds to modernist universalism with humour and satire rather than with existential *angst* as Conrad's Kurtz does. Joyce's work – from *Dubliners* and *A Portrait of the Artist as a Young Man* through *Ulysses* to *Finnegans Wake* – can be read without much strain as an Aristophanic satire on the notion of a universal culture. *Finnegans Wake* is manifestly a travesty of the Viconian notions of a universal mental language. Like *The Cantos*, *Finnegans Wake* "contains" world history and – even more than *The Cantos* – expresses the universal culture in a polyglot travesty of a universal language. The "language" of *Finnegans Wake*, manufactured by an agglutinative combination of all the European languages and many Middle Eastern and Asian ones, is unmistakably a travesty of Vico's mental language. Compared with *Finnegans Wake*, *The Cantos* are linguistically timid, merely incorporating Egyptian hieroglyphs, Chinese characters, Greek, Latin, Provençal, French,

Italian, Spanish, and German expressions into a basically English-language text. Nonetheless, the commitment to the notion of a universal culture is as unmistakable in the two works as it is in Vico, Creuzer, and Blavatsky.

Modernism, the occult, psychology, positivism, social Darwinism, and Marxism share a commitment to the universality of culture, as they share a preoccupation with the notion of history as a story. (In these days of narratology, I should perhaps add that by "story" I mean an account of events with a beginning, middle, and end. Story is understood to be helpfully explanatory and organizational, as opposed to oppressive, distorting, and hegemonic as it is in much Marxist-inspired narratology.) These shared features are, I think, more definitional than the scepticism and relativism that the scholarly community has selected as the touchstone of forward thinking in this century. Of course, each of these different groups locates the universal in a different place. For the occultist, it is most perfectly represented in the remote past. Nonetheless, for her, it is immanent in the cosmos.

Freud and Jung both place the universal component of culture in a psyche common to all humans. Freud remains materialistic, whereas Jung is principally interested in the noumenal. Freud's psyche is embodied in the individual somatic entity. Although each individual has a unique history, in Freud's theory individual biographies conform to a universal paradigm of oral, anal, and genital stages. Jung, in contrast, locates the universal in a noumenal realm that embodies itself in human psyches. Dialectical materialism, for its part, places the universal within history but retains Hegel's adaptation of Christian millenarianism and Jewish messianism by locating the universal at the conclusion of history. Nazism, in a demonic travesty of Judaism, made the noumenal immanent in history, embodied in the destiny of an "historical people," the Aryans. Although Comtean positivists and Spencerian social Darwinists also appeal to universal laws to explain historical event, their laws have little of the spiritual in them. Nonetheless, the belief in human perfectibility through the exercise of reason, and a belief in the survival of the fittest share universality and historicality with these other beliefs.

Yeats believed with Nietzsche that culture was the product of conflict, and like Nietzsche he placed the conflict outside the psyche – in history and culture. And, again like Nietzsche, Yeats was prepared to celebrate violence as an alternative manifestation of the same force or power expressed in art. A late poem, "The Long-Legged Fly," begins with Caesar in his tent:

That civilization may not sink,
Its great battle lost,
Quiet the dog, tether the pony
To a distant post;
Our master Caesar is in the tent
Where the maps are spread,
His eyes fixed upon nothing,
A hand under his head.

It ends with Michelangelo on his scaffold:

That girls at puberty may find
The first Adam in their thought,
Shut the door of the Pope's chapel,
Keep those children out,
There on that scaffolding reclines
Michael Angelo.
With no more sound than the mice make
His hand moves to and fro.

The middle stanza speaks of burning topless towers, "that face," and a child-woman dancing a little step in the street – all usually taken to be an evocation of Helen of Troy. The whole poem brilliantly encapsulates Yeats's reading of culture and history, melding military violence, sexual passion, and aesthetic expression into a manifestation deriving from a single transcendent force emblematized in the poem by the refrain: "Like a long-legged fly upon the stream / His mind moves upon silence." The stream is the flowing water of incarnate life, and hence of history. The mind is the *anima mundi* as manifest first in the culture hero (symbolized by Caesar), secondly in the anonymous beautiful woman of the middle stanza, and finally in the great artist (symbolized by Michelangelo).

Pound's position on the issue of universal culture is very little different from Yeats's, except that – true American that he was – Pound was content with a polyglot poem absorbing all cultures without troubling himself much about the crazy-quilt effect that resulted from this practice. And Pound was completely devoid of the Aristophanic mockery of the project that so clearly animated Joyce's art and that makes Wallace Stevens's treatment of this theme so delightful – and so puzzling for his readers. Pound also shared with Eliot the naïve American vanity which permitted him to believe that an individual could consciously and single-handedly produce or reformulate a culture. From at least 1933 on, Pound obviously regarded himself as the saviour of the culture of Europe and the West. In *The Pisan Cantos*, when his world had come crashing down around his ears, he still defiantly declared his faith in the old cultural imperium: "I surrender neither the empire nor the temples / plural / nor the constitution nor yet the city of Dioce" (Pound 1973a, 434).

Eliot was just as committed to the idea of a universal culture as Pound and the occult were. He even used the term favoured by the occult – "tradition" – in his early essays, trying to catch the idea of an unofficial or alternate culture which was central to occult theories. Eliot accepted the dominant view of the day that culture or tradition was the most important and leading component of the human enterprise. "Culture" was then, and remains today, a somewhat protean concept. Perhaps to avoid its shifting sense, Pound eventually adopted the term "paideuma" from Leo Frobenius, to replace "culture." He defined paideuma as "the gristly roots of ideas that are in action" (Pound 1938, 58) in an adaptation of the Fascist contempt for abstract thought. Whatever it is, "culture" is to be understood as an entity independent of and prior to the rational and technological aspects of civilization expressed in logic, mathematics, and science.

In contrast to the present intellectual climate, everyone in the modernist period – whether behaviourist, empiricist, positivist, Platonist or occultist – conceded the universality of the rational. Nietzsche's inclusion of science, mathematics, and logic in the relativized cultures had not yet "taken" at this time – even though it received a relatively accessible articulation by Lévy-Bruhl in *Les Fonctions mentales dans les sociétés inférieures* in 1910. Universality was questionable only for *culture*, which was understood as the residue of human achievement that was left after the unquestionably universal component – *science* – was subtracted. Postmodernism is genuinely distinct from modernism on this point, for like Nietzsche it relativizes all human achievement and behaviour, including the natural sciences.

Although Eliot later came to reject cultural universality in favour of a pan-European culture distinct from Asian, American, and African cultures, he was preoccupied in the period up to *The Waste Land* with the characteristically romantic problem of the relation between the individual and his culture. Like Pound, he took it for granted that culture was something that had to be laboriously acquired:

Tradition is a matter of much wider significance [than imitation of one's elders]. It cannot be inherited, and if you want it you must obtain it by great labour. It involves, in the first place, the historical sense, which ... involves a perception, not only of the pastness of the past, but of its presence; the historical sense compels a man to write not merely with his own generation in his bones, but with a feeling that the whole of the literature of Europe from Homer and within it the whole of the literature of his own country has a simultaneous existence and composes a simultaneous order. ("Tradition and Individual Talent," 1919, in Eliot [1928] 1960, 49)

This passage is very familiar to modernist scholars, but what strikes me about it is not so much its American egalitarianism – or even its modernist historicism – as its easy assumption of the romantic view of culture as a single organism. In this early period, Eliot avoids the term "culture" almost as carefully as he avoids *anima mundi*, but he does speak of collective minds in a manner slightly reminiscent of Vico and Jung: "He [the poet] must be aware that the mind of Europe – the mind of his own country – a mind which he learns in time to be much more important than his own private mind – is a mind which changes, and that this change is a development which abandons nothing *en route*, which does not superannuate either Shakespeare, or Homer, or the rock drawing of the Magdalenian draughtsmen" (51). Eliot is anxious – both early and late in his career – to insist upon the unity of culture. But he does not want a Nietzschean unity that would relativize the natural sciences. The later Eliot is more Herderian than Nietzschean, willing to achieve cultural unity by exclusion of the culturally alien.

Eliot's doctoral thesis, "Knowledge and Experience in the Philosophy of F.H. Bradley," addresses the problem of scientific knowledge in too sophisticated and intricate a manner to be summarized. However, it can certainly be characterized as a version of sceptical idealism. Eliot concedes the competing claims to knowledge of science, psychology, and metaphysics, and rejects only psychology: "There is ... nothing mental, and there is certainly no such thing as consciousness if consciousness is to be an object or something independent of the objects which it has. There are simply 'points of view,' objects, and half-objects. Science deals only with objects; psychology, in the sense of rational or faculty psychology [as opposed to what is now called neuroscience], may deal with half-objects, and metaphysics alone with the subject, or point of view" (Eliot 1964, 83). I do not think that any unambiguous conclusions about Eliot's beliefs can be drawn from this passage. Certainly, its apparent relativism is only apparent, for it is restricted to the realm of metaphysics – a realm increasingly marginal in all varieties of philosophy. (After all, he is summarizing Bradley's arguments, and Bradley was no relativist.) Nonetheless, the passage is worth citing to remind ourselves that Eliot had meditated on the issues of culture and knowledge at a level of technical sophistication far beyond that of Pound or Arnold or

Pater – and even of Coleridge, the best philosopher among English-speaking poets prior to Eliot.

Eliot famously argued that when culture is in good health, its members possess a unified sensibility and "feel their thought as immediately as the odour of a rose," with the result that their art possesses grace and beauty. This theory of unified sensibility is not original with Eliot; it is at least as old as Rousseau. However, it was enjoying a vogue at the turn of the century because of the great popularity of Bergson's vitalism, a popularity that helped to promote the analogous immanentism of the occult. A more extreme version of the theory is found in Orage's 1907 attempt to harmonize Nietzscheanism with occult theories of cognition. Orage borrows pseudo-biological theory from Maurice Bucke's *Cosmic Consciousness*, a work discussed above.

In Orage's Nietzschean version of Bucke the lowest form of intelligence is animal instinct. However, animal instinct is said to share the property of unified sensibility with those who possess cosmic consciousness:

What in the animal we name instinct is an as yet undifferentiated mode of life, in which all our faculties are, as it were, active in a single sense. Feeling, willing, and knowing are not discriminated as they are in us, but form a single strand. In the human mind, on the contrary, the various threads are separated. A certain retardation is given to various aspects of the undifferentiated instinct ... But when the mind becomes lucid, free, ethereal, the retardation may be supposed no longer to take place. The resistance is removed, and once more the passage of the instincts is unimpeded and free. Only, instead as in the animals ending in mind, they pass through mind and end in the superconsciousness.

... Now the general name for this free passage of instinct through mind is intuition; so that instinct, reason, and intuition may be said to stand for unity, disintegration, and renewed unity of the instinctual life. These phases correspond, as we have seen, to animal, human, and superman. (Orage 1907, 81)

It is not likely that Eliot's notion of the unified sensibility is derived from Orage. But we do not need Orage, for very similar ideas are found in Henri Bergson, whose work Eliot knew and admired. Nonetheless, it is worth citing Orage's rather stronger theory to demonstrate that mainstream speculation was mirrored in occult literature – and not always in a formulation easily recognizable as occult.

Eliot's argument is that because the poet's task is "to find the verbal equivalent for states of mind and feeling," and because "our civilization comprehends great variety and complexity," artistic expression "must be *difficult*" ("The Metaphysical Poets," 1921, in Eliot 1951, 289). He passes silently over the premise that the task of poetry is to express a civilization – or, to put it another way, that "states of mind and feeling" just are the culture of a civilization, and in expressing them poetry expresses the culture. On this interpretation there is very little distance between Eliot's theory of tradition and Pound's "gristly roots of ideas." Both are expressivist theories of art, and both posit a tacit, unconscious, or inarticulate foundation for culture. The expressed, conscious, and articulate aspects of culture are hence seen to be derivative and secondary, a mere "surface" beneath which lie dark, submarine depths.

Much later, Eliot makes this feature of his thought about culture explicit. *Notes Toward a Definition of Culture* is often regarded as a reactionary betrayal of his earlier cultural relativism. However, there is little reason to believe that Eliot ever was a cultural relativist. His early arguments depended upon the assumption of the universality of culture that he – like Coleridge, Arnold, and Pater – had inherited from the German Romantics. The novelty that distinguished the modernists from the Romantics and Victorians – and is easily mistaken for cultural relativism – was their discovery of non-European cultural forms of expression.

This discovery has been erroneously identified with the ethnographic work of the anthropologists, rather than with the mythographic and archaeological theories of Creuzer, Wagner, and Nietzsche as it ought to be. And it should be remembered that all of these speculators shared a belief in the psychic unity of the human species. Far from being relativists in matters of culture or psychology, they were universalists. F.B. Jevons, for example, observed in 1896 that "the study of savages still in the Stone Age has revealed the fact that not only are the implements made and used by them the same all over the world, but the institutions and conceptions by which they govern their lives have an equally strong resemblance to one another. The presumption, therefore, that our Indo-European forefathers of the Stone Age had beliefs and practices similar to those of other peoples in the same stage of development is very strong" (Leach 1985, 253).

We no longer believe that modern "savage" or "primitive" human societies are cultural fossils as the nineteenth century supposed. However, in the 1920s it was still the standard and unchallenged view. It is clearly the view reflected by Conrad in *Heart of Darkness*. What had changed by the 1920s – thanks to Wagner, Nietzsche, Freud, and Jung – was the posture of easy superiority towards these allegedly primitive cultures, a posture Jevons shared with Frazer and

Tylor. Modern European culture was thought by the whole avant-garde to be the heir – albeit a prodigal heir – of antique elements that were still observable in the cultures of India, Africa, America, and Oceania, almost all of which were believed to be wonderfully integrated. These cultures did not suffer from "dissociated sensibilities" like modern "civilized" men. This assumption is, of course, Romantic; it is Rousseauian, Creuzerian, Wagnerian, and Nietzschean.

The endemic – albeit rather soft – belief in the "spiritual" superiority of archaic and primitive culture was enthusiastically endorsed by the occult. This belief dovetailed beautifully with the occult's understanding of history as a story of decline, corruption, and decadence. All varieties of the occult believed that wisdom was a possession of the first men and that it had increasingly been lost. Jessie Weston expresses this view clearly in *From Ritual to Romance:*

The more closely one studies pre-Christian Theology, the more strongly one is impressed with the deeply, and daringly, spiritual character of its speculations, and the more doubtful it appears that such teaching can depend upon the unaided processes of human thought, or can have been evolved from such germs as we find among the supposedly "primitive" peoples, such as e.g., the Australian tribes. Are they really primitive? Or are we dealing, not with the primary elements of religion, but with the *disjecta membra* of a vanished civilization? (Weston [1920] 1957, 7)

No doubt, Weston has in mind Blavatsky's Lemurians as the vanished civilization, but it could just as well be Creuzer's Pelasgians, Nietzsche's pre-Socratic Greeks, or even Eliot's seventeenth-century Englishmen – all of whom are said to have possessed some wisdom or insight that we have lost but that we might regain by studying them. Of course, neither Nietzsche nor Eliot (nor even Creuzer) are as silly as Weston and Blavatsky in their reading of history. Nonetheless, they all share the antique view of history as a story of decline from some pure origin, rather than the Enlightenment or Spencerian view of gradual improvement on a primitive beginning – of progress or evolution. That such a pessimistic understanding of historical process is shared by such diverse thinkers as Rousseau, Nietzsche, and Derrida is no evidence that it was not also endemic in modernism.

Lucien Lévy-Bruhl was one of the most prominent theorists of cultural relativism. He called into question the principle of the psychic unity of human beings as rational creatures, or *homo sapiens*. He argued for a *mentalité primitive*, a special and irrational cognitive mode peculiar to savages. (The mark of its irrationality was its tolerance of self-contradiction – just as in the *via negativa* of the mystics.) Lévy-Bruhl's theory invoked the principle of "participation"; that is, a breaking down of the subject-object division of civilized rationality so that the primitive thinker could make no distinction between himself as knowing subject and the known as object. He likened primitive consciousness to "states such as ecstasy, that is, border states in which representation, properly so called, disappears, since the fusion between subject and object has become complete" (Lévy-Bruhl [1910] 1985, 362). According to Lévy-Bruhl, primitives think in terms of "collective representations"; that is, sensible representations of a very wide or "collective" significance to which great emotional force is attached (36–8).

Except for their empirical and contingent nature, Lévy-Bruhl's "collective representations" are equivalent to Jung's noumenal and absolute archetypes, to Freud's symbols energized by "cathexis," and to the myths and symbols of literary culture descending from Schelling and Creuzer. His privileging of ecstatic gnosis also aligns him with Nietzsche's Dionysian ecstasy. Eliot knew this work and cited it approvingly in *Knowledge and Experience* on this very point (note 105). He referred to Lèvy-Bruhl again in his review of Gilbert Murray's translation of Euripides (Eliot 1951, 62).

Wassily Kandinsky's influential essay *Concerning the Spiritual in Art* also praises the primitive sensibility, and it claims, rather like Upward, that it is re-establishing itself in the modern sensibility:

There is ... in art another kind of external similarity which is founded on a fundamental truth. When there is a similarity of inner tendency ... in any one period to that of another, the logical result will be a revival of the external forms which served to express those inner feelings in an earlier age. An example of this today is our sympathy, our spiritual relationship with the Primitives. Like ourselves, these artists sought to express in their work only internal truths, renouncing in consequence all consideration of external form. (Kandinsky [1914] 1977, 1)

Although Kandinsky's book has had a formative influence on the development of abstract expressionism, its overtly theosophical and Blavatskian character has been little noticed. Kandinsky expresses theosophical cultural history, albeit in a formulation difficult to distinguish from the Hegelian progress of spirit:

The spiritual life, to which art belongs and of which she is one of the mightiest elements, is a complicated but definite and easily definable movement forwards and upwards ...

Veiled in obscurity are the causes of this need to move ever upwards and forwards, by sweat of the brow, through sufferings and fears. When one stage has been accomplished, and many evil stones cleared from the road, some unseen and wicked hand scatters new obstacles in the way, so that the path often seems blocked and totally obliterated. But there never fails to come to the rescue some human being, like ourselves in everything except that he has in him a secret power of vision. (4)

Although Lewis and Pound printed excerpts from Kandinsky's essay in *Blast* in 1914, I do not think that Kandinsky was a source for the cultural theories of either Pound or Eliot (much less of Lewis). All the same, Kandinsky's essay is another instance of friendly relations between occultism and aesthetic theory.

Eliot certainly did not share Kandinsky's theosophical version of cultural history. On the other hand, pretty well the whole of modernism agreed with Kandinsky on the cultural superiority of the archaic if not of the primitive – once one subtracted the scientific and technological achievements of civilization. On this point, Eliot's rather delicate discussion of cultural relativism in *Knowledge and Experience* is relevant. Discussing the superiority of European knowledge to "that of the savage," he observes: "If we make no assumptions about the validity of our knowledge, the growth which we trace [in history, evolution, or the development of the child] is not the growth of knowledge at all, but is the history only of adaptation, if you like to the environment" (Eliot 1964, 85). But he does, in the end, appear to endorse a relativistic position, asserting, "All significant truths are private truths. As they become public they cease to become [*sic*] truths; they become facts, or at best part of the public character; or at worst, catchwords" (165). However, Eliot's notion of private truth belongs, I think, to Plato's famous dismissal of public truths (*Letters* 7.344c) rather than to a Nietzschean relativism.

In contrast to the painters, the poets did not succumb to the Romantic version of the primitive exemplified by Lévi-Bruhl and Kandinsky. Unlike the Romantics, who were drawn to the social and political organization of allegedly "primitive" non-Europeans, the modernists were drawn to alien high cultures that had maintained a continuity with their own "primitive" past – especially India and China – and to the archaeological past of Europe itself. Eliot had studied Indian religion and philosophy at Harvard, and at least flirted with Weston's Wagnerian and theosophical cultural history before he "betrayed" the modern taste for the esoteric and exotic by embracing Anglican Christianity.

I believe that Eliot has never been forgiven for his conversion to Christianity, just because everyone in the avant-garde – whether sceptical materialists or credulous visionaries – was antichristian. Wagner, Nietzsche, Freud, Shaw, Mead, Blavatsky, Kandinsky, Marx, and Bertrand Russell agreed on very little, but they were of one mind on the bankruptcy of Christianity. For all of them, as for Arnold, Christianity was a "creed outworn." Every *Kulturträger* had some new "creed" which he or she believed could and should replace Christianity. Comtean positivists claimed to have a science and methodology which, willy nilly, exposed all religious beliefs as mere superstition. Social Darwinians put their faith in a biological version of Adam Smith's "invisible hand." Marxists and Hegelians placed their faith in history itself.

The occult alone offered a new superstition, a new faith – one which, in the true spirit of nineteenth-century aetiology, they made prior and antipathetic to Christianity. The French and Italian occult were a little different on this point, tending to permit Catholic Christianity some share in the "tradition." However, even Schuré and Péladan wanted to reform and revitalize a religion they regarded as having fallen into an almost moribund state. They were opposed by the orthodox polemicists such as Eugène Aroux, who sought to expose Dante and the troubadours as heretics and to expunge them from the canon. Because of Pound's considerable reliance on Continental sources, he was ambivalent on this point. He tended to share in the contempt for Christianity of the occultists in the Protestant world, but persistently found virtue in Catholic authors – notably Dante.

Pound devoted much of his life to an intense (although unsystematic) study of the ancient Mediterranean world and of China in an effort to articulate his tradition. Like other occultists, he hoped to cobble together that ancient wisdom which had supposedly been obliterated by the decadence of Western civilization. He agreed with Nietzsche that the decadence began with the Greeks: "Greece rotted. The story of gk. civilization as we have it, is the record of a decadence" (Pound 1938, 309). But in his Fascist phase, he had nothing but praise for Roman and Italian civilization – the former, a distinclty un-Nietzschean posture.

Pound's economic and political involvements are an aspect of this obsessive project and not a diversion from it. The incorporation of this research into *The Cantos* has long been regarded as evidence that it was driven by the needs of the poem. However, it is my conviction that – with the exception of *The Pisan Cantos* – the poem is a creature of his cultural project, rather than the other way around. When Pound called *The Cantos* "a record of struggle," he meant his struggle to "gather from the air a live tradition" (Pound 1938, 135; 1973a, 522).

Eliot was not immune to such temptations, but he was too learned or too intelligent or too cautious to yield to them. Instead, he decided to adopt the only strategy for cultural integration that he thought held any hope of success. He opted for mainstream European culture, a culture that had been ineluctably Christian for the best part of two millennia. In doing so, Eliot did not abandon cultural relativism – as the admirers of *The Waste Land* thought. Rather, he abandoned its contrary, the doctrine of cultural universality. Eliot had never been a sceptical relativist and was in fact closer to relativism as a Christian when he adopted a cultural pluralism.

The briefest and perhaps most cogent expression of Eliot's late theory of culture is found – somewhat ironically – in the radio broadcast he made to the defeated Germans in 1946, which is printed as an appendix to *Notes Toward a Definition of Culture* (1948). There he asks himself, "What of the influences from outside Europe, of the great literature of Asia?" In his answer he mentions his "long ago" study of the ancient Indian languages and concedes that "my own poetry shows the influence of Indian thought and sensibility." He then praises the Chinese translations of Arthur Waley and of Pound (who was then under indictment for treason) and admits their influence on poetry written in English (113). But he concedes only that "every literature may influence every other" without engulfing the "unity of European culture" that arises from a shared history (114).

European culture is defined in the next lecture as "the common tradition of Christianity which has made Europe what it is" (122). "The Western world," he tells his German radio audience, "has its unity in this heritage, in Christianity and in the ancient civilizations of Greece, Rome and Israel, from which, owing to two thousand years of Christianity, we trace our descent" (123). This point is exactly the one made by Burckhardt in his 1867 lectures (later published as *Force and Freedom*), where he rejects both Herderian and Hegelian notions of culture, and argues that the past of each community is a "spiritual *continuum* which forms part of our supreme spiritual heritage" (Burckhardt 1955, 77). Eliot does not acknowledge Burckhardt, but the conformity of views is unmistakable: "What I wish to say is, that this unity in the common elements of culture, throughout many centuries, is the true bond between us. No political and economic organization, however much goodwill it commands can supply what this culture [*sic*] unity gives. If we dissipate or throw away our common patrimony of culture, then all the organization and planning of the most ingenious minds will not help us, or bring us closer together" (Eliot 1948, 123).

Eliot has been sufficiently taken to task for his "reactionary" talk about culture, for ethnocentrism, absolutism, exclusivism, elitism, and all the other "reactionary ideologies" attributed to him. I wish neither to defend him against these charges nor to add to them. My point is quite different. It is that there was no radical break in Eliot's thinking about art and culture from a preconversion clear-eyed "humane" or Nietzschean scepticism to a postconversion "elitist" credulity and blindness. Far from being an anomalous figure, Eliot is a child of his time both before and after his conversion. His oddity is that he attempts to straddle the immense gulf between organized Christianity and the fecund world of antichristian sentiment, a world which gathers together everyone from the hardest-nosed materialist and positivist to the mooniest occultist – with Marxists, Fabians, Social Democrats, Social Crediters, Utopians, social engineers, reformers, artists, and dreamers ranged in between.

Of course, he who offends everyone is not thereby correct in his views. My claim is not that Eliot's views are correct – still less that they are politically correct – but rather that his late Christian views on culture do not arise from his conversion to Anglicanism. In the first place, Christianity – whether Anglican, Roman, or Anabaptist – does not concede even the mild cultural pluralism that Eliot adopts in *Notes*. And in the second place, Christianity does not present itself as a cultural phenomenon at all. Christian revelation and the church which (by its own account) embodies it transcend history and culture, although they are in history. Christian revelation may have a role to play in the formation of culture, but for the believing Christian it is not merely an aspect of culture. To regard Christianity as a cultural phenomenon is already to be unchristian. Eliot's crime as a *Kulturträger* – if crime it be – was not that he became a Christian but that he failed to be a sceptical relativist and instead maintained the "Socratic" faith in "the preservation of learning, ... the pursuit of truth, and in so far as men are capable of it, the attainment of wisdom" (Eliot 1948, 123).

By 1946 when Eliot spoke over German radio, the avant-garde had already abandoned high modernism. Surrealism had established itself and was already becoming old hat. Existentialism was the wave of the future in literature and cinema, and postmodernism was just being born in architecture and music. These movements variously claim that the world, human reason, and culture are absurd, or pathological, or arbitrary, or relative, or reflexive – in any case, infinitely malleable. Even in such a context, Eliot's rather harmless and unsurprising "Socratism" would have generated little passion if his expression of a "personal grouse," *The Waste Land*, had not achieved the status of a canonical expression of "modern" *angst* in the face of the appalling revelation that there is no truth. It is probable that this status is based on a misreading, or a Bloomian misprision, committed by two generations of poets and scholars.

JESSIE WESTON
AND *THE WASTE LAND*

Jessie Weston does not engage in any lofty theorizing about culture or religious history. Like Kandinsky and Mead, she has no doubts about the unity of human culture. Her task is to uncover that unity hidden beneath the veil of accidental variation, deliberate occlusion, and malign oppression. In *The Quest for the Holy Grail* she articulates the standard occult belief in the existence of a secret wisdom tradition surviving underground and esoterically preserved in myth and legend:

There is a stream of tradition, running as it were underground, which from time to time rises to the surface, only to be relentlessly suppressed. It may be the Troubadours, the symbolical language of whose love poems is held to convey another, and less innocent, meaning; or the Albigenses, whose destruction the Church holds for a sacred duty. Alchemy, whose Elixir of Life and Philosopher's Stone are but names veiling a deeper and more spiritual meaning, belongs to the same family ... Of similar origin is that Free-Masonry, which outside our own Islands is even to-day reckoned as the greatest enemy of the Christian Faith, and which still employs signs and symbols identical with those known and used in the Mysteries of long-vanished faiths. (Weston [1913] 1964, 137–8)

I have no reason to believe that Eliot was familiar with this more overtly theosophical work. He referred his readers to the later and more cautious *From Ritual to Romance*. I cite this earlier study only to establish Weston's occult historiography so that we can put the matter aside. *From Ritual to Romance* is less explicit, but it would be difficult to miss its occult synopticism:

But the triumph of the new Faith once assured, the organizing, dominating influence of Imperial Rome speedily came into play. Christianity, originally an Eastern, became a Western, religion, the "Mystery" elements were frowned upon, kinship with pre-Christian faiths ignored, or denied; where the resemblances between the cults proved too striking for either of these methods such resemblances were boldly attributed to the invention of the Father of Lies himself, a cunning snare whereby to deceive unwary souls. Christianity was carefully trimmed, shaped, and forced into an Orthodox mould, and anything that refused to adapt itself to this drastic process became by that very refusal anathema to the righteous. (Weston [1920] 1957, 150–1)

For Weston, early Christianity was neither the cult of a great prophet – as the Creuzerian, Ernest Renan, argued in *La Vie de Jésus* – nor a unique incursion of divinity into the world, as Christians believe. For her, the story of Christ was just one more expression of the experience of the apotheosis of the ascending soul. Her view was Mead's, who wrote that "the religion of Mithra was one of the many forms of the Christ-mystery; and the mystery of the Christ is the mystery of man's perfectioning and final apotheosis" (Mead 1907, 46). *From Ritual to Romance* is a religious history telling the story of a vital, imaginative, and charismatic belief persecuted by a bureaucratic, self-righteous, and intolerant religion – a story of the suppression of a joyous "pagan" rite by dour medieval Catholicism. In short, it is precisely that occult religious history we found in Rossetti and his masonic sources.

I cannot imagine that Eliot was persuaded by Weston's pseudo-history, nor is it clear to me that he was attracted to her hypothesis of a suppressed pagan cult as a fiction useful to his thematic purposes. But what could it have been that Eliot expected readers of *The Waste Land* to find when they followed his instructions and consulted *From Ritual to Romance*? My guess is that he expected them to find an account of the suppression and loss of a religious faith, and perhaps also a window into the world of *Symboliste* and Wagnerian cultural fantasy. It seems unlikely that he could have imagined that his readers would mistake Weston's study for an academic and anthropological account of fisher kings and Grail legends – even though this is just what they did.

It is even possible that Eliot could have expected his readers to take note of what Weston had to say about the nature of the lost cult, dimly bodied forth in the Grail legends. The clearest insight into its nature within the work is found in the story of the dream of Chaus: Chaus enters the perilous chapel in a dream, is mortally stabbed, and then awakens dying from a magic stab wound (Weston [1920] 1957, 180–1). She comments:

For this is the story of an initiation (or perhaps it would be more correct to say the test of fitness for an initiation) *carried out on the astral plane, and reacting with fatal results upon the physical.*

We have already seen in the Naassene document that the Mystery ritual comprised a double initiation, the Lower, into the mysteries of generation, *i.e.*, of physical Life; the Higher, into the Spiritual Divine Life, where man is made one with God.

Some years ago I offered the suggestion that the test for the primary initiation, that into the sources of physical life, would probably consist in a contact with the horrors of physical death, and that the tradition of the Perilous Chapel, which survives in the Grail romances in confused and contaminated form, was a reminiscence of the test for this lower initiation. (182; Weston's emphasis)

"Astral plane" is a Blavatskian term that is difficult to miss. But perhaps Eliot did not notice even this inescapably occultist terminology. If he had done so, he would surely have found some way around giving Weston such prominence in the poem. Certainly, there are no echoes of astral experiences in *The Waste Land*. There are, however, lots of "notices" of the horrors of physical death. These charnel images are usually connected to the Grail quest and the tarot pack – elements that Eliot later said were targets of a wild-goose chase. My reading of Weston suggests that they might be better construed as elements of an initiation ritual, for that is how she construes them.

The double nature of the supposed initiation is also important to this reassessment of the relation between *The Waste Land* and *From Ritual to Romance*. Weston attaches charnel images to the lower "Mystery of Life," but it seems that it can also take erotic, or at least copulative, forms. The higher mystery, on the other hand, cannot be directly expressed, for its achievement involves being "made one with God." Its exoteric form is a sacred marriage, or *hieros gamos*, a symbolism that we have already encountered in Mead and Pound. Moreover, even the lower mystery has two forms, an exoteric and esoteric:

The Exoteric side of the cult gives us the Human, the Folk-lore, elements – the suffering King; the Waste Land; the effect upon the Folk; the task that lies before the hero; the group of Grail symbols. The Esoteric side provides us with the Mystic Meal, the Food of Life, connected in some mysterious way with a Vessel which is the centre of the cult; the combination of that vessel with a Weapon, a combination bearing a well-known "generative" significance; a double initiation into the source of the lower and higher spheres of Life (158–9).

All of the fertility cult elements upon which *Waste Land* criticism has concentrated its attention are dismissed by Weston as "Folk-lore," an exoteric disguise of no intrinsic interest. The real "meat" of the legend is the esoteric side. Here we find the mystery elements of a "mystic meal" and a symbolic expression of copulation involving lance and cup. In conformity with her theosophical friends, Weston believed that these elements – of which only the mystic meal survives in the Christian mass – represent a medieval underground survival of the genuine ancient initiation into god-wisdom suppressed by Christianity. Given that Eliot could hardly not have been aware of Pound's connection with Mead, Yeats, and their occult speculation, it is natural to suppose that he turned to Pound for help with the intricacies of this esoteric material.

Commentary on *The Waste Land* and Weston has concentrated on the exoteric and legendary aspect of the cult – the Grail legend and its fertility cult formulation in which the sexual impotence of the fisher king proves to be bad for the crops, leaving the land waste, and requiring a young, virile, questing knight to put things right through heroic acts and through marriage to some legitimate female – either the king's daughter or his consort. Some critics – notably Grover Smith – have also placed great emphasis on the tarot deck of cards. Clearly, commentaries that rely on these exoteric dimensions of the legendary material have merit. The poem has lots of waste land imagery – even a title drawing attention to the exoteric aspects of the legend. Still, the poem has never been made to fit the glove of a Grail quest with any neatness. And we should remember that the poem was not called "The Waste Land" when Eliot gave it to Pound. If we look at Pound's editing, we shall find that it tends to remove the esoteric or mystical elements of the original draft – particularly the linking of eros and apotheosis implied in the *hieros gamos* topos. When the poem issues from the hand of Pound, sexuality no longer has a transcendent function. It is merely spiritually and emotionally barren, even when, paradoxically for the fertility cult motif, it is progenitively fertile.

If we keep in mind Weston's assertion that initiation into the lower mystery of life "would probably consist in contact with the horrors of death," the pertinence of the original Conrad epigraph is evident:

Did he live his life again in every detail of desire, temptation, and surrender during that supreme moment of complete knowledge? He cried in a whisper at some image, at some vision, – he cried out twice, a cry that was no more than a breath – "The horror! the horror!" (Eliot 1971, 3)

The exchange between Pound and Eliot on this passage is worth citing:

POUND: "I doubt if Conrad is weighty enough to stand the citation."
ELIOT: "Do you mean not use the Conrad quote or simply not put Conrad's name to it? It is much the most appropriate I can find, and somewhat elucidative."
POUND: "Do as you like about Conrad; who am I to grudge him his laurel crown?" (125, n. 1)

As we know, Eliot followed Pound's initial advice and did remove the Conrad epigraph, substituting a fragment from the *Satyricon* of Petronius in which the Sibyl of Cumae is said to long for death. The "new" epigraph stresses the motif of prophecy and degeneracy more than that of an encounter with the other world, such as was inescapably evoked by the Conrad passage. In Kurtz's case, of course, there was no initiation, only death – unless we wish to count his participation in "unspeakable rites" as some sort of initiation. On the reading I am suggesting here, Kurtz's report on the experience of death would be a model of a materialistic, atheistic, doomed, and unredeemed encounter with death and the other world. Kurtz does not get past the horror to the glorious revelation beyond. Weston's initiand also encounters horrors. His surmounting of these horrors – diminished to the Chapel Perilous in the legend – is a necessary prelude to the revelation, the "full *Eidous*," as Pound calls it in canto 81 (1973a, 520).

It is important to recognize that Weston's reading of the Grail legend is not at all dark and despairing. On her reading, the legend is not only evidence of the survival of the wisdom tradition in the Dark Ages, but it is also an account of the initiation into "god-wisdom," which renders the initiate immune to the vagaries and pains of life. The legends occupy the same position in her construction of the tradition as troubadour poetry does in Pound's. Hence, her study on its own does not support a poem of religious despair such as *The Waste Land* has been understood to be. Of course, Weston's optimism about the human condition in no way invalidates pessimistic readings of Eliot's poem. It does, however, complicate a relationship long thought to be a straightforward case of poetic borrowing from scholarly research into outworn superstitions.

If we turn to the draft version of *The Waste Land*, it is clear that the London "Nighttown" episode of some fifty-five lines with which the draft version began fits this lower initiation into the mystery of life. The first-person speaker is given a bath and a meal (an exoteric form of Weston's lower mystery) by the Madame of the brothel. He does not get the girl he asks for (an ironic and exoteric failure of the *hieros gamos*) because in Madame's opinion he is too drunk. The episode ends with the speaker walking home at dawn. Pound's elision of it removes a sexual episode that contrasted with the despair, guilt, violence, and indifference that is characteristic of those sexual encounters that have survived his blue pencil.

It is true that the elided episode is hardly redemptive or transcendental. Nonetheless, it jars with the fertility cult motif of barrenness thought to govern the canonical poem. Its removal has altered the thematic thrust of the poem, and not just its length and stylistic integrity – as commentary has tended to argue. The elided episode fits Weston's account of the occult or "higher mystery" elements in the Grail legends better than anything that has remained.

The sexual episode in part 1 that does survive Pound's blue pencil is the incident of the hyacinth girl. The speaker, who has returned from the hyacinth garden with the girl, her arms full and her hair wet, confesses:

> I could not
> Speak, and my eyes failed, I was neither
> Living nor dead, and I knew nothing,
> Looking into the heart of light, the silence. (7, ll. 92–5)

These remarks have commonly been interpreted as indicative of some kind of spiritual paralysis. I have never been happy with this reading because the tone and mood of the passage are so positive. Weston's argument that the initiation into the higher mystery is expressed in erotic terms provides a persuasive alternative interpretation. The speaker's dumbness, blindness, and blankness are indices of the supreme revelation he has just experienced. He has looked into "the heart of light, the silence." That is to say, he has beheld the divine, has seen the other world. He is dumb, blind, and mindless because he is completely overwhelmed, not because he is suffering from abulia like the other denizens of the necropolitan waste land. This speaker is "dead to the world," as the charismatic Christians express their state after their parallel experience of palingenesis, or being "born again." This incident would have been the contrary of Kurtz's death – with its revelation of the darkness and horror of the other world. Kurtz looked not into the heart of light but into the heart of darkness. In this way, the Conrad epigraph was "somewhat elucidative."

In the light of our earlier discussion of Dante's role in the tradition, it seems relevant to consider here Eliot's own attitude to Dante and Dante's eroticism. Dante's Neoplatonic eroticism seems to me to be more relevant to *The Waste Land* than Wagner's *liebestod* is – *contra* Stoddard Martin and despite the number of Wagnerian allusions in the poem. Unfortunately, we have no good evidence about Eliot's attitude towards Wagner and Wagnerianism. But his admiration for Dante hardly requires demonstration. The importance of the erotic to Dante is likewise beyond dispute.

Eliot devotes considerable space in the 1929 essay, "Dante," to a consideration of how we should interpret Dante's account of his Beatrice experience, an experience undergone when they were both in their ninth year. Eliot argues that such a sexual experience is "by no means impossible or unique." He explains: "The attitude of Dante to the fundamental experience of the *Vita Nuova* can only be understood by accustoming ourselves to find meaning in *final causes* rather than in origins ... The final cause is the attraction towards God ... The love of man and woman (or for that matter of man and man) is only explained and made reasonable by the higher love, or else is simply the coupling of animals" (Eliot 1951, 273–4). There seems little question but that Eliot is endorsing the Neoplatonic, mystical, and occult practice of the exoteric expression of noumenal revelation in terms of eros. That he should do so makes him neither a full-blown mystic nor an occultist. The practice of expressing devotion in erotic imagery is at least as old as the Songs of Solomon and has been a standard component of Christian devotional poetry since the troubadours invented quasi-devotional erotic poetry in the twelfth century. We have already heard enough about that tradition, but Dante's solidarity with it – whatever character it may in truth have had – is beyond question. Eliot was aware of the esoteric readings of the troubadours and refers to it in the Dante essay. Although his remarks are characteristically cautious, they are not so very far from Pound's less measured hints about the Albigensian arcanum:

That mysterious people had a religion of their own which was thoroughly extinguished by the Inquisition; so that we hardly know more about them than about the Sumerians. I suspect that the difference between this unknown, and possibly maligned, Albigensianism and Catholicism has some correspondence with the difference between the poetry of the Provençal school and the Tuscan. The system of Dante's organization of sensibility – the contrast between higher and lower carnal love, the transition from Beatrice living to Beatrice dead, rising to the Cult of the Virgin, seems to me to be his own. (275)

That these remarks have affinities with Weston's need hardly be stressed.

Dante's account of his Beatrice experience is not dissimilar to the encounter with the hyacinth girl. Dante has just met Beatrice for the first time: "At that moment, I say most truly that the spirit of life, which hath its dwelling in the secretest chamber of the heart, began to tremble so violently that the least pulses of my body shook therewith ... At that moment the animate spirit, which dwelleth in the lofty chamber whither all the senses carry their perceptions, was filled with wonder" (*Vita nuova*, vol. 2). Of course, the psychic storm that Dante's sight of Beatrice set off is only a foretaste of the noumenal experience at the end of the *Commedia*, an account of the noumenal that Eliot praises in superlatives: "Nowhere in poetry has experience so remote from ordinary experience been expressed so concretely, by a masterly use of that imagery of *light* which is the form of certain types of mystical experience" (Eliot 1951, 267). He illustrates Dante's mastery by quoting *Paradiso* 3:85–96, but lines 55–63 are more reminiscent of *The Waste Land* passage: "From that moment my vision was greater than our speech, which fails at such a sight, and memory too fails at such excess. Like him that sees in a dream and after the dream the passion wrought by it remains and the rest returns not to his mind, such am I; for my vision almost wholly fades, and still there drops within my heart the sweetness that was born of it." Certainly, *The Waste Land* speaker does not understand the nature of his experience as Dante does. He could not speak; his eyes failed; he was neither living nor dead.

Peter Dale Scott has pointed out an even closer verbal parallel to *The Waste Land* passage in *Purgatorio* 5 (Scott 1988). Buonconte is telling Dante of his death on the battlefield: "I came, wounded in the throat, flying of foot, and bloodying the plain. There I lost sight and speech. I ended on the name of Mary and there fell and only my flesh remained" (*Purgatorio* 5:97–102). This allusion speaks of death rather than the illumination of love, but the story has a strong soteriological element. Buonconte is taken to purgatory by an angel of God and hears the lament of "he from Hell": "O thou from Heaven, why dost thou rob me? Thou carriest off with thee this man's eternal part for a little tear that takes him from me" (105–6). The Devil threatens to have his will on Buonconte's body, and Buonconte recounts to Dante that the Devil caused a storm that washed his body into the Arno river where it was buried in the muddy bottom (109–29).

The hyacinth girl incident occurs just after a Wagnerian allusion to the *liebestod* of Tristan and Isolde. Stoddard Martin seizes upon this juxtaposition to claim that "the love-tryst of the Hyacinth garden leads, like that of *Tristan*, to disaster," and he goes on to link it to the "young man carbuncular" and "civilization at a terminal stage of corruption" (Martin 1982, 215–16). But it is not at all clear that the "love-tryst" leads to any disaster, and it is unmistakably different in character from the affair of the typist and the clerk.

Although it cannot be argued that Tristan is enlightened in any mystical sense – as Dante certainly is in the *Paradiso* – a salvation analogous to that vouchsafed to Buonconte is not out of the question. Tristan and Isolde are lovers in the romantic, mystical, and tragic sense that is *echt* Wagnerian. They are manifestly not acting out of mere lust like Tereus, the young man carbuncular, and the loitering heirs of city directors. Eliot's speaker looking into the heart of light is surely undergoing the experience of Weston's "higher" erotic experience, not the "lower" carnal love. Eliot echoes Weston's distinction in the passage cited above where he speaks of "the contrast between higher and lower carnal love" in the *Vita nuova*. There is a similar erotic mysticism for Wagnerian lovers even though they can experience it only tragically. In the case of the lover of the hyacinth girl, he has had the experience but does not understand the meaning.

Eliot's "Dans le Restaurant" (from which he cribbed part 4 of *The Waste Land*) describes a more physical version of Dante's childhood experience with Beatrice. A speaker remembers a childhood adventure during a rainstorm involving himself at the age of seven and an even younger girl. They sought shelter from the rain, and he began to tickle her in order to make her laugh. In the course of this playfulness, he felt a moment of power and transport ("Je la chatouillais, pour la fair rire. / J'éprouvais un instant de puissance et de délire"). However, they were interrupted by a big dog, and he "left her in mid-course" ("Je l'ai quitté à mi-chemin"). This peculiar little anecdote surely belongs with Dante's account of his sight of Beatrice, even though it has taken a physically sensuous turn unlike anything in Dante. Dante does not invoke genitalia, groping – or even tickling – for his figuration of the erotic encounter with the noumenal. Weston's study, by contrast, does include the genital. She is quite discreet, speaking of "the sex symbols, Lance and Cup" that Christian piety confused with "the Weapon of the Crucifixion and the Cup of the Last Supper" (Weston [1920] 1957, 205).

A reader of Frazer – such as Eliot was – would not be insensitive to the power of copulative symbolism. He uses the symbolism satirically in "Mr Eliot's Morning Service" and in "Whispers of Immortality," and less narrowly in the Sweeney poems. (In "Sweeney Agonistes" he adds a dark, bestial – but comic – version of Weston's "mystic meal": Sweeney promises or threatens to play cannibal to Doris's missionary and convert her into "a nice little, white little, missionary stew.") In Frazer, the symbolism of sexuality is given a positivistic, not an esoteric, reading. Sexual rites are literal and involve the transmission of political or clerical power, not of noumenal revelation of metaphysical energy.

The second section of *The Waste Land*, "A Game of Chess," was only lightly revised, and most of the revisions are either stylistic or designed to serve consistency and the like. The two most substantive revisions do not seem to have been at Pound's request. Oddly, the original title, "In the Cage," was entirely obscure without the allusion to the Petronius citation now in the epigraph, but the title was dropped and the Petronius passage added. However, there is no discussion of either title in the Pound-Eliot exchange preserved in Valerie Eliot's facsimile edition. The other alteration was the suppression of the answer "Carrying / Away the little light dead people" to the question "What is that noise now? What is the wind doing?" (Eliot 1971, ll. 44–6).

The elided phrase is from Dante's account of Paolo and Francesca, and thus could be construed either as invoking the Wagnerian motif of *liebestod* or as an instance of a Weston/occult encounter with the other world through eros. Perhaps it was the very ambiguity of the status of the Paolo-Francesca incident that led Eliot to remove the reference to the damned lovers from the section. He retained only three evocations of love and death: the speaker's recollection of the hyacinth garden, an allusion to *The Tempest*, and the query "Are you alive, or not? Is there nothing in your head?" (19, l. 51).

Had he kept the Conrad epigraph and the Dantean allusion, the Weston motif of a transcendental experience of the other world achieved through erotic experience would have been more discernable. And the questions "Are you alive or not? Is there nothing in your head?" would have had greater resonance, for they would have evoked not only the topos of abulia, as they do now, but also – through the echo of the hyacinth garden episode – the topos of vision. However, the form in which the poem saw the light of day made it almost impossible to read the hyacinth incident as an instance of "higher" carnal love diametrically opposed to the other forms of paralysis invoked in the poem.

In the canonical poem the fertility cult understanding of sexuality seemed the appropriate interpretive device to apply. On this view, male impotence is both an index of the failure of natural fecundity and a symbol of spiritual paralysis. The failure of natural fecundity in turn leads easily to charnel images: vegetable death is a symbol as well as a possible cause of human death through starvation. Thus, the symbolism of the poem lines up neatly with a naturalistic interpretation in the best modern way.

One difficulty with this standard reading of *The Waste Land* is that most of the sexual episodes – whether narrated or merely alluded to – do not fit the pattern of male impotence, or even of female barrenness. Tereus, the young man carbuncular, Lil's husband, and the loitering heirs of city directors seem perfectly potent – and Lil at least is fertile. It has been necessary just to ignore this failure of match between the poem and its alleged mythical parallel – on the grounds, I suppose, that spiritual or emotional failures have systematically displaced merely physical ones.

No such manoeuvre is necessary if we read the mythical paradigm as an initiation rite instead of a Grail quest. Of course, the Grail quest motif does not disappear, it is merely reduced to an exoteric "vehicle" of the symbolic meaning. Weston tells us that the Grail legend is a distorted and fragmentary survival of a forgotten double initiation into the "mystery of Life" and "the mystery of Death." The former initiation is represented by a frightening encounter with emblems of death, and the second by an erotically formulated encounter with the divine. On this reading, we do not need to choose between a Grail motif and an initiation motif, but can see them as exoteric and esoteric aspects of the same sacred mystery – a mystery, moreover, which Weston tells us is not known to the authors of the Grail stories and therefore need not be known to the author of *The Waste Land* either.

On this model, the failure of the sexual encounters registered in the poem is exactly a spiritual failure rather than a sexual dysfunction as is required by the standard fertility cult reading. The male speaker (or speakers) in the poem does seem to suffer from some sexual dysfunction. If he (or they) is interpreted as the questing knight, his apparent impotence is a puzzle. If, on the other hand, he (or they) is interpreted as the initiand in a rite that leads to a revelation – or perhaps even an ascent or divination – through an *hieros gamos*, then his shyness and inactivity are appropriate. Moreover, the charnel images scattered throughout the poem become not just indices of impotence but way stations along the initiand's route to revelation – one that is not achieved in *The Waste Land* any more than it is in any of the Grail legends that Weston surveys.

In a palingenetic rite one must pass through death in order to reach the divine revelation – much as Dante passes through Hell and Purgatory, or as Odysseus nearly drowns before being rescued by Leucothea. Being born again involves "dying" first and typically includes all of the fear and loathing that we associate with death. Weston distinguished between the palingenetic rite, which leads only to a lower initiation into the mystery of life, and the *hieros gamos*, which leads to a higher initiation into the mystery of death. In *The Waste Land* both forms are dysfunctional. Neither the journey, or quest, nor the erotic encounter is fully achieved. If the speaker is the candidate for initiation, we can read his sexual problems as an index of his unpreparedness for "the full *eidous*" – as Pound describes the vision in canto 81 (1973a, 520). On the same sort of reading, the sexual potency of the others is an index of their lower hylic condition. Hellenic and occult mythographers give just this reading to Circe's transformation of Odysseus's men into swine – a fate Odysseus escapes through the protection of Hermes' *moly*. For them, eros is just sex.

An interesting parallel text for *The Waste Land* is Jessie Weston's story "The Ruined Temple" (*Quest* 7, 1916, 127–39). This tale is her own fictionalization of the esoteric sense of the Grail legends set in England during World War I. A young man comes upon an ancient ruined temple on the British coast. The narrator speculates that it may have been a Druid temple or perhaps testimony of Phoenician voyagers, worshippers of Adonis, who may have brought an esoteric cult to ancient Britain. The young man falls asleep and dreams that he undergoes an initiation rite that begins with a meal prepared by a host who is described as "both priest and king." The events proceed as in a dream, and after the meal the young man encounters at different times charnel images and temptresses. The dream concludes with the dreamer suddenly finding himself part of a group clad all in white. The dreamer and the others witness the display, or *epopteia*, of a "gleaming fiery heart." He awakens transfigured.

Weston's story is not a source for *The Waste Land*. Even if Eliot had read it – and I have no reason to believe that he did – it could not have contributed much to his formulation of the Weston and Wagner material in *The Waste Land*. However, the story is instructive in placing these Weston motifs in a different context from the Grail quest. Some of the elements Pound removed from the poem – the brothel scene, the meal, and shipwreck – bear strong affinities with the initiation formula of Weston's story. The complete absence of any quest or journey elements in Weston's story also reflects the relative paucity of these elements in *The Waste Land*. Of course, Weston's story belongs to vision literature as *The Waste Land* does not. In sharp contrast to the denizens of Eliot's poem, her dreamer *is* transfigured.

There are other elements of the draft version Eliot gave to Pound that support a reading of sexual activity in the symbolism of the *hieros gamos* of the mysteries, as opposed to that of Frazerian fertility cults. One of the least ambiguous is in the Fresca episode (which Pound persuaded Eliot to excise):

> Fresca! in other time or place had been
> A meek and lowly weeping Magdalene;
> More sinned against than sinning, bruised and marred,
> The lazy laughing Jenny of the bard.

(The same eternal and consuming itch
Can make a martyr, or plain simple bitch). (Eliot 1971, 27, ll. 42–7)

Fresca is just an empty-headed party girl. These lines tell us that in other times and places, sexual appetite has led to some kinds of transcendence: the sainthood of the prostitute Mary Magdalene, the muselike inspiration that Rossetti's Jenny (Elizabeth Siddal) brought to the Pre-Raphaelites, the martyrdom that Salome's dance earned John the Baptist. However one reads these lines, it is difficult to make them fit the fertility cult paradigm. They can be read as expressing abhorrence of sexuality and are occasionally construed as symptomatic of Eliot's personal sexual difficulties. But if we have in mind Weston's esoteric understanding of eros, these lines can be less tendentiously read as registering the loss of sanctity suffered by eros in modern culture and society.

Because it sanctifies sexuality, the occult, hierogamic view of eros shares more common ground with Christian sexual phobias than it does with the emotional and spiritual indifference of Fresca and the young man carbuncular who populate Eliot's waste land. The taboos that surround sexual behaviour surely reflect the mystery and sanctity that surround birth, copulation, and death as much as a bourgeois fear of scandal. Sexual encounters in *The Waste Land* exemplify the loss of sanctity suffered by eros rather more clearly than they exemplify a sexual dysfunction. But the standard fertility cult reading of the Weston paradigm requires sexual dysfunction.

Another passage in the elided Fresca episode alludes indirectly to the *hieros gamos* of Anchises and Aphrodite, whose issue was Aeneas, by means of Aphrodite's theophany to her son, Aeneas, rather than to Anchises. The incident is placed in apposition to the Fresca passage. They are much revised as they appear in the 1971 facsimile:

To Aeneas, in an unfamiliar place,
Appeared his mother, with an altered face,
He knew the goddess by her smooth celestial pace.
So the close rabble identify a goddess or a star.
In silent rapture worship from afar. (29, ll. 18–20)

In a crossed-out version the last two lines read, "So the sweating rabble in the cinema / Sees on the screen a goddess or a star."

The satirical intention and mocking tone of this passage do not remove the pertinence of the motif of the transcendent potential of eros upon which the convention of *hieros gamos* depends. The comparison of Aphrodite to a movie star further underlines the theme of the loss of sanctity of eros without a corresponding loss of its compelling power. Pound's blue-pencilling of the whole section no doubt removed some indifferent verse, but it also removed an attention to the motif of erotic revelation that fits Weston's initiation paradigm better than it fits the Grail legend.

Pound persuaded Eliot to drop the long first-person narrative of a sea disaster with which "Death by Water" opened in the draft version. These lines do not seem objectionable on stylistic grounds. We have no record of what Pound objected to in them. Clearly, they do not fit the Grail paradigm at all well. Indeed, they do not even fit the esoteric *hieros gamos* paradigm well. They present a first-person account of death by drowning and conclude with the lines "And if Another knows, I know not, / Who only know that there is no more noise now" (61, ll. 81–2). The know-nothingness of this speaker is reminiscent of the condition of the speaker remembering the hyacinth girl. In both cases we have a report on an encounter with the other world. This excised one, however, is on a palingenetic, or death and rebirth, model – as the title of the section "Death by Water" underlines – rather than an erotic, *hieros gamos* model. But even here, the erotic is not completely absent. The speaker, like Prufrock, and like Weston's dreamer in "The Ruined Temple," does see

> Three women leaning forward, with white hair
> Streaming behind, who sang above the wind
> A song that charmed my senses, while I was
> Frightened beyond fear, horrified past horror, calm,
> (Nothing was real) for, I thought, now, when
> I like, I can wake up and end the dream. (59, ll. 67–72)

These lines, if retained, would have picked up the Conrad epigraph as well as the Rhine-maiden allusions. Of course, the title, "Death by Water," is retained and still directs the reader to the Christian palingenetic rite of baptism, in which the "initiand" (the infant) is "drowned" and reborn to a new life. In the published poem we are left with the drowned Phoenician sailor, a poor candidate for a palingenetic revelation parallel to the erotic revelation of part 1. The elision of this passage removes not only the motif of palingenesis but also the clearest representation in the manuscript of the topos of transcendence and revelation.

It is also an incident that has no parallel in either Weston or Frazer. For the motif of magical boats and sirens, the reader would proceed from the Odyssey to Shelley, Keats, Tennyson, Wagner, and the *Symbolistes*. Pound's editing tended to block such routes of allusion in favour of more sceptical and pessimistic ones. Martin, for some reason, does not consider the manuscript versions in his discussion of Wagner in *The Waste Land*. He concentrates on *Parsifal*, thereby remaining within the reading of the poem as Grail literature. He also accepts the standard pessimistic and disillusioned reading. He sees Wagnerian opera as presenting "an idealistic and hopeful program for the future age," while Eliot's poem presents a contrasting "hyper-realistic and hopeless assessment of the effect of the past age" (Martin 1982, 224–5).

Eliot, we must presume, was not as antipathetic to the topos of transcendence as Pound's editing would suggest that Pound himself was. Perhaps Eliot was persuaded to remove this palingenetic episode in order to achieve greater focus and concentration. Valerie Eliot reports that her husband was depressed by Pound's negative reaction to it and offered to omit Phlebas as well. Pound replied, "I do advise keeping Phlebas. In fact I more'n advise. Phlebas is an integral part of the poem; the card pack introduces him, the drowned phoen. sailor. And he is needed ABsolootly where he is. Must stay in" (Eliot 1971, 61 n.2). From this advice, it would seem that Pound gave greater prominence to the tarot pack as a structural device than he did to the encounter with death within a transcendent or palingenetic framework. In the published version, the death of Phlebas unmistakably evokes the transmigration of the soul as understood by theosophy. We are told that he "passed the stages of his age and youth / Entering the whirlpool." This is just how Mead and Upward describe the soul's passage from the earthly to the spiritual realm through a vortex, or "whirl-swirl." However, Phlebas's passage may simply be a return to the hylic realm. The motif of rebirth to a higher life – which was inescapably evoked by the shipwreck account – is only very weakly suggested.

Pound's editing greatly reduces the palingenetic and erotic representations of transcendence that Eliot seems to have adapted from Weston's characterization of the ancient initiation rites in *Ritual to Romance*. The elisions have left a poem that depicts a bleak, hopeless, and wasted world occupied by the spiritually dead. Although one should not make too much of the fragments that Valerie Eliot published together with *The Waste Land* drafts, it is worth noting that "The Death of St Narcissus," "Exequy," "The Death of the Duchess," "Elegy," and "Dirge" are all poems of death overpassed in one way or another. They all fall within the horizon of palingenesis, even though, properly speaking, palingenesis involves a death to *this* life and rebirth to a *higher* life – whether that be Heaven or simply a transfigured life here on earth, such as that enjoyed by the charismatic or "born again" Christian. Although Eliot may never have intended them for *The Waste Land*, their presence amongst the drafts lends support to my supposition that he had not originally envisaged a poem of sceptical pessimism.

Of course, palingenetic experiences are not uniformly bright and cheerful. It would be wrong to suppose that a palingenetic reading would resist the despairing elements of the poem. Weston is quite explicit about the alarming nature of her putative initiation rite:

I believe it to be essentially a Mystery tradition; the Otherworld is not a myth, but a reality, and in all ages there have been souls who have been willing to brave the great adventure, and to risk all for the chance of bringing back with them some assurance of the future life. Naturally these ventures passed into tradition with the men who risked them. The early races of men became semi-mythic, their beliefs, their experiences, receded into a land of mist, where their figures assumed fantastic outlines, and the record of their deeds departed more and more widely from historic accuracy. (Weston [1920] 1957, 186)

Although Prufrock is manifestly not one of these souls, in his allusions to Lazarus and John the Baptist he invokes the tradition of spiritual heroism to which Weston refers. Christ himself is the type of this hero: he dies, descends "into the Netherworld, passing through the abodes of the Lost, finally reaching Paradise, and returning to earth after Three Days" (184). This is Weston's description of *The Purgatory of St Patrick*. She does not draw attention to the congruence between it and the story of Christ's death and resurrection, even though that is obviously the model for the legend.

Eliot must have been receptive to this component of Weston's book. The fragments cited above, as well as "The Love Song of J. Alfred Prufrock," were all written long before he could have read *From Ritual to Romance*, and they all invoke the mainstream tradition of a revelatory encounter with death. Prufrock self-mockingly imagines himself saying, "I am Lazarus, come from the dead, / Come back to tell you all, I shall tell you all." The denizens of Eliot's poetry up to and including *The Waste Land* never achieve any revelation, but they do feel the lack of it. Weston's book explained the failure of revelation to penetrate the modern world in a manner that was usable precisely because it was not mainstream and not Christian. Weston's arguments for a lost mystery religion – like the Grail legend itself and the tarot pack – provided Eliot with a framework that was as factitious as the *Odyssey* was for Joyce's *Ulysses*.

Of course, Joyce's *Ulysses* was a model that Eliot and Pound both had in mind. Yeats's creation of his own framework of historical cones and cycles for his poetry was still in embryo in 1921. G.M. Harper has calculated that between 24 October 1917 and 4 June 1921, Yeats devoted some 450 sessions to communication with his Instructors and asked 8672 recorded questions, the answers to which occupied some 3672 pages (Harper 1981). How much Pound knew of this in 1921 is an intriguing question to which I do not have an answer, but it is implausible to suppose that he knew nothing of it.

In 1921, *The Cantos* were already well begun, although still struc-tured around the apparition of ghosts, and they were certainly informed by Pound's occult understanding of the secret history of Europe. Neither Pound nor Yeats regarded their frameworks as fac-titious, but Joyce certainly did, and Eliot was self-consciously imi-tating Joyce, not Pound. However, even if the frame is recognized as factitious, the choice of an allusive frame as an interpretive device is not neutral. The selection of Weston's esoteric model ineluctably draws *The Waste Land* into the sphere of the literature of transcen-dence and revelation, just as Joyce's selection of the *Odyssey* drew his novel into the sphere of epic, and Pound's choice of the evocation of ghosts drew *The Cantos* into the sphere of dream vision.

If *The Waste Land* were patterned on palingenetic revelation, the last section ought to invoke or represent the other world, even if only ironically. It seems to me that both the title and the content of part 5 fit this expectation better than those set up by the Grail quest pattern. The title "What the Thunder Said" surely suggests that we will hear the voice of God, even though all we hear is thunder, a traditional voice of God, which does render unto us a cryptic and Hindu revelation. The opening lines of part 5 (which escaped Pound's blue pencil virtually unscathed) evoke Christianity's central palinge-netic story, Christ's passion and death:

> After the torchlight on sweaty faces,
> After the frosty silence in the gardens
> After the agony in stony places
> The shouting and the crying
> Prison and palace and reverberation
> Of thunder of spring over distant mountains;
> He who was living is now dead,
> We who were living are now dying
> With a little patience. (Eliot 1971, 83, ll. 1–9)

These lines evoke Christ's arrest in the garden of Gethsemane, his scourging and trial, his death, and the portents of thunder and earthquake which revealed who he was – the son of God – but not that he would triumph and return from the grave on Easter Sunday. *The Waste Land*, of course, does not fulfil the palingenetic pattern. There is no resurrection, only death and perhaps a descent. In Grail terms, the poem stops in the Chapel Perilous; in terms of Christ's passion, it stops on Easter Saturday while Christ is, according to tradition, harrowing Hell. The reader is left in doubt, as the apostles were, with the Saviour dead, and only obscure and ambiguous messages left as a guide – messages typified in the poem by the voice of the thunder.

In the note to part 5, Eliot says that there are three themes: "the journey to Emmaus, the approach to the Chapel Perilous (see Miss Weston's book), and the present decay of eastern Europe." The first theme is a test case for my argument. In Luke, the risen Christ appears walking beside Cleopas and Simon on Easter Sunday as they journey to Emmaus, still disbelieving the accounts of Christ's empty tomb. They fail to recognize him until he later breaks bread with them: "And when he had sat down with them at table, he took bread and said the blessing; he broke the bread and offered it to them. Then their eyes were opened, and they recognized him; and he vanished from their sight" (Luke 24:30–1). On the road to Emmaus the apostles are still in despair, ignorance, and darkness, and they cannot even recognize the risen Christ who walks beside them. The revelation has not yet come to them, although it is at hand. Similarly, the quester (esoterically an initiand) in the Chapel Perilous is at the low point of the whole quest (esoterically a rite). He experiences the terrors of death and has no hint of the bliss of the revelation still to come. Weston is most specific about encounters with the other world in the chapter entitled "The Perilous Chapel." She draws on this account in "The Ruined Temple."

If we pursue Eliot's note to line 424 where he recommends Weston's chapter on the fisher king as an appropriate gloss for the lines "I sat upon the shore / Fishing, with the arid plain behind me / Shall I at least set my lands in order?" we find that it is mostly about the mystic meal – a fish meal – and not at all about the restoration of the wasted land by the revived potency of the king. The following is a summation of the chapter's argument: "But at certain mystic banquets priests and initiates partook of this otherwise forbidden food, in the belief that they thus partook of the flesh of the goddess" (Weston [1920] 1957, 133). The fisher king himself is, as it were, the provisioner of this mystic meal and is "not merely a deeply symbolic figure, but the essential centre of the whole cult, a being semi-divine, semi-human, standing between his people and land, and the unseen forces which control their destiny (136)." In short, he is the Divine

Man, the Superman of the occult revelation. Orpheus, Hercules, Hermes, Zoroaster, Aeneas, and Christ are types of the Divine Man, who is nothing other than divinized man.

The Emmaus episode, ending as it does with a meal, underlines the mystical equivalence of Christ and the fisher king in Weston's reading of the Grail legend. However, in *The Waste Land* he is still fishing. He has not yet "saved" his people – just as the risen Christ has not yet been recognized on the road to Emmaus. The soteriological as well as revelatory elements of the Grail legend as Weston understood it are unrealized in Eliot's poem. We remain "in the middest." In terms of the Gospels, we remain in the doubt and uncertainty of Easter Saturday *before* the revelation of Christ's resurrection and our ultimate salvation.

Finally, the line "These fragments I have shored against my ruins" – whether spoken by the fisher king, a quester, an initiand, or some other – can refer either to the poem itself or to the fragments of religious belief that are encrusted in the poem like raisins in a loaf of bread. If we adopt the latter hypothesis, Weston once again appears relevant. In the introduction to *From Ritual to Romance* she writes:

The more closely one studies pre-Christian Theology, the more strongly one is impressed with the deeply, and daringly, spiritual character of its speculations, and the more doubtful it appears that such teaching can depend upon the unaided processes of human thought, or can have been evolved from such germs as we find among the supposedly "primitive" people, such as *e.g.*, the Australian tribes. Are they really primitive? Or are we dealing, not with the primary elements of religion, but with the *disjecta membra* of a vanished civilization? Certain it is that so far as historical evidence goes our earliest records point to the recognition of a spiritual, not of a material, origin of the human race; the Sumerian and Babylonian Psalms were not composed by men who believed themselves the descendants of "witchetty grubs." (7)

In this diffusionist and anti-Darwinian account of religious and biological history, Weston is reflecting Blavatskian "ethnological" theories. Allegedly following the Bible, the *Corpus Hermeticum*, and the Kabbala, Blavatsky claims that there are seven independent human "evolutions." Against Darwin, she insists that all human races precede "every mammalian – the anthropoid included – in the animal kingdom." Each of the seven evolutions is described as a "primeval" man issuing from nature and "Creative Spirits" or gods (Blavatsky 1888, 2:1–2).

I do not suppose for a moment that Eliot shared such an eccentric belief. What I do suppose is that he wanted and expected readers of *The Waste Land* to discover the poem's relation to theosophical fantasies. Weston's theosophy was to be read as a symptom of the spiritual decay that Eliot's poem – on any reading – evokes and bemoans. Eliot could not have regarded her theosophical account as a credible explanation of that decay. Even Pound seems not to have been interested in her account. The very implausibility of Weston's thesis is, I think, much of the point of the allusion. Here I find myself in agreement with Kenner's later position on Weston's relevance to *The Waste Land*: "The situation is plainly impossible; the poem that speaks to it is plainly grotesque ... The poem is a grotesquerie, often nearly a parody; Eliot even told Arnold Bennett that yes, the notes were a skit, but not more so than some of the poem itself" (Kenner 1971, 443). Weston provided Eliot with a framework that permitted the interpenetration and overlap of Christian, classical, and medieval legendary material in an "ordered" if not orderly manner – which interpenetration yields a rhetorical structure that mimes the confused spiritual state of modern man and (most probably) of the author of *The Waste Land*.

As I suggested at the outset, none of the arguments or evidence presented here requires rejection or even correction of the consensual reading of *The Waste Land*. It does not do so because the pertinence of the occult Weston bears on the original draft submitted to Ezra Pound more than on the canonical poem. This discussion does, however, challenge the consensual dismissal of the relevance of Weston's book; and, by implication, challenges the axiom of textual autonomy that has been responsible in considerable part for critical neglect of *From Ritual to Romance*.

Furthermore, the fact that Weston's book presents an occult view of religion and history is not without consequences for literary scholarship. It leads to a more plausible account of the principles governing Pound's editing of the poem than any put forward thus far, and accounts for some elements of the poem's obscurity on contingent historical grounds rather than on deliberate thematic or rhetorical strategies. By which I mean that the obscurity of the poem is to some degree an artifact of the conflicting thematic biases of Pound and Eliot and not entirely a product of a deliberate stylistic program.

A rereading of Weston may also help to illuminate the poem's obscurity a little. It might be claimed that the prominence assigned by Eliot to Tiresias makes more sense if the poem is thought to appeal to the paradigm of an initiation rather than to a quest. Tiresias has no role in quest literature, but his residence in the underworld and his complete sexual experience make him a suitable hierophant for an initiation into the mysteries of life and death. He is absent from part 5, perhaps because he represents Western culture, as Virgil represents pagan culture in the *Commedia*. The pagan Virgil is displaced by the Christian Beatrice in the *Paradiso*. Similarly, the pagan Tiresias does not hear what the thunder said.

Of course, the author of *The Waste Land* does not have Dante's religious confidence. Instead of ending with a beatific vision, Eliot's little epic concludes with a babel of voices – only one of which is God's. God's voice speaks a single monosyllable, "DA," which is translated into three Sanskrit words: *Datta, Dayadhvam,* and *Damyata*. These words are in turn glossed by cryptic anecdotes, which may or may not bespeak a new religious dispensation, combining Christianity, paganism, and Hinduism.

Part 5 of *The Waste Land* can be read as the assembling of those very fragments of a faith forgotten that Blavatskian theosophy itself gathered together: Mediterranean paganism, Gnostic Christianity, troubadour mysticism, and Buddhism. Such a reading is so much at odds with the critical consensus on the poem that it can be put forward only tentatively and under the rubric of ironic detachment. The odd collection of cultural detritus that Eliot assembles in the poem conforms uncannily to that assembled by the theosophists – including the Indian component, which we have not examined in this study. Blavatsky and Olcott founded their movement in New York, but it had no success until they transplanted it to Ceylon and redubbed it "Esoteric Buddhism." Eliot's sources are Hindu, not Buddhist. Of course, Buddhism bears much the same relation to Hinduism as Christianity does to Judaism. From the European perspective of the poem, the two could count as more or less interchangeable.

On this reading, the babel with which the poem concludes becomes an index of the religious confusion of the period, a confusion typified by the theosophical movement, upon which the poem draws through Jessie Weston. Of course, Eliot is endorsing neither theosophy nor confusion. But by the same token, he is not expressing Nietzschean sceptical relativism either. The poem is an anguished exploration of religious doubt and confusion and is neither a positivistic travesty of superstition and credulity nor an affirmation of Christian, pagan, or Hindu belief. Once it was so spectacularly successful as a Nietzschean travesty of religious belief, it was necessary that Pound and Eliot save the appearances by dissociating the poem and themselves from the circles of "excited reverie" that gave birth to it.

Conclusion

Much work remains to be done before we understand the cultural and political turmoil of this century. The purpose of this study has been to demonstrate that literary scholarship has systematically misconstrued the career of Ezra Pound. This misconstrual is important because it is only a special case of a broader misconstrual of the phenomenon of aesthetic modernism generally by New Criticism.

Even though my subject has been literary modernism, I began with the Enlightenment and the French Revolution, because I think that is where my particular story begins. It is also the period when the breach between religion and natural philosophy first opened wide in modern history. Philosophy, religion, and art had been the three pillars of European culture prior to that breach. Art and religion had much more to say to one another than art and philosophy had, despite frequent quarrels, for they both articulated and expressed society's emotional life, a role that institutionalized religion has largely ceased to fulfil.

Neoclassicism accepted the "scientific" values that excluded emotion from the arts and religion alike. It banished passion and superstition from the arts. However, the banishment of passion from art could not be maintained. Romanticism celebrated passion rather than reason, and directed its hostility to church and crown rather than to religion and superstition. The Romantic artist tended to claim access to truth *through* passion, placing himself in open conflict with science and religion alike. The Romantic artist reclaimed the ancient role of the teacher of mankind – one long since usurped by priests and philosophers. Some artists sought to make their vision compatible with Christianity, as Wordsworth and Coleridge did. Others – like Blake and Shelley – regarded themselves as prophets who spoke with greater authority than mere priests and theologians. Clearly, Eliot chose the path of Wordsworth and Coleridge, while Yeats and Pound chose that of Blake and Shelley.

I have argued that modernism continued the Romantic celebration of passion, revelation, and revolution, and found much of its inspiration in many of the same sources as the Romantics – in Neoplatonism, Gnosticism, the Kabbala, and Swedenborg. These sources have been obscured by modernist scholarship's fixation on nineteenth- and twentieth-century archaeology, anthropology, and comparative religion.

The modern occult makes a claim for itself that overlaps in many places with the claims of the Romantic and modern artist. Both the artist and the occultist claim access to truth through passion or ecstasy rather than through labour and thought. Both regard themselves as prophets, even though the occult prophet is more insistent than the poet that she is the hierophant of the one true revelation. In this respect, the occultist tends to be foundational and to assert cognitive hegemony much like religion, philosophy, and science. The visionary poet is more likely to be more tolerant of variety in vision, and highly eclectic in his articulation of it.

Romanticism modulates into aestheticism when the artist's attention is drawn to the aesthetic residue of religion – that is to say, everything in religion except its metaphysical and moral teachings. The stories and myths, rituals and music, art and architecture of Christianity, paganism, Islam, Judaism, Hinduism, and "savages" are all equally valued by the aesthete. The secular arts, religion, dream, and hallucination are all thought to belong to a single imaginitive realm, thereby enfolding religion, art, and psychology into a single field of inquiry.

The aesthete's valuation of the trappings of religion is difficult to distinguish from the occult's synoptic approach to the religions and rituals of the world, and neither can be isolated from the psychological and anthropological study of these same activities. Religion, art, psychology, and vision are not so much distinct discourses as distinct communities of interpreters – veritable instances of what Stanley Fish calls "interpretive communities" (Fish 1980, 171).

The rationale of my study has been to abandon the normative procedure of selection followed by standard literary and intellectual history. In short, I have not restricted my research to approved discourses but have deliberately concentrated on authors and texts that have been excluded from the canon of works worthy of scholarly attention. Of course, I have not selected all disregarded texts but have picked out those whose filiation with one another and with modernist artists could be established. Such a procedure has produced a portrait of the modern age at variance with the standard view, which I suggest is a product of modernist ideology itself.

The world would be a simpler place if the scientific epistemé were always accompanied by one social and political ideology, the aesthetic by another, and the occult by a third. Alas, no such simple alignment is supported by the historical record. Nor does any other alignment have superior predictive power. Despite postmodernism's claim that Enlightenment values invariably produce oppressive hegemonic power structures, my belief is that ideas have no causal role to play in history. Ideas and ideologies only legitimize actions. The *causes* of human acts are motives. Motives are always complex and are seldom accessible to inquiry – even to the inquiry of the actor himself or herself. Even within the magic circle of discourse, ideology cannot be relied upon to account for all of its features. Accident, ignorance, and error must be permitted their legitimate role in the generation of discourse – especially of literary discourse – and an even greater role in its reception. The historian who traces the tortuous path of accident, ignorance, and error, as I have tried to do, risks producing a shaggier story than a rival guided by the laser of hegemonic necessity.

Cluttered as the scene is, it is possible to divide the political spectrum into "conservative" forces, for whom the old forms of belief and worship must be protected against Enlightenment scepticism, and "progressive" forces, for whom the old forms are revealed by sceptical inquiry to be at best socially useful fossils of a dead faith and at worst cynical legitimations of oppressive power structures. For a very long time, mainstream academic opinion has identified Enlightenment rational scepticism with liberty and social equity – with social "progress." Postmodernism has adopted the Nietzschean critique of Enlightenment rationalism in which the rational scepticism of the Enlightenment is identified with a cultural absolutism legitimizing hierarchical and hegemonic power structures. European military, political, economic, and cultural domination of the rest of the world is cited as a case in point.

On an Enlightenment or rational and empirical reading of world history, the European conquest of the world would be seen as a result of the superiority of its philosophy, science, and political structures. The empiricist would argue that a science and philosophy that merely legitimated conquest and exploitation would not thereby produce it, and he would point out that it is not absolutely clear that the indigenous ideologies of Asia, Africa, the Americas, and Oceania uniformly dislegitimate conquest and exploitation. He would take Western medicine, its pharmacological and surgical practices, as an example. For the empiricist, Western medicine has greater therapeutic success than the herbal and homeopathic procedures of the rest of the world because it has a more accurate understanding of biochemistry, biology, and anatomy than "traditional" medicines do. In short, he would claim that it was more true. And he would reject as inadequate the ideological or reflexive analysis that Western medicine has greater success in reversing pathology because in accordance with Western ideology it is intrusive, aggressive, and violent.

I start with the Enlightenment because that is when rational empiricism begins its conquest of Europe, and thence of the world. The conquest has been military, political, economic, social, and cultural. Since 1945 all five aspects of this conquest have been identified with the United States of America much more than with Western Europe. The United States is today the greatest military and economic power in the world, and it is also – as a nation founded on Enlightenment principles – the least traditional and most volatile in its social and cultural practices. Inheriting the Enlightenment contempt for traditional practices, the United States seems to have been largely insulated from convulsive attempts to alter or preserve those practices that have racked most of the rest of the world. The American Revolutionary War and the Civil War were certainly convulsive struggles, but they were not joined between philosophies or ideologies. Except for these two great traumas, the Americans have been spared the convulsions that have torn Europe, Latin America, and Asia for the last two centuries.

Convulsive confrontations are the province of the historian. The literary scholar's province is the peaceful movements attempting to influence the course of events by persuasion and argument. Examples of peaceful resistance to the Enlightenment in nineteenth-century England are the Oxford Movement, the Pre-Raphaelite Brotherhood, aestheticism, and the arts and crafts movement. In the United States, transcendentalism, populism, fundamentalism, and the beat and hippie movements may also be seen as counter-Enlightenment. Typically, they mix aesthetic, social, and political agendas, although populism is almost exclusively political in the United States and – prior to Reaganism – fundamentalism was almost exclusively social. The beat and hippie movements – like their European predecessors – combine aesthetic, social, and political agendas.

As has often been observed, fascism and nazism can also be seen as movements defined by their resistance to Enlightenment values. To this extent, these conservative ideologies shared some common ground with aestheticism and modernism. However, fascism and nazism were tyrannical or totalitarian political movements hostile to the artistic movements that were contemporary with them. Fascism, nazism, and communism regarded the arts as given over to scepticism and licence, and were either hostile or indifferent to even the most friendly modernist artists. Most artists were appalled at the brutality and violence unleashed by Mussolini, Hitler, and Stalin – whatever their political sympathies. Some, however, were not, and Pound is one of those who was not repelled by the infliction of pain and death on millions of men, women, and children.

In addition to the rejection of emotion and the irrational, the Enlightenment exposes sanctified tradition and convention to cold, rational scrutiny. Literary culture has fought to preserve and rediscover just these "irrational" traditions and conventions, and characteristically regards European civilization as a pathological condition resulting from some collective trauma. This idea received its modern formulation from Giambattista Vico and Jean Jacques Rousseau, and was adopted by Marx, Nietzsche, and Freud.

Following Rousseau, Wordsworth looked "below" the educated classes to discover innocence in the child and in the untutored peasant who was still untouched by the trauma of civilization. A generation later, Byron looked south to the Mediterranean and found his "free spirits" (to apply a Nietzschean term anachronistically) among "uncivilized" Greek and Arab adventurers. Ruskin, Morris, and the Pre-Raphaelites turned to the past and celebrated untutored medieval craftsmen. The Pre-Raphaelite Brotherhood (possibly taking some hints from Gabriele Rossetti) imagined medieval painters to have been as innocent of the laws of perspective as Wordsworth's peasants were of the laws of physics, or as Byron's corsairs were of moral laws.

The modernists clearly belong to this series. They looked to the Hellenistic world of immanentist and pantheist theology, and to prehistoric and barbaric sacrificial rites – both of which were newly accessible by virtue of the labours of nineteenth-century archaeologists, mythographers, anthropologists, and religious historians. Ironically, the novelty and "scientific" status of this knowledge of antiquity permitted the modernists to disguise themselves as promoters of Enlightenment progress. Modernism was able to represent, for the first time since the Enlightenment, ancient discarded superstition as the latest thing.

I have gone to great lengths to document the perception that the modern "discovery" of the irrational was a broadly based cultural movement embracing philosophy and psychology as well as the professionally backward-looking disciplines of history, anthropology, and archaeology. The excited speculations of occultists, metahistorians, and Masons were able to hide themselves within mainstream scholarship in this century, as they had always failed to do in the past, because their field of inquiry overlapped with the mainstream disciplines of religious history, psychology, and anthropology.

Whether the unenlightened society is found within or without Europe, in the present or in the past, in the individual or in conventional practices, it is always characterized by a failure or evasion of rationality and calculation. In D.H. Lawrence's phrase, the reason is regarded as a "bit and a bridle" on the soul. Psychoanalysis effectively removed this constraint for mainstream scholarship. But once rationality is removed, it is difficult to find the means of discriminating between the profound and the silly. Within organized religions, mysticism, irrationality, and credulity are cosseted by doctrine and hierarchical authority. But no such constraints apply to the "churchless" literary and aesthetic "tradition."

I do not want to complicate the story unnecessarily by a return to a discussion of the way in which psychoanalysis fits. For the most part, modernism kept its distance from both Freud and Jung. Nonetheless, it is apparent that the Freudian subconscious and the Jungian unconscious either evade or dislocate logic and calculation much in the manner that children, peasants, savages, and primitives are thought to do. The very labelling of these psychic realms participates in the general supposition of higher and lower capacities shared by the Enlightenment and its opponents. It is hierarchization that is at issue. The resistance to the Enlightenment places greater value on the untutored, instinctive, or intuitive, while the Enlightenment places greater value on reason, logic, or calculation. It is striking that all accept the bifurcation of the human psyche into antipathetic capacities or processes. They disagree only about which ones to privilege.

Modernism represented itself as a champion of Enlightenment values by claiming to be the aesthetic expression of scientific materialism and analytic philosophy. It cunningly deployed the doctrines of artistic impersonality and aesthetic autonomy as an earnest of the "scientific" status of the arts. These doctrines coincidentally sheltered artists from any careful investigation of their "belief systems." Literary historical studies were commonly decried by the New Critical students of modernism as "mere source hunting" or "merely biographical," or as having fallen into the "genetic fallacy" – all implicitly appealing to the decontextualism of analytic philosophy.

Modernism also exploited the apparent immateriality of quantum physics and the apparent irrationality of relativity theory. These supposed features of the latest scientific developments licensed all sorts of mystical and transcendental speculation that the "narrowly" mechanistic Cartesian and Newtonian universe had forbidden. Radiation, the "fourth dimension," and relativity all seemed to leave epistemic room for soul, or spirit, or even an astral realm. At the very least, modernism fostered a scepticism about scientific materialism that mirrored Enlightenment scepticism about religion. On this construction it can be seen that postmodernism's revival of Nietzschean scepticism towards science is in fact contiguous with modernism, rather than the radical departure it claims to be.

There are genuine discontinuities between modernism and postmodernism. Modernism was committed to stylistic severity and tolerated metaphysical and epistemological absolutism. Aesthetic postmodernism is playful in tone where modernism was ironic; it is baroque in style where modernism was classically severe; and solipsistic where modernism was occult or mystical. Modernism and postmodernism are, however, similar in that neither places any principled or institutional constraints on belief or behaviour. In contrast to Enlightenment rationality, "Socratism," or "logocentrism," they both permit free rein for emotion and passion.

Politics is the realm most securely identified with the Enlightenment, and a realm where the free rein of passion has been deplored by almost all shades of opinion on the grounds that passion and irrationality ineluctably produce violence in the political sphere. Rationality and dispassion have been regarded as a specific against political passions at least since Aristotle. To be "enlightened" in common parlance means to be capable of rising above narrow passions such as self-interest, prejudicial dislikes or hatreds, and the fear of the unfamiliar. In contrast, to be "poetic" or "artistic" means to be passionate, to be "involved," in contrast to cold, rational dispassionate science. Somehow we have imagined that the artistic cultivation of passion, sensitivity, and sensuality could be achieved without fear of an attendant cultivation of credulity and violence. We have tended to forget that hatred is just as surely a passion as love is. Or – much more darkly – to suppose that love and hatred always find their proper object.

The "case" of Ezra Pound calls such "romantic" hopefulness into question at the same time as it offends the modernist doctrine of aesthetic autonomy. The counter-Enlightenment renders the artist a spiritual and moral athlete endowed with superior sensibility and insight, just as the physical athlete is endowed with superior coordination and strength. On this view, someone who endorses racism and mass murder cannot be an artist, and Ezra Pound must be either not a poet or not a Fascist. Unfortunately, the community of scholars has been unable to reach a consensus on which is the case.

If we adopt the Eliotic model of aesthetic autonomy canonized by New Criticism, the poet is merely a medium (merely a neutral sensibility, much as the scientist was said to be a neutral intelligence), then his moral failings have no pertinence to the value of his art. This is one of the yields of the doctrine of aesthetic autonomy. When we are speaking of personal failures such as dishonesty, sexual licence, rudeness, or poor grooming, this defence is reasonably persuasive. However, when we are speaking of racism, war, and genocide, the defence of aesthetic autonomy becomes monstrous. Many adherents to the doctrine of aesthetic autonomy endorse the normative corollary that artworks ought not to express the beliefs and opinions of their authors. Hence, any study that attempts to elucidate some principled relation between opinions expressed casually by the author and those derivable from his artworks is considered to be in poor taste. Such a general prohibition of the consideration of "biographical" evidence has tended to protect Pound's literary reputation from the worst consequences of his extraliterary conduct.

It has to be admitted that Pound himself maintained no such distinction between his poetic expression and his prose propagandizing. Even the most devout New Critic has been unable to maintain the fiction that Pound's prose pronouncements on Social Credit are unrelated to his verse pronouncements in *The Cantos*, or that unflattering references to Churchill and Roosevelt in *The Cantos* are to be rigorously distinguished from lexically similar pronouncements in conversation, correspondence, and journalistic essays. The "romantic" argument runs as follows: if Pound was an evil or credulous man – and there is strong evidence that he was one or the other – then he must have been a bad poet. Pound's defenders simply invert the argument: if Pound was a fine poet – and there is strong evidence that he was – he must have been a good and wise man. The possibility that he was a fine poet and also credulous or even malicious is tacitly ruled out of court as an inadmissible conclusion. Even though such a conclusion is an uncomfortable one, to rule it out in advance does not serve the cause of truth and accuracy.

The difference between the scholarly reception of Pound and of Yeats is instructive. Because Yeats's mysticism and superstition were apparent and public from the very beginning of his career, Yeats scholars could not deny his occultism. The best they could do was cautiously de-emphasize it or claim that it was not important to the poetry – even though it is manifest in virtually every line he wrote. The strategy has worked very well because, despite his occultism, Yeats's place in the canon is secure. Incredibly, Eliot's Anglicanism has caused his reputation more harm than Yeats's occultism has caused his. The explanation is that mysticism and occultism are tacitly recognized as proper components of literary culture. They are regarded as worthy – or at least tolerable – allies in the resistance to Enlightenment rationality. Yeats's only fault was to be too overt and to associate with mystics and occultists, most of whom were not themselves artists or were second and third rate.

The critical reception of Yeats is also instructive in the area of political passion. As long as Yeats's retrograde political views – that is, his metahistoricism and celebration of race and violence – could be construed as the expression of an oppressed people's struggle against a foreign hegemony, they were readily approved. But after Irish independence, Yeats's political passions were seen as nationalistic and Herderian rather than Jacobin and Voltairian. Thus, we find much more anguished discussion of Yeats's alleged "fascism" than we do of his undoubted occultism. And this is the case despite the very great probability that his political opinions were a direct product of his occultist understanding of culture and history.

The scholarly community has been content to regard the occultism of Yeats and Pound as defamatory gossip that could safely be disregarded or marginalized. Even those hostile to modernism, to Yeats, or to Pound, seldom attack the two poets as mystics and occultists. When occult components of their work are discussed, it is most frequently by those friendly to occultism. Scholars who find occultism disreputable tend to shy away from any evidence of it that they happen to stumble upon. This scholarly bashfulness about the occult is in strong contrast to the indignation – or intense embarrassment – that accompanies the exposure of "conservative" political views in Yeats, Pound, or Eliot.

The difference between our response to failures of rationality and failures of Jacobinism is most sharply illustrated by the case of Eliot. On the strength of the putatively sceptical and relativistic *Waste Land*, Eliot was adopted by the Enlightened and rational academic establishment as their spokesman. His subsequent descent into credulity and superstition – as his conversion to Anglicanism seems to have been taken – has received more condemnation than Yeats's far more extreme mooniness. Eliot's political conservatism – even though far less retrograde than Yeats's – has also received more negative notice. Part of the explanation is to be found in the different constitution of the two communities of readers. Eliot attracted sceptics and relativists as well as those seeking alternatives to established religions. Yeats attracted few if any of such sceptical readers.

Pound, who was adopted by the same community that adopted Eliot (albeit with reservations and caveats) has never received anything like the same amount and severity of criticism for his very clearly stated mystical and occult views as Eliot has for his Anglicanism – a discrepancy I find astonishing. The occult elements of Pound's poetry and of his literary and cultural theories have been much noted but have been allowed to pass muster as nothing other than standard literariness brought to a new pitch of intensity – or even (in cases already noted) as scepticism. Pound's political views are another matter. But even here the heat applied to him has arisen more from his possibly treasonous behaviour and from his expressions of anti-Semitism than from the ideological content of his writings. For the most part, Pound's ideological positions on economics, history, and culture have received favourable notice.* Attempts to identify his ideology as Fascist typically proceed backwards from his behaviour during and after the war, behaviour that was not only disloyal to duly constituted American political authority but also was morally outrageous. The striking feature of Pound's critical reception is that it has been so favourable, given the many black marks he has against him.

Within modernism, Pound's critical success – uneven as it has been – is consistent with modernism's decontextualism and absolute standards of aesthetic excellence. Pound's critical success is a straightforward consequence of the formal excellences of his poetry, quite independently of any thematic content it might be supposed to have. However, this posture is no longer viable. No one in the academy believes any longer in absolute standards of excellence, and few accept modernism's formalist suppression of the aesthetic relevance of theme or content.

I do think that Pound was a very great literary talent, an opinion supported by the consensual judgment of his peers – of Yeats, Eliot, and Williams, and of younger poets in virtually every country in Europe, in the Americas, and even in the Orient. Such testimony cannot be decisive, but neither can it be ignored. It is sufficient, I think, to count as at least a partial explanation of the survival of Pound's work in the literary universe. However, this is not the explanation that I have articulated in these pages. My explanation is thematic and hence a-modernist. I argue that Pound's work captures and expresses a set of passions, fears, hopes, and errors that were

---

* Massimo Bacigalupo and Robert Casillo are strong exceptions to this rule. Both scholars find Pound's work to be infected root and branch with fascism and anti-Semitism. I think they both go much too far, but their very strong censure is a natural consequence of the precedent lack of scholarly candour.

ubiquitous in the political and cultural history of the first half of the century. I make this claim at the same time as I argue that Pound's "world view" is deeply indebted to occult speculation on the one hand and to conspiracy theories of history on the other.

There will no doubt be those who would wish to keep the separation of sense and nonsense, virtue and vice, truth and error much cleaner than my story will permit and who would wish me to say, "*This* is worth retaining, and *that* should be discarded." Indeed, I myself am one of these. I would much prefer an intellectual climate like the modernist one in which I came of age, when such separations were thought to be clean and sharp, when it was thought that ideology and theory were as distinct as opinion and knowledge. Although I do not "hail the postmodern," it has inescapably purged the academy of "naïvely" positive views about knowledge and belief.

Modernism did – as postmodernism alleges – adhere to Enlightenment universalism. In this respect it shared an ideological component of scientific materialism and was antipathetic to Nietzschean scepticism and relativism, despite allegations to the contrary. But its universalism was Platonic and metaphysical rather than empirical and rational like modern scientific universalism. Modernism was not – as it pretended to be – an expression of Enlightenment rationalism. But it was a genuine expression of Enlightenment optimism, and it swam against the wave of pessimism that swept over Europe in the wake of the Great War, rather than drifting with it.

Bibliography

Abrams, M.H. 1971. *Natural Supernaturalism: Tradition and Revolution in Romantic Literature*. New York: Norton.

Adams, Hazard. 1986. *Philosophy of the Literary Symbolic*. Tallahasee: University Presses of Florida.

Adams, John Quincy. 1847. *Letters on the Masonic Institution*. Boston: T. R. Marvin.

Alleau, René. 1977. *La Science des symboles*. Paris: Payot.

Amadou, Robert, and Robert Kanters, eds. 1955. *Anthologie littéraire de l'occultisme*. Paris: Seghers.

Andler, Charles. 1958. *Nietzsche, sa vie et sa pensée*. 3 vols. Paris: Librairie Gallimard.

Aroux, Eugène. 1854. *Dante hérétique, révolutionnaire et socialiste*. Paris: Jules Reynouard.

– 1856. *Clef de la comédie anti-catholique de Dante Alighieri, pasteur de l'église albigeoise dans la ville de Florence, affilié à l'ordre du Temple*. Paris: Jules Reynouard.

– 1857a. *L'Hérésie de Dante démontré par Francesca da Rimini, devenue un moyen de propagande vaudoise et coup d'oeil sur les romans du St-Graal*. Paris: Mme veuve Jules Reynouard.

– 1857b. *Preuves de l'hérésie de Dante notamment au sujet d'une fusion opéré vers 1312 entre la massenie Albigeoise, les Temples et les Gibelins*. Paris: Mme veuve Jules Reynouard.

Assoun, Paul-Laurent. 1980. *Freud et Nietzsche*. Paris: Presses Universitaires de France.

Bacigalupo, Massimo. 1980. *The Formèd Trace: The Later Poetry of Ezra Pound*. New York: Columbia University Press.

Balzac, Honoré [1835] 1950. *Séraphita*, ed. Marcel Bouteron. Paris: Gallimard.

Barruel, Abbé. 1797–98. *Memoirs Illustrating the History of Jacobinism*. 4 vols. London.

Barzun, Jacques. [1932] 1960. *The French Race*. Reprint. Port Washington, N.Y.: Kennikat Press.

– [1937] 1965. *Race: A Study in Superstition*. New York: Harper & Row.

Bays, Gwendolyn. 1964. *The Orphic Vision: Seer Poets from Novalis to Rimbaud*. Lincoln: University of Nebraska Press.

Belperron, Pierre. 1942. *La Croisade contre les albigeois*. Paris: Plon.

Bernard, David. 1829. *Light on Masonry*. Utica: William Williams.

Bernstein, Michael André. 1980. *The Tale of the Tribe: Ezra Pound and the Modern Verse Epic*. Princeton: Princeton University Press.

Bertholet, Edouard. 1952, 1955, 1958. *La Pensée et les secrets du Sar Joséphin Péladan*. 4 vols. Lausanne: Editions Rosicruciennes.

Blavatsky, Helena. [1888] 1963. *The Secret Doctrine*. 2 vols. Pasadena, Calif.: Theosophical University Press.

Bloom, Allan. 1987. *The Closing of the American Mind*. New York: Simon and Schuster.

Bloom, Clive. 1986. *The "Occult" Experience and the New Criticism*. Sussex: Harvester Press.

Bloom, Harold. 1964. "Myth, Vision, Allegory." *Yale Review* 54(Autumn: 143–9.

Boulton, James, ed. 1979. *The Letters of D.H. Lawrence*. Vol. 1. Cambridge: Cambridge University Press.

Brooks, Cleanth. [1939] 1968. "*The Waste Land:* Critique of the Myth." Reprinted in *A Collection of Critical Essays on The Waste Land*, ed. Jay Martin, 59–86. Englewood Cliffs, N.J.: Prentice-Hall.

Bucke, Richard Maurice. [1900] 1961. *Cosmic Consciousness: A Study in the Evolution of the Human Mind*. Reprint. Secaucus, N.J.: Citadel Press.

Bulwer-Lytton, Edward Lord Lytton. [1845] 1853. *Zanoni*. Reprint. London: George Routledge & Sons.

– [1871] 1979. *The Coming Race*. Reprint. Santa Barbara: Woodbridge.

Burckhardt, Jacob. 1935. *The Civilization of the Renaissance in Italy*, trans. S.G.C. Middlemore. New York: Albert & Charles Boni.

– 1955. *Force and Freedom*, ed. James Hastings Nichols. New York: Meridian Books.

Bush, Ronald. 1976. *The Genesis of Ezra Pound's Cantos*. Princeton: Princeton University Press.

Campbell, Joseph. [1969] 1976. *The Masks of God: Primitive Mythology*. Reprint. London: Penguin Books.

Carpenter, Humphrey. 1988. *A Serious Character: The Life of Ezra Pound*. London: Faber and Faber.

Casillo, Robert. 1983. "Anti-Semitism, Castration and Usury in Ezra Pound." *Criticism* 25(Summer): 239–65.

– 1984. "Plastic Demons: The Scapegoating Process in Ezra Pound." *Criticism* 26(Fall): 355–82.

– 1988. *The Genealogy of Demons: Anti-Semitism, Fascism and the Myths of Ezra Pound*. Chicago: Northwestern University Press.

Cassirer, Ernst. 1946. *The Myth of the State*. New Haven: Yale University Press.

Cellier, Léon. 1953. *Fabre d'Olivet: Contribution à l'étude des aspects religieux du romantisme*. Paris: Librairie Nizet.

– 1977. *Parcours Initiatiques*. Neuchatel: Presses Universitaires de Grenoble.

Chace, William. 1973. *The Political Identities of Ezra Pound and T.S. Eliot*. Stanford: Stanford University Press.

Chamberlain, Houston Stewart. 1968. *Foundations of the Nineteenth Century*, trans. John Lees. Introduction by George L. Mosse. New York: Howard Fertig.

Chandler, Albert R. 1945. *Rosenberg's Nazi Myth*. Ithaca, N.Y.: Cornell University Press.

Chiari, Joseph. 1970. *The Aesthetics of Modernism*. London: Vision Press.

Conrad, Joseph. [1902] 1973. *Heart of Darkness*. Reprint. London: Penguin Books.

Cooper-Oakley, Isabel. [1900] 1977. *Masonry & Medieval Mysticism*. London: Theosophical Publishing House.

Cornell, Kenneth. 1951. *The Symbolist Movement*. New Haven: Yale University Press.

Dante Alighieri. 1939. *The Divine Comedy*. 3 vols, trans. John D. Sinclair. London: The Bodley Head.

– 1947. *La Vita nuova*, trans. D.G. Rossetti. In *The Portable Dante*, ed. Paolo Milano. New York: Viking Press.

Darnton, Robert. 1968. *Mesmerism and the End of the Enlightenment in France*. Cambridge, Mass.: Harvard University Press.

Davenport, Guy, ed. 1963. *The Intelligence of Louis Agassiz*. Boston: Beacon Press.

Davie, Donald. 1972. "The *Cantos*: Toward a Pedestrian Reading." *Paideuma* 1 (Spring/Summer): 55–62.

Delavenay, Emile. 1971. *D.H. Lawrence and Edward Carpenter: A Study in Edwardian Transition*. London: Heinemann.

Derrida, Jacques. 1976. *Of Grammatology*, trans. G.C. Spivak. Baltimore: Johns Hopkins University Press.

– 1978. *Writing and Difference*, trans. Allan Bass. Chicago: University of Chicago Press.

– 1979. *Spurs: Nietzsche's Styles*, trans. Barbara Harlow. Chicago: University of Chicago Press.

Doob, Leonard W., ed. 1978. *"Ezra Pound Speaking": Radio Speeches of World War II*. Westport, Conn.: Greenwood Press.

Doolittle, Hilda. 1979. *End to Torment*, ed. Norman Holmes Pearson. New York: New Directions.

Doyon, René Louis. 1946. *La Douloureuse Aventure de Péladan*. Paris: La Connaissance.

Dray, W.H. 1964. *Philosophy of History*. Englewood Cliffs, N.J.: Prentice-Hall.

Dudek, Louis, ed. 1974. *DK / Some Letters of Ezra Pound*. Montreal: DC Books.

Dunbar, Janet. 1963. *Mrs G.B.S: A Biographical Portrait of Charlotte Shaw*. London: George G. Harrap.

Durand, Gilbert. 1976. *L'Imagination symbolique*. Paris: Presses Universités.

– 1979. *Figures mythiques et visages de l'oeuvre de la mythocritique*. Paris: Berg International, L'Île Verte.

Duvernoy, Jean. 1976. *Le Catharisme: La Religion des Cathares*. Paris: Privat.

– 1979. *Le Catharisme: L'Historie des Cathares*. Paris: Privat.

Eliade, Mircea. 1976. *Occultism, Witchcraft and Cultural Fashions*. Chicago: University of Chicago Press.

– 1977. *No Souvenirs: Journal, 1957–69*, trans. Fred H. Johnson, Jr. San Fransisco: Harper & Row.

Eliot, T.S. [1928] 1960. *The Sacred Wood*. Reprint. London: Methuen.

– 1948. *Notes Toward a Definition of Culture*. London: Faber.

– 1951. *Selected Essays*. London: Faber.

– 1961. *On Poetry and Poets*. New York: Noonday Press.

– 1964. *Knowledge and Experience in the Philosophy of F.H. Bradley*. London: Faber.

– 1971. *The Waste Land: A Facsimile and Transcript of the Original Drafts*, ed. Valerie Eliot. London: Faber.

– 1975. *Selected Prose of T.S. Eliot*, ed. Frank Kermode. London: Faber.

– 1988. *The Letters of T.S. Eliot*, ed. Valerie Eliot. Vol. 1, 1898–1922. New York: Harcourt Brace Jovanovich.

Elliott, Angela. 1989. "The Word Comprehensive: Gnostic Light in *The Cantos*." *Paideuma* 18(Winter): 7–57.

Ellmann, Richard. 1948. *Yeats: The Man and the Mask*. London & New York: Macmillan.

– 1954. *The Identity of Yeats*. New York: Oxford University Press.

–, ed. 1969. *The Artist as Critic: Critical Writings of Oscar Wilde*. New York: Random House.

Ellwood, Robert, Jr. 1973. *Religious and Spiritual Groups in Modern America*. Englewood Cliffs, N.J.: Prentice-Hall.

Fabre d'Olivet. [1813, 1st French ed.; trans. 1917] 1925. *The Golden Verses of Pythagoras*, trans. Nayàn Louise Redfield. Reprint. New York: Putnam.

– 1921. *The Hebraic Tongue Restored*, trans. Nayàn Louise Redfield. New York: Putnam.

Finlay, John L. 1972. *Social Credit: The English Origins*. Montreal: McGill-Queen's University Press.

Fish, Stanley. 1980. *Is There a Text in This Class?* Cambridge, Mass.: Harvard University Press.

Foucault, Michel. 1969. *L'Archéologie du savoir*. Paris: Gallimard.

French, William, and Timothy Materer. 1982. "Far Flung Vortices and Ezra's 'Hindoo' Yogi." *Paideuma* 11(Spring/Summer): 39–53.

Frère, Jean-Claude. 1974. *Nazisme et sociétés secrètes*, Paris: Culture, Art, Loisirs.

Freud, Sigmund. [1900, trans. 1953] 1976. *The Interpretation of Dreams*, trans. James Strachey. Reprint. London: Penguin.

Frye, Northrop. 1982. *The Great Code*. Toronto: Academic Press Canada.

Fussell, Paul. 1975. *The Great War and Modern Memory*. Oxford: Oxford University Press.

Gallup, Donald. 1969. *A Bibliography of Ezra Pound*. London: Rupert Hart-Davis.

Gibbons, Tom. 1972. "*The Waste Land* Tarot Identified." *Journal of Modern Literature* 2 (November): 560–5.

Gobineau, Artur, comte de. 1983. *Oeuvres*, vol. 1, ed. Jean Gaulmier. Paris: Gallimard.

Goblet, Comte d'Alviella. 1903. *Eleusinia: De Quelques problèmes relatifs aux Mystères d'Eleusis*. Paris: Ernest Leroux.

Godlovich, Stan. 1987. "Aesthetic Judgement and Hindsight." *Journal of Aesthetics and Art Criticism* 45(Winter): 75–83.

Goodrick-Clarke, Nicholas. 1985. *The Occult Roots of Nazism: The Ariosophists of Austria and Germany, 1890–1935*. Willingborough, Northants: Aquarian Press.

Gordon, Lyndall. 1977. *Eliot's Early Years*. Oxford: Oxford University Press.

Gourmont, Remy de. [1922] 1950. *The Natural Philosophy of Love*, trans. Ezra Pound. Reprint. New York: Collier Books.

Grant, Michael, ed. 1982. *T.S. Eliot: The Critical Heritage*. Vol. 1. London: Routledge & Kegan Paul.

Guigniaut, Joseph Daniel. 1825–51. *Religions de l'antiquité*. 9 vols. Paris. (A translation, with commentary and notes, of Friedrich Creuzer, *Symbolik und Mythologie*.)

Guthrie, W.K.C. 1967. "Introductory Memoir." In F.M. Cornford, *The Unwritten Philosophy and Other Essays*. Cambridge: Cambridge University Press.

Hangest, Germain d'. 1961. *Walter Pater: L'Homme et l'oeuvre*. Paris: Didier.

Harmon, William. 1976. "T.S. Eliot, Anthropologist and Primitive." *American Anthropologist* 74(December): 797–811.

Harper, George Mills, ed. 1975. *Yeats and the Occult*. Toronto: Macmillan.

– 1981. "Unbelievers in the House: Yeats's Automatic Script." In *W.B. Yeats: The Occult and Philosophical Backgrounds*, ed. T.R. Spirey. Atlanta: Georgia State University.

Harrison, Jane. [1911] 1963. *Themis: A Study of the Social Origins of Greek Religion*. Reprint. London: Merlin Press.

Harrison, John. R. 1966. *The Reactionaries*. London: Victor Gollancz.

Hastings, Beatrice. 1936. *The Old "New Age": Orage and Others*. London: Blue Moon Press.

Heiden, Konrad. [1944] 1969. *Der Fuehrer: Hitler's Rise to Power*, trans. Ralph Manheim. Reprint. Boston: Beacon Press.

Henricksen, Bruce. 1978. "*Heart of Darkness* and the Gnostic Myth." *Mosaic* 11(Summer): 35–44.

Hesse, Eva. 1969. *New Approaches to Ezra Pound*. London: Faber & Faber.

Heyman, Katherine Ruth. 1921. *The Relation of Ultramodern to Archaic Music*. Boston: Small, Maynard & Co.

Hoffman, Daniel. 1967. *Barbarous Knowledge*. New York: Oxford University Press.

Hollinrake, Roger. 1982. *Nietzsche, Wagner, and the Philosophy of Pessimism*. London: Allen & Unwin.

Hough, Graham. 1984. *The Mystery Religion of W.B. Yeats*. Sussex: Harvester Press.

Houston, John Porter. 1980. *French Symbolism and the Modernist Movement: A Study of Poetic*. Baton Rouge: Louisiana State University Press.

Hueffer, Francis. [1878] 1977. *The Troubadours: A History of Provençal Life and Literature in the Middle Ages*. Reprint. New York: AMS Press.

Husserl, Edmund. 1962. *Ideas: General Introduction to Pure Phenomenology*, trans. W.R. Boyce Gibson. New York: Collier Books.

Hutchins, Patricia. 1965. *Ezra Pound's Kensington: An Exploration, 1885–1913*. Chicago: Henry Regnery.

Huxley, Aldous. [1946] 1985. *The Perennial Philosophy*. Reprint. London: Triad Grafton.

Hynes, Samuel. 1968. *The Edwardian Turn of Mind*. Princeton: Princeton University Press.

Iser, Wolfgang. 1960. *Walter Pater: Die Autonomie des Asthetischen*. Tübingen: Max Niemeyer Verlag.

Jameson, Frederic. 1972. *The Prison-House of Language*. Princeton: Princeton University Press.

Janz, Kurt Paul. 1978, 1979. *Friedrich Nietzsche: Biographie*. 3 vols. München: Carl Hanser Verlag.

Jenkins, Ralph. 1969. "Theosophy in 'Scylla and Charybdis.'" *Modern Fiction Studies* 15(Spring): 35–48.

Jung, Carl. 1965. *Memories, Dreams, Reflections*, ed. Amiela Jaffé. New York: Vintage Books.

– 1977. *Psychology and the Occult*, trans. R.F.C. Hull. Bollingen series 20. Princeton: Princeton University Press.

Kandinsky, Wassily. [1914] 1977. *Concerning the Spiritual in Art*, trans. M.T.H. Sadler. Reprint. New York: Dover Publications.

Kazin, Alfred. 1986. "The Fascination and Terror of Ezra Pound." *New York Review of Books* 33(3 March): 16–24.

Kenner, Hugh. 1959. *The Invisible Poet*. New York: Ivan Obolensky.

– 1971. *The Pound Era*. Berkeley & Los Angeles: University of California Press.

Kerényi, Karl. 1967. *Eleusis: Archetypal Image of Mother and Daughter*, trans. Ralph Mannheim. Bollingen Series 65. New York: Pantheon Books.

King, Francis. 1970. *Ritual Magic in England: 1887 to the Present Day*. London: Neville Spearman.

Knox, Bryant. 1974. "Allen Upward and Ezra Pound." *Paideuma* 3(Spring): 71–84.

Kuhn, Alvin Boyd. 1930. *Theosophy: A Modern Revival of Ancient Wisdom*. New York: Henry Holt.

Kuhn, Thomas S. 1970. *The Structure of Scientific Revolutions*. 2d ed. Chicago: University of Chicago Press.

– 1977. *The Essential Tension: Selected Studies in Scientific Tradition and Change*. Chicago: University of Chicago Press.

Lauber, John. 1978. "Pound's *Cantos*: A Fascist Epic." *Journal of American Studies* 12(April): 3–21.

Leach, Sir Edmund. 1985. "The Anthroplogy of Religion." In *Nineteenth-Century Religious Thought in the West*, vol. 3, ed. Ninian Smart et al. Cambridge: Cambridge University Press.

Lentricchia, Frank. 1980. *After the New Criticism*. Chicago: University of Chicago Press.

Levenson, Michael. 1984. *A Genealogy of Modernism*. Cambridge: Cambridge University Press.

Lévy-Bruhl, Lucien. [1910] 1985. *How Natives Think*, trans. Lillian A. Clare. Reprint. Princeton: Princeton University Press.

Lewis, Wyndnam. [1927] 1957. *Time and Western Man*. Reprint. Boston: Beacon Press.

– [1931] 1972. *Hitler*. Reprint. New York: Gordon Press.

– [1939] 1972. *The Hitler Cult*. Reprint. New York: Gordon Press.

Lindberg, Kathryne V. 1987. *Reading Pound Reading Nietzsche: Modernism after Nietzsche*. New York: Oxford University Press.

Long, Rose-Carol Washton. 1980. *Kandinsky: The Development of an Abstract Style*. Oxford: Clarendon Press.

Longenbach, James. 1987. *Modernist Poetics of History: Pound, Eliot, and the Sense of the Past*. Princeton: Princeton University Press.

– 1988. *Stone Cottage: Pound, Yeats, and Modernism*. New York: Oxford University Press.

McGann, Jerome. 1988. "Ezra Pound and Evil." *London Review of Books* (7 July), 16–17.

McIntosh, Christopher. 1972. *Eliphas Lévi and the French Occult Revival*. London: Rider & Co.

Mairet, Philip. 1936. *A.R. Orage: A Memoir*. London: Dent.

Makin, Peter. 1978. *Provence and Pound*. Berkeley: University of California Press.

Marcuse, Herbert. [1955] 1974. *Eros and Civilization*. Reprint. Boston: Beacon Press.

Martin, Stoddard. 1982. *Wagner to "The Waste Land": A Study of the Relationship of Wagner to English Literature*. Totawa, N.J.: Barnes & Noble.

Materer, Timothy. 1984. "Ezra Pound and the Alchemy of the Word." *Journal of Modern Literature* 11(March): 109–24.

– 1988. "Eliot on Occultism in *Four Quartets*." T.S. Eliot Centennial Conference, Orono, Maine.

– and William French. 1982. "Far Flung Vortices and Ezra's 'Hindoo' Yogi." *Paideuma* 11(Spring/Summer): 39–53.

Mathers, S.L. MacGregor. [1887] 1968. *The Kabbalah Unveiled*. Reprint. New York: Samuel Weiser.

Matthiessen, F.O. [1935] 1958. *The Achievement of T.S. Eliot*. Reprint. New York: Oxford University Press.

Mead, George Robert Stow. 1898. "Notes on the Eleusinian Mysteries." *Theosophical Review* 22(March-August): 145–57, 232–42, 312–22.

– 1900. *Fragments of a Faith Forgotten*. London and Benares: Theosophical Publishing Society.

– 1906. *The Gnosis of the Mind*. 2d ed. London and Benares: Theosophical Publishing Society.

– 1907. *The Mysteries of Mithra*. London and Benares: Theosophical Publishing Society.

– 1913. "The Meaning of Gnosis in Higher Hellenistic Religions." *Quest* 4(July): 676–97.

Meade, Marion. 1980. *Madam Blavatsky: The Woman Behind the Myth*. New York: Putnam.

Meisel, Perry. 1987. *The Myth of the Modern: A Study of British Literature and Criticism after 1850*. New Haven: Yale University Press.

Mercier, Alain. 1969, 1974. *Les Sources ésotériques et occultes de la poésie symbolistes*. 2 vols. Paris: A.G. Nizet.

Meyers, Jeffrey. 1980. *The Enemy: A Biography of Wyndham Lewis*. London: Routledge & Kegan Paul.

Michaelis, Meir. 1978. *Mussolini and the Jews*. Oxford: Clarendon Press.

Miller, James Edwin. 1977. *T.S. Eliot's Personal Waste Land*. University Park: Pennsylvania State University Press.

Miyake, Akiko. 1991. *Ezra Pound and the Mysteries of Love: A Plan for the Cantos*. Durham: Duke University Press.

Mondolfo, Vittoria I., and Margaret Hurley. 1979. *Ezra Pound: Letters to Ibbotson, 1935–1952*. Orono, Maine: National Poetry Foundation.

Münch, Marc-Mathieu. 1976. *La "Symbolique" de Friedrich Creuzer*. Paris: Editions Orphrys.

Mundy, John Hine. 1985. *The Repression of Catharism at Toulouse*. Toronto: Pontifical Institute of Medieval Studies.

Nasgaard, Roald. 1984. *The Mystic North*. Toronto: University of Toronto Press.

Nehemas, Alexander. 1985. *Nietzsche: Life as Literature*. Cambridge, Mass.: Harvard University Press.

Nelli, René. 1968. *Ecritures Cathares*. Paris: Editions Planète.

– 1972. *Les Cathares, ou l'éternel combat*. Paris: Louis Pauwels.

– 1980. *Spiritualité de l'hérésie: Le Catharisme*. New York: AMS Press.

Nichols, Peter. 1984. *Ezra Pound: Politics, Economics, and Writing*. London: Macmillan.

Niel, Fernand. 1973. *Les Cathares de Monségur*. Paris: Seghers.

Nietzsche, Friedrich. 1922. *The Nietzsche-Wagner Correspondence*, ed. Elizabeth Foerster-Nietzsche, trans. Caroline V. Kerr. London: Duckworth.

– 1961. *Thus Spoke Zarathustra*, trans. R.J. Hollingdale. Harmondsworth: Penguin Books.

– 1967. *The Birth of Tragedy and The Case of Wagner*, trans. Walter Kaufmann. New York: Vintage Books.

– 1969. *On the Genealogy of Morals and Ecce Homo*, trans. Walter Kaufmann. New York: Vintage Books.

– 1974. *The Gay Science*, trans. with commentary by Walter Kaufmann. New York: Vintage Books.

Nock, Arthur Darby. [1928] 1964. *Early Gentile Christianity and Its Hellenistic Background*. Reprint. Harper Torchbooks.

Nordau, Max. [1895] 1913. *Degeneration*. Reprint. London: Heinemann.

Norman, Charles. [1960] rev. 1969. *Ezra Pound: A Biography*. London: Macdonald.

Olney, James. 1980. *The Rhizome and the Flower: The Perennial Philosophy, Yeats and Jung*. Berkeley: University of California Press.

Oppel, Frances Nesbitt. 1987. *Mask and Tragedy: Yeats and Nietzsche, 1902–10*. Charlottesville: University Press of Virginia.

Orage, Alfred R. 1906. *Friedrich Nietzsche: The Dionysian Spirit of the Age*. London: T.N. Foulis.

– 1907a. *Consciousness, Animal Human and Divine*. London: Theosophical Publishing Society.

– 1907b. *Nietzsche in Outline and Aphorism*. London. T.N. Foulis.

– 1932. *On Love: Freely Adapted from the Tibetan*. London: Unicorn Press.

Parker, R.A.C. 1969. *Europe 1919–1945*. London: Weidenfeld and Nicolson.

Pater, Walter. [1873] 1910. *The Renaissance: Studies in Art and Poetry*. Reprint. London: Macmillan.

– [1895] 1910. *Greek Studies*. Reprint. London: Macmillan.

Pearlman, Daniel D. 1969. *The Barb of Time*. New York: Oxford University Press.

Péladan, Joséphin. 1887. "Introduction" to *La Maison de vie*, by Dante Gabriel Rossetti; trans. into French by Clemence Couve. Paris: Alphonse Lemerre.

– [1894] 1981. *Le Théâtre complet de Wagner*. Reprint. Paris: Ressources.
– 1905a. *Le Clé de Rabelais*. Paris: E. Sansot.
– 1905b. *Origine et esthétique de la tragédie*. Paris: E. Sansot.
– 1906. *Le Secret des troubadours: De Parsifan à Don Quichotte*. Paris: E. Sansot.
Pépin, Jean. 1976. *Mythe et allégorie: Les Origines grecques et les contestation judeo-chrétiennes*. Paris: Etudes Augustiniennes.
Perkins, David. 1976. *A History of Modern Poetry*. Cambridge, Mass.: Harvard University Press.
Perl, Jeffrey M. 1984. *The Tradition of Return: The Implicit History of Modernism*. Princeton: Princeton University Press.
– 1989. *Skepticism and Modern Enmity: Before and After Eliot*. Baltimore: Johns Hopkins University Press.
Peyre, Henri. 1980, *What Is Symbolism?*, trans. Emmet Parker. Alabama: University of Alabama Press.
Pincus-Witten, Robert. 1976. *Occult Symbolism in France: Joséphin Peladan and the Salons de la Rose-Croix*. New York: Garland.
Plato. 1963. *The Collected Dialogues of Plato*, ed. Edith Hamilton and Huntington Cairns. Bollingen Series 71. Princeton: Princeton University Press.
Podro, Michael. 1982. *The Critical Historians of Art*. New Haven: Yale University Press.
Pollard, Sidney. 1968. *The Idea of Progress*. New York: Basic Books.
Popper, Karl R. [1957] 1960. *The Poverty of Historicism*. Reprint. New York: Basic Books.
– 1986. "How I See Philosophy." In *Philosophy in Britain Today*, ed. S.G. Shanker, 198–212. London: Croom Helm.
Pound, Ezra. 1906. "Interesting French Publications." *Book News Monthly* 25(Sept.): 54–5.
– [1929] 1953. *Spirit of Romance*. Reprint. New York: New Directions.
– [1935] 1970. *Jefferson and/or Mussolini*. Reprint. New York: Liveright.
– 1938. *Guide to Kulchur*. New York: New Directions.
– 1951. *The Letters of Ezra Pound 1907–1941*, ed. D.D. Paige. London: Faber.
– 1954. *Literary Essays of Ezra Pound*, ed. T.S. Eliot. London: Faber.
– 1958. *Pavannes and Divagations*. New York: New Directions.
– 1962. *Patria Mia and the Treatise on Harmony*. London: Peter Owen.
– 1973a. *The Cantos of Ezra Pound*. New York: New Directions.
– 1973b. *Selected Prose, 1909–1965*, ed. William Cookson. New York: New Directions.
– 1976. *Collected Early Poems of Ezra Pound*, ed. Michael King. New York: New Directions.
– 1977. *Ezra Pound and Music*, ed. R. Murray Schafer. New York: New Directions.
– 1984. *Ezra Pound and Dorothy Shakespear, Their Letters: 1909–1914*, ed. Omar Pound and A. Walton Litz. New York: New Directions.

– 1988. *Ezra Pound and Margaret Cravens: A Tragic Friendship 1910–1912*, ed. Omar Pound and Robert Spoo. Durham and London: Duke University Press.

– 1990. *Personae: The Shorter Poems of Ezra Pound*, revised by Lea Baechler and A. Walton Litz. New York: New Directions.

Praz, Mario. [1948] 1951. *The Romantic Agony*, trans. Angus Davidson. Reprint. Oxford: Oxford University Press.

Rainey, Lawrence S. 1991. *Ezra Pound and the Monument of Culture: Text, History, and the Malatesta Cantos*. Chicago: University of Chicago Press.

Ramacharaka, Yogi. 1903. *Fourteen Lessons in Yogi Philosophy*. Chicago: Yoga Publication Society.

Ratschow, Carl Heinz. 1985. "Friedrich Nietzsche." In *Nineteenth Century Religious Thought in the West*, vol. 3, ed. Ninian Smart et al. Cambridge: Cambridge University Press.

Read, Forrest, ed. 1967. *Pound/Joyce: The Letters of Ezra Pound to James Joyce, with Pound's Essays on Joyce*. New York: New Directions.

Redman, Tim. 1991. *Ezra Pound and Italian Fascism*. Cambridge: Cambridge University Press.

Reghellini da Schio, F.M. 1829. *La Maçonnerie considerée comme le résultat des religions égyptiens, juives et chrétiennes*. 3 vols. Brussels: H. Tarlier.

Reid, Margaret J.C. [1938] 1961. *The Arthurian Legend*. Reprint. New York: Barnes & Noble.

Reitzenstein, Richard. [1911] 1978. *Hellenistic Mystery Religions: Their Basic Ideas and Significance*. Reprint. Pittsburgh: Pickwick Press.

Renan, Ernest T. 1853. "Studies in Religious History." *Revue des deux Mondes*, 15 May. Trans. William M. Thomson. Reprint. London: Mathieson.

Roberts, Marie. 1986. *British Poets and Secret Societies*. London: Croom Helm.

Rorty, Richard. 1979. *Philosophy and the Mirror of Nature*. Princeton: Princeton University Press.

Rossetti, Gabriele. 1834. *Disquisition on the Antipapal Spirit which Produced the Reformation; Its Secret Influence on the Literature of Europe in General and of Italy in Particular*, trans. Caroline Ward. 2 vols. London: Elder Smith.

– 1935. *La Beatrice di Dante, ragionamenti critici*, with preface by Balbino Giuliano. Imola. (Includes "Storia del manoscrito" by Maria Luisa Giartosio de Courten, i–xii.)

– 1967. *Commento analitico al "Purgatorio" di Dante Alighieri*, edited with an introduction by Pompeo Giannantonio. Florence: Olschki.

Rougemont, Denis de. [1940] rev. 1956. *Passion and Society*, trans. Montgomery Belgion. London: Faber. (The same translation was published by Harcourt Brace in New York as *Love and the Western World*.)

Saurat, Denis. 1929. *Blake and Modern Thought*. London: Constable.

– 1930. *Literature and Occult Tradition: Studies in Philosophical Poetry*, trans. Dorothy Bolton. London: G. Bell & Sons.

- 1934. *A History of Religions*. London: Jonathan Cape.
- [1935] 1965. *Blake and Milton*. Reprint. New York: Russell & Russell.
- 1938. *The End of Fear*. London: Faber.

Schafer, R. Murray, ed. 1977. *Ezra Pound and Music: The Complete Criticism*. New York: New Directions.

Schneidau, Herbert. 1969. *Ezra Pound: The Image and the Real*. Baton Rouge: Louisiana State University Press.

Schopenhauer, Arthur. [1958] 1966. *The World as Will and Representation*, 2 vols, trans. E.F. Payne. Reprint. New York: Dover.

Schuré, Edouard. [1876] 1886. *Le Drame musicale*. Reprint. Paris: Perrin.
- [1889] 1927. *Les Grands Initiés: Esquisse de l'histoire secrète des religions*. Reprint. Paris: Perrin.
- 1904. *Précurseurs et révoltés*. Paris: Perrin.
- 1926. *La Genêse de la tragédie: Le Drame d'Eleusis*. Paris: Perrin.
- 1928. *La Rêve d'une vie: Confessions d'un poète*. Paris: Perrin.

Schwartz, Sanford. 1985. *The Matrix of Modernism: Pound, Eliot, and Early Twentieth Century Thought*. Princeton: Princeton University Press.

Scott, Bonnie Kime. 1978. "Joyce and the Dublin Theosophists: 'Vegetable Verse and Story.'" *Eire-Ireland* 13:54–70.

Scott, Peter Dale. 1986. "Anger and Poetic Politics in *Rock-Drill*" *San José Studies* 12(Fall): 68–82.
- 1988. "Pound in *The Waste Land*, Eliot in the *Cantos*." Paper delivered in August at the Eliot Centennial Conference, Orono, Maine.

Selver, Paul. 1959. *Orage and the New Age Circle*. London: Allen & Unwin.

Senior, John. 1959. *The Way Down and Out: The Occult in Symbolist Literature*. Ithaca, N.Y.: Cornell University Press.

Shaw, G.B.S. 1908. *The Sanity of Art: An Exposure of the Current Nonsense about Artists being Degenerate*. London: New Age Press.

Sieburth, Richard. 1978. *Instigations: Ezra Pound and Remy de Gourmont*. Cambridge, Mass.: Harvard University Press.

Sismondi, Simonde de J.C. [1826] 1973. *History of the Crusades against the Albigenses*. Reprint. New York: AMS Press.

Skaff, William. 1986. *The Philosophy of T.S. Eliot: From Skepticism to a Surrealistic Poetic 1909–1927*. Philadelphia: University of Pennsylvania Press.

Smart, Ninian, John Clayton, Steven Katz, and Patrick Sherry, eds. 1985. *Nineteenth Century Religious Thought in the West*. Vol. 3. Cambridge: Cambridge University Press.

Smith, Grover. 1983. *The Waste Land*. London: Allen & Unwin.

Sohnle, Werner Paul. 1972. *Georg Friedrich Creuzer's Symbolik und Mythologie in Frankreich*. Göttingen: Verlag Alfred Kümmerle.

Sosnowski, Andrzej. 1991. "Pound's Imagism and Emanuel Swedenborg." *Paideuma* 20(Winter): 31–8.

Spivey, Ted R., ed. 1981. *W.B. Yeats: The Occult and Philosophical Backgrounds*. Atlanta: Georgia State University.

Steiner, George. 1975. *After Babel*. Oxford: Oxford University Press.

Stock, Noel. 1970. *The Life of Ezra Pound*. New York: Pantheon Books.

Surette, Leon. 1971. "The Historical Pattern in Ezra Pound's *Cantos*." *Humanities Association Bulletin* 22(Summer): 11–21.

– 1974. "A Light from Eleusis." *Paideuma* 3(Fall 1974): 191–216.

– 1979. *A Light from Eleusis: A Study of the Cantos of Ezra Pound*. Oxford: Clarendon Press.

– 1983. "Ezra Pound and British Radicalism." *English Studies in Canada* 9(December): 435–51.

– 1986. "Economics and Eleusis." *San José Studies* 12(Fall): 58–67.

– 1988. "T.S. Eliot and J.L. Weston: A Reassessment." *Twentieth Century Literature* 34(Summer): 223–44.

– 1989. "Ezra Pound's Fascism: Aberration or Essence?" *Queen's Quarterly* 96(Autumn): 601–24.

– 1989–90. "Pound, Postmodernism, and Fascism." *University of Toronto Quarterly* 59(Winter): 60–79.

– 1991. "Yeats, Pound, and Nietzsche." *Paideuma* 20(Winter): 17–30.

Svarny, Erik. 1988. *"The Men of 1914": T.S. Eliot and Early Modernism*. Philadelphia: Open University Press.

Tedlock, E.W. Jr. 1960. "D.H. Lawrence's Annotation of Ouspensky's *Tertium Organum*." *Texas Studies in Literature and Language*, 2.

Terrell, Carroll F. 1980, 1984. *A Companion to the Cantos of Ezra Pound*. 2 vols. Berkeley: University of California Press.

Thatcher, David S. 1970. *Nietzsche in England 1890–1914*. Toronto: University of Toronto Press.

Tindall, William York. 1945. "The Symbolism of W.B. Yeats." *Accent* 5(Summer): 203–12.

– 1954. "James Joyce and the Hermetic Tradition." *Journal of the History of Ideas* 15:23–39.

– 1955. *The Literary Symbol*. Bloomington: Indiana University Press.

– 1956. *Forces in Modern British Literature, 1885–1956*. New York: Vintage Books.

– 1972. *D.H. Lawrence and Susan His Cow*. New York: Cooper Square.

Torrey, E. Fuller. 1984. *The Roots of Treason*. New York: McGraw-Hill.

Tryphonopoulos, Demetres P. 1989. *"The Cantos* as Palingenesis." *Paideuma* 18(Spring/Fall): 7–33.

– 1991. "Ezra Pound and Emanuel Swedenborg." *Paideuma* 20(Winter): 7–15.

– 1992. *The Celestial Tradition: A Study of Ezra Pound's Cantos*. Waterloo: Wilfrid Laurier University Press.

Tytell, John. 1987. *Ezra Pound: The Solitary Volcano*. New York: Doubleday.

Underhill, Evelyn. [1911, rev. 1930] 1960. *Mysticism: A Study in the Nature and Development of Man's Spiritual Consciousness*. Reprint. New York: Meridian Books.

Upward, Allen. 1908. *The New Word*. London: A.C. Fifield.

– 1921. *Some Personalites*. London: John Murray.

Valli, Luigi. 1922. *L'Allegoria di Dante secondo Giovanni Pascoli*. Bologna: Nicola Zanichelli.

– 1928, 1930. *Il Linguaggio segreto di Dante e dei fedeli d'amore*. 2 vols. Rome: Biblioteca di Filosofia e Scienza, no. 10.

Viatte, Auguste. [1928] 1965. *Les Sources occulte du romantisme, illuminisme, théosophy, 1770–1820*. Reprint. Paris: Champion 1965.

Vickery, John B. 1973. *The Literary Impact of the Golden Bough*. Princeton: Princeton University Press.

– 1983. *Myths & Texts*. Baton Rouge: Louisiana University Press.

Vico, Giambattista. [1744] 1961. *The New Science of Giambattista Vico*, trans. and abridged by Thomas Goddard Bergin and Max Harold Fisch. New York: Doubleday.

Viereck, Peter. 1961. *Metapolitics: The Roots of the Nazi Mind*. New York: Capricor Books.

Vincent, E.R. 1936. *Gabriele Rossetti in England*. Oxford: Clarendon Press.

Warner, H.J. [1922, 1928] 1967. *The Albigensian Heresy*. Reprint. New York: Russell & Russell.

Webb, James. 1974. *The Occult Underground*. La Salle, Ill.: Open Court Publishing.

– 1980. *The Harmonious Circle*. New York: Putnam.

Webster, Nesta H. [1924] 1946. *Secret Societies and Subversive Movements*. Reprint. London: Boswell Publishing.

Welch, Louise. 1982. *Orage with Gurdjieff in America*. Boston: Routledge & Kegan Paul.

Westernhagen, Curt von. 1978. *Wagner: A Biography*. 2 vols. Trans. Mary Whittal. Cambridge: Cambridge University Press.

Weston, Jessie. [1913] 1964. *The Quest of the Holy Grail*. Reprint. New York: Barnes & Noble.

– [1920] 1957. *From Ritual to Romance*. Reprint. New York: Anchor Books.

Whelan, P.T. 1988. *D.H. Lawrence: Myth and Metaphysic in the Rainbow and Women in Love*. Ann Arbor: UMI Research Press.

White, Hayden. 1973. *Metahistory: The Historical Imagination in Nineteenth-Century Europe*. Baltimore: Johns Hopkins.

Wickramasinghe, Martin. 1951. *The Mysticism of D.H. Lawrence*. Ceylon.

Wilson, Edmund. [1933] 1984. *Axel's Castle: A Study in the Imaginative Literature of 1870–1930*. Reprint. London: Fontana.

Wilson, F.A.C. 1958. *W.B. Yeats and Tradition*. London: Gollancz.

– 1960. *Yeats's Iconography*. London: Methuen.

Williams, Gertrude Marvin. 1946. *Madame Blavatsky, Priestess of the Occult*. New York: Lancer Books.

Wittgenstein, Ludwig. [1922] 1960. *Tractatus Logico Philosophicus*. Reprint. London: Routledge & Kegan Paul.

Woodman, Leonora. 1983. *Stanza My Stone: Wallace Stevens and the Hermetic Tradition*. West Lafayette, Ind.: Purdue University Press.

Yates, Frances. 1964. *Giordano Bruno and the Hermetic Tradition*. London: Routledge & Kegan Paul.

– 1972. *The Rosicrucian Enlightenment*. London: Routledge & Kegan Paul.

Yeats, William Butler. [1938, rev. 1956] 1961. *A Vision*. New York: Macmillan.

– [1950] 1958. *Collected Poems*. Reprint. London: Macmillan.

– and Edwin Ellis, eds. 1893. *The Works of William Blake*. 3 vols. London: Bernard Quarich.

Zapponi, Niccolò. 1976. *L'Italia di Ezra Pound*, Roma: Bulzoni.

Index